VULNERABLE CONSTITUTIONS

Cynthia Barounis

VULNERABLE CONSTITUTIONS

*Queerness, Disability, and
the Remaking of American Manhood*

TEMPLE UNIVERSITY PRESS
Philadelphia • Rome • Tokyo

TEMPLE UNIVERSITY PRESS
Philadelphia, Pennsylvania 19122
tupress.temple.edu

Copyright © 2019 by Temple University—Of The Commonwealth System of Higher Education
All rights reserved
Published 2019

Library of Congress Cataloging-in-Publication Data

Names: Barounis, Cynthia, 1981- author.
Title: Vulnerable constitutions : queerness, disability, and the remaking of American manhood / Cynthia Barounis.
Description: Philadelphia : Temple University Press, 2019. | Includes bibliographical references and index. |
Identifiers: LCCN 2018046408 (print) | LCCN 2018059192 (ebook) | ISBN 9781439915080 (E-book) | ISBN 9781439915066 (cloth) | ISBN 9781439915073 (pbk.)
Subjects: LCSH: American literature—20th century—History and criticism. | Masculinity in literature. | Canon (Literature)
Classification: LCC PS228.M37 (ebook) | LCC PS228.M37 B37 2019 (print) | DDC 810./902664—dc23
LC record available at https://lccn.loc.gov/2018046408

Contents

Acknowledgments — vii

Introduction: Bodies That Leak; American Masculinity and Antiprophylactic Citizenship — 1

1. "An Inherent Weakness of the Constitution": Jack London's Revolting Men — 33
2. "Love or Eugenics?": Faulkner and Fitzgerald's Crip Children — 67
3. "Not the Usual Pattern": James Baldwin and the *DSM* — 99
4. Post-AIDS Permeability: Samuel Delany and Antiprophylaxis — 133
5. Prescribing Pleasure: Asexuality, Debility, and Trans Memoir — 161

Epilogue: Against Queer Resilience — 197

Notes — 211
Bibliography — 237
Index — 255

Acknowledgments

Like the endlessly mutating bodies that I describe throughout this book, this manuscript was not crafted antiprophylactically, in isolation. It was forged through an ongoing process of collaboration, adaptation, and revision and owes its current shape to its many encounters (sometimes messy, always enriching) with others. It began as a dissertation at the University of Illinois at Chicago (UIC), and I am strongly indebted to the members of my dissertation committee who devoted generous time and energy to helping me refine my ideas. I would like to thank Judith Gardiner for pushing me to think more deeply about the intersections of masculinity, race, and class; Chris Messenger for his expansive close readings and seemingly limitless knowledge of American literature; John D'Emilio for helping me to historicize the intersections between queerness and medicine; and Jack Halberstam for encouraging me to make careful distinctions between and within identities, genres, and archives. I am particularly grateful to my dissertation chair, Lennard Davis, for his phenomenal mentorship at every stage of the process. His remarkable talent for stripping things down to the essentials benefited me immensely, particularly at critical moments when I was at risk of becoming swallowed up in the details. His unwavering confidence in both my work and my worth as disability studies scholar allowed me to approach the task of writing the dissertation with genuine enthusiasm, curiosity, and joy.

UIC's English Department, Gender and Women's Studies Program, and Graduate College provided a vibrant intellectual community as well as numerous forms of practical support as I began this project, including travel support, assistantships, and fellowship funding in my final year. During my time in Chicago, my ideas were profoundly shaped by my involvement with UIC's Project Biocultures initiative, UIC's Queer Theory Reading Group, the Chicago Disability Studies Reading Group, as well as a series of informal writing groups. These intellectual contexts were vital to the development of the book in its early stages, and I found myself frequently energized by my conversations with Liat Ben-Moshe, Jennie Berner, Eugenio DiStefano, Margaret Fink, Michael Gill, Alice Haisman, Eunjung Kim, Scott McFarland, Madeleine Monson-Rosen, Ryan Parrey-Munger, Alyson Patsavas, Stephanie Reich, and Kristy Ulibarri. My time working as a graduate assistant to Stanley Fish was memorable and instructive, and I am grateful to him for recommending that I enroll in my first disability studies course. I would also like to thank Mark Canuel for generously reading and providing feedback on an early version of Chapter 2, Ralph Cintron for his mentorship during my first two years in the program, and Sharon Holland for working closely with me around queer studies and critical race theory during our brief period of overlap at UIC.

Darrell Moore graciously allowed me to sit in on his "Sexuality and the State" graduate seminar in the Philosophy Department at DePaul University during the spring of 2009. This course, along with the related conversations about race and biopolitics that I had with H. Rakes and Marie Draz, provided a rich source of inspiration at a crucial stage of the process. In less formal settings, I enjoyed academic community and camaraderie with Ryan Brooks, Garrett Brown, Kevin Carey, Cynthia Cravens, Julie Fiorelli, Chad Heltzel, Sara Rutter, and Jay Shearer. I owe particular thanks to Megan Milks, who has watched this project develop from the beginning and been one of its most consistent and generous interlocutors. They provided feedback on multiple drafts and their creative and critical work has been an ongoing source of inspiration for my own. Our decade-long friendship continues to sustain me personally and intellectually.

I am enormously grateful to my community at Washington University in St. Louis, where I completed a Postdoctoral Fellowship in the Department of Women, Gender, and Sexuality Studies (WGSS). The reduced teaching load allowed me to devote important time and energy to the writing of this book. More importantly, the fellowship connected me with brilliant colleagues and talented students who continually inspire my thinking. My postdoctoral mentor, Linda Nicholson, provided invaluable support as I made my transition from Chicago to St. Louis and as the manuscript made its transition from dissertation to book. She carefully read multiple chapters, and her suggestions were instrumental as I refined the book's central argument. I have benefited greatly from her expansive knowledge of feminist theory, and I continue to value her kindness and friendship. Other colleagues across WGSS, English, and American Culture Studies have generously provided feedback on drafts in progress and engaged me in enlivening discussions of my work during a range of formal and informal workshops including the WGSS colloquium series and the Americanist Dinner Forum. For these contributions, I'm grateful to Jami Ake, Barbara Baumgartner, Amy Cislo, Mary Ann Dzuback, Andrea Friedman, Bill Maxwell, Jeffrey Q. McCune, Mel Micir, Amber Musser, Anca Parvulescu, Vivian Pollack, Trevor Sangrey, Susan Stiritz, and Rebecca Wanzo.

My thinking has also been enriched by conversations with a number of faculty and grad students, particularly in the context of Wash U's Voice and Sexuality Reading Group, Queer Theory Reading Group, and the Workshop for Politics, Ethics, and Society. I deeply value the interdisciplinary discussions I have had in these contexts with Britta Anderson, Iver Bernstein, Patrick Burke, Katie Collins, Kate Fama, Denise Elif Gill, Clarissa Hayward, Lorraine Krall-McCrary, Dana Logan, Jasmine Mahmoud, Paige McGinley, Ben Meiners, Emma Merrigan, Rose Miyatsu, Katherine Mooney, Sowande' Mustakeem, Erika Rodriguez, Anika Walke, Rhaisa Williams, and Beth Windle. I have especially appreciated my collaborations with Claire McKinney as we worked together to organize the Disability and Intimacy Roundtable with the support of Wash U's American Intimacies Initiative.

Scholars in disability studies, queer studies, and asexuality studies have provided important intellectual sustenance, as well as friendship, over the past ten years. I am grateful that conference travel, panel presentations, invited talks, and other shared spaces have brought me into conversation with D. L. Adams, Rachel Adams, Sarah Brophy, K. J. Cerankowski, Mel Chen, Theodora Danylevich, Allyson Day, Helen Deutsch, Jane Dryden, Elizabeth Donaldson, Julie Passanante Elman, Nirmala Erevelles, Ramzi Fawaz, Kelly Fritsch, Lezlie Frye, Robert Gould, Kristina Gupta, Lynette Jackson, Michelle Jarman, Merri Lisa Johnson, Alison Kafer, Eunjung Kim, Kateřina Kolářová, Petra Kuppers, Riva Lehrer, Robert McRuer, David Mitchell, Anna Mollow, Michael O'Rourke, Margaret Price, Ela Przybylo, Julia Miele Rodas, Ellen Samuels, Carrie Sandahl, Sami Schalk, Karin Selberg, Bethany Stevens, Sandy Sufian, Sara Vogt, and Jess Waggoner.

I am incredibly fortunate to have worked with my talented editor at Temple University Press, Sara Jo Cohen, and am deeply grateful for her ongoing commitment to the project. Her sharp critical insights challenged me in just the right ways and her careful editorial eye was instrumental as I completed my revisions; much of the book's current shape owes to her presence, support, and generosity. I am indebted to both anonymous readers for taking the time to read and comment on earlier drafts of the manuscript. Their supportive feedback and perceptive critiques were extraordinarily helpful during the final stages of the writing process. It has truly been a delight to work with Temple University Press, and I would like to give additional thanks to the Editorial Board as well as Nikki Miller, Gary Kramer, Ann-Marie Anderson, Jamie Armstrong, and Cheryl Uppling.

My journey to this book began long before grad school and I am thankful to those undergraduate mentors at Knox College who set me on an academic path and helped to ignite many of the passions that led to its creation. Thank you to Lori Schroeder for equipping me with the tools to think about "unruly bodies" a decade and a half ago. I am profoundly grateful to Rob Smith, an incredible teacher and an extraordinary mentor who gave me my first appetite for theory and criticism, along with the confidence to use my writing and voice in ways I hadn't known were possible. Quite simply, this book would not exist without him.

My sincere thanks to Tony Matelli, the Marlborough Gallery, and the Davis Museum at Wellesley College, for graciously allowing me to use an image of the *Sleepwalker* (2014) on the cover of this book. Clarice Stasz generously provided me with a high-quality image of an underwear-clad Jack London for reproduction in the book's Epilogue. Portions of some chapters have been previously published elsewhere and are reproduced here with permission from those journals and presses. "Compulsory Sexuality and Asexual/Crip Resistance in John Cameron Mitchell's *Shortbus*" was republished with permission of Taylor and Francis Group, from *Asexualities: Feminist and Queer Perspectives*, edited by K. J. Cerankowski and Megan Milks, Routledge, 2014; permission conveyed through Copyright Clearance Center, Inc. "'Not the Usual Pattern': James Baldwin, Homosexuality, and the *DSM*" was republished with permission from Wayne State University Press from *Criticism: A Quarterly for Literature and the Arts* 59, no. 3 (Summer 2017).

Outside of these institutional contexts, I have been anchored by the love and support of friends and chosen family. Claire Leeds, one of my oldest friends and favorite collaborators, has always inspired me with her strong convictions and uncompromising vision. Bill Bevis enriched my writing with his uncanny ability to recommend relevant media. My conversations with Nancy Baker were generative and helped to remind me of the value of clarity.

Gabe Sopocy has a special talent for stoking my love of language, igniting my imagination, and increasing my appetite for the absurd. Ginny Barrett has been present for so many pivotal moments, and I appreciate the way she brings good nature and much-needed pragmatism to every situation. Courtney Fayle, Robin Petrovic Gayle, and Christina Tincher have never lost touch and my friendships with them remind me that, despite so many changes, some things remain constant. During my time in St. Louis, Allison Kirschbaum provided a steady supply of adventure or advice. I have known Eileen G'Sell for two decades, and she continues to energize me with her quick wit and sharp intellect; her hospitality when I moved to St. Louis made it feel immediately like home. Lisa Carrico has been a trusted confidante and enhanced my life with her warmth, humor, and insight. And my friendship with Alyson Spurgas has transformed my life in more ways than I can name. I have benefited tremendously from her fierce emotional intelligence, her intellectual passion, her incredible loyalty, and her ability to keep me laughing.

Thank you to my parents, Tom and Diane Barounis, for teaching me from an early age to ask the big questions. Their kindness, compassion, and profound commitment to social justice has set for me the highest example, and I feel lucky to have moved through life with their unconditional love and support. My son, Noah, fills my days with limitless joy and has made my life a thousand times more interesting since he entered it two years ago. Finally, it is impossible to describe the intellectual, emotional, and practical support I have received from my partner, Stefanie Boese, who read countless drafts and always seemed to know exactly what the project (or I) needed at any given moment. Her honesty, her humor, and her ability to put everything into perspective has helped me to take myself both more and less seriously during the writing process and beyond.

VULNERABLE CONSTITUTIONS

Introduction

Bodies That Leak

American Masculinity and Antiprophylactic Citizenship

In July 2013, transgender military intelligence analyst Chelsea Manning was sentenced to thirty-five years in prison after she released thousands of classified documents to WikiLeaks three years earlier. Among the most significant records Manning leaked was a video titled "Collateral Murder," which depicted the U.S. military's indiscriminate killing of Iraqi civilians during a 2007 airstrike in Baghdad. In leaking sensitive information, Manning was accused of compromising the nation's defenses, damaging the United States' global reputation and revealing military tactics that could jeopardize the country's ability to protect itself against foreign powers. But for Manning, the opposite was true. Understanding the nation's overdeveloped defenses as a liability rather than a strength, Manning made clear that her primary patriotic duty was not to help fortify our systems of security but rather to hold the United States accountable to the global community and to its own citizens. Put another way, to spring a "leak" in our nation's figurative armor may very well have been the only way to participate in the creation of a nation worth defending. Manning's act of principled dissent—her willingness to compromise the "security" of the nation for the sake of the nation—is a provocative example of what I refer to throughout this book as *antiprophylactic citizenship*. In this model, the nation earns its vitality through an attitude of openness, an embrace of vulnerability, and willingness, when necessary, to revolt.

Vulnerable Constitutions argues that one of the central features of antiprophylactic citizenship is its sustained encounter with queerness and disability.

Though Manning came out publicly as a transgender woman following her sentencing, she was continually misgendered in early press coverage by journalists who were either unaware of or insensitive to her chosen name and pronouns.[1] Those who did take her trans identity seriously tended to present it as evidence of her impaired judgment. During the initial hearings, for example, Manning's lawyers attempted to use her recent diagnosis of gender identity disorder and its related stresses to make a case for her "diminished capacity" during the time of the document leak. Throughout the trial, Manning's mental health remained a focal point with various psychiatrists and clinical psychologists testifying that Manning "showed signs of mental instability" and delivering diagnoses that included mild fetal alcohol syndrome, "postadolescent idealism," and mild Asperger's syndrome.[2] These assessments followed an incident preceding the leak in which Manning was discovered "sitting on the floor in a fetal position in a storage room," having etched the phrase "I WANT" into a vinyl chair with an army knife.[3] Manning was thus introduced to the public in a kaleidoscope of fragments, variously understood as a dangerous traitor, a national hero, a closeted gay male soldier, and, perhaps most frequently, an improperly vetted officer with undiagnosed mental health issues who should never have been granted access to sensitive information.

Against these accounts that disqualify Manning as psychologically damaged or mentally ill, we might be tempted to present a counternarrative that insists on Manning's unimpeachable mental health. In this counternarrative, Manning's personal life and private emotions would be irrelevant to her principled decision to become a whistle-blower. But Manning's feelings of anxiety and depression—which she herself shared with various friends—cannot be extricated from the national context that framed the conditions of her military employment.[4] Against a culture that valorizes violent masculinities, produces a skyrocketing rate of transgender suicide, and requires enthusiastic complicity in the enactment of state violence, Manning's mental distress may be the *only* rational response. While those who defended Manning's actions tended to bracket or deny the queer and crip elements of her identity, this book is based on the assumption that these elements are far from incidental to her act of resistance. Manning emerges as an antiprophylactic citizen not despite her queerness, her dysphoria, or her mental health status but because of them.

Without overly politicizing Manning's deeply personal decision to transition or making presumptions regarding her mental health, we might also observe the way her act of antiprophylactic resistance appears to have coalesced around a rejection of the demands of hegemonic masculinity. Indeed, the ideal of manhood that most men are taught to strive for and emulate could be described as inherently *prophylactic*. We require male bodies to be invulnerable, impenetrable, and impervious to injury. To this end, a "real man" must be heterosexually functional and physically fit. In addition to maintaining the boundaries of his physical body, he must also control and contain his emotional response to the world, and particularly to other men. Thus a related claim that this book makes is that an antiprophylactic model of citizenship provides tools for challenging normative masculinities and, in some cases, imagining alternative queer-crip models of masculine expression.

Like the other figures I examine in this book, Manning stages an overt rejection of the demands of prophylactic masculinity. However, unlike those figures, she does not identify as male and refuses to present a redemptive narrative that recenters the masculine body as the primary site of resistance to authority. Her story demonstrates that a commitment to antiprophylactic citizenship need not necessarily be attached to cismale bodies or masculine gender expressions. I open with this example not to present Manning as a representative figure of antiprophylactic masculinity but rather to highlight from the outset both the potential and the limits of antiprophylactic *masculinity* as a concept. The men who populate this book are often attempting to redefine masculinity through antiprophylaxis, using the concept to generate new masculinities and new homosocial bonds. But Manning's transfemininity may ultimately represent a more radical horizon—or perhaps a truer commitment to antiprophylaxis—than the overtly masculine visions that dominate the book. My readings in the chapters that follow do not reflect an unqualified celebration of antiprophylactic masculinity, nor are they solely critical of it. I am interested, instead, in the necessary ambivalence that is generated from the masculinization of vulnerability, receptivity, and physical susceptibility. Mapping the varied shapes that antiprophylactic masculinity has taken over the course of the twentieth century reveals a history of both complicity and resistance, with these men both relying on and rejecting their era's reigning hegemonic ideals.

Finally, *Vulnerable Constitutions* argues that this model of masculinity and citizenship is historically contingent, having emerged alongside evolving scientific and medical conversations regarding deviant genders and sexualities. It makes the case that certain American fantasies of belonging and embodiment—from Jack London to Samuel Delany—have been profoundly influenced by the invention of sexual science and the medicalization of queer sexual and gender expressions. I do not mean to suggest, however, that the authors under examination in this book are celebrating the power of medicalization itself—to the contrary, in their works, a division often emerges between the prophylactic power of diagnosis and an alternative ethics of corporeal vulnerability in which the damaged or contaminated body is celebrated as exceeding, evading, or even transcending the doctor's gaze. In these visions, perverse sexuality, physical precarity, and bodily contamination become regenerating and robust enterprises, solidifying the bonds of American brotherhood through a renewed emphasis on vulnerability, receptivity, and risk. Thus these texts present two related but distinct versions of biopolitics—one regulatory and the other affirmative.[5] It is my argument in this book that antiprophylactic citizenship relies on a continually evolving dialectical relationship between the two. In its sustained focus on the queer body as an object of medical diagnosis, *Vulnerable Constitutions* thus engages one of the most undertheorized intersections between queerness and disability.

Masculinity as a Biosocial Enactment

We tend to think of masculinity as a single standard that individual men try (and often fail) to live up to. Thus Michael Kimmel's classic definition of masculinity as "homosocial enactment" describes relationships between men within a patriarchal culture as inherently competitive.[6] For Kimmel, it is not enough to simply be born with male privilege; instead, manhood must be continually tested, and approval is earned through repeated performances that demonstrate proximity to a hegemonic ideal. While one's proximity to that ideal can be influenced by a number of factors, including intersectionalities of race, class, sexuality, and ability, even the most privileged of men are haunted by their failure to fully measure up to the hegemonic standard; one can always be outmanned (and thus unmanned) by someone slightly more successful, more muscular, or more in control of his emotions and environment. In this schema, masculinity is both individual and generic; it transforms men into isolated competitors striving toward the same abstract goal.

Importantly, this view has its roots in psychoanalytic theory, with many early scholars of masculinity taking inspiration from Freudian models that understood men to be continually compensating for their castration anxieties and unresolved Oedipal conflicts. In an extended Freudian turn, for example, Kimmel describes masculinity as a "flight from the feminine" that is informed by little boys' need to renounce their identification with the mother under symbolic threat of castration by the father (*Gender of Desire*, 31–32). Later theorists of masculinity have taken a more nuanced psychoanalytic approach. Drawing from Judith Butler's definition of gender as a series of repetitions for which there is no authentic original, C. J. Pascoe argues that normative masculinity requires the "daily interactional work of repudiating the threatening specter of the fag" who occupies the abject negative space of masculinity's "constitutive outside" (81, 14).[7] Through the prism of psychoanalysis, masculinity is fundamentally melancholic, endlessly preoccupied with how the meager biology of the male body measures up to a larger-than-life (and necessarily unattainable) phallic ideal.

What, then, would a masculinity look like that refuses the psychoanalytic model, treats the phallic ideal with indifference, and revels in the idiosyncratic biology of the body? Susan Bordo hints at this non-Freudian, non-melancholic vision of masculinity in *The Male Body* when she distinguishes between the symbolic authority of the phallus and the "biometaphors" we use to add rhetorical flourish to the male anatomy, from the ubiquitous "throbbing member" of the romance novel genre to the "colorful crests" of male birds during mating season (88). While these biometaphors may feel phallic to the extent that they are connected to bodily competitions among men, they differ from the psychoanalytic phallus because they are anchored to the specificities of the material body. Bordo explains:

> Unlike [biometaphors], the phallus stands, not for the superior fitness of an individual male over other men, but for a *generic* male superiority—not only over females but also over other species. And unlike the biometaphors, the phallus stands for a superiority that is not just biological, but partakes of an authority beyond (and often in contest with) the power, needs, and desires of the body. The biometaphors symbolize qualities (such as sexual or reproductive potency, superior aggressiveness, the capacity to give pleasure) whose value is not unique to human cultures but is shared by many other species. The phallus, on the other hand, proclaims its kinship with higher values—with the values of "civilization" rather than "nature," with the Man who is made in God's image, not *Homo sapiens*, the human primate. (89)

If the performance anxiety encoded in the phallic ideal creates a masculinity that is individual and generic, then the masculinity of the biometaphor emerges, by contrast, as collective and heterogeneous, emerging directly from the body's organic materiality. Here, biological variation can lead to competitive clashing; however, no single individual is categorically superior and no single standard is externally imposed. Against usual psychoanalytic mechanisms of repression and deferral, the biometaphor is committed to a communal, if unruly, portrait of masculinity-as-species.

Of course, the psychoanalytic phallus is the direct descendent of the species biometaphor, and the two are not always easily disentangled. As a "powerful symbol of male sexual potency" (Bordo, 88), the biometaphor does not exactly eschew patriarchal power. Rather than a vision of queer ecological diversity (like the one documented in Joan Roughgarden's *Evolution's Rainbow*), we are left with something closer to evolutionary psychology and its problematic assertions about the "hard-wired" nature of male sexual conquest and feminine receptivity. In Bordo's own account, the biometaphor does not represent an exuberant alternative to the phallus as much as it reveals the phallus's ambivalent prehistory. To embrace a masculinity-in-the-flesh does not require one to reject "generic male superiority" and its "authority beyond" the "needs and desires of the body" (89). But it does create a noticeable gap that calls into question the relationship between the concrete materiality of the male body and the abstract nature of the privileges men are assumed to inherit. It does not automatically reinforce the phallic ideal, but it doesn't necessarily subvert it either.

It is precisely this ambivalence of the biometaphor that makes it a fitting illustration of the kind of masculinity I take as the subject of this book. Like the rhetorical flourish of the "throbbing member," Bordo's quintessential biometaphor of the human animal, this masculinity strikes a delicate balance between vulnerability and bravado. It boasts virility but is also, sometimes painfully, sensitive and exposed. The writers I examine in *Vulnerable Constitutions* do not register this duality as a contradiction. Celebrating the male body's capacity for sensation, intimacy, and receptivity (over hegemonic masculinity's commitment to mastery, aggression, and self-protection), they have a stake in redefining manhood as a site of collective consciousness that moves beyond the level of the individual. Against the traditional view of masculinity as a competitive site of "homosocial enactment," these writers refashion masculinity as a collaborative site of *biosocial* enactment.

Following Paul Rabinow's coining of the term in 1996, Nikolas Rose defines "biosociality" as the "forms of collectivization organized around the commonality of a shared somatic or genetic status" (134). Importantly, these forms of collectivization can go beyond genetics to incorporate a variety of diagnostic framings and health practices, even expanding into what Rose terms "biological citizenship" (134). As norms of political responsibility become increasingly governed by protocols related to the health and vitality of the body, we have come to articulate both our selfhood and our relationship to the state through vocabularies of biomedicine. The concept of biological citizenship can be used, for example, to describe projects as diverse as the eugenic regulation of fertility, the demands of AIDS activists in the early 1990s, or the ever-expanding digital technologies (like the Fitbit) through which we record and circulate our own vital statistics. With some notable exceptions, however, we have had few conversations that consider the status of masculinity in the era of biological citizenship.[8]

While biological citizenship most frequently describes practices of medical self-surveillance and shared conformity to medical norms, I examine the way a number of American writers have located a masculinizing power in the overt *rejection* of clinical authority and its prophylactic prohibitions. I refer to this unique form of biosociality as *antiprophylactic citizenship*. In these visions, the physical boundaries of the body are taken to parallel the figurative borders of the nation. However, against the traditional view that the masculine body (and nation) should remain impermeable and impenetrable, antiprophylactic citizenship imagines the possibilities of a masculine body that shows little regard for physical boundaries or national borders. Porous and permeable, it is defined by its receptivity to potentially contaminating outsiders.

These commitments to antiprophylaxis and physical receptivity are categorically different from the masculine bottom values described in Leo Bersani's foundational essay "Is the Rectum a Grave?" (1987), even as they share some important similarities.[9] Both, for example, share a preoccupation with violated boundaries and a related desire to sully the phallic ideal of masculine impenetrability. Written at the peak of the AIDS epidemic, as a homophobic media continued to proliferate images that framed anal-receptive sex as a site of death and disease, Bersani's essay locates a powerful psychoanalytic value in queer sexuality's proximity to the Freudian death drive. Invoking the "intolerable image of a grown man, legs high in the air, unable to refuse the suicidal ecstasy of being a woman," Bersani concludes that "the rectum is the grave in which the masculine ideal . . . of proud subjectivity is buried" (222). To allow oneself to be penetrated, then, is to access the sublime "self-shattering" pleasure related to the "radical disintegration and humiliation of the self" (212). Through the masochistic embrace of submission, the male body revels in its capacity to be temporarily violated.

Of course, many critics have noted that, far from undoing or "burying" the male ego, Bersani's model relies on the very phallic model it appears to reject. As Tan Hoang Nguyen observes, "The joyful abdication of power only makes sense in the context of those with something to give up"

(12).¹⁰ Not everyone, in other words, can enjoy the "suicidal ecstasy of being a woman," least of all, perhaps, those who live their lives as women. Moreover, Bersani masculinizes this form of masochism when he describes it as "the *jouissance* of exploded limits," and "the ecstatic suffering into which the human organism momentarily plunges when it is 'pressed' beyond a certain threshold of endurance" (217). Emphasizing valorized masculine qualities of endurance, fearlessness, and boundary-pushing, Bersani's outlaw sexualities do not so much suggest the "suicidal ecstasy of being a woman" as they do the necessity of taking it like a man.¹¹

Like Bersani, the writers I examine in this book are often engaged in a complicated attempt to remasculinize masochism. However, unlike Bersani, their visions of antiprophylactic citizenship reject psychoanalytic definitions of masculinity, being preoccupied instead with the biopolitical contexts of physical receptivity. Biopolitics refers to the way the state power has increasingly come to be exercised not through the threat of violence, punishment, or death but through the rise of expert knowledge about bodies and populations and the expansions of techniques designed to optimize human life. Because biopolitics exerts power through the *production* of sexualities rather than their repression or prohibition, it represents an explicit departure from psychoanalysis. Developing this concept in *Society Must Be Defended*, Michel Foucault famously observed that while the traditional "right of sovereignty was the right to take life or let live," biopolitical control rests instead on the "right to make live and to let die" (241). It is the "take life or let live" dimensions of the epidemic that Bersani is most preoccupied with in his essay. He shares, for example, a newspaper clipping in which an older man is pictured threatening his adult son with a shotgun. The headline reads: "I'd shoot my son if he had AIDS, says vicar!" Inspired by media like this, Bersani sought to "account for the murderous representations of homosexuals unleashed and 'legitimized' by AIDS" (221). But through a biopolitical lens, the violence of AIDS is not solely measured in "murderous" homophobic threats made against gay men (as alarming and relevant as those threats are) but in the government's "let die" attitude toward a huge swath of the queer population as officials conspicuously neglected the public health crisis. In his psychoanalytic turn, then, Bersani dodges his essay's original biopolitical context, drawing out the epidemic's figurative dimensions while overlooking its literal ones. When Bersani advocates self-annihilation, he is not advocating physical death or debility (rendered in the growing casualties of the AIDS epidemic or the government's homophobic neglect of the public health crisis); he is celebrating the death drive and the interior psychic experience of "self-shattering" it enables. But without the heroic masculinity of ecstatic bottomhood enabled by Bersani's psychoanalytic detour—a masculinity that is necessarily, in Bersani's definition, isolated, individual, and antisocial—we are left with the precarious lives, collective experience, and social movements of those living with and dying from HIV/AIDS.

In this respect, the antiprophylactic masculinities that populate this book share more in common with the rhetorics of bug chasing and barebacking documented in Tim Dean's *Unlimited Intimacy*. While "barebacking" simply refers to anal-receptive sex without a condom, its emergence as a coherent concept and practice makes sense only in a world already shaped by the AIDS epidemic, and thus, as Dean argues, it cannot be understood outside the public health panics that developed in response. Barebackers are assumed to imperil their communities through their pursuit of risky personal pleasures. Occupying an even more maligned cultural status, "bug chasers" actively seek out HIV infection, inviting the virus into their bodies with the hopes of seroconversion. Despite these differences, both groups are framed through a rhetoric of suicidal (and homicidal) recklessness, creating lines of transmission that threaten to poison or decimate an otherwise thriving gay community.

But, as Dean points out, these accusations rest on a false equivalence between HIV and death as well as on the ableist assumption that a life of disability is no life at all. Adopting the mantra "infected but not ill," (68) barebacking and bug chasing subcultures push back against these narratives by reclaiming the virus as a source of vitality and biosocial connection. Against the feminization of the bottom, barebackers "embrace risk as a test of masculinity" (51) in ways that allow HIV-positive status to signify as a type of "battle scar" (52). Bug chasers further literalize the masculinizing socialities of the virus by imagining a boundaryless "bug brotherhood" created through acts of "breeding" between men (83). As Dean observes, through bug chasing, the "feature that distinguishes gay culture from national, ethnic, or religious cultures—namely, that no one is born into gay culture and therefore that each individual must discover or invent it for him- or herself—is dissolved by gay men's breeding the virus among themselves and . . . between generations" (83). Here, the rectum functions not as a "grave" but as a "womb," birthing new forms of masculinity through the viral circulation of queer biological life. In privileging the biopolitical context of barebacking, Dean reveals the way the subculture's ethical commitments to intimacy, fraternity, and even masculinity take shape not despite barebackers' resistance to health norms but precisely because of them.

Thus my inquiry into antiprophylactic citizenship is indebted to the work of scholars of queer masculinity—including Tim Dean, David Savran, Darieck Scott, Tan Hoang Nguyen, and Amber Musser—who have called for new ways of conceptualizing male receptivity and its relationship to politicized forms of sensation, including masochism. I join these theorists in speculating on what it might mean to take seriously male vulnerability *as* vulnerability. Forging biosocial bonds through the dispersal of sensation rather than through the prophylactic channels of inheritance, through physical generation rather than through psychic repression, antiprophylactic citizenship presents a lateralized "viral" mode of political belonging—a bug brotherhood of sorts—that is imagined to transcend linear bloodlines. Open-ended and receptive, it represents a generative breaching of the barriers that separate body from environment and citizen from citizen.

Foregrounding the "viral" as a major, if often overlooked, model for conceptualizing American citizenship, my study also takes inspiration from the growing literature on the cultural politics of immunity. Scholars including Priscilla Wald, Ed Cohen, Robert Esposito, Mel Chen, Alexis Shotwell, Beth Ferri, and Neel Ahuja have revitalized critical conversations on the cultural politics of immunity over the past several years, approaching the concept through the lens of new materialism, affect, disability, and the human/animal divide.[12] In her book *Contagious: Cultures, Carriers, and the Outbreak Narrative* (2008), Priscilla Wald forwards a concept of "imagined immunities" (inspired by Benedict Anderson's "imagined communities") as a way to theorize "communal belonging in epidemiological terms" (47). These recent formulations expand and complicate the foundational literature that developed in response to the AIDS epidemic, which speculated on how national fantasies of viral transmission have come to be intertwined with anxieties around global exchange and metaphors of military defense.[13] We are accustomed, in other words, to envisioning biological immunity as a process that protects the body against threatening foreign invaders and other contaminating agents.

However, it is notable that the concept of immunity was not always associated with biological processes or prophylactic protection against others. Originating as a legal term related to the "shared duties" of citizenship, it was not until centuries later that immunity was reconceived as a biological phenomenon related to body's defenses.[14] Playing on immunity's history as a legal term, Derrida argues that "immunity" allegorizes the exceptionality of state power as it "suspends at least provisionally, democracy *for its own good*, so as to take care of it, so as to immunize it against a much worse and very likely assault" (*Rogues*, 33). It is at this moment that we witness the "suicide of democracy" with the sovereign's immunity transforming into "autoimmunity"—a body turned against itself in a spectacle of self-defense gone awry.[15] But if, for

Derrida, immunity points to the exceptionalism of the state in its capacity to act outside of the law, then Ed Cohen sees in immunity the inverse capacity to represent a form of "resistance" to the law that is both corporeal and political. As Cohen points out, one 1893 French medical dictionary defines immunity as a condition that, owing to "idiosyncrasies, age, constitution, acclimatization, or inoculation," enables "some people to escape a reigning illness" (210–211). Framing contagious diseases as a "reigning" sovereign, these texts understood the immune body as a disobedient subject whose unique constitution existed just beyond the law's reach. In these imaginings, immunity was neither the result of a military struggle against foreign invaders nor a symptom of unchecked sovereign power but rather a symptom of the sovereign's failure to rule over a heterogeneous population.

In this way, immunity's shared role as a legal and medical term make it an important organizing principle for my study. Because discourses of immunity have historically colluded to make it synonymous with security and defense, we might be inclined to see immunity as synonymous with the prophylactic sensibility, and thus in opposition to the forms of masculinity and citizenship I describe in this book. But a more careful consideration of immunity's biological mechanisms reveals that it may ultimately share more in common with the antiprophylactic sensibility. Against immunity's persistent association with the bounded body of "possessive individualism," Cohen pulls out a counterreading that understands the immune system as evidence of the "necessary intimacy of organism and environment" (5), resulting from the body's interdependence with the "vital contexts in which it necessarily exists" (14). After all, to become immune to a disease, one must first become porous, opening the body, temporarily, to potentially pathogenic others. It is to build a biological resistance based on the incorporation, rather than expulsion, of "foreign" matter. The construction of "immunity-as-defense," then, obscures the extent to which immunity is based on the ability of the body to act as a "habitat, welcoming the presence of useful, commensal organisms" (29).

As Derrida notes in *Rogues*, one of the fundamental contractions of democracy lies in its aspiration toward "two incompatible things: it has wanted, on the one hand, to welcome only men, and on the condition that they be citizens, brothers, and compeers [semblables], excluding all the others, in particular bad citizens, rogues, noncitizens, and all sorts of unlike and unrecognizable others, and, on the other hand, at the same time or by turns, it has wanted to open itself up, to offer hospitality, to all those excluded" (63). For the writers I examine in this book, democratic unity is imagined precisely as this fleshy incorporation of "bad citizens, rogues, non-citizens, and . . . recognizable others." The forms of antiprophylactic citizenship that they champion can thus be understood as attempts to undo the contradiction of democracy by committing (or attempting to commit) fully to this second impulse of unconditional "hospitality"—the desire to make the body as well as the body politic into a "welcoming habitat." If the paradox of autoimmunity is the way an organism's practices of self-defense can turn destructively back upon the organism itself, then the irony of the antiprophylactic lies in the way seemingly self-destructive or self-contaminating acts can become healthful, restorative, and crucial to the proliferation of political and biological life. As Alexis Shotwell writes in *Against Purity*, "We cannot in the end be separate from the world that constitutes us. Corporeal exceptionalism cannot be sustained because interabsorption is the way things actually are" (85). Representing a generative breaching of the barriers that separate body from environment and citizen from citizen, the "immunitary" need not signify a fortification of national boundaries. Like the "interabsorption" that is a descriptive fact of our biological entanglement with the world and with each other, immunity can also imply an antiprophylactic ethics of incorporation. Open-ended and receptive, it reflects an approach to biological life that resists objectifications of medicine by inviting contagion rather than expelling it.

Revolting Men

When disability is figured in relation to the nation and its future, it is frequently couched in a language of threat. Disability menaces the "healthy" functioning of the state, serving as a reminder of how the body politic, without proper maintenance, might ultimately turn against itself.[16] As Lennard Davis observes, "For the formation of the modern nation-state it was not simply language, but bodies and bodily practices that also had to be standardized, homogenized, and normalized" (*Bending over Backwards*, 106). The invention of the "average man" was especially useful to representative democracies like the United States as it helped reconcile the nation's paradoxical commitment to both individuality and equality and solved the related conundrum of how large groupings of individuals could ever be represented by a single person (109). Because such a portrait emphasized harmony through uniformity, revolution and other forms of "social unrest" were likened to diseases that threatened the physical health of the body politic (113). This book explores how these figurations shift when anarchy and disorder become an ideal to be embraced rather than nightmare to be avoided. To celebrate the radical heterogeneity that disability represents would mean opening up the body—and the body politic—to that which might be understood as potentially contaminating and allowing it to morph into unpredictable shapes. While the traditional function of the state has been to produce legible populations and "sanitary" citizens, the writers I examine here are preoccupied instead with the political possibilities of the "unsanitary" or unruly citizen whose capacity for political dissent—whose "revolting masculinity"—is presented as the key to recuperating the United States' own revolutionary origins.[17] In this way, the antiprophylactic citizen reclaims the American body as radically democratic, with all of the risk and messiness that "rule of the many" implies.

In his study of prerevolutionary American rhetoric, Rogan Kersh points to the "obvious difficulty in promoting ethnicity or culture as the basis for a national union" (255) as the cause of American independence rested not on the strengthening but on the *breaking* of the ethnic ties that might have otherwise bound them as subjects of English rule. This, added to the "pressing need for assistance in the independence effort from anyone willing to provide it," defined American political union as a type of statehood that rested on something other than "shared blood" (257). Because the ethnicity that the American colonists shared with their "biological forebears" could not serve as a material justification for independence (to the contrary, it worked *against* it), arguments for independence had to rely instead on a more abstract, arguably "disembodied," set of principles regarding colonial injustice, violated rights, and religious providence. Indeed, when Washington Irving described the United States as a "logocracy . . . a republic of words" (231), his terminology points to an important anxiety: that the substance binding American men to one another was ultimately more rhetorical than physical, issued from an abstract commitment to the spirit of democracy rather than grounded in the flesh.[18] Put simply, while the United States had a Constitution, it lacked a *constitution*.

But if there was an "obvious difficulty in promoting ethnicity or culture as a basis for national union," such difficulties did not mean that whiteness was unimportant—only that it had been largely disconnected from national bloodlines. American colonists, after all, still needed something that differentiated their citizenship status from the indigenous American populations they displaced and the black populations whose enslaved labor they exploited. Mapping out the relationship between whiteness and what she terms "national manhood," Dana Nelson considers the ways in which qualities of benevolence, professionalism, and rationality were coded as white and figured against the inherent irrationality and primitivism of America's indigenous and black racial others. Important to this understanding of whiteness was its global expansiveness and lack of national specificity—an expansiveness that Nelson demonstrates through an innovative reading of Delano's fraternal attachments to the Spanish captain Benito Cereno in Melville's story of the same name.[19] Reading Melville's story as an example of what she terms "fraternal melancholy," Nelson understands "national manhood" through a primarily psychoanalytic framework, in which the potential for violent conflict is repressed through the formation of ritualized melancholic identifications between white men. These ritualized structures, she argues, provided opportunities for white men to understand themselves as unified, if not in body, then in spirit.

The connections Nelson draws, however, between nineteenth-century "fraternal melancholy" and late twentieth-century idealizations of U.S. presidential power, suggest a misleading historical continuity. Ending with the 1855 publication of *Benito Cereno* and resuming with the 1997 film *Air Force One*, Nelson's archive leaves a provocative gap that overlooks the impact of that evolutionary theory and sexual science on medical and cultural constructions of American masculinity. If belief in divine "Agency" helped American forefathers ground the principles of American democratic citizenship and national manhood in the absence of an appeal to biological ancestry, then the emergence of evolutionary theory in the mid-nineteenth century weakened those religious justifications, making them less viable as anchors for national belonging. Aided by the publication of case studies of sexual neurosis by figures like Richard von Krafft-Ebing and Havelock Ellis, the development of fields like sexology and criminal anthropology competed with older forms of religiously based knowledge. In this context, sexual deviance and physical degeneracy became overlapping designations, constructed by and through the same frameworks that gave rise to the body of the "normal" citizen. By the turn of the twentieth century, these medicalized frameworks had begun to reach wider audiences with literary writers adopting and adapting the scientific vocabularies of their day.

In his Marxist history of American masculinity, Kevin Floyd contextualizes the rise of sexual science alongside the emergence of Taylorism. For Floyd, the shop floor and clinic provided mirroring systems of legibility in which bodies were classified and partitioned according to their capacity for productivity, on the one hand, and their sexual drives, on the other. As desire was increasingly "scientifically abstracted, dissociated, stripped from the male body" and made a "condition of possibility for the saturation of all bodies" it now became possible to conceive of men as objects of desire rather than desire's exclusive subjects (60). These processes of abstraction—what Floyd identifies as sites of "loss" and "wounding" (118)—resonate powerfully alongside the American anxiety around what it means to inhabit a "logocracy." But here I would add that the forms of medical objectification that abstracted the male body simultaneously endowed that body with physical substance. As I will go on to illustrate, even as it shook up the epistemological foundations of American brotherhood, the new science of bodies that took root provided new ways to legitimize and ground the abstractions of American democracy through recourse to the medicalized materiality of the body.[20] Thus while sexual science did not originate in America, I want to propose that the United States' unique genesis as a nation created a paradox for citizenship that sexual science helped resolve.

Picking up where national manhood left off, the chapters that follow progress historically and chronologically, each taking up a different moment in the twentieth century when queerness became an object of medical scrutiny. Beginning with the turn-of-the-century invention of the sexual invert, the book moves through early twentieth-century eugenic efforts to regulate women's fertility, 1950s psychiatric models of homosexuality, and millennial "post-AIDS" reclamation of viral metaphors, concluding with an exploration of the contemporary medicalization of both trans identity and low sexual desire. As my readings illustrate, when we mine these intertwined genealogies, what we discover is not simply a history of stigma but a creative refashioning of American manhood through both queerness and disability. In each of these moments, I argue, queerness has been "cripped" by vocabularies of disease, defect, and disorder and resignified by male and masculine-identified writers in ways that created a potent counternarrative of American masculinity.

My use of the term "crip" in this project, like my use of the term "queer," should be understood not as a noun but as a verb and modifier. It points not toward a coherent identity but toward practices and inflections that move both with and against the grain of compulsory able-bodiedness and across the ability/disability binary. Pioneered by Robert McRuer, Carrie Sandahl, and Alison Kafer, crip theory moves beyond disability studies' traditional focus on inclusion and visibility, urging disability scholars to adopt theorizations that shake up the epistemological foundations of disability. Without dispensing with identity-based questions and practices, crip readings are more interested in interrogating and deconstructing the performative practices through which coercive ideals of health and able-bodiedness circulate.[21] Borrowing from David Halperin's delineation of how queer theory departed from gay and lesbian studies, McRuer suggests that "crip theory might function—like the term 'queer' itself—'oppositionally and relationally but not necessarily substantively, not as a positivity but as a positionality, not as a thing, but as a resistance to the norm'" (*Crip Theory*, 31). Indeed, a cursory glance over the figures that populate this book reveals a set of bodies and archives that may not immediately read as "disabled." What basis is there, one may object, for viewing physical injuries inflicted between men (in the case of Jack London), eugenic explanations of independent female sexual expression (in the case of Faulkner), or the psychiatrization of homosexuality (in the case of Baldwin) as examples of the literary figuration of disability? Setting aside the question of who really counts as disabled, *Vulnerable Constitutions* asks which populations have been targets of medical and social scientific regulation. Tracing these questions across the twentieth- and twenty-first-century literary imagination requires engaging with a genealogy of American masculinity as it has been articulated through the politics of capacity, debility, precarity, and diagnosis.

These writers comprise an unconventional and eclectic archive, from Jack London's primitivist fantasies to James Baldwin's critiques of white liberalism and Eli Clare's self-identification as a disabled rural dyke and later as a trans man. But what all of these writers share is a unique orientation to American masculinity shaped by their identification with vulnerable or at-risk groups. Despite their diverse subject positions, each experienced disillusionment with the way abstract models of American brotherhood failed to meet the needs of a heterogeneous population. Jack London was a Socialist protesting the capitalist exploitation of working-class men; Faulkner was writing in a South devastated by the Civil War; James Baldwin was intimately aware of the gendered violence of racism; Samuel Delany witnessed the public health campaigns that targeted gay spaces rather than saving gay lives during the AIDS epidemic; and Eli Clare writes poignantly of his experience as a transgender working-class rural queer survivor of physical and sexual abuse. Fitzgerald is arguably the most conventional of the writers that I examine, but even he struggled with what it meant to take up a "feminine" sentimental mode of writing against his more "masculine" modernist contemporaries. Positioning themselves against the grain of hegemonic American culture, these writers each expose the ways standard narratives of American citizenship fail to incorporate those groups it renders disposable. They are united by their desire for an alternative account of masculinity and citizenship, one that acknowledges the toll that racism, capitalism, and heterosexism can take on the physical body as well as the psyche. Though the early figures in my study are rarely considered in relation to either queerness or disability (much less the intersection of the two), I maintain that sexual science provided an opportunity for even the most seemingly canonical writers to rewrite the story of American masculinity as a story of queer-crip rebellion.

In particular, I propose that sexual science and evolutionary discourse provided a means to account for a uniquely American biology without reverting to lines of patrilineal descent. Though we might imagine that evolutionary theory, with its commitment to biological inheritance, would solidify the links between "father" and "son" and impose a set of rigidly hierarchical taxonomies regarding the development of the human species, many of the concepts to emerge from this Darwinian moment provided resources for thinking more eccentrically about species and citizenship. Atavism, for example, provides a nonlinear map of species evolution. Referring to vestigial tails and other evolutionary throwbacks, atavism describes the way that prehistoric ancestral traits, long dormant in the DNA, can suddenly and spontaneously biologically manifest themselves in the present. As Dana Seitler notes:

> Operating less by a process of continuity than by sporadic interruption, atavism skips generations: it requires a period of latency or "intermission" before it recurs in the present. It thus belies the conception of identity as direct and individualized and of time as an unbroken continuity, instead placing human beings in a more inclusive and unpredictable history of biological origins and influences. Indeed, atavism is posed as a category of personhood that erases an immediate reproductive connection between parent and child, situating the locus of the individual's identity in a much earlier ancestral moment that is no longer secured in the past but destined to recur. (2)

By "erasing the immediate reproductive connection between parent and child," evolutionary discourses offered up a form of national embodiment that was not only grounded in unpredictable and unruly eruptions of the body but also, importantly, detached from national bloodlines. As a result, the vexed question of national birthright became gradually displaced by a more generalized politics of "life."[22]

Thus, while "national manhood" is an extremely useful lens for thinking about constructions of nineteenth-century citizenship, we need models that can also account for the enormous impact that sexual science had on American understandings of national embodiment throughout the twentieth century. As I argue in my reading of Jack London, the "fraternal melancholy" that animates the mourning of dead patriarchs requires an Oedipal structure that is actively set aside in London's articulation of antiprophylactic citizenship. While I do not claim that Oedipal narratives disappear with the emergence of twentieth-century sexual science (indeed, in my chapter on James Baldwin, I make a case for the prevalence of those narratives within the texts of Cold War sexual psychiatry), the authors I examine in this book each articulate a biopolitical counternarrative of American masculinity that is resolutely antiprophylactic. In these accounts, psychic repression (with its privileging of bonds between fathers and sons) is exchanged for the lateral sensations of male friendship.[23] If the melancholic identifications of the "national man" were based on the repression of American democratic heterogeneity, then the biosocial intimacies of antiprophylactic citizenship represent its uncensored and unconditional expression. Here, the contradictory and continually mutating will of the masses is claimed as the primary virtue of American democracy.

For an example of such values, we might briefly turn to Thomas Jefferson who, in many of his writings, framed the American Constitution as a site of continual generational revision. Writing for *The Guardian*, Michael Hardt summarizes Jefferson's views on revolution:

> The first key to understanding Jefferson's notion of transition is to recognize the continuous and dynamic relationship he poses between rebellion and constitution or, rather, between revolution and government. A conventional view of revolution conceives these terms in temporal sequence: rebellion is necessary to overthrow the old regime, but when it falls and the new government is formed, rebellion must cease. In contrast to this view, Jefferson insists on the virtue and necessity of periodic rebellion—even against the newly formed government . . . "God forbid we should ever be 20 years without such a rebellion," he writes. In Jefferson's view, rebellion should not become our constant condition; rather, it should eternally return.[24]

In Jefferson's model, the goal of democratic government is not to ensure stability across time but rather to allow room for its own periodic undoing. Like the primordial outbreaks that are "destined to recur" spontaneously in the human body, "revolution" is given here as a site of "eternal return" in which the immediate connection between "fathers" and "sons" is disavowed. Jefferson makes this point quite clearly in an 1816 letter to Samuel Kercheval that criticizes men who "look at constitutions with sanctimonious reverence" and "deem them like the ark of the covenant, too sacred to be touched" (616).

Noting that "the dead have no rights" and "no substance," Jefferson advocates instead for the rights of "present corporeal inhabitants" of the "corporeal globe" to "make the Constitution what they think will be best for them" (617). Thus against the static and predictable channels that bloodlines take, Jefferson points to a generalized politics of "life" that has no truck with dead or absent patriarchs and whose reach extends beyond the boundaries of nation to the "corporeal globe." To require today's living breathing generations to follow a dead generation's laws, Jefferson suggests, is like "requir[ing] a man to wear still the coat which fitted him as a boy" (616). In this view, if America has anything like a "national body," it is a body whose ever-changing materiality must remain unconstrained by the laws and fashions of its predecessors. In stark contrast to the usual framing of the body politic as a spiritualized sovereign head that rules over a complicit material body, this ideal of the American Constitution (both big "C" and little) prioritizes the body's fundamental elasticity. Imperfect and endlessly revisable, it opens itself up to periodic mutation and even revolt.

Scientific discussions of atavism are admittedly anachronistic to Jefferson's writings, which predate the rise of evolutionary theory by half a century. But while the similarities between atavism and periodic rebellion may remain figurative, Jefferson's experiences with the science of inoculation are likely to have directly informed his vision of an unruly American biology. Having lived through a major smallpox outbreak, Jefferson was a strong proponent of the then-controversial practice of inoculation. Because inoculation involved the deliberate transfer of infection, inoculation felt like a risky practice to many Americans who worried that these attempts to vaccinate otherwise healthy individuals would only cause the disease to spread. Protests arose to resist the practice, including the Norfolk anti-inoculation riots of 1768 and 1769, in which a prominent physician's house was set on fire after he arranged to have inoculations performed on his family and friends. Jefferson represented the physician in court, and went on to support a bill that helped to decrease restrictions on the practice.[25] Thirty-seven years later, during his presidential term, Jefferson penned a letter of gratitude to "father of immunology" Edward Jenner, who developed the first smallpox vaccine, thanking him on behalf of the "whole human family" (531) for his role in eliminating the smallpox epidemic.

On the one hand, Jefferson's alignment with medical authority and his efforts to institutionalize vaccination would seem to represent a prophylactic sensibility, protecting the population against the anticipated threat of disease and infection. But inoculation, particularly in Jefferson's era, was also fundamentally antiprophylactic to the extent that it involved the transmission of biological material across bodies and even species (indeed, the first smallpox vaccine used fluid from milkmaids' cowpox sores). Still an experimental procedure, it seemed to violate health norms in its willingness to infect an otherwise healthy individual with disease. Jefferson's attitude toward inoculation thus links national vitality to an ethics of physical receptivity and constitutional adaptability. While it may be a stretch to describe Jefferson's vision of the national body as a bug brotherhood, his vision of inoculation resonates with the bug chasing mantra: "infected but not ill" (Dean, 68). Indeed, when Jefferson critiques those who "look at constitutions with sanctimonious reverence . . . deem[ing] them . . . too sacred to be touched," (Jefferson, 616) he could just as easily be describing his attitude toward the anti-inoculation rioters set on maintaining the integrity of their physical bodies against deliberate viral transmission.[26] In this respect, antiprophylactic citizenship emerges as one of the United States' founding principles.

Cripping Queer Methodology

Presenting an evolving narrative of medicalized sexuality and antiprophylactic masculinity over the course of the twentieth and early twenty-first centuries, *Vulnerable Constitutions* extends intersectional thinking among queer and disabled scholars and activists. Despite their intertwined histories and the richness of contemporary collaborations between the two fields, queers and crips have not always been easy bedfellows. To occupy a medicalized identity is to be viewed as lacking, incomplete, and in need of "fixing." Coercive programs of sexual rehabilitation, present throughout the century and manifested most recently in the spread of religiously backed "ex-gay" therapies, remind us that these processes of medicalization are not merely rhetorical but play out materially, through the disciplining or outright social quarantine of bodies and practices at the sexual margins. Given these histories, sexual minorities have had reason to approach the diagnostic framing of queer sexuality with discomfort. Rather than providing a rich source of critique, disability is all too often understood as something that queer sexuality has liberated itself from—the estranged sibling whose kinship threatens to reveal a shameful and pathologizing past.

One of the more straightforward examples of this complicated kinship between queer and crip activism played out in 1970 and 1971 protests that led to the eventual removal of "homosexuality" from the *Diagnostic and Statistical Manual of Mental Disorders* (*DSM*). Fed up with two decades of psychiatric medicalization, gay liberationists targeted both the APA and the AMA in what might, retrospectively, be described as a series of crip activist interventions. Using Guerilla Theater and other confrontational tactics, these activists called attention to the value judgments and biases that underpinned the organizations' supposedly "objective" criteria for diagnosing mental illness. As John D'Emilio notes, at one session "a young bearded gay man danced around the auditorium in a red dress, while other homosexuals and lesbians scattered in the audience and shouted 'Genocide!' and 'Torture!' during the reading of a paper on aversion therapy" (235).[27] The gay liberationist assault on the profession followed on the heels of other contemporary critiques of psychiatric authority. The Insane Liberation Front of Portland, Oregon, had been founded in 1970, followed by the emergence of the Mental Patients' Liberation Front in both Boston and New York City in 1971.[28] Early manifestations of what would later become known as the Mad Pride movement, these activist groups protested "their negative treatment within the psychiatric system," having "shared the common experience of being treated with disrespect, disregard, and discrimination at the hands of psychiatry" (Lewis, 163). Representing a brief, albeit indirect, coalition between gay liberationists and antipsychiatry activists, this wave of protests cast a shadow on the objectivity of medicine, which was now, as Ronald Bayer puts it, "haunted by the specter of a politicized psychiatry that would be defenseless against an endless wave of protests" (141).

But when the fight to remove "homosexuality" from the *DSM* was won the following year, the victory represented not a weakening of the APA's institutional authority but, to the contrary, a strengthening of the very psychiatric models of difference that these activist efforts had meant to oppose. In a gesture of strategic flexibility, the 1972 convention organizers made room for displays and presentations by gay activists who did not target the institution of psychiatry itself but who took issue, rather, with what they saw as an error in classification. It was in this context that gay rights pioneers Frank Kameny and Barbara Gittings, founders of the Mattachine Society and Daughters of Bilitis, collaborated on an exhibit labeled with a large sign reading "Gay, Proud and Healthy," coauthoring a manifesto of the same title that they distributed alongside the display. Overturning the damaging cultural conflations of "gay," "shameful," and "sick," the document expressed a hope that psychiatrists might become allies rather than antagonists to the movement, using their institutional credibility to legitimize, rather than pathologize, same-sex desire. In an open letter published immediately following the vote to remove "homosexuality" from the *DSM*'s list of disorders, Kameny marshaled a metaphorics of "cure" that, while playful and ironic, also celebrated the APA's extraordinary ability to unravel the discursive foundations of homosexual stigma:

> At approximately 8:30 A.M. on Saturday, December 15th, 1973 . . . the APA Board of Trustees passed the Nomenclature resolution, and by unanimous vote (one abstention) passed the Civil Rights resolution, making them final, and "curing" us all, instantaneously, en masse, in one fell swoop, by semantics and by vote, instead of by therapy . . . The net effect of this resolution is to remove Homosexuality from the APA's Nomenclature . . . and from their Diagnostic and Statistical Manual of Mental Disorders ("their sickness book") thus effecting the miraculous "cure" which I promised you almost a year ago when I solicited your support for my trip to [the convention in] Hawaii.[29]

The "cure" for homosexuality, Kameny satirically observes, was not to be found in pharmaceuticals, aversion therapy, or psychoanalysis but in the APA's transformative speech act. Granted "in one fell swoop, by semantics and by vote," the resolution functioned as a linguistic magic bullet. Like a patient discharged from a hospital with a clean bill of health, the word "homosexuality" was now free to exit the "sickness book" and enter the lexicon of mainstream culture with a new (qualified) claim to normalcy.[30] The 1973 victory against the APA might thus be understood as a powerful example of what disability theorists David Mitchell and Sharon Snyder have called "methodological distancing," the process by which marginalized populations "[seek] to unmoor their identities from debilitating physical and cognitive association" (*Narrative Prosthesis*, 2). As the ultimate signifier of deficiency and inferiority, disability is often understood as "the 'real' limitation from which [these identities] must escape" (2). One of the central claims of *Vulnerable Constitutions* is that we cannot fully understand the genealogy of queer sexualities in the United States without considering historical flashpoints like this one. Perhaps more controversially, the book suggests that the history of queer sexuality in the United States is, to some extent, part of the history of disability.

A fundamentally cripistemological inquiry, *Vulnerable Constitutions* explores the grids of intelligibility through which we have made certain queer bodies "knowable" as inverts, degenerates, criminals, narcissists, and autoimmune patients. It also illustrates the way the developing science of epidemiology allowed American writers to fashion alternative—even resistant—epistemologies of queerness, disability, and masculinity. Cripistemology, as

Robert McRuer and Merri Lisa Johnson define it, activates discussion about "knowing and unknowing disability, making and unmaking disability epistemologies, and the importance of challenging subjects who confidently 'know' about 'disability,' as though it could be a thoroughly comprehended object of knowledge" (130). For McRuer and Johnson, cripistemological projects not only "attend to rejected and extraordinary bodies" but also "explore disability at the places where bodily edges and categorical distinctions blur or dissolve (where the disabled body as a literal referent is, if not dematerialized, then differently materialized" (134). In making queerness more proximate to disability, *Vulnerable Constitutions* acknowledges the way queer relationalities are conditioned by sensory states as well as epistemological sites, having as much to do with the embodied intimacies of bug chasing as with taxonomies of sexual deviance. Its chapters are based on the assumption that the biocultural intersection of science, medicine, and literature has much to tell us about the way queer bodies are de- and rematerialized within the American national imagination, particularly in relation to each other. Thus I join McRuer and Johnson, as well as writers like Jasbir Puar, David Mitchell, Sharon Snyder, Mel Chen, Alison Kafer, Lauren Berlant, Dean Spade, and Nirmala Erevelles in extending queer theory's and disability studies' recent biopolitical turns.

The biopolitical turn in disability studies has pushed the field to expand its traditional focus on questions of identity, stigma, pathology, representation, and rights to include a more fluid model of capacity and debility. The publication in 2012 of Jasbir Puar's "Coda: The Cost of Getting Better: Suicide, Sensation, Switchpoints" is emblematic of this newer approach. Puar observes that, within a neoliberal economy, "all bodies are being evaluated in relation to their success or failure in terms of health, wealth, progressive productivity, upward mobility, enhanced capacity" and thus "there is no such thing as an 'adequately abled' body anymore" (155). Rather, the body is "always debilitated in relation to its ever-expanding potentiality" (153). Focusing on the forms of "slow death," institutional neglect, and debility that are "endemic to disenfranchised communities" (155), Puar thus urges disability scholars to expand their focus beyond deviant embodiments, suggesting that "a political agenda that disavows pathology" may be less potent than one that asks: "which bodies are made to pay for 'progress'? Which debilitated bodies can be reinvigorated for neoliberalism, and which cannot?" (153). Puar is primarily interested in the way homonormative and ablenationalist projects collude in a process of capacitation, with certain respectable gay and disabled citizens folded into the life of the nation while others are cast into a sphere of debility and neglect. While these new biopolitical methodologies energized the field, some worried that they risked universalizing disability, blurring the line between disabled and nondisabled bodies in ways that took away from the specificity of disabled experience.

Puar's essay originally appeared in the queer studies journal, *GLQ*, marking an increasing disciplinary collaboration—and one might even say an increasing dissolution of the boundaries—between the fields of queer theory and disability studies. At the same time, the wariness of disability scholars to fully adopt models of debility or cripistemological frameworks appears to emerge out of a periodic disciplinary tension between the fields. This tension has historically been structured by claims about how each field either ignores the body or assigns too much critical weight to its materiality. Focusing on discursive effects, linguistic slippages, and psychoanalytic questions regarding ego formation and dissolution, many of the classic texts of queer theory—and particularly queer literary theory—have tended to displace the primacy of the physical body as a ground for identification. Conversely, while disability studies scholars have always embraced constructionist understandings of identity (pitting an essentializing "medical model" of disability against a more relativizing "social model"), for a time it seemed that the field was reluctant to relinquish the body itself as a basis for theorizing.[31] Emphasizing political economy and concrete issues of accessibility and health care, these scholars have maintained a certain (and frequently useful) stubbornness about the disabled body's materiality, which opposes queer sexuality's lack of fixity. Furthermore, while disability scholars and activists have developed a nuanced literature of critique around the medical model, scholars of sexuality studies and queer theory have only in the past several years begun to align queer struggles with a crip politics of dissent.

Attuned to both the complexities of disabled identity and experiences of debilitation, *Vulnerable Constitutions* uses both methodologies in tandem. It proceeds from the assumption that these approaches are complementary rather than contradictory and that the tension that may emerge as a result of vacillating between them is a productive one. I agree with Puar's qualification in her recent book *The Right to Maim* (2017) that "disability and debility are not at odds with each other" but are in fact "necessary supplements in an economy of injury that claims and promotes disability empowerment at the same time that it maintains the precarity of certain bodies and populations" (xvii). Indeed, against the psychoanalytic and deconstructive methodologies that have led queer theory to dismiss or misrecognize crip embodiments, biopolitics provides an opportunity for making disability legible in queer literary contexts.

Throughout this book, I model a biopolitical methodology for reading literary texts as a way of continuing to cut through these divides. A biopolitical reading practice pushes back against psychoanalysis by taking seriously the historical entanglements of queerness and disability. Often, in queer literary criticism, the disabled body functions as an invitation to uncover a hidden locus of desire and repression. In these accounts, Billy Budd's stutter is reduced to a figurative site through which the novel's homoerotic investments circulate and Tiny Tim's "active little crutch" props up nothing but the heteronormative promises of sentimental futurism.[32] Here, queerness surfaces primarily through a paranoid model premised on the management of information and the speech effects that performatively render the "secret" of same-sex desire. But when we shift our focus away from psychological depth and toward sociological breadth, forms of queerness that have flown under our critical radar begin to come into clearer focus. A biopolitical reading practice allows us, for example, to consider queerness in relation to reproduction rather than the death drive; to understand viral exchange as a building block of (rather than a catastrophe for) the creation of queer kinship networks; or to conceive of amputation as a moment of masculinization rather than as a crisis for masculinity.

I am inspired by Heather Love's suggestion that we might benefit from adopting "forms of analysis that describe patterns of behavior and visible activity but that do not traffic in speculation about interiority, meaning, or depth" ("Close Reading and Thin Description," 404). Thus while my textual analyses are clearly committed to practices of close or even "symptomatic" reading, I am careful in the chapters that follow to disentangle those readings from psychoanalytic accounts of interiority that understand queerness solely in terms of repression or the inscrutability of same-sex desire. Such reading practices not only limit the scope of our queer analyses but are often deployed in ways that either erase or appropriate disability. This book veers away from these standard queer readings by taking the clinical on its own terms. Placing deviant sexualities within their historical and biopolitical contexts, it aims to unsettle the disciplinary opposition between "material" (disabled) identities and "socially-constructed" (queer) ones.

For an early rationale of biopolitical reading, we might look to the instructive example set by Eve Sedgwick in her canonical *Touching Feeling*. Sedgwick opens her chapter on paranoid and reparative reading by calling attention to the conspiracy theories that emerged in the wake of the AIDS epidemic, noting that very little, in fact, changes if we believe that the government deliberately fashioned the virus as a way to exterminate gay men; the widespread neglect of the public health crisis revealed everything we needed to know about the expendability of gay (disabled) lives. In the following passage, which I quote at length, Sedgwick makes the biopolitical stakes of reparative reading clear:

> The force of any interpretive project of unveiling hidden violence would seem to depend on a cultural context, like the one assumed in Foucault's early works, in which violence would be deprecated and hence hidden in the first place. Why bother exposing the ruses of power in a country where, at any given moment, 40 percent of young black men are enmeshed in the penal system? In the United States and internationally, while there is plenty of hidden violence that requires exposure there is also, and increasingly, an ethos where forms of violence that are hypervisible from the start may be offered as an exemplary spectacle rather than remain to be unveiled as a scandalous secret. Human rights controversy around, for example, torture and disappearances in Argentina or the use of mass rape as part of ethnic cleansing in Bosnia marks, not an unveiling of practices that had been hidden or naturalized, but a wrestle of different frameworks of visibility.... I'm a lot less worried about being pathologized by my therapist than about my vanishing mental health coverage—and that's given the great good luck of having health insurance at all. Since the beginning of the tax revolt, the government of the United States—and, increasingly, those of other so-called liberal democracies—has been positively rushing to divest itself of answerability for care to its charges, with no other institutions proposing to fill the gap. (140)

Thus there is a strong, if often overlooked, biopolitical thrust to Sedgwick's move from the paranoid to the reparative. In Sedgwick's powerful reframing, new forms of violence need no longer move under cover, parading in plain view as measures of neoliberal security and neglect. As I suggested earlier, Bersani's turn away from biopolitics and toward psychoanalysis in "Is the Rectum a Grave?" left few frameworks for approaching the precarity of queer populations debilitated by the AIDS epidemic. I now want to invert that observation, noticing the way Sedgwick's turn away from psychoanalytic practices and toward biopolitical ones opened up new ways of thinking about queerness and disability together through an acknowledgment of debility.

Moments like this in Sedgwick's writing help speak back to Tobin Siebers's charge that *Touching Feeling* perpetuates a representational system that excludes the disabled body from the queer experience of shame. Because the affect of shame "turns on the movement between the private and public realms," Siebers argues, and because disabled bodies are always already the "public" property of the state, it carries different values and consequences for disabled people who are often, especially within institutional contexts, denied basic privacy ("Sex, Shame, and Disability Identity," 205). But Siebers's observation here is based on a relatively narrow set of paradigmatic impairments that allows him to oppose the "realness" of physical disability against the confessional mobility of the gay and lesbian closet. What of breast cancer, in this model, or environmental illness, or the forms of "biocertification" that people with nonapparent disabilities—both psychiatric and physical—must furnish in order to continue to access medical coverage and care?[33] In this context, it seems clear that the queer move toward cripistemologies is not about eliding the materiality of the body but about coming to know disability differently in ways that challenge—or at the very least throw into crisis—a set of assumptions that place the disabled body and the queer psyche on opposite sides of the signifying spectrum.

Further, if the very force of reparative reading, as Sedgwick describes it in *Touching Feeling*, is to acknowledge the impossibility of privacy and the everpresent conditions of exposure, violence, and neglect—through the continual production of precarity—then what better model is there for addressing the materiality of disabled body? Sedgwick makes these links to disability explicit toward the end of the chapter when she acknowledges how the "the brutal foreshortening of so many queer life spans . . . has deroutinized the temporality of many of us," including her own and her intimate friends' experiences with breast cancer and environmental illness (148). Here, she anticipates the contemporary discussions of capacity and debility that have marked both queer theory's and disability studies' biopolitical turns.[34]

Riffing on Jasbir Puar's intertwined concepts of homonationalism, debility, and capacitation, for example, David Mitchell and Sharon Snyder have recently coined the term "ablenationalism" to describe the neoliberal process of incorporation and exclusion in which certain capacitated disabled bodies are folded into the life of the nation while others are consigned to a sphere of neglect and abandonment. At the same time, they illustrate some of the vital ways that "disabled people's openly interdependent lives and crip/queer forms of embodiment provide alternative maps for living together" ("The Biopolitics of Disability," 3). Referring to these alternative maps as the "capacities of incapacity," Mitchell and Snyder highlight those "capabilities that exceed, and/or go unrecognized within, the normative script of biopolitics"

(3). The biopolitical visions I trace in this book grow outward from Mitchell and Snyder's alternative mappings of the "capacities of incapacity." Indeed, when Mitchell and Snyder situate disability at the "materialist edge of species innovation" (27), their observation that "species are characterized by and sustained by mutation" (vii) mirrors Jefferson's own language of constitutional adaptability. As I illustrated earlier, Jefferson resisted a reverential approach to the nation's founding documents; in his view, the most robust Constitution was one that could be dirtied, stretched, adapted, and reshaped to fit the needs of future generations. It is necessarily unruly and occasionally revolting. Vulnerability, in this context, represents neither weakness nor incapacity but a generative receptivity to the other. Thus, it is my argument throughout this book that, in addition to bringing together queer theory and disability studies, a biopolitical reading practice can help to reveal the queer-crip paradigms that are often overlooked in discussions of American citizenship.

Chapter Overview

Vulnerable Constitutions traverses the boundaries between medicine, memoir, and fiction, presenting literary readings that understand diagnostic practices as fictions in their own right, albeit ones that carry embodied material consequences. One of the book's grounding assumptions is that the American literary landscape—existing as it does at the intersection of "official" medical discourses and imagined fantasies of national subjectivity—reveals new rhetorical dimensions of the medicalized queer subject that cannot be found by focusing solely on the historical record or, for that matter, solely on the literary text. Specifically, I spotlight five moments over the past century in which the queer body or mind became an object of medical scrutiny. While we tend to focus on the way that these medical categorizations produced new forms of stigma, my readings uncover the way that these medical framings also created opportunities for imagining new sites of agency and resistance. Drawing from evolving vocabularies of disease and immunity in order embrace, rather than avoid, instances of susceptibility and risk, these writers paradoxically resist national health imperatives in the service of national vitality. Attending to what is both productive and troubling in each author's portrait of resistant queer-crip subjectivity, the book presents a nonteleological account of sexual science and its counternarratives.

Beginning with the turn-of-the-century rise of sexology, Chapter 1 locates in Jack London's fiction—*The Sea Wolf* originally published in 1904 and *Before Adam* originally published in 1906—an encounter between the diagnostic gaze and antiprophylactic body as it vacillates between two very different figurations of the queer-crip subject: the sexually inverted modern gentleman and the battered body of the homoeroticized primitive. Here, I argue that London not only uses the positive figurations of queerness and disability to elevate the working-class masculinity of his contemporaries; he also employs negative figurations of queerness and disability in order to denigrate and disqualify some of the bourgeois masculine ideals that had preceded his own era. Seizing on the recently invented condition of neurasthenia and sexual inversion, London uses sexology as a rhetorical weapon against what he viewed as the anemic and substanceless masculinity of his direct antecedents. Transforming the previously celebrated qualities of "national manhood" into a set of queer pathologies and readable symptoms, London breaks with his nineteenth-century predecessors to offer what he felt was a newer and more robust definition of American manhood. Further, while psychoanalytic paradigms make it difficult to read the presence of disability in the text as anything other than Oedipal retribution for repressed homoerotic desires, I maintain that London's representations of disability and perverse sexuality, far from emasculating his characters, are the tools through which queerly gendered men are properly masculinized. The result is an ambivalent portrait of revolutionary brotherhood—a "revolting masculinity"—that prioritizes "constitutional" plasticity as the key to embodying the United States' foundational democratic virtues.

Of course, evolutionary theory came to take on a new set of practical applications, deployed by eugenicists in an effort to contain the American body politic by policing the fertility of "degenerate" populations. Chapter 2 examines the role that the reproductive bodies of women have played in the construction of antiprophylactic citizenship, particularly in the context of the eugenic efforts during 1920s and 1930s. Contextualizing these eugenic efforts alongside the changing status of sentiment, I call attention to three pathologized figures: the perversely sexualized teenage mother, her potentially "defective" child, and the male doctor who, weakened by his sentimental attachments to women, fails to maintain properly eugenic personal and national boundaries. Here, I challenge psychoanalytic readings of Faulkner's 1931 novel *Sanctuary*, arguing that what defines Popeye's queerness in the text is not his same-sex desires but his status as the disabled child of a mother who would likely have been assigned the pathologizing label of feebleminded by eugenicists of the period. Reading F. Scott Fitzgerald's 1936 novel *Tender Is the Night* through this optic, I suggest that the novel's uneasy vacillation between science and sentiment—an opposition central to contemporaneous debates on eugenics—places reproductive anxieties, rather than homosexual panic, at the heart of the novel's gender troubles. But even as they pivot around discourses of sexuality and disability, both "mother" and "child" also function in these novels as sites of antiprophylactic democratic promise, particularly when figured in relation to a permeable male subject. Indeed, as I illustrate in my reading of Fitzgerald's *Tender Is the Night*, Dick Diver's periodic rejections of eugenic science function as a way of recuperating the "fraternal feeling," transferring democratic sentimentalism, however ambivalently, back to its "proper" location in the male body.

While the first two chapters focus on discourses of embodied deviance (the aristocratic invert and the feebleminded mother and child), Chapter 3 turns to psychiatric paradigms, focusing on the Cold War medicalization of the homosexual psyche. Historians of sexuality have often called attention to the discourses of anti-Americanism that were projected onto gay men during the McCarthy era whose duplicitous "double lives" likened their sexualities to acts of treason and espionage. Less remarked upon, however, is the way that sexual psychiatry of the 1950s set the stage for this kind of analogical thinking. Upon entering the *DSM* in 1954, "homosexuality" was no longer understood as a physical fact that presented itself on the improperly gendered body but rather as an identity stemming from sexual repression and the fastidious management of a "secret." Reading James Baldwin's 1956 novel *Giovanni's Room* through these two overlapping discourses, I examine the practices of psychiatric self-diagnosis through which Baldwin's white protagonist, David, filters not only the experience of same-sex desire but also his status as an American citizen. However, against typical psychoanalytic readings of the novel, I suggest that Baldwin uses David's conspicuous practices of self-diagnosis to enact a complicated critique of Cold War sexual psychiatry and expose the whiteness of its closet paradigm. Not simply dismissive of psychological disability, however, Baldwin takes up racialized discourses of schizophrenia in his political writing during the 1960s. Turning to these essays, I argue that Baldwin ultimately proposes a model of racial interdependence and antiprophylactic citizenship that blurs the boundaries between physical and psychic life.

Chapter 4 presents the most literal focus on antiprophylaxis, exploring queer discourses of sexual citizenship in what Eric Rofes has termed the "post-AIDS" era. With advances in drug treatments making HIV an increasingly chronic condition for those who can access them, new subcultural practices—including bug chasing and barebacking—have redefined "risk" and transmission in ways that reflect emergent desires for crip futurity. Pairing Samuel Delany's *Times Square Red, Times Square Blue* (1999) with contemporary discussions of bug chasing, I identify the text as part of a larger cultural turn by which the virus has come to organize new forms of civic life rather than signify, as it had previously, a queer politics of death and mourning. Here I argue that the forms of "gift-giving" championed in Delany's landmark text, while not literally linked to viral transmission, are nonetheless animated by a similar commitment to the antiprophylactic willingness to be "infected" with the virtues of fraternal citizenship. In this way, Delany's essay presents a vibrant countercultural—though ultimately masculinized—world of American democratic belonging that resonates with the bug chasing mantra "infected but not ill" (Dean, 68). Of course, sometimes "infected" does mean "ill," even as the experience of debility remains strikingly absent from Tim Dean's account of bug chasing. I conclude the chapter by making the stakes of this omission clear, arguing that any meaningful antiprophylactic vision must grapple with and acknowledge the (often feminized) terrain of debility.

Extending Chapter 4's exploration of neoliberalism and debility, Chapter 5 turns to two contemporary forms of queer identification that continue to be articulated within medical frameworks: asexuality and transmasculinity. Reading John Cameron Mitchell's film *Shortbus* (2006) in the context of *DSM* models of low desire, I explore the way rhetorics of sexual optimization, health, and orgasmic capacity have been instrumental in reproducing queer citizenship as an expression of political, subcultural, and psychological health. As new rehabilitative regimes have transformed sexual openness and receptivity into a biopolitical mandate, low desire has increasingly come to occupy the feminized space of debility. Thus it is crucial to clarify the forms of feminist and crip agency encoded in seemingly "antiprophylactic" acts of sexual refusal. Here, I depart from the book's primary focus on cismale authors, taking up the autobiographical works of transmasculine writers including Paul B. Preciado's *Testo Junkie* and Eli Clare's *Exile and Pride*. While Preciado and Clare take us beyond medical models of transmasculinity, rejecting a definition of trans identity based on disorder, diagnosis, and cure, they diverge in their attitude toward testosterone as a sexually capacitating substance. Unlike Preciado, who celebrates the sexually galvanizing properties of testosterone, Clare explores the way that his disabled trans embodiment has come into uneasy alignment with asexual identification, particularly around experiences of trauma, exploitation, and socioeconomic precarity. Acknowledging vulnerability without mandating openness, Clare's memoir allows us to push back against the masculinist bias of some antiprophylactic models.

This chapter thus provides a necessary account of how antiprophylactic citizenship is transformed in the context of feminist transmasculinity. Indeed, while the celebration of risk and vulnerability is often presented as the key to a more robust corporeal existence, it can also clash with those feminist and crip contexts that prioritize the cultivation of safe and accessible spaces.[35]

The book's epilogue addresses these tensions, using the recent controversy surrounding Tony Matelli's sculpture *The Sleepwalker* and the "trigger warning" debates it ignited, to critically interrogate the concept of antiprophylactic citizenship. Reading the queer backlash against trigger warnings as the most recent articulation of antiprophylactic masculinity, I explore how the ableist injunction for college students to toughen up and "overcome" their psychological disabilities sits uneasily alongside the same commentators' overt valorization of vulnerability. The resulting binary between feminine "hypersensitivity" and masculine "resilience" reminds us that a truly antiprophylactic mode of citizenship must remain open to feminist-crip insights.

A study that begins with Jack London and ends with Eli Clare may appear to track a kind of progress narrative—beginning with the most identifiably heteromasculinist figure and ending with the most identifiably radical. However, my readings make clear that it would be a mistake to view this historical trajectory as a movement from repression to liberation. Rather, what we witness with the waning of national manhood and the rise of antiprophylactic citizenship is a fraught dialectic in which American cismale writers of the twentieth century attempted to produce an in-the-flesh oppositional space of masculine affiliation that embodied the virtues of democratic rebellion while often, at the same time, containing the sexual and physical "risks" that such spaces imply. However antiprophylactic and however committed to an ethics of queer receptivity, the "vulnerable constitutions" that I describe throughout the book frequently rely on the valorization of masculine biosocial bonds, leaving us to wonder to what extent antiprophylactic citizenship is possible for or available to women. Thus, in illustrating these writers' rejection of certain modes of compulsory heterosexuality and compulsory able-bodiedness, I am not claiming their visions as unqualified acts of queer-crip subversion. I read them, instead, as densely charged and often contradictory sites for the emergence of an alternative masculinity that moves, depending on one position, both with and against the grain of hegemonic ones.

1

"An Inherent Weakness of the Constitution"

Jack London's Revolting Men

In a 1903 essay titled "What Shall Be Done with This Boy?" Jack London presents his readers with an American "constitution" in crisis. Exploring the case of a juvenile delinquent named Edgar Sonne, arrested for various petty crimes, London wonders whether Sonne's "yielding" to the temptations of theft should be viewed as the result of an "inherent weakness of the constitution itself, which cannot be cured" or as part of an "acquired and non-essential weakness of the constitution that can be cured" (73). The catalog of Sonne's physical ailments is lengthy and exhaustive: a "rottenness and irregularity of the teeth, an abnormally shaped roof of the mouth," tonsils that "were so enlarged that the passage between them was no more than an eighth of an inch wide," and a "postnasal cavity entirely filled with a growth of adenoids or tumors" whose "pressure on the brain" had begun to cause deafness and a heart problem (75). Despite these numerous signs of debility, London ultimately concludes that Sonne was "normal in the making" having "come into the world a soft and pulpy infant, to be molded by the physical and social forces which would bear upon him" (76). By the end of the essay, we are told that a "tonic treatment of the body" and "a tonsil operation" is what is needed for Sonne's mind and body to become "healthy, wholesome, and good" again (77). "Give me three months," says the doctor, "and I'll show you a transformed boy" (77).

Sonne's "constitution" is not the only one in need of repair. London frequently wrote about his disillusionment with his forefathers' failure to secure for him the abstract rights he has been promised in the U.S. Constitution.

In a 1905 Socialist speech titled "Revolution," London declares that "the comradeship of the revolution" has "proved itself mightier than the Fourth of July, spread-eagle Americanism of our forefathers" (142). In this elliptical reference to the signing of the Declaration of Independence, London pays a certain amount of tribute to the United States' revolutionary origins. But while fathers and sons might share a family resemblance, both deeply committed to principles of revolution and the legitimacy of political rebellion, London presents his own Socialist masculinity as an updated alternative to the former "spread-eagle Americanism." Though the United States may have initially been founded in rebellion, London seems to be saying, it has now matured into a fatherland that neglects the welfare of its white working-class sons. Like Sonne's debilitation, the "weakness" of the U.S. Constitution is not innate but acquired. As such, it requires an intervention that will make it "healthy, wholesome, and good" once more. This chapter argues that queerness and disability, as configured within London's writing, are absolutely essential to that process.

Such a claim may appear counterintuitive given London's privileging of "health" and normalcy in the passages quoted above (and throughout his writing), as well as his denigration of "weakness" and "degeneracy." As a member of the white working class, London found himself caught between a desire to valorize the heteromasculine and able-bodied ideals of his era—including the prophylactic containment of disability—and the necessity of validating the masculinity of laboring men who are "wrenched and distorted and twisted out of shape by toil and hardship and accident, and cast adrift by their masters like so many old horses" (126). The result is an ambivalent portrait of revolutionary brotherhood—a "revolting masculinity" whose queer and crip dimensions London both claims and disavows.[1]

Sonne is not the only male character of London's to be introduced to the reader through an exhaustive catalog of injuries. In his 1911 boxing narrative "The Mexican," London turns again to the corporeality of the battered masculine body to anchor the abstract ideals of political revolution. When Felipe Rivera, a young man whose parents have been slaughtered during Porfirio Diaz's dictatorial regime, offers his services to the revolutionary uprising against Diaz, he is first met with suspicion, then simply confusion as he shows up day after day with bruises on his body and gold to fund the revolutionary effort:

> Now he appeared with a cut lip, a blackened cheek, or a swollen ear. It was patent that he brawled, somewhere in that outside world where he ate and slept, gained money, and moved in ways unknown to them. As the time passed, he had come to set type for the little revolutionary

sheet they published weekly. There were occasions when he was unable to set type, when his knuckles were bruised and battered, when his thumbs were injured and helpless, when one arm or the other hung wearily at his side while his face was drawn with unspoken pain. (402)

What his comrades don't know, but what the reader soon finds out, is that Rivera has become a small-time champion on the boxing circuit, fighting not for glory or personal gain but to raise money for the resistance. The reader is told that "it takes money to raise a modern revolution, and . . . there were times when it appeared as if the Revolution stood or fell on no more than the matter of a few dollars" (400). At these moments, it is Rivera who "laid sixty dollars in gold" or "a thousand two-cent stamps on May Sethby's desk," allowing the revolutionaries to send the "three hundred letters, clicked out on the busy typewriters (appeals for assistance, for sanctions from the organized labor groups, requests for square news deals to the editors of newspapers, protests against the high-handed treatment of revolutionists by the United States' courts) [that] lay unmailed, awaiting postage" (400). This description of the Junta's "busy typewriters" and inert stacks of letters echo Washington Irving's accusation, a century earlier, that the government of the United States was little more than a "logocracy." The revolution, it turns out, is a revolution of words—inert and lifeless, awaiting animation. Though Rivera is a man of few words himself, and though his boxing injuries render him "unable to set type," his damaged body and his "unspoken pain" are the only things capable of placing the Junta's "three hundred letters" into productive circulation. As one awed member of the Junta describes him two pages later, Rivera is "the Revolution incarnate" (403). Giving form and weight to the Junta's abstract ideals, his battered flesh legitimizes the revolution's loftier theoretical principles by providing them with what David Mitchell and Sharon Snyder have called "an anchor in materiality."[2]

In this way, London biologizes the concept of revolt while at the same time universalizing it. Despite the story's title, revolutionary resistance, in "The Mexican," is not nationally specific. Rather, the real muscle that animates revolution issues from a primordial place where the boundaries of nation do not *yet* exist. Rivera's eyes "are savage as a wild tiger's" and he is "pitiless as steel, keen and cold as frost. He is like moonshine in a winter night when a man freezes to death on some lonely mountain top" (401). Rendered prenational and prelinguistic, Rivera's corporeality is at a fundamental disconnect from the eloquent words and specific ideologies that his brawn nonetheless succeeds in animating.[3] Indeed, much like the gold that he lays on Mary Sethby's desk, Rivera's body is presented as a raw natural substance that is (socially and arbitrarily) converted into capital. Emblematizing no particular law and no national agenda, Rivera embodies, instead, the physical force or "state of exception" that is the law's founding condition.[4]

But what, for London, is to be gained by rendering nationality irrelevant to the muscular capacity for revolt? What makes a Mexican revolutionary uprising relevant to London's reinvention of American citizenship? The process of denationalization (or perhaps more appropriately *pre*nationalization) that Rivera undergoes throughout London's story allows London to present a model of fraternity that does not rely on shared national birth or patriarchal bloodlines. As David Savran notes:

> The United States is one of the few countries that became a political unit before it became a nation. After the Revolutionary War, it was consolidated as a political, commercial, and administrative entity . . . without, however, developing either a national culture or a consensus on what the defining qualities of the nation might be. Unlike other countries, it could not stake a claim to having a unique language. It shared English with its former colonizer, Great Britain, and with colonial states in North America. (262–263)

It is as though London is asking himself what—besides the disqualified concepts of religion, language, and national birthright—is left to bind American men to one another? That binding substance is here revealed as wounds that materialize in the primordial body: the "cut lip," "blacked cheeks," and "swollen ears" that evidence a man's physical capacity to step outside of the law and resist an unjust regime of political power. By offering Rivera as "the Revolution Incarnate," London transforms the liability of American manhood (the lack of a shared national birth) into its best advantage: a form of transcendent brotherhood that anyone, from any nationality, can embody.

In claiming the primitive, London and his naturalist contemporaries were in part attempting to address a perceived "crisis" in masculinity that had developed as the nineteenth century drew to a close. The rise of evolutionary theory, the increased visibility of a muscled working class, along with the political and cultural gains of women and minorities, produced a rhetoric of crisis around American masculinity. As a result, new naturalist narratives of masculinity emerged that blamed the specialized professions for alienating men from their bodies and from each other. Professionalism was understood to be a prophylactic and insulating force, protecting men from exposure to the natural world and thus alienating them from their primitive drives and instincts. Socially constructed differences between men and women were mapped onto the evolutionary scale with "early man" embodying the supposedly masculine attributes of aggression, strength, and sexual potency and "modern man" embodying the supposedly feminine traits of gentleness, domesticity, and spirituality. In this model, civilization was thus reimagined as a sanitizing force whose domestic comforts and urban distractions severed men from their connection with the earth, their natural heterosexual desire, and, by extension, their natural claim to social power. In this new "cult of muscularity," the hallmarks of the nineteenth-century gentleman (restraint, civilization, professionalism) became reconfigured as an unhealthy overdevelopment of the mind and a shameful underdevelopment of the body.[5]

In what follows, I argue that London not only uses the positive figurations of queerness and disability to elevate the working-class masculinity of his contemporaries; he also employs negative figurations of queerness and disability in order to denigrate and disqualify some of the bourgeois masculine ideals that had preceded his own era. Seizing on the recently invented conditions of "neurasthenia" and "sexual inversion," London uses sexology as a rhetorical weapon against what he viewed as the anemic and substanceless masculinity of his direct antecedents. Transforming the previously celebrated qualities of the bourgeois patriarch into a set of queer pathologies and readable symptoms, London breaks with his nineteenth-century predecessors to offer what he felt was a newer and more robust definition of American revolutionary manhood. London's valorized version of manhood can be described as antiprophylactic to the extent that it places faith in bodily exposure and celebrates the physically fortifying, and ultimately capacitating, qualities of pain and injury. London's fiction is thus preoccupied with two recurring figures who oppose dominant ideals of health and heteronormativity: the aristocratic male invert and the lower-class brute who accumulates a vast inventory of injuries at sea and on "the road." I use these figures to unsettle London's reputation as an author singularly invested in heteromasculine "fitness," revealing instead the queer-crip paradigms of masculine embodiment that structure his work. London's harsh naturalist environments give rise to a set of violent and perversely sexualized exchanges between men. London presents his physically damaged rogues as the raw material out of which states are crafted. Like paperweights, their dense physicality is designed to anchor and stabilize the written word, providing heft and substance to the otherwise "empty" declarations of American democratic independence.

A Beastly and Inarticulate Thing

Unlike London's brief treatment of the Mexican Revolution in "The Mexican" or the dystopian portrait of oligarchic rule he paints in *The Iron Heel* (1908), London's 1904 novel *The Sea Wolf* is at a literal remove from the world of political conflict, taking place on a sealing schooner in the middle of the Pacific Ocean. It is in this remote setting that pampered aristocrat Humphrey Van Weyden is rescued from shipwreck when a seal-hunting vessel spots his body in the ocean's freezing waters. Captained by the ruthless Wolf Larsen, the vessel becomes Humphrey's unwilling home for the next several months during which time Wolf provides Humphrey with a harsh nautical education—an education that ultimately transforms Humphrey from an effete man of letters into a muscled sailor. Much of the novel centers on a set of philosophical debates staged between the intellectual gentleman Humphrey and the tyrannical and brutal Wolf. Wolf not only rejects the notion of a human spirit that transcends the body but, more importantly, refuses to acknowledge the sanctity of the abstract principles that lie behind the written law. His reign as ship's captain puts this materialism into practice: throughout the novel he delivers a set of vicious beatings to the men around him and kills several of his sailors without conscience or remorse. His frequent displays of physical violence appear to be justified not by any national, human, or spiritual law but instead by the principle through which the strong vanquish the weak—a hallmark of the period's popularized social Darwinism.[6] Throughout the novel, Wolf's philosophy is expressed through the gradual molding of Humphrey's body, which gains muscle and substance in proportion to his adoption of Wolf's staunch materialism. Indeed, when Sonne's doctor declares that in "three months," we will find him a "transformed boy," he might just as easily have been describing Humphrey's delayed coming-of-age on the waters of the Pacific (77).

In their attitudes toward the extent to which the "letter" of the law is sanctified, Humphrey and Wolf emblematize, respectively, two oppositional portraits of American masculinity: the dematerialized prophylactic manhood of the nineteenth century and the rematerialized antiprophylactic masculinity that developed around the turn of the twentieth century as its antidote. Dana Nelson has coined the term "national manhood" to describe the way in which our traditional narratives of American brotherhood are more aspirational than material. Because success within the nineteenth-century marketplace depended on emotional self-discipline and rigorous competition, white masculine bonds were more theoretical than practical, creating an "imagined fraternity" of white men that ultimately masked a larger reality of ideological conflict and socioeconomic inequality.[7] Though white fraternal unity was prized in the abstract, actual fraternal spaces and contacts—especially those occurring during the vulnerable period of a youth—were to be discouraged. For Nelson, this disconnect between the version of fraternity promised to white men and the lack of masculine camaraderie most white men experienced led to what she calls a "fraternal melancholy," an affective state that expressed this sense of disconnection and longing through ceremonial consecration of absent or dead patriarchs. Conjuring the "representative" American man as a spectralized presence, such rituals not only created a space of imagined masculine intimacy but also strengthened an American faith in the structures of representative democracy—the notion that one voice could, in fact, represent the interests of the many.

In an often ignored passage that appears early in the novel, Humphrey witnesses as Wolf verbally abuses his dying first mate—a sailor who, after going on "debauch" in "San Francisco" "had the poor taste to die . . . and leave [Wolf] short-handed" (*The Sea Wolf*, 14). I quote this passage at some length, as it is here that London launches one of his most clearly defined attacks on the national man's misplaced commitment to "fraternal melancholy" as a means of white male affiliation:

> The captain broke loose upon the dead man like a thunderclap. Oaths rolled from his lips in a continuous stream. And they were not namby-pamby oaths, or mere expressions of indecency. Each word was a blasphemy, and there were many words. They crisped and crackled like electric sparks. I had never heard anything like it in my life, nor could I have conceived it possible. With a turn for literary expression myself, and a penchant for forcible figures and phrases, I appreciated, as no other listener, I dare say, the peculiar vividness and strength and absolute blasphemy of his metaphors . . . It should be unnecessary to state, at least to my friends, that I was shocked. Oaths and vile language of any sort had always been repellent to me. I felt a wilting sensation, a sinking at the heart, and, I might just as well say, a giddiness. To me, death had always been invested with solemnity and dignity. It had been peaceful in its occurrence, sacred in its ceremonial. But death in its more sordid and terrible aspects was a thing with which I had been unacquainted till now. As I say, while I appreciated the power of the terrific denunciation that swept out of Wolf Larsen's mouth, I was inexpressibly shocked . . . But the

> dead man was unconcerned. He continued to grin with a sardonic humour, with a cynical mockery and defiance. He was master of the situation. (14–15)

If, as Nelson argues, the national man found fraternal affirmation in his "obsessive recourse to communion with dead men" (*National Manhood*, 202), then what we witness here is his failure to carry out this communion. Wolf's "blasphemy" is shocking to Humphrey not simply for its vulgarity but for the way in which it seems to actively block Humphrey's attempts to sanctify the spirit of a dead comrade—and, by extension, the spirit of representative democracy.

As a self-identified Socialist who had spent his youth shoveling coal and laboring in mills, London was well aware of the extent to which his duly elected political representatives did not actually "represent" the voices of the working class. Thus in an 1895 essay titled "What Socialism Is," London envisions a "pure democracy" in which the "supreme power rests with and is exercised directly by the people" as opposed to a "republican form of democracy, in which the supreme power rests with the people, but is indirectly exercised by them, through representatives"—representatives that may or may not ultimately vote in their constituents' best interests (57).⁸ A year later, in his 1896 piece "The Voters' Voice," London advocated again for direct legislation, expressing his distrust of the state's elected officials. Here, representative democracy emerges as a fundamentally prophylactic form of government that places a barrier between "the people" and the "supreme power" that should be theirs to exercise directly. By contrast, "pure democracy" is antiprophylactic to the extent that it opens up direct lines of contact between citizens and the laws that govern them. Paradoxically, such a democracy is "pure" by virtue of its impurities—its openness to the contaminations of a heterogeneous citizenry.

London's suspicion of representative democracy extends to the "representational" power of language itself. How else are we to understand Humphrey's page-long account of Wolf's "vulgar" and "repellent" figures of speech—words that he hears but respectfully chooses to withhold from the reader? Though "vulgar" is often linked to questions of obscenity and indecency, the concept of vulgarity primarily refers to a kind of common or distasteful accessibility that simplifies and reduces the obfuscations of high culture for easy mass consumption. When Humphrey afterward concludes that "life" in this nautical wilderness "had become cheap and tawdry, a beastly and inarticulate thing" (25) his diction suggests that he could just as easily be describing a trashy novel. Adjectives "cheap" and "tawdry" suggest a mass appeal and wide indiscriminate consumption by citizens who lack the literacy and education to select something more refined. By prophylactically censoring the "vividness and strength" of Wolf's "blasphemous metaphors," and mediating them with his own elegant figures of speech (indeed, we don't know what exactly Wolf said, just that his words "crackled like sparks"), Humphrey shields the reader from the raw force of Wolf's expressions, diluting them through the representative powers of his own elite literary imagination.

Further into the narrative, London delivers a parallel but inverse scene, this time explicitly connecting the "inarticulate" materiality of the body to the logic of political overthrow. A sailor named George Leach, responding to Wolf's abuses of power as captain, publicly curses Wolf in a speech that "ran the gamut of denunciation, rising to heights of wrath that were sublime and almost godlike, and from sheer exhaustion sinking into the vilest and most indecent abuse . . . His lips were flecked with a soapy froth, and sometimes he choked and gurgled and became inarticulate. And through it all . . . Wolf Larsen seemed lost in a great curiosity. This wild stirring of yeasty life, this terrific revolt and defiance of matter that moved, perplexed and interested him" (*The Sea Wolf*, 97). In his resistance to Wolf, Leach does not reach for the spiritualized authority of white manhood but instead embodies the primitive materiality of "matter that moved." On the one hand, Leach's "terrific revolt" here is intensely physical, requiring his devolution into something resembling a rabid animal frothing at the mouth. But the primary meaning here is, additionally, political. Like "yeast," he is engaged in an act of uprising, taking a stand against an unjust regime of power.

While this may appear to position Wolf as a figure of tyrannical rule, the passage at the same time suggests the contrary. More of a bully than a tyrant, Wolf's "great curiosity" and "interest" in Leach's "terrific revolt" registers a qualified approval of Leach's willingness to physically challenge his authority. As Agamben reminds us, the state of exception that exists at the heart of the law encompasses both revolution and tyranny. Relishing in this exceptionality, Wolf seems to celebrate the extent to which his "rule," as captain, is not based on abstract principles of justice or right but simply on his (or anyone else's) physical ability to seize power.

Thus, while it may be Leach and Wolf squaring off in this scene, the real opposition that emerges here is between the two models of American citizenship that Wolf and Humphrey each embody—an opposition, in other words, between the inarticulate and embodied revolt of the masses, and the articulate obfuscations of representative democracy. Indeed, just as Humphrey had earlier blocked the reader's exposure to the "blasphemy" of Wolf's "metaphors," he here refuses to transmit Leach's words to the reader, merely calling attention to their "vile" and "indecent" nature. Describing the froth that edges Leach's lips as "soapy," it is almost as though Humphrey takes on the role of the proverbial mother whose disciplinary response to profane language is to "wash out" her child's "mouth with soap." If Wolf represents the productive democratic discord of a violent and clamoring citizenry, then Humphrey may conversely emblematize the impotent and sanitizing gestures of the democratic "logocracy" whose elegant phrases prophylactically cover and contain a reality of conflict.

I reference "impotence" here intentionally, as London executes his critique of "national manhood" by presenting Humphrey (its emblem) as perversely asexual, improperly gendered, and endlessly diagnosable. Around this time, sexologists like Krafft-Ebing began to diagnose a set of particularly "modern" ailments like neurasthenia and sexual inversion. These "disorders" seemed to represent a by-product of modernity's unhealthy professional demands on the male body and mind. The specialized professions supposedly confined men to a solely intellectual existence, alienating them from their natural drives. Male intellectualism, in this framework, was aligned with the aristocratic detachment of effeminate dandy and his "life lived in quotation marks."[9] Thus in Oscar Wildean fashion, Humphrey admits that his appreciation of women rarely moves beyond the "aesthetic" (149). By emphasizing the way in which the "aesthetic" has supplanted the "sexual" in his appreciation of women, Humphrey explicitly links his lack of heterosexual desire with his overinvestment in linguistic style.

But it is not simply the case that modernity's drive to classify has created a vocabulary for naming Humphrey's disorder. Paradoxically, it is modernity's drive to classify that comprises the very core of Humphrey's disorder. Thus, in London's formulation, the objective scientific gaze that categorizes people and populations through the rubrics of sexual pathology does not seem to be, in the end, much different from the detached gaze of the elite literary critic whose aestheticism makes him readable as queer. Humphrey in fact slips between these two positions when, drawing from the scientific vocabularies of his day, he turns his critical eye inward, diagnosing himself as "abnormal, an 'emotionless monster,' a strange bookish creature, capable of pleasuring in sensations only of the mind" (149). To put it another way, by intellectualizing his intellectualism, Humphrey reveals the diagnostic gaze to be, itself, the site and symptom of queer pathology. It is in this way that London stages a reversal that unmasks the heteromasculine doctor as the sexually inverted male patient and the diagnostic impulse into the illness itself. A kind of literary criticism gone awry, Humphrey's effeminacy becomes the readable symptom of a life spent in the abstract realm of aesthetics.

Recalling his elite urban enclave in San Francisco, Humphrey confesses that the only brutality he has witnessed is the "brutality of the intellect" with its "cutting sarcasm," "cruel epigrams," and "occasional harsh witticisms" (101), a description that bears a striking resemblance to Washington Irving's explanation, a century earlier, that "in a logocracy, thou must know there is little or no occasion for fire-arms, or any such destructive weapons. Every offense or defensive measure is enforced by wordy battle and paper war;—he who has the longest tongue or readiest quill is sure to gain the victory" (*Salmagundi*, 110). Humphrey's "wordy" "paper wars," of course, do little to prepare him for the physical brutalities that he witnesses aboard Wolf's ship, the intensities of which cause him to long for the security of the domestic sphere:

> It had dawned upon me that I have never placed a proper valuation upon womankind. For that matter, though not amative to any considerable degree so far as I have discovered, I was never outside the atmosphere of women until now. My mother and sisters were always about me, and I was always trying to escape them, for they worried me to distraction with their solicitude for my health and with their periodic inroads on my den, when my orderly confusion, upon which I prided myself, was turned into worse confusion and less order though it looked neat enough to the eye. But now, alas, how welcome would have been the feel of their presence, the froufrou and swish-swish of their skirts which I had so cordially detested! I am sure, if I ever get home, that I shall never be irritable with them again. They may dose me and doctor me morning, noon, and night, and dust and sweep and put my den to rights every minute of the day, and I shall only lean back and survey it all and be thankful that I am possessed of a mother and some several sisters. (*The Sea Wolf*, 85)

Forty years earlier, Humphrey's knack for "surveying it all" from a position of detached intellectual authority might have been celebrated as a hallmark of masculine power.[10] This passage, however, performs a clever reversal. No longer issuing from powerful patriarchs, the medical gaze is here framed as a property of watchful maternal eyes. It is now the women who "doctor," and it is the upper-middle-class white male body that is "dosed" into a passive obsolescence. Against the grain of discourses of hysteria, which locates pathology in the female sexual anatomy, London presents these women as beings without bodies at all. Like ghosts, their spiritualized "presence" is not something one sees, examines, or symptomatizes but rather something one fetishistically "feels" by airy "swish-swish of their skirts." Additionally, by framing Humphrey's writing space as a parallel object of maternal caregiving (with his personal library receiving almost as much attention as his health), London forges an associational link between Humphrey's physical body and the papers and books that absorb it. The equation here is clear—the modern male body loses muscle and substance as it gains literacy.

Furthermore, if the nineteenth-century medical gaze was structured by a strict binary that separated the unruly body of the patient from the disembodied gaze of the physician, then what we have here is, to the contrary, a kind of replication or mirroring in which the body of the modern gentleman fails to materialize beneath the gaze of the women who "doctor and dose" him. Instead, he is feminized by the feminine gaze, his body *losing* substance the more it is subjected to his mother's and sisters' domestic surveillance. "Picture it to yourself," he, as consummate critic, directs the reader, translating his own physique into verbal portrait, "a man of ordinary stature, slender of build, and with weak, undeveloped muscles, who has lived a peaceful, placid life" (32). Thus we learn that Humphrey's "disordered" sexuality is not congenital but acquired from a lifetime of maternal pampering, which has eroded the weight and heft of his physical body. And just as Humphrey observes the failures of his sisters' attempts to add "order" to his library—their interventions, in fact, produce "less order" among his books—London implicates the maternal medical gaze as the very cause of illness. Like his workspace, Humphrey might be "neat enough to the eye," but in that very "neatness" he betrays the extent to which the prophylactic protection of the nuclear household has, ironically, transformed him into an "emotionless monster" unfit for heteronormative courtship.

Mothers are not the only pathologizing agent of the modern nuclear family—also important is Humphrey's dependence on his father's wealth. Though we are given no information about Humphrey's father, we are told that it is the "income" Humphrey receives from his father's estate, and not his occupation as a critic, that supports him financially. Humphrey's literary pursuits, which are essentially funded by his inheritance, are consequently framed not as a site of productive labor but as a parasitic drain on capital. When Humphrey answers "gentleman" to the question of what his occupation is, he reveals his faith in a patriarchal model of citizenship, one that is based not on the physical resources of the male body but the transmission of capital and status from father to son. Because this model of citizenship carries no currency in the Pacific wilderness that Humphrey now inhabits, Wolf accuses him of "standing on a dead man's legs," adding a crip dimension to the model of manhood that Humphrey embraces.[11] This observation is literalized earlier in the narrative, during Humphrey's initial shipwreck, as he finds himself "becoming hysterical," "with no sensation whatever in [his] lower limbs," and several seconds later "confesses that a madness seized me, that I shrieked aloud as the women had shrieked, and beat the water with my numb hands" (5). Meanwhile, we see a sailor "stumping gallantly around on his artificial legs and buckling life preservers on all comers" (3). Though standard psychoanalytic readings often frame questions of amputation and prosthesis through vocabularies of castration and physical lack, the sailor's "artificial legs" to the contrary function here to authorize his masculine independence. Meanwhile, Humphrey's ostensibly nondisabled body is suddenly readable through the medicalized vocabularies of hysteria. His aristocratic lack of economic self-sufficiency is rendered as a feminized disorder of the nerves and an impotent numbness below the waist, a queer paralysis compensated for (and on some level caused) by the prosthetic supports of an absent patriarch.

Thus by lampooning Humphrey's status as a purely linguistic being, a "man of letters," London stages a "representational crisis" that occurs on the level of both language and politics. Humphrey is an empty signifier of American democratic brotherhood, "neat enough to the eye" but masking a deeper social disorder. He is the theory without the practice, the word without the flesh, the letter of the law with nothing to justify it. Significantly, queerness and disability are the tools that London uses to interrogate this problem. The modern male aesthete, diagnosable as a sexual invert, becomes for London a cautionary tale about what can happen to the male body when national manhood is taken to its rational extreme. London's treatment of Humphrey's character, then, can be read as an attempt to expose the rhetorical foundations of white American brotherhood. Without a physical substance (like Rivera's primitive body) to stand in as a physical anchor for American national belonging, the masculine doctor collapses into the feminized patient, the able body becomes a site of weakness and atrophy, and the "normal" heteronormative relations between fathers, mothers, and sons collapse into the pathology of perpetual queer bachelorhood.

Crude Surgeries

If the heterosexual spaces of the modern city are presented as inherently feminine (and thus dangerously feminizing), then the perversely sexualized spaces of the sealing schooner, by contrast, are presented as inherently masculine (and thus productively masculinizing).[12] When we turn our attention to Wolf and his shipmates, we can see how London attempted to solve the fin de siècle crisis of masculinity not by purging tropes of queerness and disability but by reconfiguring those tropes through the crucible of primitivism. By the novel's conclusion, Humphrey's body has been remasculinized by its gradual exposure to physical injury and perverse sexuality. Thus queerness, in *The Sea Wolf*, is present in two forms—diagnosable inversion and the physical damage that results from violent homoerotic exchanges between men.

The homoerotic undercurrents of literary naturalism have been noticed by other scholars as well. Denise Cruz, for example, examines a set of homoerotic exchanges between the two hypermasculine protagonists in Frank Norris's *McTeague*, arguing that the triangulated queer desire that structures their friendship "shatters the myth that U.S. Naturalism's agenda can be read easily as a heterosexual remasculinization of decadent, effeminate literature" ("Reconsidering McTeague's 'Mark' and 'Mac'," 489) directing us instead to recognize the presence of "homoerotic partnerships between brawny, athletic, aggressive men" (489). In readings like this, the "homoerotic" is framed as a function of psychic repression, melancholic attachment, and "paranoid gothic" doubling. This imposes a universalizing psychoanalytic paradigm of masculinity onto naturalism's specific construction of masculinity. But when we take seriously naturalism's commitment to the body and its vigorous displacement of the psyche—trading a psychoanalytic reading practice for a biopolitical one—we are better able to locate the crip shapes queerness can take in these landscapes.

Before discussing the crip contours of these sexual exchanges, I want to point to the way that disability is remasculinized when it is transformed into physical injury or damage. In a series of passages that occur a third of the way into the narrative, Humphrey finds himself once again "shocked"—this time, not by blasphemous metaphors but by the events of a day in which "brutality had followed brutality" (*The Sea Wolf*, 101). These brutalities mainly consist of altercations between crew members that come to blows, and eventually gunshots. London's portrait of the medical treatment these men receive contrasts starkly with his earlier tribute to "womankind":

> The sound of blows and scuffling came to our ears. Both men were wounded, and [Wolf Larsen] was thrashing them for having dis-

obeyed his orders and crippled themselves in advance of the hunting season. In fact, they were badly wounded, and having thrashed them, he proceeded to operate on them in a rough surgical fashion and to dress their wounds. I served as assistant while he probed and cleansed the passages made by bullets, and I saw the two men endure his crude surgery without anesthetics and with no more to uphold them than a stiff tumbler of whiskey. (100)

This passage introduces a starkly gendered opposition. Rather than the maternal gaze that "doses" and "doctors" out of "solicitude" for the "health" of the male body, we are here presented with a hypermasculine form of care that is occasioned by violent injury and coarsely applied in a bizarre spectacle of punishment. If the feminine medical gaze led to a figurative anesthetization of Humphrey's body, rendering him "capable of pleasuring in sensations only of the mind," then this "crude surgery without anesthetics" fully materializes the male body by "prob[ing]" its injuries and prolonging its physical pain.

As Humphrey takes on more and more of the ship's responsibilities, London celebrates the way various parts of Humphrey's body become gradually materialized through the pain of injury. When Humphrey "burst[s] open the ends of his fingers" while working on a sail during a storm, he continues to work with "tears of pain running down [his] cheeks" (118). And when he begins to limp, having acquired a badly swollen knee, Wolf remarks that "the injury may cripple you some, but all the same you'll be learning to walk" (27). This observation, of course, hearkens back to Humphrey's initial framing as numb below the waist and standing on his dead father's legs. As we saw with the sailor "stumping gallantly" on "artificial legs," physical injury in this nautical wilderness is not, ultimately, disabling. It bruises temporarily but is ultimately healthful and restorative. After all, despite his commitment to baseness, Wolf is ultimately "cleansing" the passages that his instruments penetrate.[13] By contrast, bodies that are technically "able" (like Humphrey's before the shipwreck) are presented as housing disorders and pathologies.

In her book *Marked Men*, Sally Robinson connects literary depictions of wounded male bodies in late twentieth-century literature to postliberationist discourses of identity politics. She argues that in response to the claims of cultural victimhood made by various "marked" identities (women, people of color, sexual minorities), men who occupied the usually "unmarked" category of white masculinity began to engage in "an identity politics of the dominant" by making their own counterclaims of cultural victimization. Such claims, she suggests, could only be made through attempts to upstage the political "wounds" of sexism, racism, and homophobia with the "the persuasive force of corporeal pain" and the corporeality of the physically "wounded body" (20). Though Robinson's investigation centers on the postliberationist era, and on texts directly informed by identity politics discourse, her observations about the power of wounds to foster collective masculine identifications are intriguingly played out in London's preoccupation with physical injury.

Like the authors in Robinson's archive, London appears to be using the occasion of physical wounding to break the association between abstract individualism and white masculinity, marking masculine selfhood through the injuries that recorporealize it. But if the late twentieth century "masochistic . . . explorations of pain" (11) that Robinson explores signal a crisis of masculinity (treating wounds as the physical analog of cultural victimization—the perceived persecutions enacted in the name of "political correctness"), then the busted fingers and bullet wounds of London's sailors seem to serve a slightly different purpose. These wounds do not so much signal a crisis as much as resolve one, marking their characters not as afflicted "victims" but as newly masculinized subjects.[14] While this difference is partially explained through the difference in eras between Robinson's archive and mine, it may also be methodological, as Robinson's emphasis on the Freudian dimensions of masochism and the psychoanalytic dimensions of cultural trauma nonetheless make it difficult to understand physical impairment outside of the usual frameworks that understand disability as deficiency or affliction.

But in these landscapes, injury does not feminize and amputation cannot be read through its usual psychoanalytic lens as a metaphor for castration. Take for example the brief scene in which ship cook Mugridge's foot is "amputated neatly at the ankle" by shark bite, explained by Wolf as the unintended consequence of a rougher-than-usual "man-play" (*The Sea Wolf*, 21). While Scott Derrick reads this scene as illustrating the way "eroticism between men" is punished with the threat of "apocalyptic violence," (122) this formulation actually inverts the casual relationship between violence and queer desire that the novel sets up. Rather than acting as punishment for queer desire, violence is the very thing that originates and authorizes queer desire, with both states framed as natural extensions of hypermasculinity. To view amputation as castration in the narrative is to ignore the way that many of the characters are, in fact, masculinized by their disabilities. Mugridge's ultimate feminization within the narrative occurs not because of his amputated foot but *despite* his amputated foot. If anything, the severing of his foot might have redeemed his otherwise disqualified masculinity.

In the end, what feminizes Mugridge is not his injury but rather his association, however loose, with domesticity in his role as ship's cook as well as the toll that modern urban life has taken on his body. Mugridge elaborates on this toll in the following monologue: "I've been in 'orspital 'arf my bleedin' life. I've 'ad the fever in Aspinwall, in 'Avana, in New Orleans. I near died of the scurvy and was rotten with it six months in Barbadoes. Smallpox in 'Onolulu, two broken legs in Shanghai, pneumonia in Unalaska, three busted ribs an' my insides all twisted in 'Frisco. An' 'ere I am now. Look at me! Look at me! My ribs kicked loose from my back again. I'll be coughin' blood before eyght bells" (86). Important to this passage is the way it stigmatizes illness and debility as the "bad" sort of disability contrasted with the curative powers of "good" injuries like Humphrey's swollen knee. If physical injury onboard the *Ghost* is masculinized, connected to the purity of outlaw spaces, then illness and debility are, conversely, feminized as a property of the metropolis.[15] Tying each of Mugridge's ailments to a different international city accomplishes two things for London. First, it de-emphasizes the importance of national bloodlines. Though critics have made much of Mugridge's lower-class Cockney racialization, London frames him in this moment as a kind of infected citizen of the world. His damaged body is a global body whose injured materiality levels out all geographic difference—whether he falls ill in "Shanghai" or "'Frisco," the physical effects remain the same. Second, the evolving mantra of different city names testifies to the contagions of urban life, showcasing their effects on the lower-class male body. Indeed, Mugridge himself contrasts his own poverty with Humphrey's career as a gentleman, scrolling out this catalog of misfortune as an indictment of Humphrey's privileged background. But whether it is upper-class maternal pampering or lower-class contagion, London makes clear the perils of modern living.

It is precisely the absence of maternal surveillance, indeed the absence of mothers at all, that transforms the homosociality of nautical life into a form of perverse sexuality—one that is wholly different from Humphrey's more asexual queering on land. He describes his fellow sailors as: "a company of celibates, grinding harshly against one another and growing daily more calloused from the grinding. It seems to me impossible sometimes that they ever had mothers. It would appear that they are a half-brute, half-human species, a race apart, wherein there is no such thing as sex; that they are hatched out by the sun like turtle eggs, or receive life in some similar and sordid fashion" (89). What Humphrey describes here is both the nightmare and the revolutionary promise of a "race" of men who exist wholly "apart" from the constraints of the capitalist nuclear household. Indeed, the fantasy of men without mothers is, in some sense, a fantasy of a wholly anti-Freudian existence. Without mothers, there can be no Oedipus complex, no castration anxiety, no fetish, and, ultimately, no resolution in heterosexuality. Thus when Humphrey observes that, for these men, there is "no such thing as sex," he is implying neither androgyny nor asexuality but a world so fully masculinized that there is no such thing as sex *difference*. This hypermasculine "celibacy," then, is celibacy only insofar as it marks a rejection of reproductive heterosexual standards of coupling, replacing them with a markedly nonreproductive community of men growing "calloused" from their "harsh grindings" "against one another."

This image of "calloused" hypermasculine bodies is significant alongside the thematics of "numbness" that initially framed Humphrey's effeminacy. If maternal "dosing" and "doctoring" has made Humphrey "capable of pleasuring in sensations only of the mind," then the excessive physical sensation of injury (the "tears of pain" that accompany "surgery without anesthetics") results in a kind of protective armor that takes the form of a second skin. While both "numbness" and "callousing" imply a deadening of sensation, they are positioned here on opposite sides of a gendered spectrum: numbness connotes feminization, prophylaxis, and paralysis while the callous testifies to masculinity, antiprophylaxis, and endurance. That these masculine callouses are gained through a sexualized "grinding" of male bodies against each other suggests the narrative interlinkages between physical injury and queer hypermasculinity.

Looking back to the earlier passage where Wolf performed "crude surgery without anesthetics," we might, in fact, read a kind of perverse sexuality into the brutality with which he "probed and cleansed the passages made by bullets." I choose the phrase "perverse sexuality," over homoeroticism here because the materiality showcased in this passage seems to go beyond traditional understandings of homoeroticism that frame it through the infinite displacements of a repressed desire between men. Indeed, from a certain angle, there is nothing at all repressed or displaced about the intensely sexualized physical contact staged here, or between the sailors "grinding harshly against one another." For London, repression happens as an extension of the capitalist nuclear family. It is a product of modernity's commitment to style over substance, insulation over exposure, civilized restraint over primitive materiality. London has created the *Ghost* as a place absent of prohibition, and therefore, absent of repressed desire. In replacing effeminate bourgeois repression with tough primitive perversity, London attempts to rematerialize the "lost" body of the American male.

In closing, I want to turn my attention to one last scene in which issues of queer sexuality, injury, and revolution intersect in striking ways. Having been called to Wolf's cabin to dress Wolf's wounds after a bloody confrontation with a small band of mutinous sailors, Humphrey is drawn into a prolonged gaze at Wolf's naked body:

> I had never before seen him stripped, and the sight of his body quite took my breath away. It has never been my weakness to exalt the flesh—far from it; but there is enough of the artist in me to appreciate its wonder . . . Wolf Larsen was the man-type, the masculine, and almost a god in his perfectness. As he moved about or raised his arms, the great muscles leapt and moved under the satiny skin. It was the biceps that had nearly crushed out my life once, that I had seen strike so many killing blows. I could not take my eyes from him. I stood motionless, a roll of antiseptic cotton in my hand, unwinding and spilling itself down to the floor. (99)

The queer valences of this rumination have been well covered by other scholars.[16] However, in their attention to the homoerotic undercurrents of Humphrey's appraising gaze at Wolf's naked body, most of these critics have left its biopolitical dimensions unexplored. But the homoerotic gaze here is deeply intertwined with the medical gaze and we cannot fully consider one without the other. For example, though critics have remarked on the way in which Humphrey's rumination ends in a figurative climax, his "roll of antiseptic cotton . . . unwinding and spilling itself down to the floor," the medical gauze here functions as much more than a simple vehicle for the staging of a homoerotic encounter. Rather, it constitutes the precondition for that encounter, and homoeroticism, in turn, helps to reconfigure the medical gaze in important ways.

If Humphrey's medical encounters in San Francisco caused his body to erode in response to his sisters' disembodied medical gaze, then here we are given an opposite sort of mirroring with Humphrey gaining in substance and materiality the longer he stares at Wolf's hypermasculine body. No longer the passive object of maternal "solicitude," Humphrey is reinstituted as the active agent of a new kind of medical seeing, one that forces him, ironically, to acknowledge that "real" manhood inheres not in the prophylactic medical gaze but rather in the unruly physicality of the specimen under observation. Though he begins his rumination by falling back on the comfortable vantage point of the disembodied critic, the hypermasculinity of his object makes it impossible for him to stay there. As aestheticism gives way to an appreciation of Wolf's bloodied physique, Humphrey is suddenly restored to his own physical body. As if finally thawing out from the water that left him numb below the waist, his renewed sensation is registered in the highly medicalized (and, of course, sexualized) form of the white cotton that leaps out from him. No longer due to numbness or paralysis, Humphrey's "motionless[ness]" here owes instead to a heightened physical awareness.

This dynamic is reinforced when the hypermasculine Wolf swiftly takes control of the visual encounter. Humphrey self-consciously observes that Wolf "noticed me, and I became conscious that I was staring at him." From here, Humphrey and Wolf share a philosophical exchange regarding the beauty of Wolf's physique, and the encounter culminates in a bizarre moment in which Wolf flexes his muscles into an athletic pose and "commands" Humphrey to "feel them." Suddenly, it is the specimen who "commands" and the doctor who obeys. As the disembodied gaze gives way to a shared sensation of touch, Humphrey finally concedes that the human body is a function of physical utility rather than divine purpose. If the medical encounters in San Francisco led Humphrey's body to erode in response his sisters' disembodied medical gaze, then here we are given an opposite sort of mirroring with Humphrey's gaining in substance and materiality the longer he stares at Wolf's hypermasculine body. Occurring midway through the novel, this moment constitutes a thematic turning point, as it inaugurates Humphrey's ability to appreciate the flesh-as-flesh (and not merely as a container for the spirit). It constitutes his first step in the process of giving up his "lettered" self for a more physical existence, relinquishing his prophylactic investments in safety and order for a more "revolting" mode of masculinity forged through unadulterated contact between men.[17]

The Sea Wolf ultimately celebrates the revolutionary potential of bodies that, existing in an oceanic space between nations, echo a prelinguistic and prenational past. These choices would seem to universalize concepts of revolution and distance the narrative from the specific political landscape of turn-of-the-century United States. But in emptying his narrative of specific political content, London was in fact addressing a uniquely turn-of-the-century American "crisis" of masculinity. As a working-class white man, London quickly discovered the representational failure of a national manhood committed to protecting capitalist interests at the expense of the health and well-being of its labor force. In this context, queer hypermasculinity and crip embodiments became useful tropes to fuel his oppositional vision of political dissent. This vision takes shape through the construction of a set of appealing "outlaw" spaces where brotherhood appeared to exist in practice, as well as in theory—the glorified venues of nautical vessels as well as the less glorified spaces of modern prisons and "tramp" populations. But as I will go on to argue, the "road," for London, is complicated precisely because it lacks the lawless exceptionality of the ocean setting. While the transient men of the road might to some degree exist in a liberatory space outside of the law, they are also vulnerable to modernity's ostensible corruptions. I suggest in the following section that London resolves this paradox by turning to the adolescent male body as a site of queer-crip potentiality.

Becoming Men

Some nineteenth-century thinkers warned against the dangers of "crowding boys together under one roof for the purposes of education" because "the vices of young people are generally learned from each other" (Dana Nelson, *National Manhood*, 13). Against these prophylactic injunctions that warned against the transmission of "vice," London celebrated the unregulated intimacies that can develop between boys as a source of transformation, adaptability, and productive contamination. Even his adult characters find themselves experiencing a kind of second puberty that reconfigures their bodies in uncomfortable but ultimately rewarding ways. London articulates his beliefs about the redemptive power of the adolescent body perhaps most clearly in his 1906 novella *Before Adam*. The novella unfolds from the perspective of a modern man who, thanks to his college education and his fluency in modern scientific discourse, is able to retrospectively identify his boyhood nightmares as the atavistic resurgence of a set of frightening "racial memor[ies]" inherited from one of his primitive half-ape ancestors. The bulk of the novella is composed of the narrator's recounting of these memories to the reader, episodes delivered from the first-person perspective of the primordial creature that he once was. Though the modern man remains unnamed, the primordial narrator who speaks through him calls himself Big Tooth and sets the stage for his autobiography by placing himself as the orphaned offspring of a father who has met an untimely and violent end and a mother whose new mate has driven him out of their primitive dwelling. Finding companionship with a boy his age who he calls "Lop Ear," he takes us through several episodes that occur during what we might call Big Tooth's "teenage" years, scenes that are interspersed with the commentary of the modern narrator who occasionally intervenes to situate the reader back to the present.[18]

Before Adam extends *The Sea Wolf*'s rejection of psychoanalysis. While, on the one hand, it could be argued that these ape-creatures act out a sort of Oedipal drama in Big Tooth's rivalry with his stepfather, the story itself rejects even the quasi domesticity of the two-parent caregiving dynamic. Anything remotely resembling a nuclear household is disposed of as early as would be realistic (despite being taken up again toward the end of the narrative). On a broader level, the modern narrator's ability to deliver this story depends on his willingness to interpret his dreams not as ciphers of repressed desire but through a Darwinian analytic of biological coding and species memory. Explaining his duality of self (a duality that furnishes the story with not one but two first-person narrators), he explicitly suggests the limitations of psychoanalytic vocabularies. "Psychologists of the book will find fault with my way of using the phrase, 'disassociation of personality,'" he acknowledges, "I know their use of it, yet am compelled to use it in my own way in default of a better phrase" (*Before Adam*, 13). Ultimately, he finds a more satisfying answer in evolutionary theory, explaining to the reader that certain "strains of germplasm carry an excessive freightage of memories—are, to be scientific, more atavistic than other strains; and such a strain is mine" (20). If Freud interpreted frightening animal dreams in childhood as a manifestation of the repressed trauma of the "primal scene" the child has witnessed between father and mother, then that primal scene is, in this moment, strikingly reconfigured. London has stripped it of its status as metaphor, transforming it quite literally into a portrait of primordial life. We are directed to read the narrator's ape nightmares not as the psychic repressions of the child who has wandered into his parents' marital bedroom but merely as a form of biological "freightage" stamped forcefully into his flesh.[19] Put rather simplistically, Big Tooth does not fear castration as much as he fears the possibility of becoming lunch to wild predators.

This is an important point because Big Tooth's freedom from the gendering structures of the nuclear household also protect him from the feminizing effects of both maternal "solicitude" and paternal inheritance. Just as the men onboard the *Ghost* were characterized as a race "without mothers," Big Tooth is unbound by the repressive structures of the bourgeois family, released from Oedipal anxieties and repressions and, as a result, free to forge alliances with other boys his age. Thus we find him spending the majority of the narrative with his friend "Lop Ear" with whom he shares a small cave and whom considers a partner in survival. This homosocial (and occasionally homoerotic) fraternity with Lop Ear extends, importantly, beyond blood relation. They are not brothers and their kinship does not depend on a nuclear family relationship. It is based, rather, on their shared species and their practical ability to aid in each other's survival.

It is through figures like Big Tooth that London maps the mutability of adolescence onto the mutability of primitive "man," drawing a parallel between the developing body of the male individual and the developing body of the collective species. This parallel is most explicit in Big Tooth's description of the creature he calls "Red Eye":

> Red-Eye was an atavism. He was the great discordant element in our horde. He was more primitive than any of us. He did not belong with us, yet we were still so primitive ourselves that we were incapable of a cooperative effort strong enough to kill him or cast him out. Rude as was our social organization, he was, nevertheless, too rude to live in it. He tended always to destroy the horde by his unsocial acts. He was really a reversion to an earlier type, and his place was with the Tree People rather than with us who were in the process of becoming men. (103)

This "process of becoming men" is, of course, much different from the act of having actually become men. If the beastly and atavistic Red Eye does not "belong with us" because, as evolutionary forefather, his "unsocial acts" make him too much the brute, then the hypersocialized modern "man" that Big Tooth is destined to "become" does not "belong with us" either. As "civilized" evolutionary grandson, he is "hysterical" and "ill" (9), explaining to the reader: "Only once did I confide the strangeness of it all to another. He was a boy—my chum . . . He laughed at me, and jeered, and told me tales of ghosts and of the dead that walk at night. But mostly did he laugh at my feeble fancy. I told him more, and he laughed the harder. I swore in all earnestness that these things were so, and he began to look upon me queerly. Also, he gave amazing garblings of my tales to our playmates, until all began to look upon me queerly" (10). Against the portrait that the narrator paints of Big Tooth's friendship with Lop Ear, or the harmonious community of primates ("we who were in the process of becoming men"), the narrator presents to his readers a modern landscape of broken or absent masculine bonds and diagnosable male psyches. Not only has his "feeble fancy" caused his playmates to "look upon [him] queerly" but, like Humphrey, we find him continually compelling himself into series of obsessive queer self-diagnoses. Within the space of a few pages, he manages to inform the reader that, like "a two-headed calf," his duality of self makes him a "freak" (17), confessing later that "in this matter I am, as I said, a freak—a freak of heredity" (18). Soon after, he confirms once again that he is a "freak of heredity, an atavistic nightmare" (20), an admission that follows yet another reiteration that he "must again, at the risk of boring, repeat that I am, in this one thing, to be considered a freak" (19).

The extreme polarization between Red Eye's extreme atavism and the modern narrator's queer hysteria allows us to understand them as more extreme versions of the polarities that Humphrey and Wolf represent in *The Sea Wolf*. Unlike *Before Adam*, however, *The Sea Wolf* has no character serving as intermediary between them. Indeed, it is as though London took the dynamic antiprophylactic space of conflict, interaction, and molding that occurred between Humphrey and Wolf and gave it a form and voice in the figure of Big Tooth. With Big Tooth standing in more concretely as the figure of masculine evolutionary adolescence, Red Eye and the modern narrator are refigured much further apart from one another on the evolutionary timeline. Wolf may have been a brute, but Red Eye is an atavism. Humphrey may have been an "emotionless monster" but *Before Adam*'s modern narrator is a freak five times over. If London valued the liminal states of "becoming" (becoming "men," becoming civilized, or becoming citizens of a nation on the brink of political self-recognition), then perverse sexuality and physical disability exist for him not on one end or the other of the evolutionary timeline but on both ends—deviant brackets that bookend the privileged middle.

Indeed, if London had previously critiqued Humphrey's impulse to prophylactically distill and purify the "blasphemous metaphors" that come out of Wolf's mouth into a more refined mode of literary (and ultimately political) representation and narration, *Before Adam* effaces the representational agency of the modern narrator entirely. Though the story begins with a split narration, with the "I" sometimes referring to modern man plagued with an overdeveloped racial memory and other times referring to the apelike creature of his ancestral past, by the end of the narrative, the latter figure has drowned out the voice of the former. Shedding his frame narrator like an obsolete skin, Big Tooth absorbs his ancestor's verbal skill and emerges as the real narrator of the story. It is his "truth" and not his ancestral grandson's that the reader is ultimately left to contemplate. Thus the Darwinian concept of "racial memory" provides London with a curious narrative technology that renders prelinguistic man suddenly capable of speaking for himself. It is in this way that London finally achieves the democratic ideal of "direct representation" that he had earlier championed in his essay "Revolution."[20]

For London, the finished masculine body is less important than the male body in transition. In this world, fathers are less important than sons, and sons are most important *before* they become fathers. Indeed, sons find themselves most powerful when they are connected *not* to their fathers but to other boys in a fraternal bond not yet severed by the demands of the nuclear family. By calling attention to the "process of becoming men" as the precondition for social "belong[ing]," the basis upon which you can call yourself an "us," London celebrates and to some extent conflates the collective utopian potential of both the developing adolescent body and the developing body of the species. This primitive flesh can thus be interpreted as providing a physical anchor for London's adolescent collectivities and a blueprint for uniting an otherwise unrelated grouping of male bodies. Because its members understand themselves as sharing something other than blood, brotherhood is not quite the right word. Brotherhood, after all, reinforces the importance of patrilineal inheritance—a model that London was attempting to reject. The alliances that London imagines, then, might be more accurately termed "boyhoods." Resembling Jefferson's vision of constitutional adaptability, the primitive framing of these boyhoods ultimately suggests the mutability of political structures and allegorizes the utopian promise of a society engaged in a powerful transition from one social organization to the next.

Indeed, though London shares many philosophies and strategies of representation with his naturalist counterparts, one thing that sets him apart is his unrelenting utopianism. Stephen Crane gives us urban degeneration and battles that mark the end of romantic heroism. Norris offers a pessimistic and brutalizing account of urban domestic life. London, however, presents many of his primitives, not as sites of degeneration but as the hopeful foundation for revolution, the raw materials out of which a socially just future might be built. His revolutionary optimism carried, for the public, strong and exciting associations with youth. The day after London published his 1895 essay, "What Socialism Is," Jonah Raskin notes in his introduction to *The Radical Jack London*, "The Examiner ran a colorful profile of London as the 'Boy Socialist'" (55). Echoing (intentionally or not) the titles of nineteenth-century "penny dreadfuls" (including *Boy Pirate* and *Boy Highwayman*), London's image as the youthful, charismatic "Boy Socialist" did important ideological work by distancing the Socialist movement from the specter of menacing outlaw adulthood.[21] It offered London a way to carve a space in opposition to the outdated male aristocrat while, at the same time, escaping the "cliche of the bearded, bomb-throwing anarchist" (Raskin, 56). Raskin relates the way in which "two bold headlines reinforce[d] the positive spin: 'The Boy Socialist Defines the Meaning and Intent of the New Philosophy' and 'A Youth with Up-to-Date Ideas Who Will Make a Lasting Impression on the Twentieth Century'" (56). In this way, London's identification as Boy Socialist enabled him to preserve the revolution as protean or embryonic, a figure not yet perverted into the full-grown "anarchist" whose "beard" and "bombs" placed him fully outside of the law. Further, by framing the United States at the turn of the twentieth century as a male body engaged in a powerful transition from one century to the next, London also helped to construct a set of analogies between the transitory body of the human "primitive," the transitory body of the pubescent male, and the turn-of-the-century changes in the American sociopolitical landscape. As Boy Socialist, London became spokesperson for the vibrant fraternity of adolescents whose "elastic" bodies separate the old (Red Eye) from the new (Big Tooth's eventual descendent), the forefathers of yesterday from the future sons of tomorrow, the utterly prehistoric from the excessively modern.

Just as Big Tooth rejects the pure animality of his *ancestral* forefathers, London rejects (or at the very least, revises) the philosophies of his *political* "forefathers" who, in his view, no longer represent universal sovereign right. In a 1905 speech titled "Revolution" (delivered between the publication of *The Sea Wolf* and *Before Adam*), London declares that "the comradeship of the revolution is alive and warm. It passes over geographical lines, transcends race prejudice, and has even proved itself mightier than the Fourth of July, spread-eagle Americanism of our forefathers" (142). A term originating in the late 1850s, "spread-eagleism" was commonly used during the late nineteenth century to refer to the practice of being "bombastic, extravagant, ridiculously boastful, esp. in laudation of the United States," deriving from the sixteenth- and seventeenth-century representation of the spread eagle, and its later adoption as the Great Seal of the United States. Of course, the phrase spread-eagle also carries with it a suggestive set of connotations regarding punishment and physical vulnerability, as another late eighteenth-century use of the term "spread-eagle" referred directly to penal practices. A spread-eagle was a "person secured with the arms and legs stretched out, esp. in order to be flogged," and, in its verb form, to spread-eagle was to "tie up (a person) for punishment."[22] London's choice of "spread-eagle Americanism" over "American spread-eagleism" gestures toward the latter definition, and, in doing so, enacts a subtle critique of the American justice system's power to "discipline and punish." At the same time, the imprecision of London's syntax allows for a potential blurring of roles—who exactly is spread-eagle here? Thus London may have also intended to evoke the image of the forefathers themselves, spread-eagle and vulnerable to the physical force of the law they themselves embody.

London's account of his own experiences with the United States penal system in his 1907 memoir *The Road*, reveal his sharp disillusionment with his forefathers to secure for him the abstract rights he has been promised in the

Constitution. Having taken to the "road" at the age of eighteen, London was arrested for vagrancy and placed in prison without trial. As if to deliver the testimony he was denied in a court of law, he declares to the reader "now I shall faithfully describe what took place in that court-room, for know that my patriotic American citizenship there received a shock from which it never recovered" (70). Like Humphrey's "shock" in the face of Wolf's blasphemous metaphors, London's "shock" at this moment relates to his realization that the white national manhood that he had believed to be anchored in the bedrock of principle was nothing more than a mirage of words. London elaborates on the fundamental constitutional rights he had been denied by the state's legal arm: "The right to a fair trial," he argues, is a right that "those ancestors of mine had fought and died for . . . This was my heritage, stained sacred by their blood, and it devolved upon me to stand up for it" (71). Importantly, in referring to his ancestors' blood, London is not making an appeal to the importance of patrilineal blood ties—birthrights passed from fathers to sons—but rather to a national covenant sealed through sacrificial wounds.

Note, too, the way that London's use of the term "devolved" itself semantically devolves into its own opposite. Though London feels that, as heir to his forefathers' legacy, it has devolved upon him (in other words, been delegated to him) to defend the constitutional rights that his forefathers' spilled blood has made sacred, the following page documents a very different sort of "devolution," consistent with its alternative definition as a "degeneration," or "retrograde evolution." Like Humphrey staring at the body of the dead sailor, London at this moment registers his discovery that, far removed from the "sacred" and "ceremonial" promises of dead men, his life had become "cheap and tawdry, a beastly and inarticulate thing." His attempts to defend his constitutional rights rendered irrelevant, he finds himself forming a fraternal bond with a fellow inmate whom he describes as "a brute-beast, wholly unmoral, and with all the passion and turgid violence of the brute-beast" (73). Doubly defined here as a "brute-beast," this inmate becomes London's "meat," (73) and the subsequent scenes present an almost literal devolution in which the prison emerges as a sort of wild jungle whose brutalities, occurring within the physical structures of law (the prison) and yet wholly outside of any transcendent principles of law (ethical notions of universal right and wrong), reflect the provisional status of all law. The alliances London makes with other male inmates in this penal jungle are what he credits, in the end, as large part of what ensured his survival.

Thus London launches a continual and impassioned critique of the rhetorical nature of male democratic citizenship, which gave lip service to white male fraternity while at the same time depicting unruly intimacies among men as an antiprophylactic threat. *The Road* (1907), London's memoir of his experience of "tramping," is suggestive of some of the ways that freedom of the tramp population, unfettered by the demands of marriage, capitalism, and the nuclear family, includes the freedom to embrace perverse or transgressive sexualities. It is striking that London dedicated his memoir to Josiah Flynt given Flynt's pathologizing treatment of the tramp population in his 1901 essay "Homosexuality among Tramps" (included in the appendix of Havelock Ellis, ed.'s *Studies in the Psychology of Sex*). "Every hobo in the United States," Flynt warns, "knows what 'unnatural intercourse' means" with "every tenth man practic[ing] and defend[ing] his conduct" (360). These "sexually perverted men," Flynt argues, are not only "abnormally masculine," (364) but, importantly, they make a practice of seducing young boys of the slums by sharing "stories about life 'on the road,' how they can ride on the railways for nothing . . . The tramp, of course, continues to excite his imagination with stories and caresses, and some fine night there is one boy less in the town" (360). Unlike the congenital invert, Flynt warns, any working-class boy who romantically hopes for better circumstances might find the homosocial (and ultimately homosexual) world of tramping an appealing alternative to the capitalist world of heterodomesticity and wage labor. In this respect, both Flynt and London are interested in the mutability of the youthful masculine body. But while Flynt identifies that underworld as a site of potential sexual corruption and "perversion," London ambivalently claims it as a site of political redemption.

This is not to say, however, that there is nothing alarmist in London's characterizations of "the road." As if to offset the revolutionary possibility he had previously located in the perversely sexualized and battered bodies of his male characters, London here warns of the threat that outlaw spaces can pose to the healthy development of the white male body:

> Saddest of all, is the training school of the "Road." Man, vicious and corrupt, the incarnation of all that is vile and loathsome, is a melancholy object; but how much more, is innocent youth, rapidly becoming so! Modification by environment: O pregnant term! . . . we, Americans . . . allow in our midst the annual prostitution of tens of thousands of souls. Boy tramps or "Road-kids" abound in our land. They are children, embryonic souls—the most plastic of fabrics. Flung into existence, ready to tear aside the veil of the future; with the mighty pulse of the dawning twentieth century throbbing about him . . . they are cast out, by the cruel society which gave them birth, into a nether world of outlawry and darkness. (*The Road*, 70)

If the savage nautical wilderness of the *Ghost* molds Humphrey's underdeveloped body in ways that enable him to "stand on his own two legs," then the "training school of the 'Road'" results in something that more closely resembles Mugridge's urban degradation. Poised between the nineteenth and the twentieth centuries, the innocence of childhood and the inevitable "corruptions" of adulthood, London's "embryonic souls" are vulnerably exposed to the capitalist economies that "modify" them. Physical injury and perverse sexuality may have carried a kind of curative or capacitating power in the lawless spaces of the ocean, but, resituated within the "cruel society" of an established nation, it can only serve as an index of the damage inflicted by a capitalist economy that relies on the labor of bodies that it treats, ultimately, as disposable.

Though London often acknowledges the vulnerability of the "tramp population," he nonetheless celebrates their "shifting" qualities and dynamic capacity to adapt. In "How I Became a Socialist," for example, he confesses that in his younger days, he ascribed to an "individualism" and "bourgeois ethics" that caused him to dismiss disability as something that did not belong to the authentically masculine body. Crediting his "good health and hard muscles" to his "boyhood hustling newspapers on the streets of a healthy Western city," London recalls being certain that he "should continue to travel with unfailing health, without accidents, and with muscles ever vigorous. . . . I could see myself only raging through life without end like one of Nietzsche's blond beasts, lustfully roving and conquering by sheer superiority and strength."[23] This evolutionary paradigm of fitness, however, is compromised the moment he, at eighteen years old, "took it into [his] head to go tramping" ("How I Became a Socialist," 126). He writes that he "found there all sorts of men, many of whom had once been as good as myself and just as blond-beastly; sailor-men, soldier-men, labor-men, all wrenched and distorted and twisted out of shape by toil and hardship and accident, and cast adrift by their masters like so many old horses" (126). In this framework, disability and debilitation are distanced from constitutional deviance; unlike true "degenerates," these men are previously healthy masculine specimens who have been contaminated by their urban environments.

Thus emerges a gendered and racialized split between constitutional and acquired pathology, with the white male body granted the privilege of antiprophylactic adaptability. The evolutionary dynamism of the white tramp, London argues, contrasts markedly with the inert passivity of the "stationary Negro population," reflecting instead the "the indomitability of the Teuton" (66). We have on the one hand the London who asserts in 1905 that the "comradeship of the revolution . . . passes over geographical lines" and "transcends race prejudice," and the London who in 1899 declares in a letter to Cloudesley Johns, "I do not believe in the universal brotherhood of man ... I believe my race is the salt of the earth," adding later that year that Socialism isn't open to every man, but rather exists to move the higher races forward and leave the weaker ones behind (Kershaw, 102). No longer universal and expansive, brotherhood here is demarcated, contained, and protected. What on the one hand looks like a liberatory queer and crip sensibility that existed in the liminal and lawless spaces—between the human and the animal, the legal and the extralegal, the child and the adult— begins here to look instead like the vertex of a parabola, the human genealogical timeline bent into the graphical equivalent of Galton's bell curve.

A Transformed Boy

How are we to distinguish, then, between London's queer-crip revolutionary boyhoods and the ranks of a heteromasculine citizenry that Sonne, after his "tonic treatment," will finally be fit to join? What is the difference, in other words, between the antiprophylactic openness of "we who are in the process of becoming men" and the closed body of the "transformed boy"? To answer this question, we might briefly, in conclusion, return to the ending of *The Sea Wolf,* which effectively neutralizes the queer-crip materiality it has previously invoked as a model for revolution. Critics have often identified the novel itself as moving in two distinctly opposite directions, with its bleak, deterministic naturalistic setup fundamentally at odds with its romantic resolution, which begins the moment that the intellectual and ethereal female castaway Maud Brewster is introduced into the *Ghost*'s homosocial environment. Maud, it has been generally noted, functions as a kind of catalyst that, introduced late in the character experiment, neutralizes its tensions. Ambrose Bierce, upon being sent a review copy of the novel, "confes[ses] to an overwhelming contempt for both sexless lovers" whose "absurd suppressions" and "impossible proprieties" distract from the "tremendous creation" that is "Wolf Larsen." Indeed, just as Maud declares in the novel's last line her relief at the appearance of the steamship that will "rescue us from ourselves," the heterosexual subplot that Maud initiates may have been the only way London could rescue his text from its own ambivalent creations. That is to say, Humphrey's inevitable return to San Francisco sets up the conditions for the narrative to ultimately disavow the "revolting" bodies that it had previously championed as an alternative to modernity and national belonging. The approaching steamship suggests that the *Ghost* has, all along, been less of an alternative to national belonging than a sort of unorthodox "training school" that has refitted Humphrey for the citizenship from which he had previously been disqualified. Just as the heterosexual household ended up producing its own opposite (the queer and the crip), the outlaw spaces of the sea similarly produce a newly able and resolutely heterosexual American political subject.

In setting up a marriage plot between Humphrey and Maud, London resolves the problem of both the New Woman and the male invert simultaneously.[24] As an unmarried woman and a well-known poet, Maud's independence and intellectualism may have, in San Francisco, been medicalized as unhealthy, masculine, and even lesbian. But onboard the *Ghost*, she is rendered a creature infinitely more fragile and ethereal than Humphrey ever was. With her feminine physical "dependence" on Humphrey reinforcing Humphrey's newly acquired masculine independence, Humphrey and Maud's respective queerness is effectively canceled out by their gendering effect on one another.[25] Indeed, on nearly every level, queer desire is framed in the narrative as the preceding instance, if not the precondition, of heterosexuality. Several scholars have pointed to the triangulated gaze that reveals Humphrey's eventual desire for Maud as an extension and rerouting of his original attraction to Wolf. Furthermore, Humphrey's primal dubbing of Maud as his "mate" toward the end of the narrative both replaces and intensifies the homoerotic implications of an earlier scene in which Wolf tells Humphrey that he has been promoted to the position of "mate" aboard the ship.[26]

Just as perverse sexuality is transformed, ultimately, into the fire that fuels a renewed commitment to heteronormative coupling, so too does disability intervene a final time to neutralize the very revolt it had initially emblematized. As Humphrey discovers Maud unwillingly "crushed in the embrace of Wolf's arms," Humphrey strikes his first blow of the narrative, punching Wolf and then stabbing him in the shoulder (*The Sea Wolf,* 174). The ultimate victor of this fight, however, is not Humphrey but a brain tumor that, we later learn, Wolf had been previously diagnosed with but had not disclosed to his crew. Having caused him only occasional headaches until now, Wolf's tumor produces a sudden searing pain at the moment that Humphrey launches his attack. Reacting to the sudden onset of pain, Wolf "grope[s] about in a dazed sort of way," (174) and eventually "grow[s] limp" (175). The scene of combat is suspended, along with Humphrey's knife which, poised midair, would have otherwise struck a killing blow.

Humphrey's willingness to engage in an act of violent revolt against Wolf is what finally marks him, at this moment, as a fully masculinized being. The emergence of Wolf's tumor here both supports and contains that masculinity, kicking in as a sort of security system or safety valve that places appropriate limits on Humphrey's actions. Interrupting the arc of Humphrey's knife, the tumor conveniently ensures that Humphrey's newfound masculine independence does not—as Wolf's has—transgress the abstract principles of right and wrong. By denying Wolf a violent death by overthrow, London assures his readers that the queer-crip materiality he has introduced in the novel should not, ultimately, be viewed as a viable alternative to national manhood. Rather, he directs his readers to view that materiality as the raw substance out of which the rehabilitated American masculinity of the twentieth century might be built.

Thus in one final medical exchange, we find Wolf back in his role as patient, but this time it is his deathbed, and now it is the heterosexual couple, working cooperatively, who tend to him. As Wolf's body gradually gives itself over to blindness, then paralysis, Wolf and Maud are free to once again embrace the sanctity of the law and perform acts of liberal benevolence, bestowing charity upon a "feeble" body whose impairment exists in contrast to their own robust health (217). Humphrey concludes that "somewhere in that tomb of the flesh still dwelt the soul of the man," whose "fierce intelligence . . . burned on in silence and in darkness. And it was disembodied" (246). When Wolf dies peacefully in his bunk, Humphrey and Maud together observe that he has now become a "free spirit" (251).[27] This closing observation, along with the makeshift funeral that he and Maud fashion for Wolf's body, allows Humphrey to access the fraternal melancholy that he was denied in the first scene as he witnessed the "sordid" death of the sailor. It enables him, finally, to make death "sacred in its ceremonial."

That Wolf's stubbornly material body has finally transformed into a vehicle for meaning rather than a thing-in-itself seems to justify Humphrey's own transformation, establishing that a white man can indeed incorporate a little bit of primitivism without sliding all the way down the evolutionary ladder, emerging instead as a newly fortified white heterosexual able-bodied subject. Earlier in the novel, women had been presented as exclusively spiritual beings, feminizing and dematerializing everything they "dosed" and "doctored" while men, meanwhile, had been presented as exclusively physical beings, materializing and masculinizing one another through injury. Heterosexual contact, of course, is a difficult prospect in a world where anything feminine is feminizing and anything masculine is masculinizing. But if the men onboard the *Ghost* were once a "race apart," in which there was "no such thing" as sex difference, Wolf's new duality (he is both "flesh" and "spirit") makes possible Humphrey's eventual romantic union with Maud (as "man" and "woman"). "The youth of the race seemed burgeoning in me, over-civilized man that I was" (201), confesses Humphrey as he contemplates the way his rough maritime education has newly fitted his body for heterosexual marriage.

A number of scholars, including Jack Halberstam, Kathryn Bond Stockton, Sarah Gleeson-White, and Julie Passanante Elman have pointed to the way that the body in adolescence temporarily resists physical and sexual normativity. Demonstrating the contingency and mutability of desire and embodiment, the adolescent body represents a space of transgressive possibility before the adult imposition of compulsory heterosexuality and compulsory able-bodiedness. Thus Sarah Gleeson-White provocatively suggests that "we might define the freak, like the adolescent, according to physical distortion and in opposition to the 'normal' body" (20). Elman's study more explicitly links the queerness of the adolescent body to disability and medicalized constructions of abnormality. Of course, not all adolescent bodies enjoy the same access to rebellion. Halberstam is careful to distinguish between the male adolescent of "literary and cinematic history . . . a sullen and recalcitrant white youth who says no to paternal authority," (206) and the "rogue tomboy" who finds herself caught between either "assimilat[ing] to the demands of femininity" or "imagining a queer future for her butch body" ("Oh Bondage, Up Yours!" 208). Unlike the female tomboy, whose adolescent rebellion necessarily constitutes a rejection of gender norms, London's queer-crip male adolescents share more in common with the "recalcitrant white youth" whose unruliness ultimately adheres to traditional gender norms ("boys will be boys"). If the female tomboy is subversive because she precedes the normative imperatives of heterosexual femininity, then London's adolescent boys present an inverse temporality, with the normatively gendered boy continually menaced by a potentially effeminizing adulthood.

Thus while it may be tempting to identify in London's queer-crip primitivism a radically affirmative biopolitics or a form of queer posthumanism, it's crucial that we remain wary of paradigms that read instability through the lens of subversion. Dana Seitler, for example, locates *The Sea Wolf* among a set of other "atavistic embraces" that transgress the human/animal divide. But what we see in London's writing is less a deconstruction of the human than a clever (if not always successful) negotiation of the contradictions that threaten white masculinity. London's continual appeal to the natural world ultimately anchors normative gender constructions rather than destabilizing them, with physical vulnerability and mutability presented as beneficial only when it takes place outside of national boundaries (whether in a nautical or primordial context). Within the structures of the nation, such vulnerability is stigmatized as debility and pathology. It is in this way that the queer-crip exchanges essential to the "process of becoming men" ultimately give way to the capacitated heterosexual body of the "transformed boy."

2

"Love or Eugenics?"

Faulkner and Fitzgerald's Crip Children

CLOVER:
My figure discloses no finicky poses
No curve so soft and fair
No fashionable bustle but plenty of muscle,
And avoirdupois to spare.
The rouge and the powder that make you look louder
I always scorn to use.
I'd rather be lorn with the face I was born with,
A face never meant to abuse.

CELESTE:
Now I'm a most popular, tippular, toppular
Maiden born to vex.
And yet he prefers me and always avers me
The queen of the feminine sex.
You scorn good cosmetics in verses ascetic
But there's a reason alack!
For powder looks smart on, with something to start on,
A something you certainly lack.

CHORUS:
Ladies,
Here's a problem none of you can flee,
Men, which would you like to have come and pour your tea?
Kisses that set your heart aflame,
Or love from a prophylactic dame.
Ladies,
Take your choice of what your style shall be.

—F. SCOTT FITZGERALD, "Love or Eugenics," written for the college musical *Fie! Fie! Fi-Fi!* (1914)

In 1914, while he was a student at Princeton, F. Scott Fitzgerald penned the plot and lyrics for a university-sponsored musical playfully titled *Fie! Fie! Fi-Fi!* One of the musical's numbers, titled "Love or Eugenics," drew inspiration from contemporary discussions of the eugenic control of fertility, presenting with flamboyant irreverence the dichotomy that framed many of the more official debates on the subject. In her reading of the song, Daylanne English points to the way Fitzgerald "pits the plain, muscled dame and her 'ascetic verses' (Clover) against the 'queen of the feminine sex' (Celeste) with the natural choice for men being obvious" (67). English thus concludes that Fitzgerald "mocks and rejects eugenics's programmatic, constrained approach to sex and reproduction. What real man, after all, would want a 'prophylactic dame'? Rendering women more like men, leveling sexual difference, strikes Fitzgerald as quite unsexy" (77). Suggesting that the heart might be a better judge than the head, Fitzgerald thus presents feminine beauty and aesthetics as an appealing alternative to the "prophylactic" rationality of eugenic breeding.

In addition to reflecting the sensibilities of the young Fitzgerald, the "choice" presented here also distills the fluctuating status of sentiment as a national discourse in the first decades of the twentieth century. In the early American republic, sentiment was celebrated as an instrument of democratic inclusion. In the absence of national bloodlines, it was "fraternal feeling" that promised to bind male citizens to one another by "eras[ing] differences and creat[ing] a shared social being" (Dill, 710).[1] But while sympathetic bonds may have functioned as a powerful tool for uniting citizens across differences, those same bonds were also understood to be dangerous in excess, with "right" feelings of fraternal love and affection occasionally threatening to transgress into "wrong" feelings of lust and violence. Thus Elizabeth Dill questions what she sees as a "false rift between the sensational and the sentimental" arguing that these opposite affective registers reveal the paradoxes and anxieties of American democracy. Without appropriate boundaries, what begins as "heartfelt democracy" (713) can easily slip into incest and interclass intimacy and the dream of national harmony might collapse into the nightmare of social discord and mob rule. These tensions were exacerbated by the late nineteenth- and early twentieth-century transformation of emotions into clinical entities. As medical experts including Sigmund Freud and Richard von Krafft-Ebing related concepts like "love" to the physical (and pathologized) drives of the human body, there suddenly seemed to be little separating the transcendent qualities of sentimental affiliation from the diagnosable impulses of the melancholic, the hysteric, or the pervert.[2] Indeed, as

Fred Kaplan notes in *Sacred Tears*, sentimentality was not viewed negatively until the late nineteenth century when it became increasingly understood as an "excessive indulgence" or "insincere display" that placed one "in opposition to reason" (17). Worse, some saw sentiment as an affective mode that was fundamentally exploitative, manipulating the emotions for the sake of a particular agenda or outcome.[3]

As sympathy became increasingly discredited as a basis for national reform, the first decades of the twentieth century witnessed the decline of charitable institutions headed by women, particularly those institutions that provided a safe refuge for unmarried mothers. Throughout the nineteenth century, young unwed mothers were frequently framed through religious discourses that understood them to be either "fallen women" or innocent victims of predatory men. But by the turn of the twentieth century, emerging scientific vocabularies of deviance and degeneracy led eugenicists to cast "mother" and "child" into less flattering roles. No longer framed as innocent victims of predatory men or even as "fallen women" who succumbed to sin, unwed mothers were increasingly understood to be "delinquent daughters" whose degenerate bodies posed a hereditary threat to the national gene pool.[4] In this context, the sympathy that motivated female reformers became increasingly understood as a dangerous liability—by "saving" individual women, they appeared to be endangering the very health of the nation. As the hazards of "feminine" sympathy were pitted against the ostensibly more prudent objectivity of "masculine" medical science, the bodies of mother and child were figured as menaces to public health.

Reading these bodies as both crip and queer, this chapter locates transgressive sexuality beyond same-sex desire as it extends to certain socially disqualified reproductive bodies. Too often, particularly in psychoanalytic and antisocial strands of queer theory, the figure of the "queer" is positioned wholly outside of heterosexual reproduction and therefore is assumed to be utterly disconnected from a politics of life and futurity. In these accounts, the most notable of which occurs in Lee Edelman's now classic and widely debated polemic *No Future: Queer Theory and the Death Drive* (2004), a dichotomy emerges between the heteronormative "children of tomorrow" and the "death-driven" childless queers who threaten to negate that future. Edelman argues that the Child, as inheritor of the political future, has come to be deployed as the universal icon that justifies any and every political agenda. The rhetoric is always the same; we must "make the world a better place for our children." Filtering his cultural argument through the lens of Lacanian theory, Edelman adds that our investment in the Child reveals an investment in both the "telos of the social order" (11) and "the narrative sequence of history" (10). The Child thus represents coherence, politics, identity, and successful signification—what, combined, Edelman coins "reproductive" or "sentimental futurism."

Accordingly, it is the queer that occupies the Child's abject negative space. Because gay male sexuality is perceived as occurring outside of reproduction, gay men are continually framed not only as a threat to the safety and well-being of the Child, but, even more malevolently, as "a threat to the logic of thought itself" (39). Here, Edelman playfully queers Lacan's notion of the *sinthome*, by coining the phrase "sinthomosexuality." If for Lacan, the *sinthome* is a kind of sign that does not signify, then "sinthomosexuality" reveals the extent to which the turn away from signification and toward the death drive has been culturally mapped onto homosexual bodies and practices. Figural representatives of a "culture of death," Edelman argues, queers are uniquely poised to tear apart signification, dissolve identity, and obliterate both the future and the Child upon whose shoulders the future rests. Rather than reject such figurations, Edelman urges queers to take up their abjection exuberantly. Thus Edelman famously proclaims: "Fuck the social order and the Child in whose name we're collectively terrorized; fuck Annie; fuck the waif from Les Mis; fuck the poor, innocent kid on the Net; fuck Laws both with capital ls and with small; fuck the whole network of Symbolic relations and the future that serves as its prop" (29). Here, the Child emerges as the unqualified nemesis of queerness. But what happens when the bearer of perversity *is* the child—or the mother who bears the child?[5] In her stunning memoir, *The Argonauts*, Maggie Nelson takes on the "presumed opposition of queerness and procreation (or, to put a finer edge on it, maternity)," questioning how an "experience so profoundly strange and wild and transformative" can at the same time "symbolize or enact the ultimate conformity" (13–14). Placing the "inscrutable hormonal soup" of her own pregnancy in conversation with her transmasculine partner Harry's gender transition, Nelson reveals the fundamental queerness of procreative femininity. Throughout her memoir, she illustrates the way the pregnant body's proximity to death, toxicity, pain, intimacy, and bodily transformation have the capacity to overturn the gay men's seeming monopoly on those "self-shattering" forms of queer negativity that would seem to take place only in bathhouses.

Maggie Nelson's book adds to emergent conversations in queer theory and crip theory that write the reproductive body back into narratives of sexual and bodily transgression. In her important book *Feminist, Queer, Crip*, Alison Kafer launches a more pointed critique of the whiteness and ableism embedded in Edelman's vision of reproductive futurism. Asking what Edelman's call to "fuck" both the "Child" and the "future" might mean for those children who are "already marked as having no future, as destined for decay, as always already disabled" (34), Kafer notes that "queer kids, kids of color, street kids—all of the kids cast out of reproductive futurism—have been and continue to be framed as sick, as pathological, as contagious" (32). Calling for "alternate temporalities that do not cast disabled people out of time, as the sign of the future of no future," (34) Kafer draws our attention to various disabled female bodies who are "cast out of time" as a result of their menacing procreative potential. Her case studies range from the hysterectomy and growth attenuation procedures performed on "Pillow Angel" Ashley X to the controversy generated when two deaf lesbians selected a deaf sperm donor. While the "Ashley treatment" was widely embraced as a humane solution to the assumed problem that Ashley's physically maturing body might pose to caregivers, the deaf lesbians met with disapproval and opposition in their attempt to conceive a deaf child. Both cases reveal the extent to which disabled fertility and maternity persist as an emblems of perversity.[6]

In this chapter, I continue to explore the way disability and motherhood have been written out of both queer negativity and reproductive futurism. My approach is more explicitly historical than Nelson's and Kafer's, preoccupied with how early twentieth-century eugenic framings of reproductive futurity both used and disavowed the politics of sympathy.[7] These framings ignited ableist anxieties regarding the spread of "feeblemindedness"—a category that was broadly applied to people with intellectual disabilities as well as lower-class women, black women, prostitutes, and middle-class lesbians. By writing these bodies back into our conversations about queer negativity, we are able to tell a new story about the biopolitical linkages between queerness and disability.[8] Moreover, such linkages allow us to clarify the role that procreative femininity has played in the construction of antiprophylactic citizenship.

Eugenics, as Fitzgerald's song reminds us, is a fundamentally prophylactic enterprise. Literalized through the developing technologies of birth control and medical sterilization, the prophylactic aims of eugenicists were also reinforced by vocabularies of quarantine, containment, and racial sanitation. Populations targeted by eugenic initiatives were not simply understood as carriers of disease; named as constitutional degenerates, they were understood to *be* the disease. William Faulkner's *Sanctuary* (1931) and F. Scott Fitzgerald's *Tender Is the Night* (1934) both reveal, in markedly different ways, the extent to which procreative femininity was queered during this era. For Faulkner and Fitzgerald, the contaminating procreative bodies of women function as objects rather than subjects of antiprophylactic citizenship. Ambivalently embraced by a set of male characters who are faced with the choice between "love" and "eugenics"—with all of the health risks that the choice of "love" entails—the bodies of mother and child provide opportunities to either comply with or rebel against medical authority and its prophylactic mandates. In this framing, procreative femininity is antiprophylactic only insofar as it is the disease agent that prophylactic medicine was committed to guarding against. Inspiring openness and receptivity and inviting men to experience psychological and bodily encounters with contagion and otherness, mother and child set the stage, in these narratives, for the performance and cultivation of antiprophylactic masculinity.

Sanctuary's Sterilizations

> Birth control and contraception cannot be depended upon to *save us from the children* of the very groups whom we are most eager to restrict.
>
> —Rabbi Sidney Goldstein, speaking in support of more widespread sterilization of the unfit (1936, emphasis added)[9]

Amid the barrage of horrors that the reader encounters in William Faulkner's 1931 novel *Sanctuary*—from the rape of Temple Drake to the murder of the "halfwit" Tommy to the instances of sadism outlined in Popeye's psychobiography—it could be argued the most horrific moments confront the reader, ironically, in the form of Ruby Goodwin's sickly infant. From our introduction to Ruby's child nine pages into the novel to the "fretful sound" of "whimpering" we hear upon the infant's exit from the narrative roughly three hundred pages later, the sickly child becomes the refrain to which the narrative continually and compulsively returns. On two separate instances, we witness the infant lying "in a sort of drugged immobility" (116, 269) and in one of those instances we gaze upon "its pinched face slick with faint moisture, its hair a damp whisper of shadow across its gaunt, veined skull, a thin crescent of white showing beneath its lead-colored eyes" (116). Later, we observe that "its eyes were half open, the balls rolled back into the skull so that only the white showed, in color like weak milk" (161). "Weak milk," in this context, suggests a form of maternal failure that is linked to limited resources, sapped vitality, and failed or tainted transmission. In opposition to past sentimental framings of the child as the hopeful instrument of the future, Faulkner gives us an infant already infected by the vices of the present and—we are led to assume—barred from the traditional narrative arc of maturity and adulthood.

Popeye, *Sanctuary*'s central villain, is partly to blame for the infant's feeble state. Popeye, exists at the heart of Yoknapatawpha County's criminal underworld; he not only runs a bootlegging operation but is connected to an underground prostitution ring. Early in the novel, Popeye murders his associate Tommy in order to gain access to the corn crib where Tommy has hidden Temple Drake, a University of Mississippi coed with a reputation for associating with the wrong kind of men. Though impotent, Popeye rapes Temple with a phallic substitute (a corn cob), eventually stashing her away in a brothel where he voyeuristically watches her encounters with a series of men more virile than himself. Meanwhile, Popeye pins Tommy's murder on the sympathetic character of Lee Goodwin, father to the sickly infant described above. Horace Benbow, Goodwin's defense attorney and the novel's central narrative consciousness, worries that Goodwin's conviction may result in the death of Ruby's child.

Edelman's own brief engagement with *Sanctuary*'s infant exemplifies what is most seductive in his account of reproductive futurism, as well as what is most troubling. In a lengthy footnote, Edelman discusses "the defectiveness of Popeye's masculinity," revealed in his inability to perform heterosexually as well as "the sexual parasitism that binds him like a shadow . . . in too intimate a union with other men" (179). This, coupled with the indirect threat that he poses to Ruby Goodwin's child, allows us to understand him as a "sinthomosexual." With a "face like stamped tin," Popeye is a mask that hides nothing, a symbol without a referent, a signifier with no signified. Furthermore, his willingness to let Goodwin take the blame for Tommy's murder ultimately jeopardizes the reproductive futurity of the nuclear family. "Though Popeye, of course, has no literal responsibility for the illness of the child," Edelman contends, "he embodies the 'evil' whose outcome the infant's cadaverous torpor conveys" (179). Thus, for Edelman, Popeye constitutes the novel's antisocial, homosexual villain; his victory over Goodwin would spell the demise of Ruby's infant just as surely as his downfall would secure the child's future.

Edelman's reading of *Sanctuary* opens up a set of useful questions, but in his exclusive focus on (white male) homosexuality as the only imaginable source of sexual transgression, Edelman forecloses the more interesting site of queerness in the text. Indeed, given the provocative connotations of the term "reproductive futurism" (as well as the crip resonances of the term "defectiveness") it is surprising that a discussion of eugenics does not appear anywhere in Edelman's book. The regulation of fertility has historically been, after all, a politics that is wholly future-driven and largely invested in securing that future by curtailing the reproduction of populations deemed "defective." But if reproductive futurism, in Edelman's account, rests on the sentimental premise that we must make the future better for our children, then the future-oriented politics of eugenics rests on the similar but somewhat inverted notion that we must, in fact, rid ourselves of our sentimental attachments to the child. For the eugenicist, the collective future rests less on the project of making the world better *for* our children than on the project of making the world better *through* our children—that is, through the utilitarian manufacture of better, "fitter" children.

In this context, Edelman's naming of reproductive futurism as "sentimental futurism" (48) feels inaccurate, considering the notoriously unstable historical relationship between sentimentality and rhetorics of national futurity. Consider, for example, Francis Galton's 1873 rumination on the limits of "kindness": "I do not see why any insolence of caste should prevent the gifted class, when they had the power, from treating their compatriots with all kindness, so long as they maintained celibacy. But if these [compatriots] continued to procreate children inferior in moral, intellectual and physical qualities, it is easy to believe that the time may come when such persons would be considered as enemies to the State, and to have forfeited all claims to kindness" (307). These remarks reflect a nascent skepticism toward sentiment as a national project. By the 1920s, most eugenicists agreed that the time had indeed come to regard women who gave birth to allegedly "inferior" children as "enemies to the state" who had "forfeited all claims to kindness." Documenting Ivey Lewis's role in incorporating eugenic science into Southern university curricula, Gregory Dorr explains that "Lewis regarded as 'sentimentalists' those who viewed racial inequalities as the result of prejudice rather than biology," and criticized, in 1924, what he saw as "the large class of the falsely sentimental" (279). Describing the utilitarian logic presented in student papers written under this curriculum, Dorr observes that these students advocated genocide as "the best solution for racial problems," and disparaged the effectiveness of "'sentimentalist' social interventions," which in their view, "artificially prolonged the lives of the unfit" (284). Sentimentalism emerges here as a dirty word and as an emotion fraught with social peril. Against these dangers emerged the utilitarian objectivity of the medical expert who was willing to put the good of the nation before his own emotional biases.

Given this political backdrop, it becomes impossible to talk about reproductive futurism in Faulkner's novel without addressing the eugenic anxieties that inform the markedly unsentimental portrait of the baby imperiled by Popeye's queerness.[10] Indeed, as Horace contemplates the desperation of the situation in which he has become entangled, his rumination is accompanied by a set of disturbing eugenic, and even genocidal, undertones: "He thought of [Temple], Popeye, the woman, the child, Goodwin, all put into a single chamber, bare, lethal, immediate and profound: a single blotting instant between the indignation and the surprise. And I too; thinking how that were the only solution. Removed, cauterized out of the old and tragic flank of the world" (221). Described through a vocabulary that suggests removal, purification, and even extermination, the prophylactic future that Horace wants to save for Ruby Goodwin's baby suddenly begins to look a lot like a future where the Ruby Goodwins of the world are no longer *having* babies. During the 1920s, Ruby Goodwin would in fact have been a likely subject of eugenic regulation—women with a history of prostitution were among the first candidates for what was called "prophylactic institutionalization" and even enforced sterilization under many Southern initiatives of the time.[11]

In her study of how the profession of prostitution evolved in America between 1900 and 1918, Ruth Rosen emphasizes the rhetorical links that were forged between the criminal sexuality of the prostitute and vocabularies of disability. "By 1913," Rosen writes, "twelve states had laws that permitted the sterilization of criminals, idiots, the feeble-minded, imbeciles, syphilitics, moral and sexual perverts, epileptics, and rapists" (21). The grouping together of all of these categories attests to the extent to which the perversely sexualized figure of the prostitute was marked with the additional stigma of disability, allowing reformers to diagnose women's sexual nonconformity as evidence of genetic weakness. Around this time, roughly fifteen thousand prostitutes were imprisoned as a result of these laws.[12] Legal measures like this, along with the frequent institutionalization and sterilization of prostitutes, Rosen argues, "reflected a society that increasingly associated degeneracy with poverty and gradually sought means to control the sexual behavior of the poor" (21).

Concepts of "childhood" and "sympathy" are notably reconfigured in these discourses. Rosen includes, for example, a quote from a Massachusetts investigator who, in 1914, came to the following conclusion with regard to the prostitutes he had examined: "The general moral insensibility, the boldness, egotism and vanity, the love of notoriety, the lack of shame or remorse, the absence of even a pretence of affection or sympathy for their children or for their parents, the desire for immediate pleasure without regard for consequences, the lack of forethought or anxiety about the future—all cardinal symptoms of feeble-mindedness—were strikingly evident in every one of the 154 women" (22–23). This passage rehearses the logic of sentimental futurism; the prostitute, as she is described here, "lacks" many things, but central among them is the average person's "forethought or anxiety about the future." This disregard for the future is tied to her inability to feel "sympathy" for her "children." Indeed, if we were to replace the word "women" in this passage with "homosexual men," it would be difficult to tell this passage from the many cited in Edelman's account. It is clear here that homosexuality isn't the only perverse sexuality to be culturally framed as a kind of death-driven commitment to antifuturity: the prostitute described here occupies a similar relationship to sexual stigma. Notably, she not only lacks sympathy for her children but also lacks sympathy for the parents to whom she is herself a "delinquent daughter." Thus she is not only a feebleminded mother but also, herself, a sexually perverse child who menaces the nation's collective future. Unlike the homosexual, then, the prostitute's sexual stigma does not issue from the fact that she cannot produce children but, to the contrary, the fear that—as a child of inferior stock—she will produce other children like herself.

Even more striking is the way this passage works against its own logic. While the prostitute's gendered perversity is evidenced by her supposed lack of sympathy toward her children, the same lack of sympathy was, ironically, the very thing that was required of the medical professionals assigned to evaluate whether she qualified for eugenic sterilization. This hard-lined utilitarian logic was famously showcased in the 1927 Supreme Court ruling on *Buck v. Bell*, which took place in Virginia four years before the publication of *Sanctuary*. Having borne an illegitimate child out of wedlock as a result of a rape, seventeen-year-old Carrie Buck was institutionalized by her adoptive family. During her institutionalization, Buck was labeled "feebleminded" and sterilized without her consent.[13] Significantly, Buck's biological mother had been a prostitute, and because Buck's pregnancy was attributed to a constitutional predisposition toward promiscuity, all three—mother, daughter, and grandchild—were declared "feebleminded." Buck brought her lawsuit to the Supreme Court in 1927, but the court upheld Virginia's compulsory sterilization statute. Regarding the ruling, Justice Oliver Wendell Holmes Jr. made the famous declaration that "three generations of imbeciles are enough."[14]

Keeping this in mind, we can reframe the binary oppositions that structure Edelman's reading of Popeye's relationship to the Child. Popeye, as

Sanctuary's perversely sexualized villain, does not threaten the sentimental futurity of the child as much as he is *himself* a perversely sexualized child whose very presence in the world is understood to place future generations at risk. Put another way, Popeye does indeed cast a menacing shadow over Ruby Goodwin's baby, but only insofar as he embodies precisely the kind of monster that such "feebleminded" infants will inevitably grow up to be. He does not threaten the child with death as much as he represents the perversity of its continued life.

This continuity between Ruby's feeble infant and Popeye's queer adulthood is suggested through a set of images that bind them figuratively to one another. The image of the infant's "pinched face slick with faint moisture, its hair a damp whisper of shadow across its gaunt, veined skull" (116) is provocatively mirrored in Popeye's death scene as the executioner "drag[s] [the rope] over Popeye's sleek, oiled head, breaking his hair loose" (315). This causes Popeye to "jerk his neck forward in little jerks," (316) a gesture that echoes a much earlier description of the infant: "It was still whimpering now and then, tossing its thin body in sudden jerks" (133). Edelman himself notes the similarities between descriptions of Popeye's eyes and the "lead-colored" eyes of the infant, but he concludes that such similarities merely demonstrate Popeye's malevolent influence upon the otherwise innocent infant. These parallels go much deeper, however, marking "the child" itself as the very emblem (rather than the victim) of perversity.

Indeed, when Holmes declared that "three generations of imbeciles are enough," he could just as easily have been referring to Popeye's own perverse genealogy, celebrating Popeye's impotence and early death as the welcome end to a defective genetic legacy. As we learn in the psychobiography that concludes the narrative, Popeye's grandmother was a pyromaniac and his mother was a mentally unstable syphilitic who conceived him out of wedlock. Popeye himself, meanwhile, is presented as a sociopathic child who never possessed any sentimental claim on innocence. Following a particularly devastating fire set by Popeye's grandmother, we find that

> there were times when [Popeye's mother] still believed that the child had perished, even though she held it in her arms crooning above it. Popeye might well have been dead. He had no hair at all until he was five years old, by which time he was already a kind of day pupil at an institution: an undersized, weak child with a stomach so delicate that the slightest deviation from a strict regimen fixed for him by the doctor would throw him into convulsions. "Alcohol would kill him like

strychnine," the doctor said. "And he will never be a man, properly speaking. With care, he will live some time longer. But he will never be any older than he is now." (308)

Popeye's "weak" and "undersized" body, his "delicate" stomach, and his arrested physical development mark his queerness with the additional stigma of disability.[15] The queer-crip child of an unwed "feebleminded" mother, he is the last gasp of a degenerate family line. A boy who will never grow into manhood, he is a patrilineal dead end. Thus, while no sterilization literally occurs within the novel, the narrative itself imposes a form of sterilization upon Popeye whose impotence ensures that his genes will not pass into future generations.

When the narrator informs the reader that "Popeye might well have been dead," then, this "death" should not be read as the queer jouissance that emerges in the wake of a transgressive embrace of the Freudian death drive. Rendered by the narrative in far more biopolitical terms, Popeye's relation to death might be understood more as a kind of negative relation to birth. The death that enfolds Popeye and Ruby Goodwin's child is not about the end of life but about the beginning, gesturing not toward the gallows but toward the female reproductive body and the question of "who should and should not inhabit the world."[16] As we witness Popeye at his own execution, with a rope around his neck, we find that he "stood rigid, as though he had an egg balanced on his head" (316). That Faulkner evokes such a bizarre image of female fertility in the moment before the sheriff "spring[s] the trap" seems to suggest that Popeye's execution, in the end, has more to do with birth than death. It is less a matter of retributive justice than of biopolitical management, a retroactive sterilization to correct the error of his conception.

Thus despite Edelman's contention that the cultural imperative has always been to "save" the future for the children, in *Sanctuary* we find a very different invocation to "save" the future *from* the children. As Rabbi Sidney Goldstein declared in 1936, in support of a measure that would lead to more widespread sterilization of the unfit, "birth control and contraception cannot be depended upon to save us from the children of the very groups whom we are most eager to restrict" (219). The children that the future needs saving from, in these accounts, are the children of prostitutes, the children of the lower class, the children of African Americans, the children of immigrants, and, crucially, the children of people with disabilities to whom the rest of these populations were likened. We might say that these perversely sexualized populations are less death-driven than life-driven. It is not their relation to death that must be policed but their relation to an unruly form of queer-crip life.

Rereading Benjy

Faulkner's own attitude toward eugenic philosophy is unclear in *Sanctuary* as the novel provides no real moral center to guide its readers' attitude toward these issues—even the status of Horace Benbow's benevolence toward Ruby Goodwin is compromised by his own incestuous family drama, foregrounded more heavily in earlier drafts of the novel.[17] Though Scott DeShong argues that the novel's horrors function to intensify the reader's empathy, it's hard to ignore the sensationalism with which its acts of violence are presented.[18] *Sanctuary* is unique among Faulkner's works for its extreme exteriority and its use of horror to both attract and repel its readers. Faulkner himself admitted that *Sanctuary* had been a "cheap idea," "deliberately conceived to make money," explaining, "I chose what I thought would be the right answer and invented the most horrific tale I could imagine and wrote it in about three weeks."[19] Unlike his more widely read *The Sound and the Fury* (1929), *Sanctuary* trades sympathetic identification for a superficial Gothic thrill. And yet the two novels traverse strikingly similar ground. Might we, after all, see in Popeye's diagnosis as a child who "will never be a man" and "will never be any older than he is now" echoes of Benjy Compson whose arrested intellectual development has kept him at the age of "three years old" for "thirty years" (17)? Both men are described as perpetual children who will never reach adulthood and both, to some extent, have been made to signify the end of a tainted family line.

Reading Popeye and Benjy as Gothic and sentimentalized inversions of one another, we can see the way Benjy's literal sterilization in *The Sound and the Fury* anticipates Popeye's more figurative sterilization in *Sanctuary*. If Popeye is a perversely sexualized adult doomed to perpetually inhabit the physical body of a child, then Benjy provide a purified alternative: his disability, scholars often note, allows him to carry the innocence of childhood into a body that has physically matured into adulthood.[20] It is precisely this mismatch between Benjy's childlike interiority and his exterior appearance of adulthood that leads the schoolgirls he approaches to misread his attempts at communication as sexual advances—an incident that leads to his castration and to the possibility of institutionalization. A sentimental child himself, he is mistaken for a perversely sexualized predator of children.[21] Unlike Popeye, Benjy's sexual innocence is guaranteed by the narrative, and Faulkner makes clear the extent to which his sterilization is a violation of his bodily rights.

David Mitchell and Sharon Snyder have persuasively argued that Benjy's disability becomes, for Faulkner, less a source of pathologization and stigma than a kind of litmus test of the other characters' ethical integrity, pointing out that "all of the Compson family members are explicitly judged in relation to their ability to imagine Benjy's humanity" (167). Characters like Caddy and Dilsey, who treat Benjy with sympathy and oppose his sterilization and institutionalization, are awarded greater moral authority than characters, like Jason, who operate as mouthpieces for eugenic ideology. Jason rejects outright any overtures of "sympathy" even (or especially) when those overtures are directed toward his own family. "They never started soon enough with their cutting, and they quit too quick" (263), declares Jason at the conclusion of his narration, epitomizing the callous utilitarianism that emblematized the period's eugenic thinking. If Faulkner's attitude toward eugenics is unclear in *Sanctuary*, *The Sound and the Fury* demonstrates a more straightforwardly critical attitude toward philosophies that biologize poverty and initiatives that advocated the sterilization and institutionalization of the "unfit."

Faulkner's sympathetic approach to Benjy's character is not unproblematic from a disability studies perspective. Maria Truchan-Tataryn points out that Faulkner's childlike rendering of Benjy's innocent and "mindless" affinity with the animal world performs a kind of representational violence against intellectually disabled people even as he attempts to give intellectually disabled people a voice though Benjy's character. "Though others are judged by the way they approach 'the idiot,'" she argues, these judgments "demarcate the humanity of others" while failing to illuminate the humanity of Benjy himself. Truchan-Tataryn cites an early reviewer of the novel who suggests that Benjy is "as beautiful as one of the helpless angels," possessing an "innocence" that is "terrible as well as pathetic" (163). Though critical responses like these ostensibly value Benjy's pastoral innocence, they also reinscribe a problematic sentimental framing of disability through the registers of pity and inspiration. Caught between sentimental models of pity and the callous interventions of eugenic medicine, Benjy—like Ruby Goodwin's baby and even like Popeye himself—exists on both sides of reproductive futurism's binary as both the menaced and vulnerable child and the menacing and sexually perverse adult.[22]

And just as *Sanctuary*'s male "monsters" could be traced back to a form of dangerous female fertility, Benjy's crip embodiment is linked to the novel's figure of perverse motherhood, his sister Caddy. While Caddy is not Benjy's mother in a literal sense, the role that she plays in relation to Benjy is exceedingly maternal, and her intimate bond with him to some extent aligns her with nineteenth-century models of maternal sympathy. These bonds, however, become severed when she is finally expelled from the Compson household for conceiving a child out of wedlock. Caddy's absence, the narrative makes clear, is what ultimately motivates Benjy's disastrous attempt to communicate with the young schoolgirl—in "trying to say" that he misses his sister, he inadvertently resignifies himself as a sexual predator.

Through Caddy's exile, Faulkner allegorizes the larger historical process through which a politics of maternal sympathy was gradually replaced with the scientific regulation of female reproductive deviance.[23] Caddy is a failed maternal protectress whose embrace of Benjy is discredited the moment that her metaphoric motherhood becomes biologically literalized. A girl without a husband from a family without money, Caddy is finally just another delinquent daughter who poses a hereditary threat to the nation. Once a sympathetic mother opposing her disabled brother's sterilization, Caddy has been reduced, by the end of the narrative, to the bearer of "degenerate" offspring. Her daughter Quentin, it turns out, "inherits" Caddy's sexual delinquency but none of Caddy's compassion. Like Caddy, Quentin transgresses the boundaries of acceptable female sexuality, eventually running away from home with a circus performer. But it's important to note that Quentin expresses only disgust and annoyance with Benjy, aligning herself with Jason's suggestion that Benjy be sent to Jackson for institutionalization. If Caddy treads the line between the sympathetic womanhood of the nineteenth century and the female delinquency of the twentieth, Quentin marks the completion of the process through which a politics of sympathy is replaced with the more "objective" science of defective bodies.

But the novel's central figure of eugenic "objectivity" is not ultimately Quentin but Caddy's brother Jason. Far from objective, Jason clings to eugenic fantasies as a way of venting his anger at the white privilege that he feels has been denied him. Thus his narration reveals the fundamental contradictions and paradoxes of eugenic thought. As the white patriarch of a once wealthy family, Jason is the very portrait of the ideal American citizen whose family must be protected from the fertility of undesirable others. And yet the defects that Jason is most eager to police and restrict emerge not from outside of his family but from within it. Jason struggles with this tension, deploying the rhetorical tools of eugenics even as he finds them ultimately turning back upon himself. As Quentin makes her escape with her red-tied suitor, Jason thinks:

> You can't do anything with a woman like that, if she's got it in her. If it's in her blood, you cant do anything with her. The only thing you can do is to get rid of her, let her go on and live with her own

sort. I went on to the street, but they were out of sight. And there I was, without any hat, looking like I was crazy too. Like a man would naturally think, one of them is crazy and another one drowned himself and the other one was turned out into the street by her husband, what's the reason the rest of them are not crazy too. All the time I could see them, watching me like a hawk, waiting for a chance to say Well I'm not surprised I expected it the whole time the whole family's crazy. (233)

The problem with exhorting Quentin to "go on and live with her own sort" is that eugenic logic dictates that her "sort" is the Compsons themselves. The Compson's financial decline in the post–Civil War South, compounded with the new science of heredity, has altered their relationship to American national belonging, transforming them from Southern aristocracy to potential genetic liabilities. Because the female reproductive body exists at the heart of these tensions, Caddy's out-of-wedlock pregnancy and her daughter's sexual delinquency make the two young women easy scapegoats for Jason's class frustrations. Prophylactically guarding himself from their contaminations, Jason engages in a contradictory act of declaring that "blood is blood and you cant get around it" (243) even as he rhetorically separates his own blood from his sister's and his niece's.[24]

Jason's more direct discussion of American citizenship is similarly paradoxical. After declaring that what America "needs is more white labor," Jason engages in a conversation with a drummer about crops, disparaging the "dam eastern jews" who "produce nothing" but "follow the pioneers into a new country and sell them clothes" (191). The drummer replies that Jason must be thinking of "Armenians," as a "pioneer wouldn't have any use for new clothes," and clarifies that, with his "French blood," he is properly American. Soon after, Jason reflects that while "those eastern jews have got to live too," he'll "be damned if it hasn't come to a pretty pass when any dam foreigner that cant make a living in the country where God put him, can come to this one and take money right out of an American's pockets" (192). In this confused exchange, the relationship between "blood," nationhood, and citizenship becomes muddled and it is unclear what exactly it is that blood ultimately reveals. Jews are foreigners, but French are American. The pioneers that leave the "country where God put them" to settle the New World are authentically native, but those that follow to "sell them clothes" are burdensome imposters.

The dovetailing of Jason's anti-immigration attitudes with his racism toward African Americans reflects a wider adoption of eugenic attitudes within the American South during the 1920s. With the crumbling of the Southern aristocracy following the Civil War, Southerners who clung to an outdated regionalism were seen as backward and provincial, a drag on the process of modernization that would help reunify the nation. As Dorr observes, the incorporation of eugenics into the University of Virginia curriculum "eased the merging of Virginians' regional identity with a new overarching identity of so-called pure, 100 percent Americanism. Scholars at elite northern institutions emphasized the importance of whiteness and Anglo-Saxon heritage in defining the 'American race'" (261). Thus the incorporation of eugenics into Southern public life provided an opportunity for white Southerners to reinforce their claim on Americanness, bringing themselves up to date with the policies of the North while at the same time preserving traditional racial hierarchies.[25] The embrace of Northern eugenic science, then, came in part out of a desire to demonstrate that the South was capable of modernizing itself, to prove that the South was as important a part of America as the North, and to justify antimiscegenation legislation that would, amid all of this modernization, allow policy makers to maintain a traditionally segregated South.

But while eugenic philosophy validates Jason's desire to protect "white labor," it has at the same time transformed whiteness into a more complicated category. The fact that eugenic "fitness" was a designation open *only* to white people did not make it automatically inclusive of *all* white people. As the line between acceptable and unacceptable ethnicity blurred, so did the distinctions between "fit" white families and poor "white trash." Jason never questions the authenticity of his own whiteness and his inclusion in the category of white labor, yet he is at the same time deeply aware that his whiteness does not exempt him from the contagion of feeblemindedness and that his family's poverty might well determine his own inclusion among the ranks of the degenerate. Thus when Edelman quotes David Lane's Aryan assertion that "we must secure the existence of our people and a future for white children" (66), the invocation of whiteness must be taken seriously as an important facet of the futurism that Edelman wishes to critique. Edelman's own critique of Lane forecloses that opportunity, writing "so long as 'white' is the only word that makes this credo appalling, so long as figural children continue to 'secure [our] existence' through the fantasy that we survive in them" (66). But, of course, white is *one* of the words that make the credo appalling, as it connects reproductive futurism to eugenic ideologies of racial sanitation. It reminds us that what supposedly threatens the "future of white children" is not just the "unregenerate, and unregenerating" sexuality of the queer; it is also the perceived *hyper*regenerate sexuality of racial minorities, the working class, disabled people, and prostitutes whose fertility called for prophylactic safeguards. In this context, *reproductive* futurism might be more accurately called by the name of *prophylactic* futurism.

Love-Murders

In Faulkner's fictional worlds, "eugenics" will always win out over "love" and sympathy is always already foreclosed, persisting only in his characters' nostalgia for a more secure past and their desires for impossible (interracial or incestuous) future intimacies. For Fitzgerald, however, love is ever present, flowering around his characters like the "huge horse-chestnut tree in full bloom" that Rosemary spots on a passing truck in *Tender Is the Night*, after a particularly charming night with the Divers. The seeming gulf between Faulkner's unrelenting Gothicism and Fitzgerald's lush sentimentalism, along with the two authors' regional differences, has placed them on opposite sides of the modernist canon. It feels odd to analyze Fitzgerald's sparkling New York, with its flappers and its nouveau riche, alongside the somber and desolate landscape of Faulkner's decaying South. But it is precisely these two authors' seeming diametric opposition that makes their eugenic intersections a generative site of analysis. Though Fitzgerald embraces the sentiment that Faulkner exiles from his landscapes, both authors conceive of sentiment in similar terms: as a vehicle for the antiprophylactic breaching of personal and national boundaries.

While Faulkner and Fitzgerald never met, there are several documents suggesting that Fitzgerald was reading *Sanctuary* as he composed *Tender Is the Night* and in Fitzgerald's outline for the novel, he squarely positions his own writing as the sentimental antidote to Faulkner's clinical gaze.[26] Under a section titled "Method of Dealing with Sickness Material," Fitzgerald writes, "Must avoid Faulkner attitude and not end with a novelized Krafft-Ebing—better Ophelia and her flowers" (Bruccoli, 334). This note is, of course, consistent with his more flippant championing of "love" over "eugenics" twenty years earlier. As Thomas Inge puts it, Fitzgerald attempts to avoid "sounding clinical and too deeply immersed in psychological theory the way he felt Faulkner's novels were and, if necessary, opt for the romantic description of madness and insanity." It would seem, then, that we are left with a relatively clear-cut set of oppositions: Shakespeare is preferable to Krafft-Ebing, poetry trumps pathology, aesthetics is more appealing than diagnosis, Ophelia's flowers make a welcome alternative to Temple's corn cob, and sentimental love should be chosen over the cold rationality of eugenics.[27] This continuity would appear to authorize us to read Fitzgerald's embrace of sentimentalism in *Tender Is the Night* as a more masterful rendering of his initial assertion twenty years earlier that "kisses that set your heart aflame" are superior to "love from a prophylactic dame."[28] But sympathy, the novel makes clear, has its price, and Dick Diver's sentimental identifications do not ultimately provide a viable alternative to eugenics. Fitzgerald's ambivalence about the antiprophylactic qualities of sentiment can be seen both in his celebrations of unconditional hospitality and, conversely, in his wariness of the consequences of breached boundaries, both personal and political.

Indeed, even as "love" emerges as the victor in Fitzgerald's 1918 musical exploration of "Love or Eugenics," it is at the same time aligned with the "bad" version of sentimentality that had been discredited toward the end of the nineteenth century as mere feminine artifice.[29] What Celeste has to offer here are not authentic emotional bonds but "good cosmetics." Her status as "queen of the feminine sex" depends on skill with illusion, manipulation, and subterfuge. If Clover's "eugenic" muscles masculinize her as a kind of New Woman (and on some level queers her by making her an inappropriate object of the heterosexual male gaze), then Celeste's feminine superficiality reveals the ostensible frailty of the appropriately gendered female body, a lack which must be made up for with "rouge and powder."[30] These are traits you might not want to pass to your future offspring but that should nonetheless, in the logic of the song, excite the sexual imagination of any red-blooded American male. The choice of "love" over eugenics, then, is obvious only insofar as love is equated with the feminine mystifications of charm that tempt the American male away from his reproductive duty to the race.

We can see, then, how the dichotomy Fitzgerald sketches out here is not simple binary as much as it is a gendered minefield. Congealing some of these tensions is a photograph of Fitzgerald himself, costumed as a call girl for *Fie! Fie! Fi-Fi!* and looking every bit the "queen of the feminine sex." If eugenic muscles only look good on men, then we might also infer that sentimental charm, intended as a form of feminine adornment, looks queer on men. In *Tender Is the Night and F. Scott Fitzgerald's Sentimental Identities*, Christian Messenger argues that "Fitzgerald's intimation was that his fictional authority arose from the sentimental, that he was best there, while he also held to the counterbelief that the sentimental was 'vicious' rather than 'whole-souled' [34], and was cheapened through the 'harlot's mind' [69] of Hollywood, as well as darkened and imbricated by sympathy's twinning with its inevitable counterparts of seduction and emasculation" (61). Identifying Fitzgerald's vacillation between the "whole-souled" and "vicious" character of sentiment,

Messenger suggests that Dick's charm is both appealing and dangerous, allowing him to possess women but also leading him down a path of uneasy identifications with gay men and incestuous fathers and into a world of decadence and degeneracy. Sentiment, in this framework, can be restorative, but it can just as easily function as a form of "vicious" contamination.[31] Though Fitzgerald is committed to a sentimental rather than sexological rendering of his characters, "whole-souled" masculine fellow feeling is always in danger of slipping into those vicious, "cheapened" forms of sentiment that provide an occasion for sexual transgressions, miscegenation, and other queer intimacies.

A more pointedly biopolitical reading of the novel reveals Fitzgerald's troubled relationship to sympathy to be indicative not only of his own psychological investments but of a historical moment in the United States in which sentimentalist policies were dismissed as a political liability. A sympathetic approach to immigration and reproduction threatened the purity of national bloodlines by allowing racial mixing, welcoming the wrong kind of whites, and failing to sterilize the unfit. Against the "soft-hearted" liberal impulse to open up the national gene pool to outsiders, eugenicists thus warned of the grave dangers of sentiment. As Robert Ward proclaims in 1917:

> I do not believe that *sentiment* can solve grave national problems. I do not believe that the indiscriminate kindness we may seem to be able to show to some thousands, or millions, of Europeans and Asiatic immigrants can in any conceivable way counterbalance the harm that these people may do our race if large numbers of them are mentally and physically unfit . . . It is in the highest degree ungenerous for us, who are the *custodians of the future* heritage of our race, to permit to land on our shores mental and physical defectives who . . . will tremendously increase all our *future problems* of public and private philanthropy. We have no right to addle any additional burdens upon the already overburdened *coming generations of America*." (quoted in Ordover, *American Eugenics*, emphasis added, 52)

Madison Grant similarly observes that "the *maudlin sentimentalism* that has made America 'an asylum for the oppressed' [is] sweeping the nation toward a racial abyss. If the Melting Pot is allowed to boil without control, and we continue to follow our national model and deliberately blind ourselves to all 'distinctions of race, creed, or color,' the type of native American of Colonial descent will become as extinct as the Athenian age of Pericles and the Viking of the days of Rollo" (quoted in Ordover, emphasis added, 51–52). Note the way that Edelman's notion of reproductive futurism surfaces within these passages. Eugenics and tighter restrictions on immigration are here framed as the future-driven politics that will make the United States safe for future white nondisabled children. It is the vaccine that will immunize the "coming generations" and secure the "future heritage of our race." But Ward and Grant's strain of "futurism" is by no means "sentimental" and has a much more complicated relationship to reproduction than simple affirmation of childbearing. If Ward argues against letting the "unfit" land on American shores, then Grant warns of racial interbreeding that will happen once they're here, transforming America's melting pot into a volatile chemistry experiment. In this framing, sentiment threatens to "sweep the nation toward a racial abyss."

The process though which sentimental identification with the other slips into sensationalist anxieties about the mixing of bloodlines is most clearly allegorized through the body of *Tender*'s child figure, Rosemary, a starlet who encounters the Divers on the French Riviera after she has gained fame through her Hollywood role as *Daddy's Girl*. As the novel opens we are given a relatively simple binary; Rosemary is the sentimentalized child of reproductive futurism's claim on the social; she is imperiled by racial otherness and protected through ethnocentric exclusionism. Indeed, our first portrait of Rosemary retains traces of an almost Victorian sentimental sensibility. She is described as having "magic in her pink palms and her cheeks lit to a lovely flame, like the thrilling flush of children after their cold baths in the evening . . . Her eyes were bright, big, clear, wet, and shining, the color of her cheeks was real, breaking close to the surface from the strong young pump of her heart. Her body hovered delicately on the last edge of childhood—she was almost eighteen, nearly complete but the dew was still on her" (3). Although Rosemary "hovers" dangerously close to the precipice of adulthood, she is able to access the status of the Child through sentiment. Because we have not yet witnessed Dick's son bathing in the "dirty suds" of a child who has picked up some "Asiatic" disease, the invocation of "children after their cold baths" connotes racial and sexual purity (264). If sentiment, as some critics have argued, is designed to be registered visibly on the surface of the skin (often through physical tears), then Rosemary's "thrilling flush" and her "clear," "wet," and "shining" eyes mark her physically as a creature of sympathy.[32] Later we find Rosemary "as dewy with belief as a child from one of Burnett's vicious tracts," a framing that hints at the dangers of sentimentalism.[33] But here at least, Fitzgerald's ornate prose suggests that he has made good on his promise to circumvent medicalization by emphasizing "Ophelia and her flowers." As Rosemary enjoys the water, "embracing it, wallowing in it" (5), the beach on the Riviera takes on the "purity" of the Aryan gene pool.

Thus it is not surprising the first threat to Rosemary's safety comes in the form of a man of "indeterminate nationality" who warns her that the water has sharks. If the water is a gene pool, then sharks represent that which threatens to taint it with the wrong kind of blood. The same racial threat hovers in the air as Rosemary takes her place on the beach "between the dark people and the light" (6) and worries about getting a sunburn because, as Mrs. Abrams warns her, "*your* skin is important" (7); presumably, she means that Rosemary's skin must remain light so she can assume future roles playing an approximation of "Daddy's Girl." In order to remain a child, one must safeguard one's whiteness and avoid becoming "dark." Sentimental childhood must finally be protected eugenically from the contaminations of race.

To this effect, Dick "arrang[es] an umbrella to clip a square of sunlight off of Rosemary's shoulder," as Tommy Barban catalogs (and evokes a certain anxiety over) the different nationalities that have been mixed together on the Riviera. The umbrella functions as an emblem of American racial exclusionism under which the "clamor of Empire" (13) can be re-created even while vacationing abroad: "They obviously formed a self-sufficient little group, and once their umbrellas, bamboo rugs, dogs, and children were set in place the part of the plage was literally fenced in" (16). Later they form "so bright a unit that Rosemary felt an impatient disregard for all who were not at their table. They had been two days in Paris, but actually they were still under the beach umbrella" (52). Rosemary's imagined fantasy of the Divers ends with a return to the safety and protection of the Child: "She thought of [the Divers] both together, heard them still singing faintly a song like rising smoke, like a hymn, very remote in time and far away. Their children slept, their gate was shut for the night" (40). Whether under the umbrella's protective shade or "fenced in" by a gate that is "shut for the night," the Divers' colorful entourage provides a tightly sealed space of American racial exclusionism.

But ironically, it is also Rosemary's intimacy with the Divers that leads to the materialization of a dead black man in Rosemary's bed. After beginning an extramarital affair with Rosemary in her hotel room, the couple is interrupted by Dick's friend Abe North and Jules Peterson, a black shoe polish salesman who had recently testified against a prominent business owner. Rosemary later returns to her room to find Peterson's bloody corpse in her bed, an event that appears to transform her sentimental romance with Dick into a nightmarish racial scandal. No longer the sentimental child whose vulnerable "skin" needs protection, Rosemary faces the possibility that the newspapers will paint her, instead, as a delinquent girl whose transgressive sexuality jeopardizes the racial health of the body politic. The swift succession with which Rosemary's romantic affair with Dick is replaced by Peterson's bloody corpse signals the extent to which, by 1934, the grand gestures of sentiment had collapsed into the specter of miscegenation and criminal female sexuality.

The presence of Peterson's murdered body on Rosemary's bed, coupled with the threat of a media scandal for Rosemary, invokes the specter of two early twentieth-century "love-murders" that received sensationalized attention in the press. One of these accounts centered on the 1909 murder of Elise Siegel in New York's Chinatown by her Chinese lover Leon Ling. The murder was framed as evidence of the inherent perversity and unassimilability of Chinese men and as a testament to the dangers of racial mixing. Occurring between the 1882 passing of the Chinese Exclusion Act and the Immigration Act of 1924, the murder contributed to anti-Chinese sentiment and led to the imposition of even stricter controls on immigration.[34] As Douglas Baynton points out, immigrants entering the country at Ellis Island during this period were subject to medical scrutiny and rigorous tests to determine their level of "fitness," with certain ethnicities being regularly pronounced more defective than others. Thus, not only were people with disabilities being excluded from citizenship during this time but the concept of disability was also being applied to people from "undesirable" ethnicities as a pretense for their exclusion.

The other "love-murder" occurred in 1892 when nineteen-year-old Alice Mitchell allegedly killed her seventeen-year-old lover Freda Ward. While the sensationalized coverage of Alice Mitchell's trial does not deal with miscegenation explicitly, it was nonetheless overlaid with a set of anxieties that linked female sexual transgression with disability and foreignness. Both reflecting and constructing the new lesbian identities that were emerging at the turn of the twentieth century, the press coverage used Mitchell's "love-murder" to support the medical construction of lesbianism as a diagnosable mental disorder. Nineteenth-century romantic friendship had been previously perceived as innocent sympathetic affinity between young women. But by the twentieth century, the emerging science of sexuality had placed these intimate bonds between women within a new pathologizing medical framework of sexual inversion and predatory seduction. In these discourses, the gender cross-identifying lesbian was a true constitutional deviant while her gender-conforming lover was an otherwise "normal" woman who had fallen prey to the "inverted" woman's masculine charms.[35] Lisa Duggan thus reads the trial coverage as an example of the ways in which the murder "persisted as a topic of newspaper sensationalism and of scientific sexology," pointing out that Mitchell was not ultimately brought before a criminal court but rather "declared 'presently insane'" and "confined to the state lunatic asylum as dangerous to the community" (795). Thus the slippage of the sentimental into the sensational was connected to the pathologizing narratives of sexual science. In her rejection of traditional structures of heteronormative reproduction, Mitchell was not a "fallen woman" in need of religious compassion but a monstrous member of a new queer-crip species.

In addition to the Jules Peterson incident, there are only two instances in *Tender* where the term "murder" is invoked. The first takes place during an acting lesson, in which Dick offhandedly mentions that it is the responsibility of the actress to "get the audience's attention back on herself, away from the murdered Chinese or whatever the thing is," a statement that bears traces of Elsie Siegel's Chinatown murder twenty-five years earlier (288). The second instance is even more provocative as it initiates a series of female parings which, presented in quick succession, provide a condensed thematization of the historical process by which "romantic friendship" between women transformed into a criminalized and diagnosable female sexuality.

We encounter the first of these pairings when Tommy Barban and Nicole Diver, having just begun their affair, hear a commotion outside of their hotel room. As it continues, Tommy exclaims, "My God, has there been a murder?" Upon investigating the source of "increasing clamor," Tommy opens the window to find "two women on the balcony below . . . talking about weather and tipping back and forth in American rocking chairs" (295). Though brief, this placid image of female companionship might be understood in relation to the nineteenth-century model of romantic friendship through which the public made sense of intimacy between women. Chatting about the weather in their "American rocking chairs," their maternal serenity empties the relationship of any potentially threatening sexual connotations.[36] Looking past them, however, Tommy discovers the real source of the commotion as two American sailors trade blows before a cheering crowd. "They have *poules* [prostitutes] with them," Tommy notes, "I have heard about this now—the women follow them from place to place wherever the ship goes. But what women! One would think with their pay they could find better women!" (296). Soon after this rumination, Tommy and Nicole discover:

> two girls, young, thin and barbaric, unfound rather than lost, in the hall. One of them wept chokingly.

"Kwee wave off your porch?" implored the other in passionate American. "Kwee please? Wave at the boy friends? Kwee, please. The other rooms is all locked."

"With pleasure," Tommy said.

The girls rushed out on the balcony and presently their voices struck a loud treble over the din. . . . One of the girls hoisted her skirt suddenly, pulled and ripped at her pink step-ins and tore them to a sizable flag; then, screaming "Ben! Ben!" she waved it wildly. As Tommy and Nicole left the room it still fluttered against the blue sky. Oh, say can you see the tender color of remembered flesh?—while at the stern of the battleship arose in rivalry the Star-Spangled Banner. (297)

Note the swiftness with which the initial image of romantic friendship (two women chatting benignly in rocking chairs) has here been replaced by a more unruly female pairing (two girls "wildly" waving their undergarments at departing sailors). Embodying the sexual license of a younger generation of American women, their infiltration of the heteronormative bedroom signals an uneasy shift in gender norms. Rhetorically and thematically linked to the sexually delinquent prostitutes Tommy has just described, they make a very different spectacle than the matronly pair in the balcony below them. With their "flag-like" underwear billowing against the sky to the tune of the national anthem, they are a parody of American patriotism, emblematizing the nation while simultaneously threatening its undoing.[37]

But if the young age of the two girls on the balcony to some extent "excuses" or makes understandable their lack of sexual discipline (girls, after all, will be girls), then Lady Caroline and Mary North's antics five pages later reveal what can happen when youthful sexual license is carried into adulthood. Late at night, Dick is called to the police station to help Mary North and Lady Caroline who had "pretended to be sailors on leave" and "picked up two silly girls" (303). Though the incident is more of a "lark" than an expression of lesbian desire or identity, the "stunt" nevertheless brings this cycle of female pairings to a conclusion by conjuring the specter of the predatory cross-identifying lesbian whose medical profile was widely circulated during the Alice Mitchell case. No longer chatting about the weather in rocking chairs or waving their undergarments to American sailors from a stranger's balcony, this female pairing has now morphed into the sailors themselves. Preying on innocent girls, they produce a potential newspaper scandal that Dick must once again contain. "You're an insanity doctor, aren't you?" Lady Caroline wryly jokes to Dick, "You ought to be able to help us." The help that Dick offers, however, is more political than medical, as he uses money and persuasion to make the record of his friends' transgression, like Jules Peterson's body, disappear.

Thus, in this swift succession of scenes, Fitzgerald presents to the reader a condensed history of female delinquency, from its "innocent" genesis in romantic friendship, to its ambivalent expression in young girls' increased sexual latitude, to, finally, the disordered and criminal sexuality of the cross-identifying lesbian. Thus, by linking Rosemary, through Jules Peterson, to the era's racially and sexually charged "love-murders," Fitzgerald registers a set of national anxieties regarding racial mixing, gender-crossing, medical diagnosis, and masculine decline.[38] But perhaps the novel's most notable "love" crime is the one that is chronicled in Devereaux Warren's confession to Nicole's psychiatrists:

> After her mother died when she was little she used to come into my bed every morning, sometimes she'd sleep in my bed. I was sorry for the little thing. Oh, after that, whenever we went places together, we used to hold hands. She used to sing to me. We used to say, "Now let's not pay attention to anyone else this afternoon—let's just have each other—or this morning you're mine." A broken sarcasm came into his voice. "People used to say what a wonderful father and daughter we were—they used to wipe their eyes. We were just like lovers—and then we were lovers—and ten minutes after it happened I could have shot myself—except I'm just such a Goddamned degenerate I didn't have the nerve to do it." (129)

Devereaux Warren's language is saturated with the language of sentiment; like one of "Mrs. Burnett's vicious tracts," the portrait that he paints evokes sympathy: a motherless child, a "wonderful father and daughter," the physical tears issuing from the eyes of strangers.[39] But just as Dick's attempts to protect Rosemary through a "rare atmosphere" of sentiment result in a black man staining her sheets with blood, the sentimental narrative that constructs Nicole and Devereaux Warren as a "wonderful father and daughter" collapses inward on itself, transforming the safety of the metaphor "like lovers" into the literal act of incest: "—and then we were lovers." Whether it's Alice Mitchell, Leon Ling, Jules Peterson, or Devereaux Warren, the ending is always the same: bloody sheets left over as evidence of a degenerate love that has gone too far. Despite Fitzgerald's initial notes to the contrary, it would seem that we begin with "Ophelia and her flowers" but end up with "a novelized Krafft-Ebing."

Prophylactic Dames

What, then, is the relationship between gender and the antiprophylactic in Fitzgerald's work? While the perversely sexualized girl is presented as a contaminating agent in these narratives, it is ultimately Dick's male body that flexibly embodies the dynamism of antiprophylactic openness. As a doctor, Dick is expected to apply a cold scientific gaze to the patients under his care; as a sentimentalist, however, he continually fails to maintain these boundaries. As Dick's sentimental identifications with potentially "delinquent" women increase, he becomes increasingly readable as the figural embodiment of a nation whose racial borders have been penetrated by undesirable populations. Thus we might read the following description of Dick's psyche as a passage with broad biopolitical ramifications: "In the broken universe of the war's ending—in such contacts the personalities had seemed to press up so close to him that he became the personality itself—there seemed some necessity of taking all or nothing; it was as if for the remainder of his life he was condemned to carry with him the egos of certain people early met and early loved, and to be only as complete as they were complete themselves" (245). In his reading of this scene, Chris Messenger observes that "Dick's sentimental 'carrying' of the egos allows him to produce belief and master his psyche's production while usurping all the bodies as desiring subject," conceiving of Dick's recourse to charm as both narcissism and melancholia (71).

The implications of this reading deepen when we consider Dick's melancholic incorporation of others' egos in the context of the era's obsession with eugenic fitness. The fact that Dick's psychic incorporation is figured as a burden (he is "condemned" to carry others' egos) implies the dead weight of dependent populations and the draining of national resources. Even Nicole realizes that "there was a pleasingness about [Dick] that simply had to be used" (87), and indeed, by the end of the narrative, Nicole leaves Dick emptied of resources and contemplating her fear of "what the stricken man above [Dick] would feed on while she must still continue her dry suckling at his lean chest" (279). Musing about Dick, Rosemary wonders, "When people have so much for outsiders, doesn't it indicate a lack of inner intensity?" (75). Considering these observations against the backdrop of eugenic policy, we can see how Dick's willingness to let "outsiders" enter his ego and make use of his psychic resources might, beyond its psychoanalytic dimensions, indicate the sapping away of the national vitality by parasitic populations. In his sentimental or sympathetic acts of incorporation, Dick's psyche metonymically transforms into a national melting pot of all of the egos that he is "condemned to carry" and incorporate within himself—one that, in Grant's formulation, is allowed to "boil without control." Dick's sentiment, in other words, allegorizes him as a figure for the United States itself.[40] He embodies a masculine citizenship that aspires to provide unconditional hospitality but finds itself depleted by the gains of the (lesbian) New Woman and the incoming hordes of feebleminded immigrants.

And yet, Fitzgerald can never quite bring himself to disavow these practices of male sympathy, nor does he ever fully embrace the prophylactic impulse behind medicine's management of perversely sexualized populations. But far from feminizing him, what we witness instead in these moments is a process by which sentiment is remasculinized while the ostensibly masculine commitment to eugenic "objectivity" is projected onto the female body. Consider, for example, the language that Fitzgerald uses to describe Dick's identification with Nicole: "Men were for that, beam and idea, girder and logarithm; but somehow Dick and Nicole had become one and equal, not opposite and complementary; she was Dick too, the draught in the marrow of his bones. He could not watch her disintegrations without participating in them. His intuition rilled out of him as tenderness and compassion" (191). Initially, this passage reads as a straightforward description of feminized masculinity, with Dick opting to identify with and incorporate the New Woman into his own psyche in ways that predict his own "disintegration." And yet there is a qualified approval in Fitzgerald's lyrical description of Dick's "intuition" which "rill[s] out of him as tenderness and compassion." Against the nobility of this phrase, the abstractions of "beam and idea, girder and logarithm" sound sterile and substanceless. Rather than using sentiment to question Dick's masculinity, Fitzgerald is using sentiment to redefine masculinity. Like the "fellow feeling" that had bound male citizens to one another in earlier eras, Dick's compassion is subtly reframed as a commendable, if outdated, masculine virtue. But in his attempt to remasculinize love, Fitzgerald must also feminize eugenics, making women "prophylactic dames" who function as a "girder and logarithm." Thus Nicole's maternal presence is accompanied not by domestic warmth, but by a hard rationality that is more characteristic of male scientism. She "bring[s] up children she could only pretend gently to love" (180), and she takes Lanier and Topsy on an "organized romp" during which she reacts to Kaethe with the revulsion of a person who fears contagion (240).

Thus while Dick's eczema-encrusted female patient would seem to emblematize a form of unruly female embodiment that contrasts with masculinized medical discipline, Dick's unprofessional practices (or at least fantasies) of empathy complicate this reading. Dick is, after all, the eczema woman's doctor; it is his medical authority that diagnoses her illness and his fidelity to the male medical establishment that causes a much more paternalistic tone to creep into his interactions with her. "You are sick," he tells the woman "mechanically" (185). As he leaves the room, he punctuates the episode with a moral: "We must all try to be good" (185).[41] These moments to some extent recall the utilitarian logic embedded in Robert Ward's appeal to eugenics as a form of social ethics. But between these statements we find in Dick a much different sensibility: "He wanted to gather her up in his arms, as he so often had Nicole, and cherish even her mistakes, so deeply were they a part of her" (185). This moment of antiprophylactic acceptance provides a sharp contrast to Dick's status as a clinical psychologist and highlights the two opposing polarities between which the novel's commitments vacillate.

Indeed, the great irony of Fitzgerald's framing of his patient's eczema is that the cure has not treated an illness; it has created an illness. In her biography of Zelda Fitzgerald, Sally Cline notes that "Zelda's doctors believed her recovery depended on a 'successful' marriage, so they advised her against conflicts with Scott" and believed that "the propensity towards homosexuality and menstrual disturbances noted in female schizophrenics indicated endocrine or chemical imbalances." Listing several invasive chemical treatments that Zelda's body was subjected to, she hypothesizes, along with Scott, that Zelda's painful eczema might have been "caused by a lack of elimination of poison" (283). If we can hypothesize that Fitzgerald was drawing from his wife's eczema in his writing of Dick's unnamed patient, then what emerges is a portrait of a female body poisoned by medical prophylaxis and rehabilitated by the affective openness of a sympathetic masculinity. We can consider this alongside Dick's encounter with a "normal and conscientious" father who "had tried to protect a nervous brood from life's troubles and had succeeded merely in preventing them from developing powers of adjustment to life's inevitable surprises" (186). Prophylactic protection of the child nearly always, in *Tender Is the Night*, collapses into the very thing that puts the child at risk.

Similarly, sentiment continually emerges as both a balm and a threat, like the "brutal sunshine" (4) that causes Rosemary to "feel her skin broiling a little bit" (6) or Dick's "carnivals of affection" that resemble massacres (27). If eugenic prophylaxis sacrifices today's children to the ghostly bounties of the future, then sympathy threatens to ruin the children of the future by spoiling the children of today. Ultimately in *Tender*, no child is safe. Whether it is Lanier bathing in his oxymoronic "dirty suds," Baby Warren waltzing with a bloated spleen, Rosemary catching pneumonia on her movie set, or Nicole's "moving childish smile that was like all the lost youth in the world" (134), we are met with a parade of children who are continually imperiled by the very kinship structures designed to keep them safe. Thus when the "three children sledding past shouted a warning in some strange language" (173), we might read it as a siren signal to every child whose existence reproductive futurism both depends on and obliterates.

For Faulkner and Fitzgerald, children are both vulnerable to contamination and themselves carriers of contagion and in their works there is a jarring swiftness with which sympathy becomes love, love becomes perversity, and the perversely sexualized adolescent girl becomes the bearer of unfit children. These narrative progressions reveal that there is no inherent political content to sentiment and no singular cause whose badge bears the insignia of the baby's face. Neither is queerness easily located in the body of the gay man. Ironically, *Tender*'s two gay men, Campion and Dumphrey, are among the only adults who never put a child at risk; meanwhile, the gay youth Francisco, whom Dick is called upon to treat, brings a mature and balanced perspective to the novel that is unmatched by any of his heteronormative counterparts. While the icon of the Child has certainly been put in the service of heteronormative—sometimes even fiercely homophobic agendas—gay men are not the only demographic that have been "collectively terrorized" under reproductive futurism's flag. But by acknowledging those sexualities whose very link to reproduction is what makes them "queer," we can continue the cultural work that queer theory, at its best, enables.

In "Unspeakable Conversations," Harriet McBryde Johnson describes her professional encounter with Peter Singer, a philosopher and one of the disability studies' notorious foes. McBryde Johnson begins her essay provocatively: "He insists he doesn't want to kill me. He simply thinks it would have been better, all things considered, to have given my parents the option of killing the baby I once was, and to let other parents kill similar babies as they come along and thereby avoid the suffering that comes with lives like mine and satisfy the reasonable preferences of parents for a different kind of child. It has nothing to do with me. I should not feel threatened" (573). When Singer professes that McBryde Johnson's parents ought to have been given the option of "killing the baby [she] once was," he is nowhere close to taking up Edelman's rallying cry to "fuck the social order and the Child in whose name we're collectively terrorized" (29). Singer's utilitarian approach to disabled children is, of course, markedly different from the eugenic philosophies that preceded him. As a twenty-first-century philosopher, he is less concerned with the racial composition of the nation and more concerned with questions regarding the relationship between available resources and quality of life. What remains strikingly similar, however, is a logic that prizes the "reasonable" preferences of parents (and professionals whose diagnosis are believed to predict quality of life) over other individuals' ostensibly "unreasonable" emotional attachments to the value of disabled life.

Like fitness, the notion of a measurable quality of life creates a fixed scale of worth that does not often correspond to the experience of those it describes. McBryde Johnson explains that because "the sight of me is routinely discombobulating" for many she encounters, she finds herself in the continual "tedious" position of explaining that "I enjoy my life, that it's a great sensual pleasure to zoom by power chair on these delicious muggy streets, that I have no more reason to kill myself than most people." The "sensual pleasure" McBryde Johnson describes here—real, felt, unquantifiable—fundamentally shifts the terms of the debate. Rejecting both sentimental and utilitarian approaches to her disability, she reveals the choice between love and eugenics to be a red herring. Instead, she chooses to "invoke the muck and mess and undeniable reality of disabled lives well lived" (585). To "invoke the muck and mess" of "disabled lives well lived" is not to "shatter the self" or to transcend the ego through a temporary foray into queer self-debasement. More radically, it is to persist in imagining a future for unimaginable subjectivities: the queer-crip child who "fuck[s] the social order" precisely by having been allowed to grow up.

3

"Not the Usual Pattern"

James Baldwin and the DSM

You can't know anything about life and suppose you can get through it clean. The most monstrous people are those who think they are going to . . . And this is terribly dangerous, because it means that when the trouble comes, and trouble always comes, you won't survive it. It means that if your son dies, you may go to pieces or find the nearest psychiatrist or the nearest church, but you won't survive it on your own. If you don't survive your trouble out of your own resources, you have not really survived it; you have merely closed yourself against it . . . For example, right now you find the most unexpected people building bomb shelters, which is very close to being a crime. It is a private panic which creates a public delusion that some of us will be saved by bomb shelters.

—JAMES BALDWIN, "The Uses of the Blues" (1964)

James Baldwin's attitude toward psychiatry was a complicated one. Though not entirely dismissive of psychoanalysis, Baldwin was keenly aware of the way psychiatric discourses could function in ways that isolate and insulate citizens from one another. In the epigraph above, taken from Baldwin's 1964 essay "The Uses of the Blues," Baldwin aligns the psychiatric profession with the prophylactic impulse to "close yourself against" those challenges that would have otherwise helped you generate the coping mechanisms necessary for "survival" (80). Those citizens who run to the "nearest psychiatrist," Baldwin seems to imply, are the same people who are inclined to build "bomb shelters," (80) with both venues designed to "shelter" individuals from the contexts of their environment, and from each other. Resembling the ableist injunction to toughen up in the face of adversity, this logic risks perpetuating stigma around those who seek mental health treatments. However, rather than simply romanticizing states of precarity and risk, Baldwin grounds his observations with the acknowledgment that total security (both physical and national) must be recognized as a "public delusion"—one that exacts a violent cost in the physical and psychological degradation of black lives. Disability occupies a curious place in this vision, with psychological and physical vulnerability presented both as an index of social injustice and as a valuable resource for rethinking the structures of American community.

The first half of this chapter explores Baldwin's complicated relationship to *DSM* models of homosexuality popularized during the 1950s and 1960s. From its first entrance into the *Diagnostic and Statistical Manual of Mental Disorders* (*DSM*) in 1952 to its eventual removal in 1973, "homosexuality" spent twenty-one years classified by the American Psychiatric Association as a psychological disorder. Psychiatric models of homosexuality contrasted with previous discourses of sexual inversion in significant ways, with medical professionals generally believing inversion to be a property of the physical body. The mental disorder of homosexuality, by contrast, was understood to be a "sickness of the mind," stemming from early childhood psychological trauma.[1] Many literary and cultural representations from the period—from mainstream cinema to the lesbian pulp novels of Ann Bannon—reinforced this portrait of homosexuality as the expression of psychological maladjustment.[2]

I argue that Baldwin's 1956 novel *Giovanni's Room* is crucially engaged with this queer moment in the history of medicine. However, unlike standard critiques of sexual psychiatry, Baldwin's novel remains relatively unconcerned with the shaming effects of the *DSM*'s diagnostic labeling. Though it is common in scholarship on *Giovanni's Room* to understand Baldwin's protagonist David as a self-hating homosexual, or even further, to understand Baldwin himself as ambivalently reinforcing psychiatric models of same-sex desire, such readings miss the extent to which the novel continually critiques the way its narrator, David, fashions himself as the model homosexual patient to be diagnosed by the reader. Framed through psychoanalysis as the outcome of bourgeois family drama gone awry, the diagnosis of homosexuality was, after all, applied primarily to white middle-class subjects who were assumed to possess a more complex psychological interiority than their nonwhite and working-class counterparts. Placing David's practices of self-diagnosis within the context of Cold War paranoia and the rise of the closet paradigm, my reading reframes *Giovanni's Room* as an exploration of how these diagnostic criteria might function, for some gay subjects, as a counterintuitive site of racial and class privilege—one which cleansed same-sex desire of many of its previous associations with effeminacy, poverty, interracial intimacy, and prostitution. For Baldwin, what makes David "monstrous" is not his sexual repression, but his quintessentially American assumption that he can "get through [life] clean." In this way, Baldwin reveals that it is much more than the shame (or its failure to be converted into pride) that is at stake in David's continual rehearsal of his psychosexual backstory.

In the second half of the chapter, I turn from 1950s constructions of white homosexuality to the racialization of schizophrenia during the civil rights era. If Cold War discourses of paranoia directed white men to continually "read" one another (and themselves) for evidence of homosexual repression or the presence of sexual double life, then during the 1960s, paranoia became clinically attached to the bodies of black militants whose feelings of persecution were diagnosed as delusional. In his political writing during this period, Baldwin drew from these discourses to create a portrait of black schizophrenia that contrasts markedly with David's practices of self-diagnosis: if David's "paranoia" functions prophylactically, then the "paranoia" of black militants constitutes a legitimate response to institutional racism. The inevitability of psychic injury in a segregated America, Baldwin suggests, makes prophylactic protection impossible for black subjects who are always already vulnerable to physical and psychological violence.

In a provocative scene that occurs in Baldwin's 1963 novel, *Another Country*, Baldwin uses psychiatric paradigms of homosexuality to dramatize and critique the prophylactic impulses of white liberalism. In it, white bohemians Eric and Cass find themselves on the verge of an unlikely love affair—unlikely because Cass is a married woman and Eric is a gay man. Before they begin their sexual encounter, Eric explains to Cass that their affair must remain temporary because his French lover, Yves, will be arriving in New York soon. No matter what Yves "think[s] of the States," Eric explains, his love for Yves has made Eric "responsible for him when he gets here" (289). Eric's sense of responsibility for Yves, it's important to point out, escapes both the rhetoric of dependence and burden that characterize some discussions of immigration as well as the rhetoric of autonomy, independence, and the American Dream that characterizes others. Eric's responsibility for Yves is based, rather, on an ethic of queer interdependence in which the two men rely on each other for various forms of material and emotional support. When Eric casually adds that Yves "hates his mother," Cass's reply (and the subsequent exchange between the two) reveals the extent to which clinical psychiatric understandings of homosexuality had made their way into popular consciousness:

> "That's not the usual pattern, is it?" Then she wished that she had held her tongue, or could call the words back. But it was too late,

really, to do more than blandly compound her error: "I mean, from what we're told, most men with a sexual bias toward men love their mothers and hate their fathers."

"We haven't been told much," he observed, mildly sardonic. "I used to know street boys in Paris who hadn't had any opportunity to hate their mother or their fathers. Of course, they hated *les flics*—the cops—and I suppose some safe slug of an American would work it out that they hated the cops because they were father figures . . . but it seems just as likely to me that they hated the cops because the cops liked to beat the shit out of them." (289–290)

Here Cass, a straight woman, finds herself "caught" in the attempt to sanitize and fortify the "naturalness" of her heterosexual identity against a pathologizing view of Eric and Yves' homosexual otherness. But her knee-jerk Freudian explanation not only fails to account for Yves's family dynamic (since he hates the wrong parent); it outright backfires. It is in that backfiring that Baldwin deftly reverses the usual scene of sexual "outing": revelation emerges not from the scandalous declaration of homosexual difference (a "bias toward men") but rather, ironically, from Cass's unintentional eruption of heterosexist bias. Indeed, we might view Cass's rhetorical deployment of pop psychiatry as a kind of preventive measure: the precoital prophylactic that promises to protect her against the complicated web of queer relationality that her intimacy with Eric threatens to fold her into.

Baldwin's intention here, however, is neither to condemn Cass nor to transform Eric into the bearer of moral authority. Instead, these moments of interpersonal alienation lead his characters toward alternative (and ultimately productive) sites of social revelation. In this sense, Eric becomes a sort of anti-Freudian Freudian analyst. Refusing to take Cass's psychiatric speculations at face value, he asks her instead to address the wider social unconscious that lies beneath the comfortable psychiatric narrative she has just related. Reading past the surface of Cass's psychiatric text, Eric uncovers an important set of unresolved political and class conflicts which, taken seriously, means that gay sexuality can no longer be reducible to the psychic complexity of white bourgeois men with father issues. Instead, gay sexuality must be contextualized socially and politically in relation to the economically disadvantaged street kids and the institutionalized forms of violence they experience when faced with officers of the law—a law that can't, in their case, be counted on for protection. If Cass describes a version of selfhood that is self-contained (to discover who you are, you must examine the depths of your psyche), then

Eric mines its meanings to create an opposing version of selfhood that is ultimately social and dialectical (to discover who you are, you must examine your political and ethical relation to others).

Eric's political reframing of homosexuality as a relational practice rather than a static identity causes Cass to consequently question her own class status in relation to the police, as "it had never entered her mind to feel menaced by one" and "and if a policeman . . . seemed to forget his place, it was easy enough to make him remember it" (290). This rumination pushes Cass's frame of reference beyond the interiority of the individual, forcing her instead to interrogate her own position within a network of social relations: the street boys are subject to the power of the cops, and the cops, as members of the working class, have less financial and social capital than Cass. Eric may not be a street boy but his sexuality still makes him vulnerable to the police in a way that Cass is not. At the same time, Eric's gender places him in a position of privilege within a patriarchal society, even as his sexuality complicates that privilege.[3] Thus what had begun as a sexual exchange between equals has now been revealed as a complicated and politically fraught union between differently empowered political subjects. Ironically, however, this realization does not block intimacy but enables it. If Cass had originally attempted to wield psychiatry as a kind of epistemological prophylactic, shielding her against a complex web of queer relationality, she now allows Eric's "wonder," during the subsequent scene of lovemaking, to "infect her" (291). Put simply, the scene suggests that medical discourses sanitize and separate individuals while deeper political revelations enable subjects to enter into productive intimate exchanges.

But if *Another Country*'s urban setting and multiracial cast of characters seems to lend it more readily to intersectional analyses, *Giovanni's Room* has appeared to be more resistant to such readings. This is partly owing to Baldwin's choice of subject matter (white homosexuals in Paris), a choice that surprised and dismayed audiences who had pigeonholed Baldwin as an author of "the black experience."[4] Some critics took the lack of African American characters in the text as evidence of Baldwin's desire to focus exclusively on the complexities of same-sex desire without the distractions of racial controversy. Others have more persuasively pointed out the racialized dimensions of the text, examining the construction of David's Nordic and Anglo ancestry in relation to Giovanni's ethnic Mediterranean difference.[5] To most critics, however, the novel's racial and class consciousness seems negligible in comparison to the more radical queer achievement represented by the publication of *Another Country* seven years after the publication of *Giovanni's Room*. I would contend, however, that *Giovanni's Room* is best understood not as a timid, ambivalent warm-up to the more politically brave *Another Country* but as an extensive and inverted telling of the same narrative, related from the opposite perspective but fashioning, more subtly, the same critique.

In these commitments, Baldwin's work consistently breaks down the categories upon which his contemporaries relied. Baldwin's queerness, for example, and his openness to interracial collaborations brought him under attack by Black Nationalists like Eldridge Cleaver who interpreted his intimacies with white people as evidence of "racial death wish."[6] Conversely, Baldwin's canonization within an LGBT literary tradition has often served as a way of muting the pointed racial critiques that his novels offer, with gay and lesbian readers either tokenizing Baldwin (his racial difference simply illustrating the diversity of the gay and lesbian canon) or ignoring the way that his status as a black man had, in various ways, complicated his sense of identification with the gay community. These conflicts and intersections have played an enormous role in shaping Baldwin's reception in both literary and political circles. His status as a black man writing in a white gay canon, a gay man writing in a straight black canon, and a political activist publishing literary masterpieces has sparked seemingly endless debates regarding the slippery intersectionalities that frame his work. While such debates have been necessary and productive, they have also led Baldwin scholarship into an intersectional rut with the tension between the signifiers "black" and "queer" overdetermining the way scholars have received and responded to his work. To get out of this rut, I believe that we need to begin thinking in new ways about Baldwin's work, expanding our frames of reference beyond (without at the same time abandoning) the important critical observations that queer-of-color scholars have made about Baldwin's dueling dual identities. Considering Baldwin through the lens of disability studies, and particularly through the often ignored critical intersections between queer sexuality and the history of psychiatry, provides such an opportunity.

Mummy Issues

The plot of *Giovanni's Room* unfolds through a series of flashbacks recounted in the first person by David, an upper-middle-class white American living in Paris. David begins his story by relating a set of early events and impressions that he believes have set the stage for his flight to Europe. Key among those impressions are his status as the only child of a widowed father and his having once had sex, during his teenage years, with his male friend Joey. Frightened and secretive about both the encounter and its implications, David travels to Europe and proposes marriage to the first American woman that he meets during his travels. He finds himself alone, however, for a brief period of time while his potential fiancée, Hella, travels to Spain to think over his proposal. The main action of the novel takes place during this interval. Soon after Hella's departure, David meets Giovanni, the Italian bartender of a gay establishment, and the two men begin a passionate love affair. But, unable to come to terms with his sexuality and desperate to protect his reputation, David ultimately abandons Giovanni for Hella when she returns to Paris. Without David, the poverty-stricken Giovanni is forced to accept the sexual advances of wealthy Parisian men in exchange for a small measure of financial security. When David finds out that Giovanni has been sentenced to death, having murdered his boss, Guillaume, after a particularly exploitative sexual exchange, his guilt over Giovanni causes his relationship with Hella to fall apart. In the novel's final scene, David—alone and depressed on the night of Giovanni's execution—struggles to make sense of his own role in Giovanni's death.

Significantly, the first dozen pages of *Giovanni's Room* read more like a case history or a medical chart than the opening of a novel. Before we know almost anything about David, we are briefed on the death of his mother when he was five years old and his boyhood nightmares of her "putrescent" corpse, which, David recalls, "opened, as I clawed and cried, into a breach so enormous as to swallow me alive" (16). We are also told that David's aunt Ellen (his father's sister) appeared to replace David's mother as a caregiver. Ellen, we are told, "flirted" with her brother's party guests in a "nerve-wracking kind of way," with a "mouth redder than any blood" and a voice going "on and on like a razor blade on glass" (17). Finally, David describes his experience of feeling "exhausted and appalled" (21) by his father's insistence on treating him like a "buddy" and the uncomfortable "masculine candor" about women that existed between them. It is not difficult to read into these brief recollections a distilled portrait of Freudian angst. David's dream of his mother's powerful and suffocating corpse represents an inverted incestuous longing; Ellen's "blood red" "razorblade" mouth stands in for the resulting threat of castration; and the fraught intimacy with his father constitutes a failed Oedipal bond that does nothing to protect him against the force of his childhood fantasies.

Understanding his homosexuality as a horror of femininity and castration, David thus recites the common medical narrative that dominated popular understandings of same-sex desire during the 1950s. Indeed, the same year that Baldwin published *Giovanni's Room*, Edmund Bergler published his influential study titled *Homosexuality: Disease or Way of Life?* (1956) in which he defined homosexuality as a "neurotic disease" caused by an "unsolved masochistic conflict with the mother of earliest infancy" (263).[7] These understandings grew out of psychiatric professionals' interest in (and oversimplification of) Freud's earlier theories of sexuality.[8] As Simon LeVay notes, "the real psychoanalytic attack on homosexuality was initiated by Freud's followers, particularly those working in the United States" (75). With the 1940 publication of Sando Rador's article "A Critical Examination of the Concept of Bisexuality," homosexuality became redefined as an inherently pathological (and curable) disorder that results when a child has been frightened away from heterosexual contact. These figures were joined by others in the profession, most notably Irving Bieber, Charles Socarides, Lionel Ovesey, and Edward Glover all of whom categorized homosexuality as a form of sexual psychopathology characterized by a "phobic response to members of the opposite sex" (29).[9]

Summarizing these thinkers' interpretation of Freud's fourth theory of homosexuality, Kenneth Lewes explains that "the homosexual lover is not drawn to his object through preference, but is impelled to it by the horror of the mutilated female genitals and the possibility of suffering a similar fate, a force that operates each time a homosexual object choice is made or a heterosexual one repudiated" (31). David's first queer encounter, narrated directly before his psychobiography, reproduces this Freudian logic. After their lovemaking, David looks upon Joey's naked body and sees "the black opening of a cavern in which I would be tortured till madness came, in which I would lose my manhood" (14). Like the "enormous breach" that opens up within his mother's corpse and threatens to devour him, Joey's body becomes a similarly ravenous "opening" that threatens castration. Indeed, "fear of engulfment by women" is listed second among psychologist Charles Socarides's fifteen pathological characteristics of the male homosexual in his 1978 book *Homosexuality*. Sex with men, for David, can only represent the pathological attempt to negotiate an Oedipal drama gone awry.

Such discourses gained credibility with the first publication of the *DSM* in 1952, which included "homosexuality" among its index of treatable mental illnesses. The publication of the *DSM* was itself a significant moment in the history of psychiatry, not only grounding the institutional authority of the APA but creating, for the first time, a standardized and mainstreamed rubric for the classification, diagnosis, and treatment of mental disorders. Homosexual patients during this period were subjected to hypnosis, electroshock treatment, and aversion therapy, as well as psychoanalytic treatments intended to facilitate heterosexual adjustment.[10] The *DSM*, it's important to add, was not simply a medical text but a best seller, helping to convert psychiatric vocabularies of disorder into the popular parlance of the upper middle class. Like Cass, David is likely to have been literate in the mainstreamed psychological account of "disordered" homosexuality and to have fashioned his understanding of himself and his desires through its vocabularies.

The diagnosability of David's homosexuality is a point that has been noted by other critics as well. However, most of these accounts view David's confession as a sincere attempt (on his own part and Baldwin's) to negotiate and come to terms with a stigmatized sexual identity. Mae Henderson, for example, sees in David's narration a "variation on the classic psychological explanation for homosexuality" which she describes in detail:

> Following the fashionable Freudian formulation of homosexuality, the narrator's ambivalence toward the mother, coupled with his father's distance, creates a confusion for young David that is compounded by the brief, but frightening, adolescent homosexual encounter with a childhood schoolmate, Joey . . . The union between David and Giovanni, thus, figures that of a motherless son and a childless father, a configuration suggesting a symbolic displacement of the Freudian Family Romance. (317)

Though Henderson's reading here is cleverly attuned to the "fashionable Freudian formulations" that the novel, on its surface, presents, the implications of those formulations may extend beyond the process through which Baldwin grappled with his own same-sex desire. Though he "masks in whiteface his first explicit treatment of homosexuality," Henderson argues, "the act of writing *Giovanni's Room* represents a significant step for the author in understanding his own homosexuality and reconciling himself with a vision of America" (326).[11] But I would argue that Baldwin's narrative "whiteface" is not intended to pass as or "mask" anything. Rather, as a racial masquerade, it uses a drag-like irony to *unmask* the white privilege of its narrator.

While both David and Giovanni's personal histories are consistent with psychiatric narratives of homosexuality that were popular during the 1950s—narratives that located same-sex desire as evidence of a traumatic disruption of the nuclear family—I believe that Baldwin was up to something a bit more shrewd in his representations of David's "disordered" sexuality. Might we detect a level of wry performativity—or at the very least, overstatement—in the textbook clarity with which Baldwin has David present his psychobiography?

Though David, as a gay man, would appear on the surface to have more in common with Eric than Cass, his obedient conformity to a psychiatric origin story actually places him more in line with Cass's lapse into Freudianism; he is all too aware that what he has presented the reader with conforms precisely to the "usual pattern" of unresolved Oedipal conflict.

Indeed, what is perhaps most striking about David's psychosexual ruminations is their dense concentration at the outset of the narrative and the lack of subtlety with which the psychological etiology of David's disordered sexuality is fashioned. It's certainly possible to chalk up this Freudian overkill to Baldwin's youth and lack of experience as a novelist, but looking at the subtlety and complexity of Baldwin's entire body of work suggests otherwise. I put forth instead the following possibility: in having David obediently deliver a prepackaged "explanation" for his homosexuality, Baldwin's priority is not to provide insight into the bearing that David's psychological past has on his sexual present. Instead, he is inviting the reader to view in David's overwrought Freudianism a calculated performance of medical literacy. A perfectly disciplined subject, David asserts himself as the ideal patient; however, his dutiful repetition of the standard psychiatric narrative necessarily overdetermines the information he provides, making the standard Freudian analysis impossible. In other words, David's conscious insistence on the Freudian origins of his desires automatically rules out their usefulness as an explanatory tool. David's professed castration anxieties and unresolved Oedipal conflicts become the text rather than the subtext. Consequently, the reader is asked to read *through* David's neatly packaged account of his "disorder" to the historical unconscious that strains below its surface.

What kind of historical unconscious, then, is being "repressed" by David's airtight prophylactic account of his own psychosexual trauma? David's commitment to psychiatric models of gay identity obscures the practices of cross-gendered identifications and working-class associations that dominated public understandings of deviant sexuality before they were displaced by newer psychiatric designations. In other words, while both the invert and the homosexual were diagnosable, it was only the homosexual whose diagnosability was compatible with traditional masculinity. But the version of homosexuality and same-sex desire that David is committed to relies on a gay/straight binary that had, in fact, only recently emerged at the time of his narration. As historians like George Chauncey have pointed out, models for understanding male same-sex sexuality in the United States before World War II were both highly gendered and often deeply inflected by social class. During these decades, male queerness was understood by medical professionals primarily through the model of gender inversion, focusing on effeminate men whom the larger public termed (and many of whom self-identified) as "fairies." Elaborating on what he calls the "working-class bachelor culture" of the early twentieth century, Chauncey explains the social dynamics through which working-class fairies partnered with traditionally masculine men in brief encounters that occasionally may have involved an exchange of money. These masculine men were often sailors or engaged in other transient or low-paying occupations that made them less likely to be married or tied to the domestic sphere. In these instances, taking the active sexual role in a same-sex encounter did not threaten masculinity and even potentially amplified it. Thus fairy culture, as Chauncey describes it, had more in common with female prostitute culture than with modern gay identity.

This history provides an important context for reading the anxieties that accompany David's brief exchange of looks with an American sailor he sees "dressed all in white, coming across the boulevard" (88):

> He seemed—somehow—younger than I had ever been, and blonder and more beautiful, and he wore his masculinity as unequivocally as he wore his skin . . . I wondered if my father had ever been like that, if I had ever been like that—though it was hard to imagine, for this boy, striding across the avenue like light itself, any antecedents, any connections at all. We came abreast and, as though he had seen some all-revealing panic in my eyes, he gave me a look contemptuously lewd and knowing; just such a look as he might have given, but a few hours ago, to the desperately well-dressed nymphomaniac or trollop who was trying to make him believe she was a lady. (88)

Though David wants to understand his relation to the sailor's untarnished butch exterior as a relation of sameness (with the sailor's masculinity acting as a mirror to his own), he finds himself ultimately perceiving this encounter through a framework of difference more consistent with earlier understandings of bachelor subculture that Chauncey describes. The sailor's "unequivocal" masculinity can only diminish David's sense of his manhood, and the sailor's freedom from "antecedents" can only emphasize David's own fraught relation to the fairies and trade who were his genealogical forebears. The "panic" that David feels here is ultimately not the panic of homosexual disclosure but the panic of being read as a fairy.

It is also, I would add, the panic of social class. By comparing himself to the "desperately well-dressed . . . trollop," David underscores the extent to which many male fairies were understood as inhabiting a similar category as lower-class women, and female prostitutes in particular. Both subcultures, Chauncey points out, drew sexually from a similar pool of men, both were assumed to have "loose morals," and both were vulnerable to physical and sexual violence. Consequently, both adopted a working-class femininity marked by the toughness of the streets. Thus when David imagines the look the sailor may have given to the "trollop who was trying to make him believe she was a lady," there are not one but two forms of impersonation evoked—that of a lower-class woman "masquerading" as an upper-class one, and that of a biologically male "fairy," adopting the style and mannerisms of a "lady."

With this in mind, I want to consider a scene that occurs early in the novel. Visiting a local gay bar with his gay friend Jacques, David engages in an intense flirtation with the bartender, Giovanni. Because David's sexuality had been a source of speculation among the bar patrons, the courtship attracts notice with one particularly flamboyant patron approaching David in order to tease him. As he approaches, David records his reaction in the following hyperbolically Gothic terms that evoke Frankenstein's famous first description of his monster:

> It looked like a mummy or a zombie—this was the first overwhelming impression—of something walking after it had been put to death . . . It carried a glass, it walked on its toes, the flat hips moved with a dead, horrifying lasciviousness . . . It glittered in the dim light; the thin black hair was violent with oil, combed forward, hanging in bangs; the eyelids gleamed with mascara, the mouth raged with lipstick, the face was white and thoroughly bloodless with some kind of foundation cream; it stank of powder and gardenia-like perfume. The shirt, open coquettishly to the navel, revealed a hairless chest and a silver crucifix; the shirt was covered with round paper-thin wafers, red and green and orange and yellow and blue, which stormed in the light and made one feel that the mummy might, at any moment, disappear in flame. A red sash was around the waist, the clinging pants were a surprisingly somber grey. He wore buckles on his shoes. (41)

Like the classically theorized feminine object of the voyeuristic male gaze, the patron's body is fragmented into bits of clothing and isolated body parts, but these parts fail to produce in David the desire aroused by the traditional "fetish" object. If the psychosexually healthy male is able to neutralize the threat of castration through recourse to the fetish, these fragments of feminine artifice (perfume, cosmetics, revealing attire) are attached not to desire but to death. The cosmetics worn by the "zombie" (lipstick, mascara, foundation cream) feel more like the work of a mortician preparing a body for a public viewing than the trade secrets of the glamour model. Rather than the flawless skin and objectified curves of the female movie star, we are given only the "stink" of "bloodless" flesh and the "horrifying lasciviousness" of "dead" hips.

This Gothic rendering is, of course, entirely consistent with David's earlier Freudian projections that rationalized his homosexuality as a phobic response to femininity. The memory of his dead mother's decaying corpse might be easily transposed onto the "mummy" (mommy?) who stands before him at this moment. That this mummy's "mouth raged with lipstick" echoes David's earlier description of his Aunt Ellen, whose mouth, "redder than any blood," carries with it the (perpetually unresolved) threat of castration. This threat is confirmed by abrupt introduction of the word "he" in the final line—the feminine subject, it turns out, was a castrated male all along. But as I have suggested above, this too-easy textbook Freudianism obscures the real source of David's anxieties in this scene. This is not, after all, one of David's childhood nightmares. What David is presented with in this moment is not the horror of the corpse but, to the contrary, the camp theatricality of the fairy. David does not fear that castration will transform him into a woman; he fears that attraction to Giovanni's masculinity will transform him into the effeminate creature that stands before him. Thus he speculates that the "insistent possibilities" Giovanni has inspired in him are now "as visible as the wafers on the shirt of the flaming princess" (44).

Indeed, when David offhandedly describes the "band of disgusting fairies" that his friend Jacques runs with, his revulsion is mixed with uneasy recognition. He confesses that he "always found it difficult to believe that they ever went to bed with anybody, for a man who wanted a woman would certainly have rather had a real one and a man who wanted a man would certainly not want one of them" (30). Later he confides in the reader his own discomfort upon encountering a boy dressed in drag: "His utter grotesqueness made me uneasy; perhaps in the same way that the sight of monkeys eating their own excrement turns some people's stomachs. They might not mind so much if monkeys did not—so grotesquely—resemble humans" (30). These "silly old queens" who seem to periodically surround and haunt David function as a set of historical mirrors; lurking around every corner, they remind David that it was not very long ago that attractions like his—to masculine men—were considered to be symptoms of a feminized lower-class physiology, rather than evidence of a traumatized masculine psyche. Thus if earlier models were marked by messier gender identifications, interracial intimacies, and complicated class dynamics, then the new gay male subculture that began to emerge during the 1940s and 1950s was one that offered the possibility of more cleanly sanitized boundaries. It is those prophylactic boundaries that are really at stake for David and those boundaries that his diagnostic performances are meant to fortify. By presenting to the reader the psychiatric origins of his sexually disordered psyche, David produces not a confession but an alibi—a discursive smoke screen that ironically protects his racial and class privilege even while seeming to call it into question.

Disagreeable Mirrors

Feminization and class status are not the only anxieties at play in David's brief exchange with the sailor, discussed earlier, who "strid[es] across the avenue like light itself" (88). Equally important in this description is David's preoccupation with race. "Dressed in white," the sailor is described as "blonder and more beautiful" than David himself "had ever been" (88). Thus when David explains that the sailor "wore his masculinity as unequivocally as he wore his skin," we can only assume that the whiteness of that skin has something to do with the confidence behind his masculinity (88). Had David succeeded in situating his desire for the sailor along a post–World War II model of gender and racial sameness, then the sailor's whiteness would have amplified, rather than diminished, David's own. However, because all of David's encounters are haunted by the specter of a past in which queer sexuality was understood through a lens of difference rather than sameness, David finds a failed mirror in the sailor's whiteness. Finding it "hard to imagine" that he and the sailor were ever the same, David can only feel like a darkened silhouette standing in his relief.[12]

In his 1965 essay "The White Man's Guilt," Baldwin speculates that his own black skin may serve as a "disagreeable mirror" to his white acquaintances who are reminded of their complicity with racist structures.[13] Though mirrors are typically identified with sameness and introspection—enabling self-knowledge by producing a self-identical image—Baldwin suggests that to know the self, one must look outward rather than inward, acknowledging one's position in relation to others. Thus David's problem is not that he spends too much time on "self-reflection" but that he is relying on the wrong mirrors to tell him the truth about himself. Sameness fails to produce recognition, while otherness, ironically, has the potential to produce an unbearably sharp portrait of the individual in the context of their privilege. It is this latter portrait that David avoids in the novel's opening scene as he transforms a transparent glass window pane (which might have afforded a broader view of Paris's social heterogeneity) into the singularly reflective surface of a mirror: "I watch my reflection in the darkening gleam of the window pane. My reflection is tall, perhaps rather like an arrow, my blond hair gleams. My face is like a face you have seen many times. My ancestors conquered a continent, pushing across death-laden plains, until they came to an ocean which faced away from Europe into a darker past" (9). In this brief and frequently discussed reflection on race, David both insists upon and expresses anxiety about the status of his whiteness.

Not surprisingly, this moment has, for many scholars, provided an opening through which the novel's racial politics can be glimpsed. Mae Henderson, for example, has compared Baldwin's opening lines to Fitzgerald's closing lines in *The Great Gatsby*. If, in the closing image of *Gatsby*, Henderson suggests, Fitzgerald "captures the innocence and freshness of the New World encounter," then Baldwin's opening image by contrast "evokes a vision of the ravages and destruction consequent upon its discovery, the blood-guilt of its violent colonial origins" (316). Bryan R. Washington adds that it is here that "David acknowledges his complicity with racial conquest. And his recognition marks the beginning of an associative pattern compelling the reader to explore the connections linking Giovanni's persecution with the African-American's" (72). Similarly, Robert Reid-Pharr compares Giovanni's exploitation (both sexual and economic) by wealthy white men to the exploited and commodified bodies of black slaves. While all of these critics rightly observe that Baldwin has racialized the sexual dynamic between David and Giovanni, it is curious that they have kept their observations regarding that racialization consistent with the timeline that David, as narrator, has presented to the reader. When we liken Giovanni to an African American slave or the colonially exploited native, we may be making the mistake of taking at face value the version of whiteness that David wishes to insist upon, while ignoring the racial politics he wishes to obscure. When David insists on his ancestral connections to the original European settlers of America, he not only perpetuates eugenic understandings of his own normalcy and fitness but attaches himself (albeit through guilt rather than innocence) to a long line of white precursors.

By facing toward a "darker" and more distant past, David may thus be evading the complicated knot of queer interracial intimacy and prostitution that directly preceded (and partially constituted) his own era. Raised in New

York, presumably during the 1930s, David would likely have come of age in close proximity to Harlem with its queer and racially mixed sexual subcultures.[14] Thus, as Sharon Holland points out, Europe "offers David another space of privilege and becomes a new symbol of whiteness" after America has become "tainted" by David's "queer act with a 'brown' body" (276). These anxieties, I would argue, help to account for both the novel's Parisian backdrop and David's obsession with what it means to be an American—an issue that he takes up almost as frequently as the question of his sexuality. Not only is the difference between American "innocence" and European experience and tradition foregrounded in many of David's conversations with the Italian Giovanni, but David himself confesses to feeling a vacillation between his identification with Americans on the one hand and his total alienation from them on the other. Visiting the American embassy soon after beginning his affair with Giovanni, David observes that the "disquietingly cheerful horde" of Americans that stand before him "struck the eye, at once as a unit. At home I could have distinguished patterns, habits, accents of speech . . . now everybody sounded, unless I listened hard, as though they had just arrived from Nebraska" (86). Though this description registers a certain alienation from Americans, it also produces a level of comfort—unlike Harlem's gender and racial crossings, this portrait of Americans is one of familiarity and homogeneity.

Ironically such a purified vision of American identity is, for David, only possible when taking up a traitorously non-American subjectivity. By framing himself as "outside" of Americanness, David echoes the Cold War conflation of closeted homosexuality with foreignness, defection, and even espionage. During the period's "lavender scare"—in which masses of gay men and lesbians were purged from government positions—anti-Communist anxieties about foreign infiltration were mapped onto the image of the duplicitous homosexual who lives a secretive double life. Like the spy or double agent, it was believed, the homosexual could blend into mainstream society, all the while bearing a different allegiance and harboring a foreign/sexual secret. Understood, furthermore, as promiscuous, alcoholic, and vulnerable to blackmail, it was widely believed that gay men could not be trusted with classified information and that they therefore posed a serious threat to national security.[15]

Notably, these framings relied in part on new psychiatric explanations of gay desire. Now understood as an expression of psychological trauma rather than a manifestation of physiological difference, queer desire was no longer believed to be immediately readable on the body of the sexual "deviant." In this framework, detecting a hidden homosexual identity meant carefully reading through an elaborate web of signs and clues. One predictable consequence of this redefinition was a certain paranoia regarding the "undercover" nature of the homosexual man, who could now assume the disguise of "normal" masculinity. Thus one short propaganda film from 1961 warns of a new "sickness," one that is "not visible like small pox but no less dangerous and contagious: a sickness of the mind." Framing this "sickness of the mind" as a threat to corruptible American boys, the film concludes: "One never knows when a homosexual is about. He may appear normal and it may be too late when you discover he is mentally ill."[16] No longer a "fairy" inhabiting an urban sexual underground, the homosexual was thought to emerge from (and move undetected within) the heart of suburban America. Pairing easily with anti-Communist sentiment, psychiatry thus helped to construct a gay/traitor subject who, despite posing a threat to American masculinity, embodied all of its conventional hegemonic attributes.[17] "My face," David tells the reader in the opening passage, "is like a face you have seen many times" (9). The implication here is that David's typical appearance hides an atypical psychology—a loose translation might be, "though I walk among you, I am not one of you." Baldwin seems to suggest, however, that we not underestimate the cultural capital that such a "typical" appearance might carry. While David's doubts about his Americanness could reflect internalized Cold War homophobia, those doubts also, ironically, function to further reinforce his masculinity and his whiteness. Casting himself as traitorously closeted and placing an ocean between himself and the fairy culture of New York, David makes his queer desires compatible with the outward image of hegemonic American masculinity.

Thus while Chris Freeman has noted the "overwhelming sense [of] claustrophobia" (141) that permeates *Giovanni's Room*, I believe that we should understand David's narrative excursions into the suffocating spaces of his psyche as being fueled not by claustrophobia but by what Marlon B. Ross has termed "claustrophilia." Ross defines claustrophilia as "a fixation on the closet function as the grounding principle for sexual experience, knowledge, and politics," adding that such a fixation ultimately prevents queer critics from fully engaging with "potential insights from race theory and class analysis" ("Beyond the Closet as a Raceless Paradigm," 162). Against the "always known" physiology of the black body, Ross argues, the homosexual psyche emerges in traditional queer accounts as a site that is rich with implication and the lure of unknowing. There is more than a passing resemblance, he suggestively argues, between the epistemology of the "closet" and the practices of "close reading" that queer scholars apply to a "closed-off" modernist canon in order to mine the sexual subtexts that exist in the elite imaginations of figures like Henry James and Marcel Proust. Bryan R. Washington, for example, might be understood as engaging in a form of literary claustrophilia when he argues that *Giovanni's Room* can be read as a "revision" of Henry James's canonical gay text "The Beast in the Jungle." As James's brasher and more liberated literary successor, Washington suggests, Baldwin "nam[es] what the Master will not name" (71), and, in doing so, throws open the closet doors. But *Giovanni's Room*, as I have suggested, is less concerned with giving voice to the "love that dare not speak its name" than it is with exposing the ideologies of gender, race, and class that govern the very logic of the closet. Protective rather than stifling, David's closet can be understood as a site of intense claustrophilia, both for himself and for many of the novel's critics who mine its exhaustive psychoanalytic subtexts.

Similar to the "bomb shelters" that Baldwin derides in "The Uses of the Blues," this psychiatric closet functions as an extreme prophylactic technology. The prophylactic function of the closet becomes clear in David's description of the room he and Giovanni share:

> To begin with, the room was not large enough for two. It looked out on a small courtyard. "Looked out" means only that the room had two windows, against which the courtyard malevolently pressed, encroaching day by day, as though it had confused itself with a jungle. We, or rather Giovanni, kept the windows closed most of the time; he had never bought any curtains, neither did we buy any while I was in the room; to insure privacy, Giovanni had obscured the window panes with a heavy, white cleaning polish. We sometimes heard children playing outside our window, sometimes strange shapes loomed against it. (82)

Personifying the windows as a pair of eyes that "looked out" into the courtyard, this description suggests that we understand the cleaning polish as more than simply an attempt at privacy. A hygienic barrier to keep the outside world from peering *in*, the cleaning polish has the additional virtue of keep David and Giovanni from peering *out* onto the racialized "jungle" of courtyard. By effectively shutting the eyes of the room, David and Giovanni participate in the "ignorance effects" that Sedgwick has identified as the "epistemological privilege of unknowing" held by those in power, which enables those subjects to evade culpability in a range of situations (5). David's "ignorance" of the courtyard, I would argue, is played out in every other act of willful "ignorance" that I have outlined in this chapter. What ultimately horrifies David is not what exists inside of his closet but what that closet locks out—the deviantly gendered fairies, the black-and-tan speakeasies of Harlem, as well as the street boys who, as Eric described earlier to Cass, are too busy clashing with the police to worry about hating either their mothers or their fathers. These are the "strange shapes" that "loom against" the sanitized windows of David's closet, no matter how many layers of cleaning polish lay primed there. Built from psychoanalytic vocabularies, this closet is "not large enough for two," accommodating one (white) race, one (middle) class, and one (same-sex) model of queer desire.

Furthermore, in constructing Giovanni's room as a space of sameness on the level of race, gender, and class, David attempts not only to block out the power dynamics that mark the world *outside* of the room but also to level out the power differential that emerges between the two men *inside* of it. Because David's financial resources make finding a job unnecessary for him, Giovanni's work schedule leaves David alone at home for long periods of time. As David takes on more domestic tasks, he begins to feel feminized by what he perceives to be a gendered division of labor that has left Giovanni's masculinity intact. At the same time, Giovanni's very real poverty intervenes to reveal the starkness of the two men's class differences. Appearances may lead David to become anxious that he is being "bought" and therefore feminized by Giovanni; in the end, however, it is Giovanni who must prostitute himself to rich white men after David abandons him. Unlike *Another Country*'s Eric, who sees himself as being responsible for Yves, David can only, ultimately, conceive of his relationship with Giovanni in two ways. At the outset, he mistakenly understands it as the meeting of equals; as it progresses, he mistakenly understands it as the burden of dependency. Giovanni is understood either as an autonomous white subject or a dependent subject of color. But for David to take seriously the differences between himself and Giovanni, he would need to interrogate and address the power differential that exists between them. He would need, in other words, to look into the "disagreeable mirror" that Giovanni's body presents. David's failure to do so allegorizes, for Baldwin, white liberalism's failure to enact a genuinely transformative politics.

Thus, unlike other gay critics of "disordered" homosexuality, Baldwin appears less concerned with the extent to which these models have caused white subjects to feel shame about their desires and more interested in the way that those models have perpetuated a problematic division between the "sophisticated" interiority of white subjects and the "primitive" sexuality of their lower-class and African American counterparts.[18] It is not the psychosexual traumas of his early childhood that David is unable to reconcile in *Giovanni's Room* but the threateningly diverse sexual heterogeneity of the queer underground—a heterogeneity attended not only by differences in race and gender but also by differing access to social power and resources. What ultimately horrifies David is not the same-sex desire that exists *inside* of his closet but the multiple forms of racial, sexual, and class differences that "encroach" upon it from the outside. Holding onto a rigidly Anglo-American masculine ethic of progress, independence, and privatized ownership, David prophylactically insulates himself from the obligations and mutual reciprocities that would later come to inform feminist and crip models of interdependence. It is in this way that Baldwin's novel encourages us to move past the outworn binary that pits pride and progress against isolation and shame and to recommit to the coalitional possibilities that exist beyond the logic of the closet.

Psyches That Matter

The portrait I have presented of David in *Giovanni's Room* is admittedly double-edged in usefulness for disability studies and disability activism. On the one hand, the novel would seem to fall in line with disability scholars' critique of the medical model, with Baldwin deftly unveiling the ideologies and historical repressions that construct certain behaviors and desires as objectively diagnosable. At the same time, Baldwin's casting of David as an unreliable source of information about his own mental distress sits uncomfortably with the important insights of scholars like Margaret Price, Anna Mollow, and Ellen Samuels who have suggested that we need to do a better job of believing the accounts of people with nonapparent disabilities.[19] Because these individuals do not consistently bear the outward markings of stigma, their claims of difference are met with the suspicion of fraudulence or the assumption that they are psychosomatically inflating the significance of their symptoms.[20] Thus, rather than having a diagnosis imposed on them, individuals with nonapparent disabilities frequently find that, to the contrary, a much needed diagnosis is being withheld.

It's also important to point out that antipsychiatry movements have a complicated relationship with disability activism. Merri Lisa Johnson points to this dissonance in her discussion of the "label rip," a protest action in which psychiatric survivors gathered at the APA's headquarters, tearing apart sheets of paper bearing the names of their diagnoses. To what extent, Johnson asks, does the "ripping up" of a diagnostic label require an active disidentification with disability? How might we measure the empowerment of rejecting a diagnosis against the empowerment of claiming one? Noting that the "*DSM* debates" are "not [her] drama," Johnson recalls the way she "welcome[ed] the epiphany of [her] diagnosis with joy," claiming it both personally and publicly in the writing of her memoir of borderline personality disorder (BPD):

> By claiming the label "borderline" in the title, I deliberately risked the penalty of stigma, joining the ranks of other queer, feminist, and crip artists who use vulnerability to challenge the application of stigma to unruly or rejected bodies . . . Instead of ripping the label up and throwing it away, the memoir performs a label c/rip: reassigning meaning to BPD by turning with tenderness toward the strange spasticity of emotion dysregulation, much as Eli Clare does with cerebral palsy, or the late Cheryl Marie Wade with her anomalous hands.

In David's insistence on the extent to which his symptoms match a set of diagnostic criteria, we might ask, isn't he also "claiming disability" and "risk[ing] the penalty of stigma" that it carries? An odd bedfellow to Johnson, David appears to embrace "the epiphany of his diagnosis," finding it a useful tool for understanding his alienation. And like David, Johnson is met with a set of critics who understand her embrace of a BPD diagnosis as an example of false consciousness and internalized oppression.[21] In this context, how might we disentangle Baldwin's own investments in categories of mental disability—as they emerge in *Giovanni's Room* and elsewhere in his writing?

While my analysis in the previous sections might suggest that we read Baldwin's novel as a wholesale rejection of psychological vocabularies, it would be a mistake to argue that Baldwin was uninterested in psychological interiority or psychiatric designations, particularly as they reflected on the complex relationality between black and white subjects in America.[22] Baldwin believed deeply in what he referred to as the "American psychology," whose central feature he described as "a kind of perpetual, hidden, festering, and entirely unadmitted guilt" ("The Uses of the Blues," 76). For white Americans in particular, Baldwin observes, guilt is an appealing affect because it does not require meaningful action. A "luxury" that traffics in regret and remorse, it allows well-meaning citizens to feel badly about past racial injustices without "taki[ing] great chances" with their own material comfort in the present (76). David's attachment to guilt in *Giovanni's Room* is therefore psychologically important to Baldwin not for what it tells us about his "homosexual psyche" but for what it reveals about his prophylactic American psychology. Baldwin is not, in other words, disputing the value of claiming a damaged psyche;

rather, he is challenging the belief that psychological damage emerges exclusively from within a private and protected realm beyond the political (in David's case, the white nuclear family and its psychosexual dynamics).

What makes David's narration troubling, then, is not his preoccupation with his own mental health but his fidelity to the medicalized framework that actively excludes black men like Baldwin from understanding their mind as something that "matters." Indeed, black citizens' psychic life matters a great deal to Baldwin and a significant portion of his writing is devoted to the question of how much psychological injury African American subjects (and particularly African American men) can continue to endure. In "The Harlem Ghetto," for instance, Baldwin speculates that "in every act of violence, particularly violence against white men, Negroes feel a certain thrill of identification, a wish to have done it themselves" (64). Baldwin's racialized spin on the concept of Freudian "wish fulfillment" relocates feelings of repressed hostility to a broader landscape of racial injustice and social unrest. And unlike David, who understands his flight to Paris as an escape from his own Freudian demons, Baldwin frames his own parallel flight to Paris in 1948 explicitly as a reaction to American racism, as the suicide of an African American friend caused him to "doubt" his "ability to survive" in the United States.[23]

Of course, during the 1960s, the psychology of black men had become a focal point of psychiatric medicine as "paranoia" migrated from discourses of white homosexuality to discourses of black schizophrenia. If the Cold War vocabulary of "hidden secrets" and treasonous "double lives" directed social paranoia toward the duplicitous and repressed behavior of the white homosexual man, then the following decade increasingly located paranoia within the psyche of the African American militant who was thought to entertain delusional fantasies about racial injustice. As Jonathan Metzl observes, during the 1960s "psychiatry's focus on angry black bodies *produced* new categories of schizophrenic illness," transforming schizophrenia into "a rhetorically black disease" (105). Thus the revised criteria for schizophrenia, developed throughout the decade and set in print in the 1968 edition of the *DSM*, traded a gender neutral (or even arguably feminized) language of "emotional disharmony" for a new emphasis on "masculinized hostility, violence, and aggression" as key diagnostic criteria. Believing racial protests to be a symptom (and even a cause) of a paranoid state of mind, psychiatrists dubbed schizophrenia the "protest psychosis" and pharmaceutical ads circulated that featured politically charged images of black militancy. One ad, for example, featured an "angry, hostile African American man with a clenched, inverted, Black Power fist," against an "orange, burning, urban setting [that] appears to directly reference civil unrest" (102). In the context of these new discourses, diagnoses of schizophrenia were disproportionately applied to black men in ways that discredited collective responses to institutionalized racism, including acts of organized rebellion.

But if the feminist romanticization of hysteria often overlooked the "real madwoman in the attic," then we must also tread carefully when celebrating a framework that aligns schizophrenia with virtues of black masculine revolt.[24] While these redefined psychiatric vocabularies may reveal much about the anxieties that white Americans were projecting onto the bodies of black men, those same black men were also often experiencing mental distress in very real ways. In "A Challenge to Bicentennial Candidates," for example, Baldwin narrates the way his own father went "mad and died in Bedlam because, being black, he was always 'the last to be hired and the first to be fired'" (126). Baldwin goes on to describe his father as a "big, strong, handsome, healthy black man" who struggled to psychologically survive a system that forced him on welfare and, in so doing, naturalized his status as a racialized "burden" to the state. "No wonder he died in an American asylum," Baldwin reflects, "and at the expense, needless to say, of the so-victimized American taxpayer" (127). Baldwin sardonically concludes that he is "saddened indeed to be forced to recognize that my father's anguish—to say nothing of my brothers'—has cost the Republic so dearly" (128).

Written on the occasion of America's bicentennial and rhetorically directed toward the political "candidates," Baldwin's reflection on his family's collective mental anguish—and its perceived costs to the American taxpayer—doubles as a searing indictment of American democracy. Indeed, Baldwin's brief parenthetical aside that his "father was also an American taxpayer, and he paid at an astronomical rate" (126) carries an intriguing echo of the pre–Revolutionary War slogan "no taxation without representation," which provided a justification for principled revolt against British colonial power.[25] This paradox of black American citizenship—wherein black subjects are required to pay into a system that fails to protect them—is showcased even more explicitly in Baldwin's 1963 "Talk to Teachers." Here, Baldwin similarly connects psychological disability (and schizophrenia specifically) to principled revolt in ways that vacillate uneasily between metaphorical appropriation and embodied experience. He writes:

> Any Negro who is born in this country and undergoes the American educational system runs the risk of becoming schizophrenic. On the one hand he is born in the shadow of the stars and stripes and . . . he

pledges allegiance to that flag which guarantees "liberty and justice for all." He is part of a country in which anyone can become president, and so forth. But on the other hand he is also assured by his country and his countrymen . . . that the value he has as a black man is proven by one thing only—his devotion to white people. (679)

In this framework, "schizophrenia" refers to the potent disconnect between the promise and reality of American citizenship for young African American men. It also reflects what Baldwin calls "the paradox of education" in which the education that is intended to transform children into good adult citizens also, ironically, arms them with the tools to critically examine and ultimately resist the culture that is educating them (685). Thus if he "intends to get to be a man," Baldwin continues, the black child "must never make peace" with the "criminal conspiracy to destroy him" (685). In this way, Baldwin reverses the valence of the "protest psychosis," redefining paranoia not as evidence of an irrational mind but, instead, as the hallmark of political self-knowledge and collective consciousness.

The same year as his "Talk to Teachers," Baldwin published an impassioned polemic titled "We Can Change the Country," which draws upon similar themes but calls more directly for revolutionary action. Advocating a "nationwide" "campaign of civil disobedience" (61), Baldwin here argues that "if the government does not represent us, if it insists on representing a handful of nostalgic Southern colonels, the government will be replaced" (62). Pointing to the massive toll that American racism has taken on black youths, he continues:

> We are here not only to mourn those children, who cannot really be mourned. We are here to begin to achieve the American Revolution. It is time that we the people took the government and the country into our own hands. It is perfectly possible to tap the energy of this country. There is a vast amount of energy here, and we can change and save ourselves. We don't have to be at the mercy forever of these sordid political machines. The future is going to be worse than the past if we do not let the people who represent us know that it is our country. A government and a nation are not synonymous. We can change the government, and we will. (63–64)

Baldwin's attention to children who "cannot really be mourned" evokes Agamben's account of the "bare life," which, in being "killed but not sacrificed," (*Homo Sacer*, 85) functions as a physical "bearer of the link between violence and law" (65).[26] For Agamben, this link points to the law's exceptionality and is evident not only in the extralegal overreach of state power but also, paradoxically, in acts of revolutionary uprising against state authority. The "vast amount of energy" that Baldwin wishes to "tap" into issues not from the outmoded "political machines" of dead patriarchs but from the biopolitical vitality of the present moment. Like London's "comradeship of the revolution," it is "alive and warm" and "mightier than the Fourth of July, spread-eagle Americanism of our forefathers" (142).[27] Indeed, though James Baldwin and Jack London make exceedingly odd bedfellows, they echo remarkably similar sentiments in their distrust of the American government, particularly in its failure to protect those American bodies that are perceived as disposable.

Of course, Baldwin and London differ in their understanding of exactly what those forefathers looked like and what their sacrifices were. In the same essay, for example, Baldwin prefaces his plea for a new American revolution with the reminder that "I am an American. My forefathers bled and suffered and died to create this nation, and if my forefathers had not dammed all those rivers and picked all that cotton and laid all that track, there would not be an American economy today" ("We Can Change the Country," 60). If London saw the citizenship rights denied to him as part of his "heritage, stained sacred by [his ancestors'] blood" (*The Road*, 71), then Baldwin knew all too well that his own "heritage" traced back to the always already disqualified three-fifths humanity of his enslaved ancestors. If the black boy educated in America constantly "runs the risk of becoming schizophrenic," it is because of his ongoing awareness of his disposability in the eyes of a law that purports to protect him. What for London became a moment of crisis—a "shock" to his "patriotic American citizenship . . . which it never recovered" (70)—constitutes for Baldwin a perpetual state of physical and psychological precarity.

Thus, despite his powerful rhetoric of protest and revolution, Baldwin is not simply celebrating the "schizophrenic" African American psyche as a site of automatic "outlaw" agency. Like Baldwin's father, the black man experiencing depression or psychosis may very well be more likely to "die in an asylum" than to proudly subvert America's institutionalized racism from within. In this respect, Baldwin appears to anticipate Lauren Berlant's notion of "slow death" when he claims in the same essay that "there are several concrete and dangerous things that we must do to prevent the murder—and please remember there are several million ways to murder—of future children . . . And one of them, and perhaps the most important, is to take a very hard look at our economic structure and our political institutions" (61). Baldwin's provocative aside about the "several million ways to murder" children calls up a more gradual temporality of injury in which violence, rather than occurring in short dramatic bursts, constitutes a more prolonged process "wearing down" against smaller systemic aggressions.

Thus while the spectacle of lynching might be the most obvious and visible example of racialized violence, Baldwin is also interested in the subtler ways that black men have experienced debilitation, often at the hands of psychiatric authority. Both "We Can Change the Country" and "Talk to Teachers" were written in 1963, a moment when national news stories increasingly featured violent crimes committed by black male "schizophrenics" who were subsequently medicated and institutionalized. In 1962, for example, boxing champion Eddie Machen made news after his "life went into a downward spiral" following a career-altering loss. Found in "a parked car with a loaded gun, muttering about committing suicide," he was "bundled off to Napa State Hospital," where he was "described by doctors as an 'acute schizophrenic'" and "committed to a mental hospital" (quoted in Metzl, 111). As Baldwin was well aware, such "slow deaths" are crucial to acknowledge if we are to understand psychic life and political life as mutually intertwined.

In his 1969 essay "The Price May Be Too High," Baldwin goes further in addressing the inextricability of political and psychic life when he theorizes that the "black artist," too, may be in "perpetual danger of lapsing into schizophrenia" (106). In order to "reach something of the truth, and to tell it," Baldwin observes, he must "deal not only with his public discontent and daily danger but also with the dimensions of his private disaster. How, given the conditions of his life here, is he to distinguish between the two?" From a disability studies perspective, Baldwin's use of schizophrenia to mark the precarious position of the black artist would be easy to dismiss as an act of metaphorical appropriation or "narrative prosthesis" that obscures the experience of the ordinary schizophrenic subject. As Catherine Prendergast has persuasively argued, postmodern theory is notorious for its "aestheticization of the schizophrenic experience," with writers like Fredric Jameson, Jean Baudrillard, and Gilles Deleuze and Félix Guattari understanding schizophrenia as "always/already artistic, always/already literary, always/already metaphorical" (58). These "metaphorical entrapments," she suggests, present a "stable" and largely inaccurate outline of the schizophrenic subject, which makes us unable to see the "ordinary" and "unexceptional" ways that schizophrenia is experienced by those who have it (58). While Prendergast identifies a very real and troubling trend within postmodern theory, closer attention to Baldwin's phrasing suggests a more nuanced approach to mental distress, with ideology and activism ("public discontent") inseparable from bodily precarity ("daily danger") and psychic interiority ("the dimensions of his private disaster").

Baldwin's male schizophrenic, in other words, is no mere aesthetic flourish or textual strategy. He is exceedingly real and remarkably unexceptional in his capacity to be biopolitically disciplined en masse by law enforcement working in tandem with psychiatric authorities. Thus in his different analysis of white homosexuality and black schizophrenia, Baldwin is not presenting the latter as the subversive alternative to the former; rather, he is concerned with broader cultural practices through which citizens orient themselves toward medicine. Presenting the black male schizophrenic as simultaneously "unexceptional" and as emblematic of the law's exceptionality, Baldwin rejects psychiatry's disciplinary power while at the same time claiming the injured or "broken" psyche as a tool for collective resistance.

The Pain Which Saves Your Life

While I've spent most of the chapter outlining Baldwin's resistance to a prophylactic sensibility, I want to conclude by elaborating his explicitly antiprophylactic vision of American democracy and citizenship. In his book *Awakening to Race* (2012), Jack Turner explores the way Baldwin urges Americans to give up their sense of safety and security to make room for a new world order. Turner proposes that we understand Baldwin as a key "theorist of democratic reconstitution" whose work takes up and revises Thomas Jefferson's and Thomas Paine's belief in the necessity of periodic revolution within the body politic. The right of "each generation" to "reconstitute its world" is for all three thinkers "founded not in the authority of its illustrious founders but in the principles of human equality and creative individuality" (100). But while Jefferson and Paine were not especially concerned with how such reconstitutions might reconfigure race relations, Turner is careful to note that Baldwin's embrace of the concept was motivated by the possibility that reconstitution might tear the foundation away from white privilege, particularly as it manifests in white liberalism's evasions of responsibility. "What Baldwin pinpoints," Turner writes, "is the personal disposition required to make democratic reconstitution work: detachment from the things we think guarantee our safety, and a willingness to surrender to others what their effectual freedom requires" (103). Turner does not explicitly address the role that medicalization and disability might play in this vision of democratic reconstitution. However, Baldwin's belief that we "detach from the things we think guarantee our safety" resonates strongly with an ethics of antiprophylactic citizenship. Applying epidemiological paradigms to psychological well-being, Baldwin ultimately suggests that national transformation is enacted only when American individuals open themselves up to corporeal and psychic contamination. The resulting immunity is fashioned not through the hygienic exclusion of outsiders, but through an interdependent embrace of vulnerability and exposure.

There are, of course, important differences between embracing risk and simply being subject to it. In "Notes of a Native Son," for example, Baldwin dramatizes the choice between fighting racism and internalizing it as a choice that is no choice at all, with each option simply leading to a different form of precarity:

> One is always in the position of having to decide between amputation and gangrene. Amputation is swift but time may prove that the amputation was not necessary—or one may delay the amputation too long. Gangrene is slow, but it is impossible to be sure that one is reading one's symptoms right. The idea of going through life as a cripple is more than one can bear, and equally unbearable is the risk of swelling up slowly, in agony, with poison. And the trouble, finally, is that the risks are real even if the choices do not exist. (83)

Baldwin's metaphor here is troubled by the ableist assumption that the life of a "cripple" is "more than one can bear." But though amputation is invoked as an index of racism's warping effects on the racialized individual, it is also presented, however subtly, as a means of survival—a strategy through which an always already vulnerable or "contaminated" body can effectively manage psychological toxicity. Observing that "the risks are real even if the choices do not exist," Baldwin frames antiprophylaxis not as a fetishized postmodern subjectivity but as an ongoing state of vulnerable and troubled agency.

Baldwin gives this process a slightly more optimistic spin in "The Artist's Struggle for Integrity," published eight years later in 1963. Describing privileged Americans, including many of his "public and technical allies," as "panic-stricken at the very first hint of pain" and "determined to believe that they can make suffering obsolete," Baldwin laments that too many citizens fail to understand a "very physiological fact: that the pain which signals a toothache is a pain which saves your life" (36). Later in the same essay, he adds that the "time has come, it seems to me, to recognize that the framework in which we operate weighs on us too heavily to be borne and is about to kill us" (56–57). Here, Baldwin presents a clear critique of what we might call the "prophylactic" sensibility: the tendency to disavow pain and discomfort in ways that, ironically, result in the infection's amplification into disease and death. Political stasis does not guarantee stability; rather, it causes the body politic to buckle under the "weight" of its outdated "frameworks." In order to enact meaningful political change, then, toxicity must be acknowledged, and even valued and embraced for its ability to disrupt existing structures. Metaphors like these also provide Baldwin with a form of embodiment that transgresses racial divisions without transcending the body itself. Anyone, after all, regardless of their race, can step on a rusty nail or experience a tooth infection. The gangrene example that he provides is interesting precisely because of its universalizing potential, allowing Baldwin to break down the essentializing boundaries that separate black and white without capitulating to a disembodied color-blind liberalism.[28]

Baldwin's framing of racial injury as disability also revises the disability imagery of his Black naturalist predecessors. In his study of Baldwin's relationship to black manhood, for example, Keith Clark examines Baldwin's relation to authors like Richard Wright and Ralph Ellison whose commitment to naturalism and the politics of protest caused them to create characters who find themselves continually "deformed" or "crippled" by their toxic urban environments. The limitation of these naturalist representations, Clark argues, is their authors' investment in ideologies of American individualism: freedom is defined through a set of isolated, singular men who find themselves at odds with their communities as they struggle to access their place in the American dream. Baldwin's work provides a counterpoint to this individualism, Clark suggests, by merging homosexual intimacy with something that looks like homosocial solidarity, thereby showcasing the nurturing bonds that can exist in politically productive ways among black men. Redefining these masculine bonds as a potentially feminist (or at the very least, nonpatriarchal) site of community, Clark suggests that Baldwin and a handful of his contemporaries "negate . . . deformation" by defining their community through "healing rituals" and a larger ethics of care.

Baldwin's revision of the naturalist tradition—his refutation of American individualism, self-reliance, and independence and his emphasis on the importance of reciprocal responsibility, unconditional hospitality, and care—aligns him to some extent with disability theories of interdependence. In *The Rejected Body*, feminist disability theorist Susan Wendell explores the way in which "societies that regard independence as a central virtue . . .

tend to diminish the esteem of people who cannot live without a great deal of help from others" and "undervalue relationships of dependency or interdependence" (145). Through theories of interdependence, disabled people are reconceived as agents within a community rather than dependent populations whose needs are a burden upon the otherwise self-sufficient individuals who care for them. Like Wendell's critique of individualism and her alternative theorization of interdependence, Baldwin refuses to counter discourses of African American economic dependency with a striving toward African American individualism and independence. Rather he rejects altogether the binary between independence and dependence, emphasizing instead an ethics of responsibility and care that acknowledges the interrelationality between organism and environment.

Thus Andrew Shin and Barbara Judson locate in Baldwin's work an "emphasis on the pleasures of nurturance as opposed to mastery" and a "repudiat[ion] of masculine autonomy," values that Baldwin tends to express through "the messiness of bodily odor and fluid—a convergence of bodies that opposes the formulations of white liberalism and black radicalism. He does not invoke the cult of the primitive as a reservoir of primal energy capable of bursting through social restraint; instead, he marshals love as the glue of a just society. The exchange of odors between men cuts across racial, class, and sexual lines" (251). Shin and Judson's invocation of "love as the glue of a just society" echoes Fitzgerald's ambivalent presentation of "love" as an alternative to the antiprophylactic ethos of "eugenics." In this account of Baldwin's writing and others, we find that the democratic American body is not a "body" at all; rather it is a set of "messy" antiprophylactic encounters among differently racialized, sexualized, and gendered bodies that, for Baldwin, form the ground of an ethical American democracy.[29]

An ethic of antiprophylactic citizenship might even, in Baldwin's vision, "infect" the structures of psychiatry whose practices Baldwin frequently aligns with "antiseptic passivity of American life" ("Theater," 25). In his review of Stuart David Engstrand's 1946 *The Sling and the Arrow*, for example, Baldwin describes the play as

> the carefully documented study of a schizophrenic personality. From the first page to the last it is a masterpiece of correct and faintly disturbing detail; the progress of the disease is recorded with cold and merciless accuracy . . . his story is very slickly contrived indeed, and Herbert's downfall as final—and as right—as any of our psychiatrically conscious millions could wish. . . . We are not asked to consider

a personality but an abnormal psychology, not a study of human helplessness but a carefully embroidered case history... Here is no illumination, no pity, no terror. One closes this neat and empty volume untouched, indifferent, leaving Herbert floundering in his irrelevant hell, knowing that this happens seldom and can never happen to us. (304)

In his description of Engstrand's "slickly contrived" and "carefully embroidered case history," Baldwin dismisses practices of psychiatric diagnosis—and their literary popularization—as bourgeois prophylactic technologies. "Embroidery," after all, not only connotes domestic comforts but also hints at a cloth barrier that can be draped or held over a surface to avoid damage or contamination. Like a monogrammed handkerchief held over the mouth, Herbert's "abnormal psychology" insulates the reader against potential infection, leaving them "untouched, indifferent" and certain that it "can never happen to [them]" (304).

Against this antiseptic view of psychiatry, Baldwin offers, in other essays, a vision of psychological healing that cedes therapeutic control to the black subject—who turns out to be exceedingly qualified to rehabilitate the white liberal from his or her own prophylactic investments. Addressing his white contemporaries in "From *Nationalism, Colonialism, and the United States: One Minute to Twelve*," Baldwin observes that black people have been given a "terrifying advantage" as they have been forced to "spend their lives outwitting and watching white people. I had to know what you were doing before you did it" (17). Having become, by necessity, an expert reader of the white psyche, Baldwin presents himself as a kind of political psychotherapist. But unlike Engstrand's "slickly contrived" case history, which allows the reader to walk away "untouched," Baldwin's racialized "therapy" involves a difficult act of mutual risk-taking. As Baldwin notes in "The White Problem": "The price for this transformation is high. White people will have to ask themselves precisely why they found it necessary to invent the nigger... Black people will have to do something very hard, too, which is to allow the white citizen his first awkward steps toward maturity. We have, indeed, functioned in this country in precisely that way for a very long time—we were the first psychiatrists here" (97). Here, Baldwin playfully reverses the usual doctor/patient configuration, with the black "psychiatrist" allowing the white person their "first awkward steps toward maturity." This is no flippant thought experiment. Acknowledging that the "price for this transformation will be high," that it will indeed place both "doctor" and "patient" in a precarious position, Baldwin frames this mutual vulnerability as a necessary intervention into race relations. The net result of this unconventional "therapy" is not medical mastery but a conversational ethics that relies upon the acknowledged mutuality of pain, vulnerability, and precarity as a site of antiprophylactic connection between citizens.[30]

In "The Artist's Struggle," Baldwin directly addresses the political possibilities of pain, arguing that "your pain is trivial except insofar as you can use it to connect with other people's pain; and insofar as you can do that with your pain, you can be released from it" (52–53). Like the "pain of a toothache," which ultimately "saves your life," the collective pain that Baldwin describes here carries a nationally redemptive quality. In its nationally cohesive qualities, the pain that Baldwin depicts here is similar to the "madness of art," which Baldwin describes in "As Much Truth as One Can Bear" as a force with the capacity to

> bring, inexorably, to the light at last the truth about our despairing young, our bewildered lovers, our defeated junkies, our demoralized young executives, our psychiatrists, and politicians, cities, towns, suburbs, and interracial housing projects. There is a thread which unites them all and which unites every one of us. We have been both searching and evading the terms of this union for many generations. We are the generation that must throw everything into the endeavor to remake America into what we say we want it to be. Without this endeavor, we will perish. However immoral or subversive this may sound to some, it is the writer who must always remember that morality, if it is to remain or become morality, must be perpetually examined, cracked, changed, made new. He must remember . . . that life is dangerous, and that without the joyful acceptance of this danger, there can never be any safety for anyone, ever, anywhere. (41)

In an expansive Whitmanesque turn to catalog rhetoric, Baldwin's democratically lateralizes "psychiatrists" among the "defeated junkies," "bewildered lovers," and "despairing young." Each of these populations occupy "the generation that must remake America" and each carries equal responsibility to "examine," "crack," and "change" the established order. "Madness" is presented here as that which not only cures the psychiatrist but immunizes the country against the disaster that will cause it to "perish." In this context, risk is not presented as a singular, exceptional act that one "takes" but is understood as an ongoing condition of precarity and personal divestment—a condition that "threads" through "us all" in ways that create the possibility of national "union." Presenting a fraught dialectic between the disciplinary practices of psychiatric diagnosis and the affective contours of psychic injury, Baldwin thus invites his white liberal counterparts to relinquish those defenses—physical, psychological, and political—whose danger lies in their promise of safety.

4

Post-AIDS Permeability

Samuel Delany and Antiprophylaxis

"A vector!" he whispered, urgently. "Forget about typhus, or smallpox, or flu. They're rank amateurs! Wallies who give the show away with all their sneezing and flaking and shitting. To be sure, AIDS uses blood and sex, but it's so damn savage, it forced us to become aware of it, to develop tests, to begin the long, slow process of isolating it. But ALAS—"

"Alas?"

"A-L-A-S." He grinned. "It's what I've named the new virus I've isolated, Forry. It stands for 'Acquired Lavish Altruism Syndrome' . . . What if some virus one day stumbled on a way to make people enjoy giving blood?"

—DAVID BRIN, "The Giving Plague" (1988)

In his short story "The Giving Plague," science fiction writer David Brin imagines a future world in which altruism is contagious. No mere metaphor (like the cliché that "happiness is infectious"), Acquired Lavish Altruism Syndrome (ALAS) originates from a blood-borne pathogen. Because the virus manifests as intense desire to donate blood, it not only cultivates in its "victims" an altruistic self-image but also spreads rapidly among and between populations. The British scientist, Les, celebrates the utopian potential of his discovery, imagining ALAS as an agent of world peace, a "final opportunity . . . to learn to cooperate" before "selfishness and greed" succeed in "destroying the planet" (17). The American narrator Forry, on the other hand, is "spooked" by the virus's threat to his autonomy. A status-obsessed individualist, the only potential that Forry sees in ALAS is the Nobel Prize its discovery might win him. Hoping to take credit for Les's discovery, Forry begins to plot the murder of his colleague. However, before he is able to execute his plan, a new global pandemic emerges that not only diverts the narrator's energies but also results in a spike in blood transfusions. By the story's conclusion, the virus has spread to a quarter of the world's population.

The narrator reflects: "Peace treaties were signed. Citizens of the industrial nations voted temporary cuts in their standards of living in order to fight poverty and save the environment. Suddenly, it seemed, we'd all grown up" (24). Forging a counterintuitive link between antiprophylaxis and the utopian future, ALAS produces a cooperative global community founded upon viral bonds.

Originally appearing in 1988, "The Giving Plague" is easy to read as a provocative reimagining of the AIDS epidemic, though Brin is careful to distinguish his fictionalized virus from the 'real' one. If AIDS is "savage" and destructive, erupting visibly and violently on the bodies of its "victims," then ALAS, by contrast, is civilized and cooperative, the invisible hand quietly shepherding its converts into noble humanitarian action. But in transforming the ravages of AIDS into the utopian promise of ALAS, a "selfish" epidemic into a "giving plague," Brin anticipates some of the ways in which the discourses of HIV/AIDS would be newly invested, over a decade later, with utopian promise. While the cooperative world that Brin's story anticipates is far from having arrived, recent subcultural practices—including bug chasing and barebacking—have shifted the meanings of HIV in ways that emphasize its generative community-building properties. Tim Dean, for example, observes that "Bug chasers replace one story about the queer future with another. In place of the stock narrative about inevitable sickness and death, they have invented a story about kinship and life—a different version of the queer future to which HIV transmission nevertheless remains central . . . We might say that bug chasers are living a different mythology of HIV, one that treats the virus as a gift rather than as a punishment" (*Unlimited Intimacy*, 69). With the introduction of newer and more effective treatments in 1996, HIV diagnosis was, for many, no longer a death sentence but a new way of life. In contrast to the twin concepts of "mourning" and "militancy" that fueled early AIDS activism and organizing, these later interventions tended to emphasize questions of risk management, sex education, and routinized practices of personal safety.[1] Noting the way the "specific psychology of risk pioneered within AIDS education resonates . . . with the developing political culture of risk and security in advanced capitalist societies in general," Andrew Ross frames this shift as a sapping away of the "frankly utopian energies and desires" that had previously powered gay liberation movements (398).[2] But what Ross may not have anticipated were some of the "frankly utopian" discourses of queer citizenship that did emerge directly out of this new biopoliticization of serostatus, including a very literal commitment to antiprophylaxis.

These antiprophylactic commitments pushed back against many of the safe sex campaigns that emerged as a response to the epidemic—campaigns that were, themselves, pushing back against the public health crackdown on gay bathhouses and other sites of public sex. Though the ostensible goal of the imperative toward safer sex among gay men was to preserve the lives and health of those in the community, these imperatives were also frequently perceived as creating a set of prophylactic barriers that resulted in the death—or, at the very least, the dampening—of the very practices that constituted those communities as such.[3] Douglas Crimp observes that:

> alongside the dismal toll of death, what many of us have lost is a culture of sexual possibility: back rooms, tea rooms, bookstores, movie houses, and baths; the trucks, the pier, the ramble, the dunes. Sex was everywhere for us, and everything we wanted to venture: golden showers and water sports, cocksucking and rimming, fucking and fist fucking. Now our untamed impulses are either proscribed once again or shielded from us by latex. Even Crisco, the lube we used because it was edible, is now forbidden because it breaks down the rubber. Sex toys are no longer added enhancements; they're safer substitutes. ("Mourning and Militancy," 11)

Crimp's nostalgia for the lost intimacies of the bathhouses echoes other scholars' portraits of pre-AIDS sexual subcultures as nonhierarchical sites of democratic brotherhood. In 1982, for example, Dennis Altman, described the bathhouses as partaking in "Whitmanesque democracy, a desire to know and trust other men in a type of brotherhood far removed from the male bondage of rank, hierarchy, and competition that characterise much of the outside world" (79–80).[4] In this context, latex is framed not as a symbol of sexual pleasure but rather a metonym for the broader antisex moralism that places a "shield" between queer male subjects. Prescribing a set of boundaries around desire, these safer sex substitutes appeared to simply be another part of the prophylactic apparatus through which public health discourses intruded upon and stamped out the vitality of these previously unfettered sites of masculine intimacy and abundance.

In this chapter, I examine the contours of antiprophylactic citizenship in the "post-AIDS" era by reading Samuel Delany's *Times Square Red, Times Square Blue* (1999) alongside contemporary discourses of barebacking and bug chasing. Though it was published after the "Protease Moment," Delany's memoir spans several decades, recalling his experiences of public sex in the porn theaters from the 1960s through the 1990s. Against the current gentrified landscape of Times Square, Delany affectionately recalls a vibrant sexual community structured by an ethics of democratic inclusivity, neighborly goodwill, and eccentric practices of physical and material exchange. While the forms of gift-giving championed in Delany's landmark text are not literally linked to viral transmission, they are animated by similar commitments to the antiprophylactic, as they mobilize a figural logic of viral infection. While AIDS is mentioned only briefly in *Times Square Red, Times Square Blue*, I read the book as an important reimagining of the epidemic as a site of queer-crip biosociality and even futurity. Here, Delany presents bodily risk and viral transmission as figurative resources for the affective renewal of American community. At the same time, we must also contend with the way these risks tend to be gendered as masculine and framed through a rhetoric of physical and sexual capacity. Thus I conclude the chapter with a word of caution. These new queer imaginaries, if they are to live up to their "antiprophylactic" democratic promise, must also grapple with the often feminized terrain of debility as well as the unresolved tensions left over from the feminist sex wars.

Gifts That Keep on Giving

In 1996, Samuel Delany published portions of what would later become his book-length pair of essays, *Times Square Red, Times Square Blue*. During the same year, the International AIDS Conference in Vancouver initiated what Eric Rofes calls the Protease Moment. New advertisements for AIDS drugs proliferated that "consolidated conflicting images into a single, unified representation" of the AIDS public health crisis as something that was now over (29). "People with HIV," Rofes observes, now appeared "as healthy, active people bearing no obvious differences from uninfected people" (29). No longer understood as an automatic death sentence, HIV was reconfigured in the cultural imagination as a new way of life. Rofes acknowledges, of course, that to proclaim "the end of AIDS," as many newspaper headlines and cultural commentators had done during the last years of the 1990s, may seem both inaccurate and offensive to many who lack the capital or the circumstances to inhabit this "post-AIDS subjectivity." "How can some of us have this feeling that AIDS is over," Rofes asks, when "people are still dying, not only people from whom middle class white gay men separate themselves— Latinos, blacks, drug users, women, poor people—but middle class white gay men as well?" (10) Acknowledging the uneven distribution of resources and the reality of continuing AIDS casualties, both of which contradict drug companies' rosy picture of "healthy" and "active" HIV-positive individuals, Rofes explains that while AIDS itself is far from over, what has ended is the AIDS "crisis" as a specific (and often white) cultural response to an enormous (and often white) death toll. The designation of the "post-AIDs" era, then, registers more of a discursive than a material shift in the American response to the virus, with the new portrait of "life" existing uneasily against a continued, and often unacknowledged, death toll among lower income populations.

Having left behind the vocabulary of "emergency," Rofes suggests, gay men should now invest in "regenerating community and culture" through practices of low-risk promiscuity (18). For other critics like Tim Dean, writing more recently, such regenerations can also take the form of high-risk behaviors in which gay men are either indifferent to, or actively searching out, the possibility that a sexual encounter will result in seroconversion. In his 2009 study of barebacking culture, Dean explores the new and unexpected meanings attributed to condomless sex between men in the post-AIDS era.[5] Often characterized as a form of sexual Russian roulette, the practice of barebacking has been stigmatized as a negligent and even suicidal behavior, framed both by the mainstream and by members of the gay community as a chilling example of homophobic self-hatred. Who, after all, would risk infection unless they already have a death wish or a desire for self-punishment? Challenging dominant discourses that frame condomless sex between men in the era of AIDS as a form of risky or even suicidal behavior, Dean maintains that barebackers are, to the contrary, engaged in affirmative practices of subcultural solidarity. Framing the appeal of barebacking and bug chasing as the appeal of "unlimited intimacy," Dean thus reinterprets these "risky" sex practices as a means for creating alternative form of kinship and futurity. Among men who identify as bug chasers, the virus is more explicitly imagined as a life-giving agent that enables new forms of "breeding" and "fantasies of generation" between men. "What would it mean," Dean asks, "for a young gay man today to be able to trace his virus back to, say, Michel Foucault?" (89). Thus, in a "crip" twist on the politics of marriage equality, Dean remarks that bug chasers exchange "bodily fluids" rather than "wedding rings," replacing mainstream marriage and health norms with the queer "solidarity" of a "bug brotherhood." By "reasserting what might be considered a retrograde emphasis on blood or 'substance,'" Dean suggests, this new form of "biosociality" among queer men "offers a vital means of showing relatedness" (89–90, 94).[6] Here, serostatus "conversion" does not signify a rising body count but the swelling ranks of a virally bonded queer citizenry.

Written on the cusp of the "post-AIDS" era, Delany's memoir is ambivalently positioned between Rofes's championing of low-risk promiscuity and Dean's portrait of a queer-crip viral community. Documenting the public sex subcultures that flourished during the heyday of New York City's porn theater district, Delany laments the eventual erasure of these communities during the 1980s "clean up" of Times Square in the wake of the AIDS epidemic. Part memoir, part social theory, Delany's book provides a compelling account of how a dynamic sexual institution was forged at the intersections of visual culture, urban space, and, eventually, public health discourse. Interested less in the films themselves than in the way those films helped animate a set of important subcultural practices, Delany argues that the eradication of Times Square's red-light district, though enacted in the name of "public health" and "women's safety," ultimately served the interests of corporate expansion.[7] "The New Times Square," he argues, "is simply not about making the area safe for women . . . It is not about reducing the level of AIDS . . . The New Times Square is about developers doing as much demolition and renovation as possible in the neighborhood" (161).

While moments like these indicate Delany's solidarity with queer rejections of "safety" and its discourses, the claim that Delany mobilizes—even partially—an ethics of "bug chasing" might appear to be a stretch. In an interview with Thomas Long, Delany responds to Scott O'Hara's essay "Good-Bye to the Rubberman" by explicitly repudiating bug chasing as a "lunatic" practice and recounting his own refusals to have anal sex with HIV-positive men (136). At the same time, however, Delany acknowledges that he is "deeply in sympathy" with O'Hara's call for the "Negatives" to "stop whining about how hard it is to stay safe. Why don't they just get over it and get positive?" (136). Here, Delany clarifies that while he doesn't believe that "we negatives should become positive," he does believe that we should "stop whining and learn to take responsibility for learning to negotiate the sexual landscape that exists" (136). Countering mainstream misinformation about the transmissibility of the virus, Delany has often championed masturbation and other activities that, unlike anal sex, do not require men to "swath[e] themselves and their partners' bodies in rubber . . . so as to prevent literally all contact between bodies" (125). It is these low-risk, high-contact practices that Delany is most interested in chronicling in *Times Square Red, Times Square Blue*. Defining "intimacy" in much different terms than the barebacking subcultures documented in Dean's study, Delany would appear to agree with writers like Rofes who champion low-risk promiscuity as the alternative to high-risk sex or deliberate viral transmission.

What I locate in Delany's text, then, is far from any sort of straightforward ethics of bug chasing. If bug chasing literalizes a more abstract concept of community, then Delany's deliteralizes these forms of queer-crip biosociality once more, transforming the biological dynamics of HIV transmission into a figurative schema that empties the virus of its actual disease properties. It is not a virus that is exchanged in the antiprophylactic public intimacies Delany documents but rather forms of social pleasure, pedagogy, and material exchange that promise to "spread" laterally, like a pandemic, among and across populations. Part of Delany's project here is to reclaim "illness as metaphor" against the prescriptions of writers like Susan Sontag who argued that we should resist framing literal instances of disease in figurative terms. Metaphors for cancer and AIDS, Sontag observed, generally function as a source of stigma, appropriating the body of the sick person for ideological purposes in ways that strip them of their agency to describe their own relationship with their sick body. In the same interview in which Delany discusses bug chasing, he suggests that "the *controlling* metaphoric structure for AIDS from the beginning was: 'What metaphors shall we use for it?' AIDS has been from the beginning a term-in-search of a metaphor" (137). Defending one gay writer whose use of plague metaphors to describe the epidemic caused him to be "pilloried in the gay press," Delany argues that "by purging the disease of still *another* metaphor, we were all furthering the *dominant* discourse of the disease-with-*no*-fixed metaphor" (137). Delany's use of the word "purge" here suggests that we understand metaphor as a necessary linguistic contamination. To "purg[e]" our descriptions of illness and disease of their figurative dimensions, as Sontag and others do, becomes a form of prophylactic quarantine that fails to adequately challenge the "dominant discourse." Embracing AIDS metaphors rather than "purg[ing]" them, Delany reclaims the "viral" as potent symbol for the formation of affective subcultural bonds. What is championed in *Times Square Red, Times Square Blue* is the antiprophylactic willingness to be "infected"—not with the virus itself but with forms of "fellow feeling" at the heart of the American democratic project.[8]

This antiprophylactic impulse is strikingly illustrated in Delany's anecdote about his chance encounter with Russian poet Andrei Voznesensky. When Voznesensky tells Delany about his refusal to use a public urinal for fear of contracting HIV, Delany interprets Voznesensky's trepidation as a "cross-section of the process by which AIDS functions, on an international level, as a discursive tool to keep visitors to the city away from all public facilities and places where, yes, one might, if so inclined, engage in or be subject to any sort of interclass contact" (156–157). Delany's "yes" here is revealing, as it functions rhetorically and grammatically to reinforce rather than deny the linkage between public space and the possibility of infection. Delany, in other words, is not at all interested in rehearsing the medical fact, as many liberal commentators do, that one cannot get AIDS from a toilet seat. Using the potential public transmission of the virus as a metaphor for the blurring of class boundaries, he implicitly celebrates the productive border-crossings and contaminations that public spaces make possible. Delany's scant attention to HIV/AIDS or "safe sex" practices within the book itself, then, can be read less as omission than an active form of queer-crip resistance to the public health panics and rhetorics of safety through which conservative forces sought to sanitize public space and "dismantle the various institutions that promote interclass communication" (122). The promotion of "safe sex," Delany argues, tends to function as little more than extension of the conservative drive to cultivate "safe neighborhoods, safe cities, and committed (i.e., safe) relationships" (122).

It is therefore no surprise that Delany chooses the word "contact" (with its connotations of infection and transmission) to describe his vision of democratic exchange. "Contact," Delany suggests, presents a messy organic alternative to the stale and hygienic practices of professional "networking." Drawing examples from the institutionalized structures of academia, Delany frames networking in terms of the elitist commitment to self-promotion. For the networker, social exchange is purpose-driven—a means to an end. Often, too, networking proves to be ineffectual as the "supply" of opportunities available to networkers is usually much smaller than the demand. But if networking persists in the hierarchized and often elitist institutions of higher education, then "contact" is democratic insofar as it constitutes a mode of social intimacy in which members of different social classes and backgrounds can experience pleasurable, surprising, and mutually enriching connections with one another. Thus Delany's examples often combine the sexual with the quotidian:

> Contact is the conversation that starts in the line at the grocery counter with the person behind you while the clerk is changing the paper roll in the cash register. It is the pleasantries exchanged with a neighbor who has brought her chair out to take some air on the stoop . . . As well, it can be two men watching each other masturbating together in adjacent urinals at a public john . . . contact is also the intercourse—physical and conversational—that blooms in . . . public restrooms, sex movies, public parks, singles bars, and sex clubs. (123)

In all of these examples, public space provides a chance to experience pleasurable cross-class dialogue and intimacies that temporarily transcend the divisions that normally shelter citizens from one another. Indeed, if the vertical structures of networking reinforce a stagnant and static model of learning, then lateral structures of contact present fresh and exciting opportunities for the transmission and dissemination of knowledge. Ultimately the pedagogical practices to which "contact" gives rise are spontaneous and incidental; these learning opportunities occur only when members of different races, cultures, and social classes make themselves available to one another. If we define "safety" as the sanitizing of social and class boundaries, then to do away with it is no suicidal or masochistic endeavor. By rejecting the prophylactic barriers that insulate citizens from one another's differences and by making sexuality part of the ordinary exchanges between neighbors, Delany instead frames cross-race and cross-class public sex as a life giving, communal practice that allows parts of the city to "bloom."

Referring to these public sex spaces as "sexual free zones," disability scholar Chris Bell, uses *Times Square Red, Times Square Blue* to critique the way compulsory HIV disclosure ignores the way sexual free zones are rooted in an alternative ethics of risk and relationality. Reflecting on his own experiences of condomless sex as an HIV-positive African American man, Bell considers the ways that certain state laws make nondisclosure of HIV-positive status a prosecutable offense, regardless of the context of the encounter or the level of risk involved in the individual sexual exchange. "People do not always disclose their status in sexual free zones," Bell argues, "But that does not mean that they are lacking in moral fiber. It implies that those acting in sexual free zones realize that they are occupying a space in which the rules ('read: family values') of the outside are not in effect" (223). Bell thus praises Delany for downplaying the question of sexual "safety," emphasizing instead the importance of protecting the autonomy of those who engage in "risky" expressions of sexual desire as well as dismantling the loaded discourses of sexual "responsibility."[9] Dean, too, cites *Times Square Red, Times Square Blue* as a useful model for formulating an ethics and rationale of queer cruising and stranger sociality. Calling Delany's subcultures "profoundly democratic" and "Whitmanesque," Dean wonders what it might mean to formulate "cruising as a way of life" (188).

However, considering the vocabulary of gift-giving that permeates bug chasing discourse, it is surprising that Dean's reading of *Times Square Red, Times Square Blue* makes no mention of the central role that *literal* acts of gift-giving play in the text. "By treating HIV as a 'gift' whose donation creates consanguineous relations among subcultural members," Dean observes early in his study, "barebackers are participating, almost invisibly, in the broader cultural enterprise of redefining kinship" (51). Delany, too, structures his vision of urban kinship around a peculiarly organic model of gift-giving that understands altruistic donation as an act that is pleasurable for both the giver and the receiver. At its best, Delany explains, "contact" involves a pleasant cross-class interaction between strangers that results in the "easy and fun" exchange of goods or services. In its most idealized form, it involves the spontaneous alignment between one citizen's needs and another citizen's unwanted castoffs. Delany describes, for example, the editorial jobs that a straight male friend of his was able to offer several of the topless dancers that he encountered at strip clubs, a publishing job that he himself was able to secure for the client of a street hustler with whom he was acquainted, and the short bibliography of science fiction writers that he was able to jot down for the "aspiring director" in line next to him at the supermarket. Finally, he recounts an anecdote in which, ten minutes after trashing a broken vacuum cleaner, Delany encounters an Italian American man looking to sell his own wet-dry vacuum cleaner for ten dollars. What makes these encounters different from networking, Delany maintains, is their spontaneity, their cross-class dimensions, and, most important, the fact that they are motivated not by personal gain but by neighborly good will.

Might we understand the economic pleasures of "contact," therefore, as being structurally similar to the pleasures of barebacking? In both instances, acts of neighborly exchange are pleasure-driven rather than motive-driven. Fueled by a desire for neighborly intimacy, the act of social and/or physical intercourse is satisfying in its own right, requiring no external reward or incentive—and yet there exists the possibility that one participant in the exchange will nevertheless come into possession of an unexpected "donation." Without literally advocating the controversial practice of bug chasing, the text presents a "gift economy" in which what is being passed back and forth is not a virus, but rather, physical pleasure, practical knowledge, and, on a very basic level, goods and services. Figuring queer altruism in viral terms, Delany mobilizes a metaphorics of infection that empties the concept (productively and problematically) of its biological content. If, for barebackers, the virus is understood as a gift that "keeps on giving," then Delany presents us with the inverse: the altruistic "gift" between strangers is framed in viral terms as a good deed that spreads outward into the population. Contracted from the "Good Samaritans at traffic accidents" or the "neighbor who . . . lets you use her phone to call a locksmith," (125) these random acts of kindness send ripples of neighborly goodwill among the populace. "Watching the metamorphosis of such vigil and concern into considered and helpful action," Delany concludes, "is what gives one a faithful and loving attitude toward one's neighborhood, one's city, one's nation, the world" (126). Striking in this quote is not just the utopianism of Delany's vision, but the way his language of geographic expansion (from the local, to the national to the global) mimics the process by which an isolated outbreak can transform into a worldwide pandemic.

The ALAS-like pandemic of altruism that Delany imagines here might even be understood as queer-crip contestation of the shape that charity movements have taken in the age of global capitalism. As Mara Einstein illustrates in her provocative book *Compassion, Inc.*, the rise of "strategic philanthropy" over the past twenty years has enabled corporations to materially profit from global charity practices.[10] These forms of philanthropy are not only "strategic" for corporations looking to open global markets but for consumers as well. As Paul Longmore observes, the increasing commercialization of charity appeals to the American public because it takes the "self-centered" act of purchasing products—which often functions within neoliberalism as a means of fashioning and performing of one's 'unique' selfhood—and recodes them as "selfless" expressions of civic duty. On a basic material level, promotional opportunities and other monetary incentives allow consumers to "profit under the guise of helping disabled people" (Einstein, 141). Countering these neoliberal forms of strategic philanthropy with embodied practices of queer altruism, Delany purifies gift-giving of the external motivations that make it indistinguishable from "networking." Requiring that citizens be open to the generously "contaminating" reciprocities of the public sphere, Delany's book thus constructs a powerful counter to the problematic forms that disability activism can take in a globalized economy. He replaces, in other words, the rehabilitative logics of corporate "donation" with the crip virtues of a "giving plague."

Like Les, the utopian scientist in Brin's short story, Delany celebrates the infectious qualities of communalism much to the chagrin of the American capitalist forces that would shut down all sites of potential transmission. A networker par excellence and a paragon of American individualism, Brin's narrator Forry can only conceive of his professional relationship with Les as a means to an end and concludes the story clinging to false credentials: "I carry a card in my wallet that says I'm a Christian Scientist, and that my blood group is AB negative, and that I'm allergic to nearly everything . . . I won't take blood. I won't. I'll donate, but I'll never take it." Forry's refusal to receive the "gift" of blood donation mark his suspicion of communitarian values, presenting him as the embodiment of a prophylactic American individualism. But while this may be true in Forry's case, not all similar refusals are expressions of corporate privatization or neoliberal rhetorics of safety. In the section that follows, I question Delany's reliance on the assumption that good deeds are always rewarded, that a public pedagogical encounter will always result in learning—that, in short, all subjects who articulate themselves in opposition to the world of privatized capital will end up aligning harmoniously with one another. Taking seriously the refusal to make "contact," I argue that we must grapple with other less utopian possibilities of conflict and violence if we are to take antiprophylaxis seriously as a blueprint for a better world.

The Sexual Politics of Contact

The generative intimacies of contact cross lines not only of class and race but also of ability/disability. As Robert McRuer and Abby Wilkerson have argued, what often goes unremarked in Delany's essay is the "disability consciousness that permeates it: not only does Delany himself use a cane for mobility, but he seeks out and comes into contact with people who embody behavioral, cognitive, physical, and sensory difference" (6). These figures, among others, include a young man named Joe, nicknamed the "Mad Masturbator" because his sexual compulsions lead him to remain in the theater for hours at a time, muttering obscenities at the screen and rubbing his penis painfully raw in the process. Though some of the patrons are disturbed by Joe's "derangement . . . [his] stooped shoulders, his scrawny arms, his drooling incontinent satyriasis," Delany observes that most of the customers let him be, some of them even extending a friendly greeting as they walk in. "Two months later," Delany narrates, "the city closed the Variety Photoplays" when "city inspectors noted . . . 'a hundred and fifty acts of unsafe sex,'" adding: "what accommodations, if any, Joe was able to make for his condition, I cannot even imagine" (73). Against a gentrified landscape hostile to disability accommodations, Delany thus recollects the porn theaters as a place of radical accessibility for the crip sexual body.

And yet, from a feminist perspective, Joe, the "Mad Masturbator," is one of the most perplexing figures in Delany's narrative. One the one hand, the porn theater offers an important "accommodation" for Joe's sexual compulsions by providing a nonjudgmental space of inclusion and limited freedom from biopolitical disciplinary control. In the homosocial space of the porn theater, Joe can enjoy some measure of protection from the doctors and law enforcement officials who misunderstand his condition. But while Joe's compulsive behavior showcases the crip dimensions of Delany's sexual democracy, those compulsions are also gendered in ways that might be difficult for a feminist reader to immediately reconcile. Delany relates a few of the phrases that he hears Joe directing toward the movie screen: "them fuckin' tits, man—oh, shit, them tits! Go on, sit on my face bitch" (67). The difficulty in separating the objectifying language Joe uses from the sexual compulsions that frame his disability opens up a set of knotty questions about the potential limits of "contact" as a theoretical or political paradigm. If, as Delany argues, the porn theaters provide a space where intimate encounters between strangers can function as a friendly social glue that binds men to one another (across the usual divisions of race, class, and ability), then how are we to respond to expressions of sexuality that make these spaces potentially unwelcoming to women? In asking this question, my intention is neither to villainize Joe nor to dismiss his legitimate need for accommodation but rather to complicate a set of the dichotomies that reappear throughout *Times Square Red, Times Square Blue*. Constructing too neat an opposition between the democratic potential of public sex and neoliberalism's commitment to corporate privatization, Delany often leaves the sexual politics of "contact" undertheorized. Here, the prophylactic sensibility is implicitly gendered as feminine, making women's affective desires for bodily autonomy and privacy synonymous with neoliberalism's commitment to individualism and privatization.

These implications are, on the one hand, understandable given the complicated and often divisive role that second-wave feminists played in the sex wars. Only ten years earlier, Catharine MacKinnon had controversially identified pornography as the place where "one learns that forcible violation of women is the essence of sex" (329). Identifying male sexuality as the primary instrument of gender hierarchy, MacKinnon joined Andrea Dworkin, Adrienne Rich, Susan Griffin and others in condemning pornography as the main site through which misogynist fantasies of sexual domination and exploitation played out. As Robin Morgan famously put it, "pornography is the theory, rape is the practice."[11] While gay male sexual subcultures were not the direct target of anti-pornography feminism, there was ultimately little distinction being made in these rhetorics between the largely same-sex cruising culture of the porn theaters and the more clearly hetero(sexist) exchanges that characterized the culture of the commercial sex industry.[12] Indeed, in her canonical "Compulsory Heterosexuality and Lesbian Existence," Adrienne Rich argued for the "dissociation of lesbian from male homosexual values and allegiances," pointing to "women's lack of economic and cultural privilege relative to men" and disparaging the "the prevalence of anonymous sex," "the justification of pederasty," and the "pronounced ageism in male homosexual standards of sexual attractiveness" (649–650). This fraught history contextualizes Delany's seeming disregard for "women's safety." Presenting promiscuity as pedagogy and reframing the porn theater as a site of altruistic egalitarian exchange, Delany implicitly counters anti-porn feminists' portrait of gay male sexuality as an extension of heterosexuality's commitment to hierarchical relations.

Thirty-five years later, it has become routine to denounce the insights of MacKinnon and Dworkin as examples of short-sighted feminist prudery. And indeed, there is much to critique.[13] But is it possible, in the context of Delany's analysis, to take a concern for "women's safety" seriously without capitulating to the moral and health panics that he so usefully critiques? What is the relationship between the heterosexist encounters taking place *on* the movie screen and the male same-sex encounters taking place *off* of it? Can a feminist reading of *Times Square Red, Times Square Blue* be undertaken without resurrecting the clichéd and reactionary image of the predatory underclass rapist and the helpless upper-class (nearly always white) female victim? What modes of analysis, in other words, are available to us for theorizing "safety" and "privacy" in a way that does not place feminist insights at odds with theories of crip and queer citizenship?

One way out of this bind is to subject Delany's text to some of the same critiques that have been made of lesbian feminism's own commitment to sexual utopianism. Ironically, what writers like Delany and Rich share is their commitment to a globalizing framework of egalitarian sexuality. While Rich's portrait of feminist eroticism rests on a racially transcendent and geographically expansive "lesbian continuum," Delany's blooms in the organic pedagogical intimacies shared between men in "free zones" of interclass contact. Just as Rich's model purports to encompass all women without addressing the structural differences in their racial, class, or geographic milieu, Delany's model purports to encompass all *human* subjects without addressing key differences in gender. Finally, and perhaps most importantly, both accounts create a perplexing binary between "right" and "wrong" approaches to sexuality. Policed in Rich's account are forms of desire and identification that appear to, but do not always, align with patriarchy. And as I go on to argue, policed in Delany's are those forms of sexual refusal that appear to, but do not always, align with the homophobic and conservative forces of corporate capitalism.

However, while radical feminism has, over the years, come under heavy fire by third-wave feminists for its theoretical shortcomings, *Times Square Red, Times Square Blue* has received almost exclusive praise from queer scholars.[14] By troubling Delany's text from a feminist standpoint, it is not my intention to simply rehash an old political debate between "pro" and "anti" sex positions but to develop new ways of talking about sexuality that cut through these binaries. In what follows, I discuss a couple of episodes in which feminism comes into uneasy—but perhaps productive—conflict with the queer and sometimes crip world of democratic sexual exchange that Delany celebrates. These conflicts are not easily resolved but addressing them brings us closer to developing an interpretive framework that guards against conservative co-optations of "women's safety" while still critiquing the implicit masculinization of Delany's model of contact.

The conflict between Delany's politics of "contact" and a feminist analysis of gender is showcased most clearly, perhaps, in his encounter with a young man named Rannit. Having developed a casual sexual relationship with Rannit inside one of the theaters, the two men decide to have lunch together one day. The excursion brings to Delany's attention a habit of Rannit's of which he had been previously unaware: "In the seventy-five yard walk . . . Rannit managed to brush up against three women on the street, dragging his hand across their hip as he passed, and, once, as he was going into the pizza place, outright grabbing a young woman's behind. She turned and gave him a sharp, disgusted look. He grinned at her, then at me" (86–87). Appalled by what he observes and refusing to celebrate or encourage Rannit's acts of street harassment and assault, Delany attempts over lunch to engage him in a conversation about his compulsions. Though he makes little headway in helping Rannit to understand why his actions toward women are inappropriate, Delany uses this encounter to highlight the informal but important civic value of public sexuality. Delany describes Rannit as "a guy I'm unlikely to invite to my house. But that still doesn't mean that the sex between us wasn't fulfilling and mutually satisfying. And who knows: if we continue running into each other . . . maybe I'll be a good influence. Perhaps I'll begin to get across to him some idea that there are other ways to behave in this society that might satisfy the largely heterosexual components of his desire, ways that are a good deal more socially acceptable than touching up women in the street" (88). This account raises questions about what precisely it means to conceive of sexual exchange as an extension of civic dialogue. Does this encounter constitute a moment of "contact" *despi*te Rannit's misogynist treatment of women? Or does "contact" happen here precisely *because* clashing ideologies are brought together within a network of intimacy through which pedagogy, as well as pleasure, can productively flow? Delany seems to conceive of his friendship with Rannit as falling under the latter rubric, their friendly exchange of sexual pleasure leading to a productive dialogue in which Delany can exert a "good influence" over Rannit's misguided beliefs about acceptable conduct toward women.

However, the reasoning that Delany uses to persuade Rannit to end his street harassment suggests the limits of "contact" as a pedagogical tool. Delany tells Rannit "there are a lot better ways to go about getting yourself laid than that," and later, "you're going to get in trouble. What happens when some woman calls the police on you?" (87). This dialogue, while well-intentioned, does not ultimately provide Rannit with a feminist education. If Rannit learns anything from the exchange with Delany, it's not a lesson about sexual politics, gender privilege, or the systemic violation of women's bodies in public and in private. It's a lesson, rather, about how to "satisfy the largely heterosexual components of his desire" within the acceptable limits of the law. After all, if second-wave feminism taught us anything, it's that there are plenty of "socially acceptable," and indeed, institutionalized, ways to infringe on women's sexual autonomy. Though Delany at one point observes that Rannit's behaviors "seemed a cross between social and obsessive, rather than in any way sexually gratifying," he seems uninterested in connecting that observation to the radical feminist belief that social practices like rape and sexual assault are indeed more social than sexual, an assertion of social power wedded to an intricate set of compulsory (or even "compulsive") institutionalized practices and representations. Though Delany may have been attempting to influence Rannit's behavior by meeting him on his own terms, he ultimately allows his own example of civic exchange to be emptied of much of its civic value.

This breakdown in feminist pedagogy extends to Delany's framing of the films themselves. Acknowledging the sexism of most of the commercial pornography of the 1970s and 1980s, Delany suggests that the films nonetheless challenged gender norms in potentially transformative ways. Conducting an unofficial experiment during the 1980s in response to the tours that WAP (Women Against Pornography) was leading through the area, Delany recalls comparing six mainstream films in the movie theaters in New York with six of the films playing in the porn theaters. The pornographic films, Delany reports, represented a greater number of women as "having a profession," more instances of "friendships between women," and more frequently ended with more women "getting what they want" (79).[15] Delany does not, however, discuss what precisely it is that the women are represented as "wanting" in these films, nor does he engage with the common feminist argument that heterosexual sex scenes in pornographic films can often function as a form of discipline, in which professional women are "taken down" and intimacy between women is disrupted and disqualified by the eventual intrusion of the male member.[16]

More than simply overlooking feminist critiques of pornography, however, Delany suggests that the films that were screened in the porn theaters may have actually provided a "tremendous sexual education for their working class audience" (78). Observing the way pornography diversified the sexual act into a "a four part act, oral and genital, where everyone gets a chance to be on top" (78), Delany suggests that the sex acts represented in the films may have helped to normalize and destigmatize nonmissionary sex positions in ways that were liberating to both men and women. He elaborates:

> Generally, I suspect, pornography improved our vision of sex all of the country, making it friendlier, more relaxed, and more playful—qualities of sex that, till then, had been often reserved to a distressingly limited section of the better-read and more imaginative members of the mercantile middle classes. For the first year or two the theaters operated, the entire working class audience would break out laughing at everything save male superior fucking . . . By the seventies' end, though, only a few chuckles sounded out now—at the cunnilingus passages. And in the first year or two of the eighties, even those stopped . . . I think, under pressure of those films, many guys simply found themselves changing what turned them on. (78)

Here, Delany both replicates and reverses the logic of second-wave feminist condemnations of pornography. What for writers like Dworkin and MacKinnon was most dangerous about pornography—its ability to act as an instructive primer for how to treat women—for Delany becomes its greatest virtue. Both, in other words, understand pornography as a genre with a relatively direct and unmediated relation to the public it reaches, its transmission of social values resulting in a predictable set of real-world consequences. If antiporn feminists saw pornography as a violent and patriarchal sex education for men, then Delany sees in those same films a sexual pedagogy committed to nonpatriarchal egalitarian values. If for Robin Morgan, "porn is the theory" and "rape is the practice," then for Delany, we might say that "porn is the theory" and "democracy is the practice." Notably, Delany's description here resonates with his invocation, elsewhere in the text, of the infectious qualities of altruistic exchange. Like the good deed whose effects ripple concentrically outward into the population, we are here given a new attitude toward sex that originates with a privileged sliver of the educated elite ("the more imaginative members of the mercantile middle classes"), spreads to the working class, and ultimately "improve[s] our vision of sex all of the country."[17]

Delany is not the only one to conceive of pornography as a site of democratic sexual abundance. Steven Marcus has used the term "pornucopia" to discuss pornography's frequent framing of sexuality as an endless and communally shared resource. "Everyone," Marcus writes, "is always ready for anything, and everyone is infinitely generous with his substance . . . No one is really jealous, possessive, or even angry" (273). Marty Klein adds that "the most straightforward narrative for pornography is erotic abundance. In the world that porn depicts, there is more than enough of everything," creating "a world of erotic surplus in which all choices are possible" (249).[18] This pornucopic world of erotic surplus is, for both Marcus and Klein, limited to the fictional world of fantasy, as it differs markedly from what Klein calls the "sexual economy" of dominant culture where "female eroticism" is understood to be a "precious" and "scarce commodity" (252). In almost identical terms, Delany describes what he sees as the "system of artificial heterosexual scarcity," which he blames for some of the street harassment women experience. Were heterosexual women to adopt a similar approach to sexuality as gay male culture, he speculates, the whistles and catcalls that women regularly encounter on the street would likely either disappear or at the very least lose their "hostile tenor" (197). Envisioning a "situation of greater sexual availability" for all genders, Delany takes a step further than either Klein or Marcus in envisioning what a fantasized "pornucopia" might look like in embodied material practice.[19]

Delany's championing of an expansive democratic sexuality to be shared by all genders is, of course, a worthy political goal. But bringing that world into being requires that we first contend with the patriarchal ideologies that underlie the very logic of "abundance" and heterosexual "scarcity." As Adrienne Rich pointed out twenty years before the publication of Delany's essay, compulsory heterosexuality is culturally enforced precisely through "the mystique of the overpowering, all-conquering male sex drive, the penis-with-a-life-of-its-own," a mystique grounded in "the law of male sex-right to women" (645). When we frame sexual violence as primarily a problem of men's limited sexual access to women (rather than a problem of sexual entitlement), we miss an opportunity to critique and dismantle the structures of compulsory heterosexuality that create this "mystique" in the first place. Indeed, Delany's arguments about the feminist pedagogical value of the films is somewhat belied by his own observation earlier in the piece that the forms of homosexual and homosocial bonding that take place inside the theaters in many ways "depend entirely on the absence of 'the woman'—or at least depend on flattening 'the woman' till she is only an image on a screen, whether of light or memory, reduced to 'pure' 'sexuality,' till, a magical essence, a mystical energy, she pervades, grounds, even fuels the entire process, from which she is corporally, intellectually, emotionally, and politically absent" (25). We might recognize in this description the classic traits of what Eve Sedgwick identified in 1992 as "male homosocial desire" as it is triangulated through the figure of the woman.[20]

In a peculiar attempt, perhaps, to resolve the dissonance between this portrait of marginalized femininity and the subversive forms of sexual education that he claims the films enable, Delany attempts to transform this "corporally, intellectually, emotionally, and politically absent" woman into a "present" one. In the pages that follow, Delany recounts an episode in which he allowed a curious female friend to accompany him to the porn theaters one afternoon. Ana's interest in the space is more anthropological than sexual, motivated by a desire to observe for herself the practices that Delany had related to her in conversation. As she tours the aisles and observes various sexual exchanges taking place around her, she is propositioned by a couple of men who politely accept her rejections. "It was more relaxed than I thought it would be," she observes afterward, "I thought it was going to be more frenetic—people just grabbing each other and throwing them down in the shadows and having their way. But it was so easy going" (30). This anecdote serves an important purpose in Delany's narrative as it appears to demonstrate how "safe" the porn theaters actually are for women. If the dominant rhetoric has painted these spaces as dangerous havens for sexual predators, then Delany's recounting of Ana's reaction frames them instead as a neighborly space of social and sexual exchange—spaces where female agency can be easily exercised. But when Delany asks Ana if she would ever consider returning, she says "no," adding later, "I was scared to death!" (30). Ana's affective relation to the porn theater (one of fear) thus appears at odds with her intellectual perception of the space's "easygoing" atmosphere. Privileging Ana's intellectual response over her affective one, Delany is quick to imply that Ana's fear is irrational and ultimately prophylactic. When prompted, Ana is unable to point to "anything in particular that scared [her]," leading Delany to chalk up much of her anxiety to the "fear of the outside that she brought within" (32). Delany concludes that "despite Ana's assertion from more than twenty years ago" that she felt uncomfortable in the theater, he doesn't see "any reason that a woman (or women) couldn't take any (or every) role I've already described or will go on to describe for any (and every) male theater patron" (32). But to produce the diversely gendered sexual subculture that Delany envisions, we may need to do more than simply encourage women to check their anxieties at the door or "educate" them to be less afraid of strange men in dark places.[21]

Taking an additive approach ("the more the merrier"), Delany seems unwilling to acknowledge the structural overhaul that may be necessary to make these spaces of "contact" truly inclusive of and accessible to women.[22] As Kendall Thomas observes in his 1996 interview with Jocelyn Taylor (founder of one of the first New York City lesbian sex parties): "The culture of public sex is definitely gendered; even within the queer world, the possibilities are not identical, and therefore the efforts to create a public sexual space for women must be qualitatively different. Although it would be important not to exaggerate the degree of safety that gay men have, one must meet needs that simply aren't present in the culture in which men can move freely, through the night, in and out of doors" (64). As Kendall's observation suggests, terms like "safety" and "privacy" might hold more radical feminist meanings and associations that are not simply reducible to the corporate privatization. It is these qualitative differences that seem to get lost in Delany's indiscriminate Whitmanesque model of contact. Presenting antiprophylactic citizenship in primarily masculine terms, Delany only conceives of "privacy" as a version of capitalist "privatization" and only understands "safety" as a neoliberal buzzword designed to stamp out interclass contact. While anti-porn feminism may have brought discussions of sexuality in directions that were often divisive and counterproductive, we may still do well to remain wary of theoretical paradigms that celebrate the inherently subversive power of public sexuality while ignoring the power relations that structure it. We must, in other words, trouble some of the institutional and activist binaries that have dominated the terms of the conversation if we are to forge coalitions across political lines. It may ultimately be in the lowering of our disciplinary barriers, rather than our sexual ones, that we access the most powerfully "antiprophylactic" moments of contact.

The Walking Wounded

Over the past several years, queer scholars like Dean Spade, Christina Hanhardt, and Margot Weiss have carefully untangled the slippery rhetorical formulations that promote the "safety" of certain populations while mandating forms of structural violence that endanger others.[23] In this context, Delany's memoir does powerful and necessary work, revealing the way redevelopment efforts projected the specter of menace and threat onto the very populations it menaced and threatened. Behind the appeal to "clean up" Times Square was an unspoken appeal to take out "trash"—those individuals whose lives are considered disposable in the eyes of capitalism. But while the appeal to safety and privacy can often collude with corporate logics, we must also grapple with the extent to which the transgressive valorization of risk can align with neoliberal logics of capacitation. I would like to conclude my reading of *Times Square Red, Times Square Blue* by illustrating the ways in which Delany's text genders debility and capacity, assigning debility to the province of the feminine while presenting a valorized portrait of capacitated crip masculinity.

With this in mind, I want to turn to Delany's account of his trip to visit his ailing mother, accompanied by his longtime lover and acquaintance Arly, whom he met in the porn theaters. Significantly, Arly is introduced in the text through his disability:

> And then there was Arly, who'd lost a leg at five when his crazed, drunken father flung him under an oncoming subway . . . I met him when he was twenty-one or twenty-two and he would come in to settle in the Cameo's balcony. Good-looking, friendly, and extremely agile on his one-stick crutch, for the first three times I talked to him, he claimed to be too tired for sex. Finally, I assumed he just wasn't available, when, the next time he passed me in the balcony aisle, suddenly he seized my arm to explain in a low, excited voice . . . that he was more highly sexed than most men, and thus anyone who sat with him but stayed only through one of his orgasms would (in his words) "drive me crazy, man. It makes me wanna *die*—" he dragged down on my arm at the emphasis—"if I can't come three or four times, you know? I mean, I wanna die. So if you wanna do me, man, you got to stay with me till I come at least three times, huh?" (50)

In what follows, Delany verifies Arly's claim to be "highly sexed," describing Arly's capacity to have five or six orgasms over the course of a "two- or two-and-a-half hour session" (50). As their sexual relationship progresses, Delany recalls that "a couple of times Arly came to my five-flight walk up writer's digs. With his one leg and single-stem homemade crutch, he took my steps three at a bound" (51). From a traditional disability studies perspective, this framing might read as a positive, even subversive, example of disability representation. Against a pervasive cultural ideology that understands disabled bodies as sexually broken, lacking in libido, and inappropriate as either subjects or objects of desire, Arly's "highly-sexed" crip body is unapologetically sexual. Far from amputation's usual status as a signifier of castration or emasculation, Arly's amputation is consistent with his masculinity and his sexual virility. His disability does not inhibit his ability to function within the queer sexual spaces of the porn theater. To the contrary, Delany describes his and Arly's mutual pleasure as Delany "mov[ed] into his open fly to rub the irregular flesh of his stump, while it flexed and shifted in response" (51). The sexualization of Arly's disability within these spaces establishes them as nonhierarchical sites of sexual expression and bodily diversity.

But importantly, while Arly is disabled, he is not described as being debilitated. Just as his body is capable of multiple orgasms, his desire for queer sex seemingly allows him to nimbly ascend the stairs to Delany's fifth-floor apartment. In this respect, his physical capacity is representationally linked to his orgasmic capacity. A kind of sexual supercrip, he thus performs a queer twist on the overcoming narrative, heroically transcending access barriers through the sheer force of his unbounded libido. Arly thus bears a unique form a biocapital within the sexual economy of the porn theaters. Indeed, even as Delany's text powerfully positions itself against the logic of neoliberalism, his language nonetheless echoes its numerical metrics for assessing biopolitical value. Fast-forwarding a decade, Delany observes: "Now at thirty, Arly was good-looking, with a hard body, and a solid ten inches, uncut; and while a few people were put off by the missing leg, he seldom lacked for takers. He demanded endurance. But he was attractive enough—and big enough—that he could afford to be choosy" (51). Thirty-years old, ten inches long, averaging three orgasms per hour, and able to take the stairs three steps at a time, Arly's body confronts us as a kind of mathematical proof of its own productivity. Rather than requiring care, he "demands endurance." In his sexual insatiability and seemingly endless orgasmic potentiality, he is identifiable as *Times Square Red, Times Square Blue*'s ultimate figure of crip capacity.

Arly's crip capacity is rendered all the more capacious as it is paired with the book's ultimate figure of feminized debility: Delany's mother following her stroke. Immediately after introducing Arly, Delany presents the following description, which I quote at length:

> In July of 1987, at a pre-theater dinner in Greenwich Village with two of her oldest friends, on her way to the lady's room at Gavin's restaurant, my mother suffered a massive stroke that kept her at St. Luke's hospital for ten months, then put her in the Park Shore Manor nursing home, paralyzed on her right side and unable to speak, write anything other than incoherent progressions of letters, or respond directly to verbal instructions. In this state, wheelchair-bound and incontinent, she remained for the final eight years of her life.

The incident, as do such medical catastrophes—with hospital visits, medical consultations, visits with lawyers in a cluttered upstairs Harlem office, conservatorship papers, trips down with lawyer and doctor to the city courthouse for competency hearings in the courtroom off the echoing second-floor rotunda, and yes, the resultant emotional strain—simply excised, as with a pair of sheers, a productive ten months from my sister's life and mine.

I am convinced that, in Kafka's Die Verwandlung, Gregor Samsa's transformation stands for just such a catastrophe, fallen on one or another family member: a stroke, a crippling accident, insanity . . . an irrevocable change that does not (immediately kill) but leaves, rather, an incomprehensible creature to be dealt with one way or another by all who remain, a creature wholly alien yet somehow recognizable in fifty little ways—a hand gesture, a shake of the head, a sudden single phrase ("I know") muttered thirty-seven times, a smile, a moue—as the subject he or she once was. (52)

There is, of course, an obvious ableism in this portrait, which frames disability in terms of "catastrophe," burden, and dehumanization ("an incomprehensible creature to be dealt with"). More precisely, I am interested in the way this passage works alongside the preceding description of Arly to mark and maintain a curious distinction between the geographies of capacitated masculinity and the feminized terrain of debility. "Agile on his one-stick crutch," Arly embodies a fantasy of unfettered mobility that contrasts sharply with Delany's account of his mother's "paralyzed" and "wheelchair-bound" body. While Arly's disability is woven into the fabric of porn theaters' queer socialities, Delany's mother's stroke is presented as a socially isolating condition, leaving her "unable to speak, write . . . or respond directly to verbal instructions." She is literally a subject of slow death, stubbornly persisting eight months beyond what should have been, it is implied, her proper "catastrophic" end. In this way, the text's own swift movement from Arly's disability to Delany's mother's stroke registers the broader parallel movement that Puar observes "from the subject of disability to the subject of prognosis" (165). Against the seemingly constant forward-motion of Arly's disabled body in space, Delany's description of his mother resonates instead with the lagging temporalities of debility and its impersonal administrative landscapes.

Indeed, in a book that is continually attuned to the vital textures of New York City's built environment (from the darkened interiors of the porn theater to the stoops of 42nd Street), Delany's brief detour into the "cluttered upstairs" law offices of Harlem and the "echoing second-floor rotunda" of the city courthouse presents the book's sole engagement with the spaces of bureaucracy. While the antiprophylactic outlaw atmosphere of the porn theater transforms strangers into intimates, the sterile administrative spaces of the court perform an inverse operation, transforming intimates into strangers—"creature[s] wholly alien yet somehow familiar." In the porn theaters, physical amputation does not register a lack, signifying instead as an exceptional site of masculine virility. Rather, it is the antiseptic corridors of the legal apparatus of the state that perform the more profound amputation, "excis[ing], as with a pair of sheers, a productive ten months" from Delany's and his sister's lives. Losing a leg, as Arly has, in a spontaneous spectacle of trauma, does not diminish the male body but regenerates its vital capacities. Worse than losing a leg, Delany implies, is losing months of one's life to the bureaucratic intrusions of the state, with its numerous metrics for assessing competency, managing finances, and determining inheritance. This is a safer, cleaner incision; it may not produce immediate harm, but it saps energy and wears down productivity one court appearance at a time.

In their inverse relations to productivity, optimism, and bodily capacity, Arly and Delany's mother become what Puar calls the "good and bad subjects" regulated by the "modulation and surveillance of affect" in which "affect entails not only a dissolution of the subject but, more significantly, a dissolution of the stable contours of the organic body, as forces of energy are transmitted, shared, circulated" (154–155). The scene thus concludes with Delany accepting Arly's offer to accompany him on his next visit to see his mother, and noticing Arly's capacitating effect on her debilitated body:

> In my mom's room on the seventh floor, Arly became a one-legged whirlwind, straightening her pillow, putting things right on the table beside her bed—the crutch was left in the corner now: in such small spaces he found it easier to maneuver without it—telling her how well she looked, smoothing up her covers, reassuring her that she'd soon be well. Mom's sluggishness over the first fifteen minutes of our visit gave way to a bright-eyed attention, as if by osmosis she absorbed his energy and cheerfulness. (54)

Afterward, the trio leave to get ice cream, and Arly leads a brief sing-along during the excursion. Delany observes, "In her orange robe in the wheelchair, her paralyzed arm belted with white Velcro into its fiberglass brace, Mom 'la-la-ed' along" (54). Revitalized by Arly's infectious energy, Delany's mother is momentarily capacitated. She is transformed from one of debility's bad subjects into, if not a good subject, at the very least a momentarily *better* subject in her receptivity to the "forces of energy [that] are transmitted, shared, circulated" through Arly's affective orientation to the world. In this way, Arly bears out Puar's suspicion that queerness, too, can "operate as a machine of regenerative productivity" (153). But even as their bodily edges blur during this affective exchange, Arly and Delany's mother persist as two ends of a gendered spectrum in which antiprophylactic masculinity corrects or compensates for a prophylactic femininity marked by debility, sterility, unresponsiveness, uncooperativeness, and even refusal.

In this context, the bug chasing mantra "infected but not ill" raises questions about how, if at all, debility fits into the structures of antiprophylactic citizenship. Sometimes infected *does* mean ill, even as Delany's account of Arly's relentless energy would seem to tell us otherwise. Sometimes an amputee will say no to a flight of stairs, and sometimes a positive attitude is not enough to convert "sluggishness" into "bright-eyed attention" in the aftermath of a stroke. Indeed, if for bug chasers "the rectum is a womb"—a site for proliferating viral bonds and new forms of queer life—then we might pair this observation with Maggie Nelson's reflection in *The Argonauts* that pregnancy was her "first sustained encounter with the pendulous, the slow, the exhausted, the disabled. I had always presumed that giving birth would make me feel invincible, and ample, like fisting. But even now, two years out, my insides feel more quivery than lush. I've begun to give myself over to the idea that sensation might be forever changed, that this sensitivity is now mine, ours, to work with. Can fragility feel as hot as bravado?" (86). Nelson's "fragility" emerges here as an affective mode of feminist-crip relationality that displaces queer theory's more glorified accounts of masochism. Rather than the "ample" sensations of fisting—sensations that testify to openness, receptivity, and endurance—we are given "quivery" "insides" and a "sensitivity" that must be carefully "worked with" and negotiated between partners. I will return to this language of sensitivity in my epilogue on trigger warning discourse. Here, I want to highlight how Delany's text—as well as the other works I've discussed throughout this book—stages an uneasy vacillation between the kinds of "fragility" and "bravado" that Nelson describes. If these writers tend to valorize risk as an inherently vital or life-giving enterprise, it is because they are often already writing from the place of debility, slow death, precarity, and neglect. As I argued in my reading of Jack London's fictional and autobiographical writings, London vitalizes injury precisely as a complicated response to capitalism's debilitation of male workers whose bodies are "wrenched and distorted and twisted out of shape by toil and hardship and accident, and cast adrift by their masters like so many old horses" (126). Claiming antiprophylactic citizenship thus provides an opportunity for male writers to generate fantasies (or epidemiologies) of belonging in which individual acts of risk-taking outweigh the biopolitical control of populations, affective experience compensates for precarious existence, and the spectacle of masculine vulnerability displaces a feminized temporality of chronic and unresolvable symptoms.[24]

Indeed, despite Delany's frequent descriptions of Arly's crip invincibility, it's important to remember that, from the vantage point of neoliberalism as a system, Arly's biocapital is more figurative than literal. During these vignettes, Delany provides glimpses of Arly's history of panhandling and his alcoholism; as he confides in Delany, "Scotch is what saved me from being a crackhead!" (54). In these moments, Arly is recognizable as a member of those populations who experience "slow death"—the wearing away of precarious subjects under capitalism. Choosing whiskey over crack, he exercises what Berlant refers to as "lateral agency," the power to develop coping mechanisms that occupy a "shifting sensual space between pleasure and numbness" ("Slow Death," 779). I am not arguing that one portrait of Arly is more or less authentic than the other. However, I am interested in Arly's figural status in the text as a subject who moves back and forth between "fragility" and "bravado," and who materializes a certain fantasy of crip capacity against the debilitating structures of neoliberalism.

The tensions that frame Arly's shifting orientation toward biopower are threaded throughout *Times Square Red, Times Square Blue*. Existing alongside Delany's antiprophylactic vision of sexual democracy and affective abundance—his celebration of capacitated disability—are brief acknowledgments that such visions emerge against a landscape of debility and slow death. Delany refers to the mid-1980s in the porn theaters as the "'Great Winnowing,' from crack and AIDS—with crack very much the leading villain of the two. If I gather the tragedies, most of the ones I remember come from that period" (41). "Winnowing," of course, lacks the antiprophylactic glamor of the pandemic. As I argued earlier, the vocabulary of contagion offers Delany a powerful model for redefining social intimacy and citizenship. Contagion is proliferative, vital, and always mutating; it promises to expand laterally across larger and larger radiuses, gathering momentum, touching everyone. Winnowing, by contrast, implies dwindling numbers, depleted resources, and a slowly shrinking radius. Here, we are in the realm of the chronic rather than the contagious, a distinction that Delany underscores in his emphasis on crack, rather than AIDS, as the "leading villain" of the period.

It is in this context that we learn the story of Kevin, a "teak-colored, muscle-bound little powerhouse" (42) whose "big hands," "full mouth," and "general masculine gentleness" make him an "exemplar of male beauty" (41). Years later, Delany encounters a "dirty and ragged" Kevin, homeless and rooting through dumpsters before "shambl[ing] off" (42). While "the gentleness was still there," Delany notes, "the power was gone" (42). There is also the example of Joey-Who-Needs-a-Bath, another figure of sexual insatiability: "I have never known anyone who could get into sex more than he could. I mean, that boy *loved* to come!" (47). Delany's friend relates the news of Joey's premature death at twenty-nine, "Frozen to death in a hallway—with a heart attack. I think the drugs must have weakened his system" (48). These figures reveal the slow temporalities of structural violence and their capacity to create constitutional vulnerability or "weaken[ed] systems." Their vulnerability does not lie primarily in their status as potential targets of racist or homophobic hate crimes, though many of them are men of color and nearly all of them enjoy queer sex. What ultimately causes the decline of these physically vital and sexually potent male "powerhouse[s]" is the *make live, let die* logic of capitalism with its everyday neglect of marginalized populations.

Elsewhere, Delany refers to some of the more exceptional figures who inhabit Times Square as the "walking wounded" (89). Though he does not elaborate, the phrase is striking in the way that it seems to describe both the capacitated masculinity of Arly ("agile on his one-stick crutch") and the debilitated masculinity of Joey ("the drugs must have weakened his system"). Indeed, what is perhaps most compelling about antiprophylactic citizenship is its celebration of "risk" in relation to bodies that may not always be exercising absolute agency in their exposure to potential harm. For these reasons, it is crucial that we continue to center debility and chronicity in our analyses, even or especially when they are characterized by slow death or a gradual wearing away of vitality. Some risks promise to fold us into national or subcultural life, while others are occasioned by conditions of precarity and neglect. There are meaningful differences as well as powerful overlaps between the pleasures of taking risks and the experience of being at risk. Tracing these connections requires that we tread carefully around the kinds of de facto values we might be tempted to assign to experiences of safety, violence, vulnerability, and exposure.

5

Prescribing Pleasure

Asexuality, Debility, and Trans Memoir

What does antiprophylactic masculinity look like in the absence of cismen? One of the paradoxes of antiprophylactic masculinity is its tendency, despite its queer-crip commitments, to emerge as a *capacitated* masculinity constructed at the expense of—or in relief against—a rejected portrait of feminized debility. Vitalized by vulnerability and regenerated by risk, it is a masculinity that invites contagion in the name of health. A proliferator of queer life, the antiprophylactic citizen finds power in a perpetual stance of openness, permeability, and consent—a preparedness to say "yes" to every form of sensation and intimacy being offered. In the previous chapters, antiprophylactic citizenship emerged as a function of the cismale body's willingness to become uncharacteristically porous, receptive, and violable. But the appeal of violability is less legible, arguably, for transmen and ciswomen who are at a much greater risk of sexual violence and other forms of feminized and feminizing trauma. This chapter explores the status of antiprophylactic citizenship as a troubled horizon of possibility for female, asexual, and transmasculine bodies.

The association between trans subjectivities and corporeal transformation allows some transmasculine practices to map fairly easily onto the structures of antiprophylactic citizenship. While plenty of trans individuals choose not to modify their bodies through hormones or surgery, there is a certain antiprophylactic ethos in opening up the body to testosterone. In addition to transgressing bodily boundaries, these chemical encounters have the potential to disrupt medical authority as well. Beyond testosterone's prescribed function as a treatment for gender dysphoria, and against those forms of medical gatekeeping that have required trans individuals to conform to appropriate diagnostic criteria in order to access surgery and hormones, some critics have argued for approaching testosterone not as a medication but as an intoxicant. In this framework, one incorporates new hormones into the body not to "fix" a misaligned gender but rather to access new forms of bodily sensation and queer sociality through the alteration of consciousness. Here, testosterone becomes everything doctors assure us it's not: an instrument of pleasure, a controlled substance, an aphrodisiac, and, above all, a method for exercising the freedom to perform unsanctioned experiments with our physiologies.

It is this antiprophylactic model of transmasculinity that we are presented with in Paul B. Preciado's provocative and influential *Testo Junkie*. First published in Spanish in 2008, with the English edition following in 2013, *Testo Junkie* was composed alongside Preciado's own experiments with testogel and thus reads both as an experimental trans memoir and as a theoretical treatise on the history of sexuality. Proposing a politics of "voluntary autointoxication" (351), Preciado presents his own experimentation with testogel—which he applied to his female body during the writing of the book—as a blueprint for how we might "use our living bodies as biopolitical platforms to test the pharmacopornopolitical effects" of a variety of substances (352). Against the *DSM*'s diagnostic categorization and treatment of gender variance through the rubric of gender identity disorder, Preciado advocates a model that understands sex hormones as recreational—even addictive—substances for individual consumption. "Either I declare myself to be transsexual," he writes, "or I declare myself to be drugged and psychotic" (256). Choosing the latter designation, identifying as a "testo junkie" rather than as transsexual, Preciado describes what it feels like to "get roaring drunk on masculinity" (396). Treating testosterone as just another object of economic circulation, he displaces the authority of medicine to act as a cultural gatekeeper.

Describing the effects of testosterone on his body, Preciado recounts how "an extraordinary lucidity settles in, gradually, accompanied by an explosion of the desire to fuck, walk, go out everywhere in the city. This is the climax in which the spiritual force of the testosterone mixing with my blood takes to the fore. Absolutely all the unpleasant sensations disappear. . . . Nothing but the feeling of strength reflecting the increased capacity of my muscles, my brain" (21). Testosterone emerges here as a capacitating substance, both physically and sexually. Rather than curing a disordered body of gender dysphoria, it functions as a performance-enhancing drug, activating a "desire to fuck" and facilitating a "climax" that is both spiritual and sexual. This framework is, indeed, intoxicating. If Gayle Rubin's "Thinking Sex" drew criticism from transgender scholars like Susan Stryker for "categoriz[ing] transgender practices as sexual or erotic acts rather than expressions of gender identity or sense of self" (Stryker, 131), Preciado moves these debates full circle by recuperating trans practices as acts of erotic deviance. In this sense, he departs from trans studies' traditional focus on gender, centralizing sexuality as the locus of trans agency.

This is consistent with Preciado's overarching thesis that, within the contemporary workings of neoliberalism, sexual pleasure has become increasingly central to the apparatuses through which capitalism exercises control over and through the subject. Arguing that we currently inhabit a "pharmacopornographic era," Preciado provides an exhaustive account of the way that recent transformations in the structure of capitalism have resulted in a parallel "transformation of 'gender,' 'sex,' 'sexuality,' 'sexual identity,' and 'pleasure' into biopolitical technologies" (25). Preciado variously refers to these contemporary political currents as the "toxico-pornographic era" (53), the "pharmacopornographic regime" (234), or more simply as "biopolitical capitalism" (40). Focused on capitalism's investment in the continued production of sexual pleasure—from the technologies of pornography and birth control to the marketing of Viagra and testosterone—Preciado powerfully extends Foucault's thesis on the regulatory function of pleasure.

Alongside this analysis, however, Preciado also presents a transgressive counternarrative that valorizes the biological capacity for orgasm as the ultimate act of queer agency. Consider, for example, Preciado's discussion of "*potentia gaudendi*" (41). Loosely translated as "orgasmic force," the phrase describes "the (real or virtual) strength of a body's (total) excitation" (41). Preciado clarifies that while we should not understand the market as an "outside power coming to expropriate, repress, or control the sexual instincts of the individual," (46) orgasmic force nonetheless carries a transgressive potential in its detachment from individual bodies and identities. A "force of transformation for the world in pleasure," (41) it

> does not allow itself to be reified or transformed into private property. I can neither possess nor retain another's *potentia gaudendi*, but neither can one possess or retain what seems to be one's own. *Potentia gaudendi* exists exclusively as an event, a relation, a practice, or an evolutionary process. Orgasmic force is both the most abstract and the most material of all workforces. It is inextricably carnal and

digital, viscous yet representational by numerical values, a phantasmatic or molecular wonder that can be transformed into capital. The living pansexual body is the bioport of the orgasmic force. Thus, it cannot be reduced to a prediscursive organism; its limits do not coincide with the skin capsule that surrounds it. (43)

Refusing to recognize the skin of the body as a barrier to the circulation of pleasure, value, and sensation, orgasmic force emerges here as a fundamentally antiprophylactic energy. Not just a life force but a "workforce," it circulates simultaneously inside and outside of regulatory systems. It is both current and currency, electrically transmitting those forms of erotic sensation that maintain (or subversively rewire) the capitalist system.

But if "pharmacopornographic control infiltrates and dominates the entire flow of capital" (40), then resistance cannot be conceptualized outside of the erotic. The result is a body that is debilitated by the extent to which it does not function as a "bioport" for sexual pleasure and capacitated by the extent to which it does. Without questioning the value and factuality of Preciado's powerful autobiographical account, we might nonetheless question why it is the case that queer agency and political subversion continue to be measured through the barometer of erotic sensation. The value of testosterone, here and elsewhere in *Testo Junkie*, inheres in the extent to which it carries an orgasmic force that "can be transformed into capital." No mere side effect of somatechnic experimentation, the capacity for sexual pleasure is the constitutive feature of the empowered pharmacopornographic subject. We might then ask what it means to be an asexually identified subject in the pharmacopornographic era. What is the status of sexual refusal in an "ejaculatory" economy?

There is much to say about the evolving diagnostic criteria that have been used to name gender variance in the *DSM*. However, this chapter is primarily interested in placing antiprophylactic models of transmasculinity like this one in conversation with the simultaneous medicalization of a less visible site of queer identity: asexual femininity.[1] Both "Transsexualism" and "Inhibited Sexual Desire" entered the third edition of the *DSM* in 1980, the same moment that "Homosexuality" was in the process of being declassified as a mental disorder. Both diagnoses have gone through a series of revisions over the past two editions. "Inhibited Sexual Desire" was reclassified as "Hypoactive Sexual Desire Disorder" in 1987, with the 2013 edition incorporating the additional category of "Female Sexual Interest/Arousal Disorder."[2] In a seemingly parallel progression, the initial diagnosis of "Transsexualism" was replaced with "Gender Identity Disorder" in 1994, and finally "Gender Dysphoria" in 2013.[3] Many trans advocates celebrated the way the most recent revision traded the stigmatizing vocabulary of "disorder" for a more accurate and nuanced portrait of social and bodily discomfort.

But while the evolution of trans diagnoses would appear to reflect a progressive shift, the replacement of the unisex Hypoactive Sexual Desire Disorder (HSDD) with new gender-specific criteria seemed to breathe new life into retrograde binaries that posit essential differences between active "male" and passive "female" sexuality. Previously HSDD had been applied to both men and women, but the new diagnosis of Female Sexual Interest/Arousal Disorder (FSI/AD) redefined low female desire as a unique medical category, now distinct from the newly masculinized HSDD. In her 2013 study of the medicalization of low desire, Alyson Spurgas ("Interest, Arousal, and Shifting Diagnoses") has remarked on the ways in which the *DSM*'s evolving diagnoses describing female sexual dysfunction have promoted an "alternative model of sexual response for women" (190). Notably, while the masculine diagnosis of HSDD remains relatively brief and retains the vocabulary of "desire," the new and rather lengthy diagnosis of FSI/AD dropped the word "desire" from the criteria entirely, centering on "interest" and "arousal" instead. As Spurgas persuasively argues, the most recent model assumes that healthy female sexuality is characterized by "responsiveness, receptivity, flexibility, and complexity" (193) and is "triggered" by the complementary presence of an active and initiating male desire. Alongside these highly gendered diagnostic criteria, Spurgas observes, new therapeutic treatments have emerged that replace psychoanalytic and psychodynamic approaches with the more "goal-oriented, explicit, and systematic procedures" of cognitive behavioral therapy (198).

I would add that this shift resonates strongly with the neoliberal reframing of disability as debility, with low desire no longer signifying as the property of an abnormal or pathological body.[4] In the context of FSI/AD, low-desiring women do not have broken bodies in need of repair; rather, they have bodies that experience differential levels of orgasmic capacitation. Beyond rhetorics of function/dysfunction, presence/absence, and wholeness/lack, the insufficiently "interested" woman is instead understood primarily as a vehicle of sexual activation, production, and optimization. In this way, the alternative female sexual response model projects a fantasy of neoliberal flexibility onto the (heterosexual) female body in ways that echo Puar's framing of debility and capacity in the neoliberal era. To borrow Puar's phrasing, we might say that the low-desiring woman is always already "debilitated in relation to

[her] ever-expanding [sexual] potentiality," and, as such, she becomes "profitable for capitalism" ("The Cost of Getting Better," 153).

This chapter proposes that the differing trajectories of gender identity disorder and FSI/AD reveal much about antiprophylactic citizenship in the pharmacopornographic era. In this context, an antiprophylactic femininity, like its transmasculine counterpart, might be envisioned as a site of sexual capacitation. It is a femininity that is open, responsive, and receptive to the possibility of sexual arousal. The low-desiring woman sits uneasily in this framework. In her refusal to connect, consent, or lower her defenses in the name of queer sociality, she emerges as the ultimate symbol of prophylaxis itself, and thus as a problem body for antiprophylactic citizenship and its affective networks. Perverse in her lack of perversity, her refusal or inability to say "yes" to sex molds her into queer theory's debilitated other.

With this in mind, it is notable that Preciado's own discussion of the medicalization of low desire among women does not challenge the therapeutic models as much as it continues to highlight the capacitating value of "orgasmic force." Here, Preciado examines the U.S. FDA's 2004 refusal to approve Intrinsa, a testosterone patch designed for the treatment of women with HSDD. Preciado speculates that the reason for "turning down such a growth market" within biopolitical capitalism is based on an outdated but enduring "gender binary epistemology" (223) that could only understand Intrinsa as a dangerous "lifestyle drug" (222). We must undoubtedly work to dismantle the binary logic that understands women's sexual pleasure as inconsequential or merely supplemental to men's "primary" natural active desire. But it's also crucial to remain wary of a medical establishment that prescribes female pleasure in ways that make sexuality compulsory. Indeed, with the recent approval of Addyi—the so-called Pink Viagra—we can acknowledge that the U.S. FDA is no longer in the business of turning down such growth markets. More troublingly, unlike Viagra, Addyi directly affects a woman's neurochemistry. As Spurgas notes in a recent commentary following Addyi's historic U.S. FDA approval: "If we really cared about women, we'd focus more on their pleasure and try to dismantle some of the barriers to pleasure that women experience so regularly in our world—including gendered harassment and violence, low pay, and antiquated divisions of labor, including the disproportionate burdens of carework and emotional tending that women are expected to provide . . . let's not pretend we've come a long way, just because we now have a little pink pill to match his little blue pill" ("Solving Desire"). Unmasking the false equivalence between Viagra and Addyi as a form of faux feminist empowerment, Spurgas reminds us that while increased sexual pleasure may indeed be an effect of revolutionary politics, it can't function (at least not solely) as its biopolitical instrument.

In what follows, I interrogate some of the ways that antiprophylactic citizenship has been reproduced through ideologies of ability and optimization, including the valorization of orgasmic capacity. Reading John Cameron Mitchell's 2006 film *Shortbus* as emblematic of these tendencies, I evaluate the role that asexual politics and subjectivity play (or fail to play) in *Shortbus*'s antiprophylactic spaces. As a supportive queer community intervenes to "fix" the problem of Sophia's nonorgasmic body, the film presents the concept of "permeability" both as a queer ethos and as a rehabilitative measure. Turning back to trans theory and autobiography, the chapter concludes by focusing on Eli Clare's own complicated relationships with pleasure, debility, and trans diagnostic politics in his two works of autobiographical theory, *Exile and Pride* (1999) and *Brilliant Imperfection* (2017). Clare, like Preciado, rejects medical models of trans identity, revealing the way his own transmasculinity is embedded in complicated affective encounters with the material world. But against queer theory's orgasmic imperatives, Clare explores how his own history of low desire is fundamentally interwoven with his queer-crip identity in ways that force us to take pain and trauma seriously. While Preciado presents erotic sensation and heightened libido as the measure of a capacitated masculinity, Clare's account of stone butch untouchability carves out new spaces for theorizing the contribution that queer asexuality can make to antiprophylactic citizenship.

Capacitating Pleasures

Because rhetorics of orgasmic capacitation have emerged most visibly and aggressively in heteronormative therapeutic contexts, such rhetorics have perhaps been harder to recognize in queer theoretical discourse. In *Orgasmology*, for example, Jagose describes the forms of "orgasmic reconditioning" applied to gay men during the 1950s, which supplemented the more well-known aversion therapies. In these treatments, gay men were directed to view images of women just prior to ejaculation in an attempt to produce heterosexual desire through positive association. Currently, women with low desire are being prescribed new pharmaceutical treatments, in addition to the increasing popularity of mindfulness-based cognitive behavioral therapies. Incorporating yoga and acupuncture, these therapies train women to become orgasmic through "focusing exercises" that guide them to increased presence in and awareness of their physical bodies.[5] In these instances, the medicalized production of pleasure is oriented toward the preservation of "healthy" heterosexual marriage.[6]

Against such heteronormative prescriptions, Jagose observes, queer scholars from Foucault to Deleuze have tended to approach the study of orgasm with suspicion. Opposing the biological "reflex" of orgasm to the antiteleological intensities of "pleasure" or "desire," both Foucault and Deleuze understand orgasm as "too bound up with the regulatory and normalizing aspects of modern sexuality" (2). Resisting these writers' tendency to cast orgasm as one of queer theory's "bad objects," Jagose builds on feminist theory's recent turn to affect in order to reconsider the value of "those bundled biological mechanisms" that include orgasm (25). While Jagose herself is careful to avoid "advocat[ing] for orgasm" as a "different ground for a new political engagement" (xvi), her sampling of queer theoretical texts may risk overstating queer theory's resistance to orgasm as a theoretical figure or site of political resistance. Positioning Bersani's "influential account" of queer *jouissance* as an exception to queer theory's "anti-orgasm tendencies" (14), Jagose remains relatively silent regarding those theorists writing in Bersani's legacy—from Samuel Delany and Michael Warner to Tim Dean and Paul B. Preciado—who do, in one way or another, "advocate for orgasm" as a "different ground for a new political engagement." Focusing primarily on Foucault and Deleuze, and limiting her discussion of Warner to his cowritten article with Berlant, "What Does Queer Theory Teach Us about X," Jagose thus sidesteps some of the more prescriptive accounts that present physical receptivity as the ethical basis of queer citizenship. Such accounts tend to overlook the extent to which sexual pleasure has, itself, come to function as a disciplinary mechanism.

In 1984, Gayle Rubin's "Thinking Sex" sparked a wave of sex-positive feminist and queer scholarship regarding the subversive political value of transgressive sexual expression. Making oppression based on sexuality legible *as* oppression, Rubin's essay was primarily intended to provide a descriptive account of how members of erotic minorities are subject to discrimination, moral scapegoating, and state surveillance. However, queer theorists writing in Rubin's legacy have tended, without ignoring erotic injustice, to emphasize a more prescriptive narrative linking political subversion to queer sexual acts. Thus, in his canonical queer polemic *The Trouble with Normal*, published fifteen years later, Michael Warner positions individual acts of erotic transgression as key components of a broader "ethics of queer life" (33). This ethical vision, for Warner, places a collective value on one's willingness to embrace sex in the face of our aversion to its undignified or disreputable qualities.

More than a personal expression of desire or drive, sex emerges in here as an instrument for the ethical—and, as I will argue, the *bioethical*—production of queer citizenship.[7] In this formulation, there remains a perplexing slippage between the descriptive and the prescriptive. At what point does an "ethics" become an imperative? How have rhetorics of sexual optimization, health, and orgasmic capacity been instrumental in the reproduction of antiprophylactic queer citizenship? What forms of feminist or crip agency are readable in acts of sexual refusal?

Indeed, despite his self-described Foucauldian stance, Warner ultimately reproduces a version of the repressive hypothesis in his insistence on the extent to which the culturally enforced moralism around sexuality can "inhibit variation and restrict knowledge about the variations that do exist" (12). The result, he reflects, is a "stunting effect on people who lack resources of knowledge or of experiment" (12). In this account, power may produce "new pleasures, new identities" and "new bodies" (12), but power only truly *operates* through acts of repression, censorship, and inhibition. Benjamin Kahan has referred to this tendency as the "expressive hypothesis," a "reaction formation" in queer writing that makes sex "not just desirable (energizing) but a communitarian necessity" (4). In the shadow of the expressive hypothesis, asexual identifications and practices rarely signify as queer. More frequently, they are framed as malignant symptoms of a culture of shame and repression.

In their essay "Stunted Growth: Asexual Politics and the Rhetoric of Sexual Liberation," Megan Milks (2014) identifies the asexual as "sex positivity's scapegoat" (110). In these narratives of "suspended" "political futurity and agency," asexual subjects are always already scripted as figures "on the wrong end of the narrative of sexual liberation—the obsolescent beginning to which no one wants to return" (108). Lacking proper exposure to transgressive sexualities, politics, and communities, the asexual is thus presumed to be "not yet" sexual and "not yet" queer. Rather than constituting a legitimate site of identification, asexuality remains a site of potentiality on which a narrative of queer futurity and freedom might eventually be written. Put another way, when queer erotic life is put forward as an "ethics," then erotic refusal risks appearing unethical, or at the very least, anticommunitarian. Refusing to partake in the "special sociality" at the heart of queer life, the asexual becomes a repository for queer cultural fantasies and fears regarding the prophylactic policing of transgressive desires and practices.[8] To borrow and invert Rubin's terminology, the queer uneasiness with asexuality might be described as its own "moral panic" regarding the asexual's lack of generativity for queer kinship networks.

We might thus imagine the discourse around asexuality to find a better home among queer theories of the antisocial. Parting ways with Rubin in "Is the Rectum a Grave?" Leo Bersani (1987) rejects the "pastoral impulse" underlying feminist and queer attempts at the "redemptive reinvention of sex" (215). But in refusing to "prettify it, to romanticize it, to maintain that fucking has anything to do with community or love" (215), Bersani simply romanticizes sex differently, famously presenting it as a form of "self-shattering" that revels in "the jouissance of exploded limits" (217). The result is a self-negating experience of ego dissolution that unmasks the fundamental truth of sex: that it is "anticommunal, antiegalitarian, antinurturing, antiloving" (215). Similarly, Lee Edelman's notorious critique of reproductive futurism and appeal to the queer value of antifuturity in his 2004 *No Future* would appear to share much in common with Milks's description of the "suspended" futurity of the asexual. However, sexuality and desire ultimately comprise the core of Edelman's vision, with the sexual perversity of gay male desire emerging, exclusively, as a menace to the sentimentalized asexuality of the Child. Asexuality, rather than occupying the transgressive site of "no future," persists in Edelman's account as the very emblem of reproductive futurity. In all of these visions, queer sex is instrumental to the establishment or undoing of queer relationality. For theorists of queer subcultures, saying "yes" to queer citizenship would appear to mean saying "yes" to sex. And yet, for proponents of the antisocial thesis, saying "no" to queer citizenship would also appear to mean saying "yes" to sex.[9] Meanwhile the asexual, whose erotic refusal is understood to be neither generative nor death-driven, occupies a curious no-man's-land.

There are a small number of queer theoretical texts that do explore sexual refusal as a valuable or transgressive subjectivity. Those works, however, have tended to abstract sexual refusal from asexuality, glossing over asexuality as a lived experience, practice, and identity. Take, for example, Michael Cobb's *Single: Notes on the Uncoupled*, which powerfully critiques the hegemony of the couple form. Taking issue with the presumption that singleness is synonymous with loneliness, Cobb explores the way the refusal to connect intimately with others can open up new modes of personal and political fulfillment. Departing from standard queer critiques of monogamy and marriage, Cobb clarifies that he does not intend to "rehash a tired sexual liberation argument about . . . sex without love; sex without a relationship; and sex without the imperative of marriage" (8). Unlike writers like Warner and Delany, Cobb locates an alternative to the binary logic of the dyadic couple in a regenerating return to the "singular."

While Cobb's valorization of singularity would seem to align with asexuality studies in their mutual legitimization of erotic refusal, nowhere does Cobb explicitly recognize asexuality as a nonheteronormative expression of selfhood or acknowledge the work that asexual activists and subcultures have already done to disrupt the hegemony of the couple form. Indeed, when Cobb proposes that we begin "attaching the letter 'S' to the LGBTQ abbreviation (LGBTQS) so that [he] could affiliate those who were 'single' with the ever-elongating list of nonmajority sexualities" (5), he is only partially in earnest, referring primarily to pop cultural "single ladies" (from Bridget Jones to Beyoncé) and not to those who self-identify on the asexual spectrum. Perhaps more problematically, Cobb ignores the fact that the LGBTQIA acronym has already been expanded to include asexual identities and practices. Asexuality and singlehood are, of course, different identities, and it is not my intention to conflate them here. Instead, I want to highlight the extent to which asexuality is often written out of even those queer discourses that would appear to be allied in the struggle against compulsory sexuality. Rather than a rich elaboration of asexual lives and practices, *Single* ultimately presents a familiar narrative of individual rebellion in the face of totalitarian conformity. Against the couple's mundane routines, miniaturized pleasures, and "forced intimacy" with one another, Cobb argues, is the expansive eroticism of the singular individual whose pleasures center around desire rather than fulfillment. In turning away from society, the uncoupled individual thus experiences an "aesthetics of distance" that is erotically rich with "infinite possibilities" (107). Far from displacing sexuality and desire as the center of queer subjectivity, Cobb transforms singleness into a form of sexual exceptionalism.

Furthermore, with sexual refusal presented as a radical withdrawal from the social as such, Cobb's account of singleness is overlaid with an implicit narrative about bodily capacity. In Thomas Rogers's 2012 interview with Cobb in *Salon*, Rogers asked Cobb whether there might be some practical benefits of coupledom, including the common projection that "when we're older we'll have people around to help us do things like . . . move boxes across the floor." Playful as this inquiry was, the topic might have opened an important dialogue about disability, access, assistive technology, and the increasing privatization of carework. Cobb's response, however, reproduced a familiar American narrative of rugged self-reliance. To bring the question of physical incapacity into the conversation, he ruminates, is like

> trying to predict the future, and you could be living with someone who's blocking your happiness that's not letting you flourish. People

think, "I can endure an awful relationship for a number of years as long as they can help me move the box across the floor." But think about how often do you really move boxes that require that much assistance . . . I was just with a friend who was helping his great-aunt go to his grandma's house. She lived in this two-story house by herself, and she was able to move around and do stuff in her 90s and seemed happy.

Without placing too much emphasis on these somewhat informal remarks, I want to call attention to the implication here, and elsewhere in *Single*, that the exceptionalism of the single person is animated by, or by a property of, able-bodiedness. Framing the eventuality of physical impairment as a paranoid fantasy, Cobb reinscribes disability as the "sign of no future."[10] To even imagine a disabled future, he implies, is to construct a roadblock that inhibits one's own "flourish[ing]." And yet, even as Cobb encourages us not to "predict the future," he puts forward his own indisputable emblem of able-bodied futurity in the image of an uncoupled and self-reliant ninety-year-old woman. As the exception that fails to prove the rule that "if we live long enough, we will all become disabled," her perpetual physical mobility is presented as both the prerequisite to and the effect of living an uncoupled life. She is the nondisabled antidote to what Cobb refers to at one point in his book as the "crippled unity" of the couple (149). Indeed, Cobb's fidelity to a model of Emersonian self-reliance, both here and throughout his book, leads to an implicit suggestion that the single individual is physically capacitated by her lack of dependence on the other. Far from bearing the medicalized stigma of asexuality, she is robust in her autonomy, a powerhouse of untapped erotic potential.

Taken together, these accounts of queer erotic capacitation participate in the structures of what asexuality scholars have called "compulsory sexuality."[11] In framing sex and desire as universally positive and enriching, they not only participate in the erasure of asexual identities but also obscure some of the second wave's more pessimistic insights—that sex can often function as a source of violence and control. In a commentary in *Feminist Studies*, K. J. Cerankowski and Megan Milks suggest that a serious consideration of asexuality has the potential to "challeng[e] many of the basic tenets of pro-sex feminism—most obviously its privileging of transgressive female sexualities that are always already defined against repressive or 'anti-sex' sexualities" ("New Orientations," 656). Cerankowski and Milks are careful to acknowledge that asexuality does not automatically map onto radical feminist claims;

rather, the intersection between asexuality and feminism is one possible site for questioning the rhetoric of liberation that dominates sex-positive feminist and queer framings of sexuality as such. This approach makes legible not only lesbian resistance to compulsory *hetero*sexuality but also *asexual* resistance to a much broader set of compulsory systems governing erotic identification—systems in which even queers may sometimes find themselves complicit.

In her online essay, "The Ethical Prude: Imagining an Authentic Sex-Negative Feminism," Lisa Millbank critiques Easton and Hardy's book *The Ethical Slut* for its inability to imagine agency in sexual refusal. Taking issue with the authors' "radical proposition that sex is nice and pleasure is good for you," Millbank argues that such a proposition "create[s] space for every sexual possibility except for one: the possibility to consider whether sex may *not* be nice."[12] To consider the possibility that "sex may not be nice" is not, of course, to declare that sex is never nice, or that it is always experienced as a threat or as violence. More descriptive than prescriptive, it mandates neither pleasure nor prohibition, only the acknowledgment that there can be good reasons for turning away from sex's seemingly undeniable pleasures. If antiprophylactic masculinity requires a certain optimism that what doesn't kill you makes you stronger—building immunity and resistance through an ethics of exposure—then perhaps a feminist approach to the antiprophylactic is one that acknowledges the way past injuries have transformed our relationship to the world. It might follow calls, like Ann Cvetkovich's in *Archive of Feelings*, for a "sex positivity that can embrace negativity, including trauma" (63). Like Sara Ahmed's figure of the "feminist killjoy," Jack Halberstam's illustration of "shadow feminism" (*The Queer Art of Failure*), Sianne Ngai's extended meditation on "ugly feelings," and Heather Love's recuperation of "backwardness" (*Feeling Backward*), these feminist commitments to negativity take damage and vulnerability on its own terms. Despite the promises of queer sociability, they remind us that certain boundaries might be worth preserving.

Queer Permeability

John Cameron Mitchell's independent film *Shortbus* (2006) watches in many ways like *Times Square Red, Times Square Blue*'s younger sibling. A fictionalized document of queer public sex in contemporary New York City, the film stages a set of polymorphously perverse couplings between individuals and groups across a spectrum of genders and orientations. Throughout the film, the scenes that take place at the Shortbus gatherings are relaxed and lively, filled with unexpected connections and intimacies between characters. A salon and cabaret as well as a sex party, the intercourse that takes place within its walls is not only sexual but (in the spirit of "contact") artistic and intellectual. Echoing the salon's historical location within a broader genealogy of sexual dissent, Justin Bond describes the space as being "like the sixties, only with less hope." But its post-9/11 context is not the only thing that separates the Shortbus salon from Delany's Times Square subcultures. Unlike the porn theaters, *Shortbus*'s sex parties take place within a private residence and operate by invitation only. Notably, they are less racially and socioeconomically diverse than the porn theaters described in Delany's account, though the space does boast a greater diversity of gendered bodies.[13]

There is also a generic shift in the film's treatment of sexuality. While Delany's essay documents the sexual subcultures that organize around the screening of pornographic films, *Shortbus* itself constitutes a film that treads a fine line between art and erotica. Described by *GQ* as "the most sexually explicit film to ever go on general release," *Shortbus* pioneers in its use of frequent unsimulated sex scenes in which, Mitchell assures us, nearly all of the orgasms are real. With *Shortbus*, Linda Williams observes, "Mitchell set out to make a uniquely American film of hard-core art that might leave his viewers with a feel-good afterglow" (*Screening Sex*, 284). Taking the film as a "knowing counterpoint" to the traditional American pornographic genre, Williams notes the way that *Shortbus* is both "modeled on the quintessential pornographic narrative" but also "operates as corrective to the isolation and fixation on bodies that solitary porn can engender" (288). Indeed, one of the film's most striking twists on the pornographic narrative is its seemingly total disinterest in producing sexual arousal in the viewer. Commentators frequently observe that, despite its hardcore depiction of sex, the film is not particularly sexy. In the end, the "feel-good afterglow" that Williams points to is more sentimental than sexual, prioritizing personal/political liberation over physical release.

In the DVD commentary, Mitchell describes his attempt to invert the standard critical practice of locating sexual subtexts in seemingly nonsexual images and narratives. In making a film that is wholly about sex, he explains, sex itself can stand in as a figure for broader themes and issues. Bringing these observations to bear on a particularly memorable threesome between James, Jamie, and Ceth, Mitchell observes: "We truly are talking about the optimism of the U.S. The ingenuity. And even the position that the three of them are in is rather ingenious. There's resonances of this pursuit of happiness." Thus, for Mitchell, the gymnastic qualities of some of the film's sexual acts gesture, albeit irreverently, toward a set of reinvented American patriotic ideals. This point is humorously underscored at a different moment during the same three-way when Jamie delivers what one critic calls a "proctological rendition of the 'Star Spangled Banner,'" singing the national anthem as he performs anilingus on Ceth. Ceth soon joins the vocal performance, using James's penis as a microphone; before long, all three men are laughingly and exuberantly belting out the lyrics.[14] Though playful in tone, moments like these invite us to take seriously the film's status as a reflection on American democracy. Like Delany, Mitchell proposes a vision of antiprophylactic citizenship in which acts of civic engagement are presented through the vehicle of bodily sexual exchange.

The film's opening sequence invites us immediately to reflect on the porosity of national borders, as the camera pans across an animated model of the New York City landscape, lingering finally on the body of the Statue of Liberty. Named "mother of exiles" by Emma Lazarus in her nineteenth-century poem, the statue recalls histories of immigration that wed American identity to the promise (if not always the practice) of hospitality. After this prolonged gaze at one of our most recognizable national icons, the viewer (rendered infinitely mobile by the camera's panoramic sweep) is transported into and out of the windows of multiple apartments where a series of frustrated sex acts are taking place in isolation. These short sexual vignettes serve as our introduction to all of the principal characters. James attempts, in a series of gymnastically impressive positions, to fellate himself; Severin, a dominatrix, exchanges a set of caustic remarks with the client she is pleasuring; and Sofia and her husband copulate in a series of urgent and comically acrobatic positions. The isolated nature of these opening vignettes demonstrates a kind of prophylactic angst, showcasing sex without connection and pleasure without intimacy. But this prophylactic angst is political as well, suggesting a body politic hopelessly fragmented by a set of national and even global traumas. Between two of these bedroom vignettes, the viewer is reminded that this New York cityscape is one that is uniquely shaped (and damaged) by the 9/11 attacks. Moving across the city from James's bedroom, the frame stops for several seconds on an animated facsimile of Ground Zero. During this brief gaze at the two visible spaces where the towers used to stand, the animation dissolves into realism, and Ground Zero comes into clear photographic focus. Panning upward to a neighboring window, we witness an encounter between Severin and her client, Jesse, who between the cracks of the whip engages her in a discussion about the Iraq War. Thus psychological wounds become associated with the scarred New York landscape and sexual alienation is mapped seamlessly onto Bush-era political apathy.

It is precisely this set of early associations that allows Mitchell and his ensemble to present the literal space of *Shortbus* as both a sexual and a political antidote to this alienation. If sex between couples, in private, isolated bedrooms signifies political apathy and resignation, then the public nature of sex in *Shortbus* begins to look, strikingly, like revolution. Perhaps the most immediate connection between political resistance and public sexuality is the "Sex-Not-Bombs" room, the most explicit site of sexuality within the Shortbus salon. While other rooms witness misfired communication between friends and lovers, this public, fleshy paradise at the heart of the Shortbus salon is peaceable and serene, an edgy reinvention of the idealistic 1960s slogan "Make Love, Not War." As Sofia enters the "Sex-Not-Bombs" room for the first time, both she and the viewer are confronted with an amorphous mass of limbs; dozens of bodies intertwine in ways that are complicated and disorienting while simultaneously maintaining a cooperative unity. This is perhaps a version of what Preciado envisions when he speculates: "What if, in reality, the insatiable bodies of the multitude—their cocks, clitorises, anuses, hormones, and neurosexual synapses—what if desire, excitement, sexuality, seduction, and the pleasure of the multitude were all the mainsprings of the creation of value added to the contemporary economy? And what if cooperation were a masturbatory cooperation and not the simple cooperation of brains?" (37). The "masturbatory cooperation" of the "insatiable bodies" that populate *Shortbus*'s pansexual orgy can be read here as a cipher for how antiprophylactic citizenship might be reinvented in the pharmacopornographic era.[15]

Tobias, the elderly former mayor of New York, becomes the spokesperson for this vision of sexual citizenship during an intimate pedagogical moment with Ceth. After Ceth meets Tobias during a technological mishap involving Ceth's mobile device and Tobias's pacemaker, the two begin a conversation in which Tobias reflects:

> But you know what's the most wonderful thing about New York? It's where everyone comes to get fucked. It's one of the last places where people are still willing to bend over to let in the new. And the old. New Yorkers are very permeable . . . Therefore, we're sane. Consequently, we're the target of the impermeable. And the insane. And of course, New York is where everyone comes to be forgiven. . . . People said I didn't do enough, to help prevent the AIDS crisis, because I was in the closet. That's not true. I did the best I could. I was scared, and impermeable. Everybody knew so little then. I know even less, now.

Here, Tobias articulates an antiprophylactic vision of queer "permeability" that links sexual openness to personal and collective well-being. Permeability is presented here not only as contributing to psychological health (keeping one "sane") but also, materially, to the promotion of queer public health. Powerfully inverting the conservative logic through which the AIDS epidemic signifies as a problem of promiscuously breached bodily boundaries, Tobias reframes the transmission of the virus as a problem of personal and political "impermeability" in which not enough people, himself included, were willing to "bend over to let in the new." The "new," in this context, might be defined as new attitudes about queer desire, new political investments in the health of gay men, new forms of sex education, new prevention techniques, or new medical research into the virus. Far from representing genuine protection from the health crisis, prophylactic "impermeability" is put forth as that which most imperils the health of a population.

Psychiatric disability plays a curious role in this description, however, with the arguably crip virtues of antiprophylaxis aligned with the ableist language of "sanity." In this formulation, the "insane" are defined as those "impermeable" antisex moralists intent on preserving a white middle-class illusion of comfort and safety. While Tobias's rhetoric here is intended to address the moral panic of the AIDS epidemic, it has the unintentional effect of marginalizing those who do experience mental illness. Indeed, the equivalence between insanity and impermeability is particularly troubling in a moment when requests for psychiatric accommodations and safe pedagogical spaces for trauma survivors are routinely dismissed as expressions of bourgeois entitlement or as a mere resistance to feeling "uncomfortable."[16]

With this in mind, we might observe the prophylactic terms in which James's psychiatric distress—as well as its cure—is framed. In the video that James creates prior to his suicide attempt, he includes several shots of his antidepressant medication arranged in an eccentric flower pattern. The medication has been ineffective, this moment tells us—better used for aesthetic expression than psychiatric treatment. James's rejection of the medicalization of his distress, particularly as it is managed by a global pharmaceutical industry, resonates powerfully with antipsychiatry and psychiatric survivor movements. However, the method through which James is "cured" ultimately sidesteps a more difficult set of questions about alternative forms of support that can be offered to individuals who experience depression. Confiding in Severin, James tells her, "I never let him [Jamie] fuck me. I never let anyone fuck me," confessing later to Caleb that all of the love he sees around him "stops at my skin. I can't let it inside." James's depression is thus presented as a problem of numbness and insulation whose solution lies in the lowering of his personal and sexual boundaries—an act that will allow him to feel and connect with the world around him. In allowing Caleb to finally penetrate him, the film implies, James exchanges his stubborn commitment to individual autonomy (recall the "closed circuit" of his earlier attempt at self-fellatio) for an antiprophylactic commitment to queer sociability. But to read this moment as unquestionably redemptive is to ignore the troubling fact that Caleb has spent the majority of the film stalking James and photographing him without consent. Earlier, Caleb refuses to stop kissing James when presented with James's repeated and vigorous noes. Thus, rather than cultivating a therapeutic environment for James to work through his complicated emotions, the film presents his psychiatric rehabilitation as a function of personal willingness to finally take risks, to reject safety, to "bend over and let in the new."

Indeed, there is a certain paradox in Mitchell's prizing of physical permeability. Infectiously crip, on the one hand, and coercively rehabilitative on the other, permeability functions as a sort of inverted health balm—a welcoming of contagion that is designed to inoculate and fortify the body against disease and distress. Like the ALAS virus in Brin's story, queer permeability authorizes an outbreak of communal sentiment and sexual affect that cures social diseases.[17] But with sex acts doubling as acts of patriotism, there is a risk that practices of sexual refusal can begin to look like political apathy or civic irresponsibility. Though the Shortbus salon is presented as a sexually democratic landscape where all variations are accepted and encouraged, there is, at the same time, an implicit judgment of those unwilling or unable to open themselves up to sexual pleasure. In what follows, I turn toward a somewhat different figuration of disability within *Shortbus*—Sofia's medicalized "frigidity" and her rehabilitation (via queer sex) into a new state of health and wholeness. Presented as the central problem that the narrative must solve, Sofia's nonorgasmic body exposes the extent to which able-bodiedness, as a compulsory system, requires its subjects to be adequately sexualized.

Sexual Healing

Early in *Shortbus*, partners James and Jamie meet Sofia, a sexually frustrated sex therapist whose inability to experience orgasm has created tension within her own marriage to her husband. In an attempt to help her experience her first orgasm, the two invite Sofia to attend one of Shortbus's sex parties. It is here that Sofia meets and develops a friendship with the dominatrix, Severin, who attempts to coach Sofia in her quest for an orgasm. Though Severin's guidance proves to be mostly ineffective, Sofia does finally experience her first orgasm during the exuberant orgy that concludes the film. Focusing on Sofia's narrative arc from sexual frigidity to sexual functionality allows us to explore the ways in which discourses of queer sex-positivity can pair with the ideology of ability to produce two intimately related forms of marginalization, denying sexuality to some while making it compulsory for others.

When Sofia makes her first visit to the Shortbus salon, Justin Bond presents her with the following brief explanation of the space she is entering: "Do you know what a shortbus is? You've heard of the big yellow school bus. Well this is the short one. It's a salon for the gifted and challenged." Invoking a shared legacy of medical othering, the film urges its sexual misfits to say "no" to normalcy and "yes" to sex, banding together with their disabled counterparts for an irreverent erotic joyride. Here the historical linkages between queerness and disability are not a source of shame but rather something to be claimed, celebrated, and defiantly flaunted. But from a disability studies perspective, we might justifiably question, if the Shortbus salon is truly a space for the "gifted and challenged," why we do not see more disabled bodies populating the space. The few glimpses of physical disability we do get are brief and perplexing. A man identifying himself as an albino recognizes Jamie from the sitcom that Jamie had starred in as a child, but their brief interaction functions more as comic relief than social commentary ("I'm an albino!" had been Jamie's character's catch phrase).[18] And while a pacemaker malfunction throws the elderly Tobias into the arms of young and nondisabled Ceth, the arguably crip kiss they share remains relatively chaste, with Ceth saving most of his actual bending over for his encounter with James and Jamie later that night.

Furthermore, as the camera traverses the spaces of the salon, the bodies that we see are, for the most part, young and fit, often displaying feats of impressive flexibility and athleticism. One notable exception to this homogeneity of body types occurs when the camera briefly lingers on a sexual pairing between a fat individual and a thin one. But, tellingly, both individuals are shot from the neck down, revealing their bodies but not their faces. Given how frequently the camera seems to linger on faces throughout the film (often sealing a set of intimate bonds between characters via the exchange of long, wordless looks), these faceless bodies stand out as being outside of its erotic fold, objects rather than subjects. We might almost read their presence as a kind of superficial "proof" of the film's commitment to diversity, eccentric furnishings that decorate rather than truly inhabit the space of the salon. In these ways, the film falls short of forging the connections between queerness and disability that its vocabulary so suggestively gestures toward. This absence of physically disabled bodies in the Shortbus salon perpetuates what Russell Shuttleworth has referred to as the "imposition of asexuality" onto disabled bodies—the ubiquitous representation of people with disabilities as undesirable as well as uninterested in or incapable of sexual expression.

It's important to note, too, that the same ideology that imposes asexuality on certain disabled bodies can also impose sexuality on certain nondisabled bodies. As Tobin Siebers observes, the "ideology of ability" creates the assumption that "the more healthy a person is, the better the sex life is supposed to be. Whence the imperative in today's culture to 'work on' one's sex life,' to 'improve' or 'better' it, to do special exercises or adopt a special diet . . . all for the purpose of discovering 'the ultimate pleasure'" ("A Sexual Culture for Disabled People," 40–42). In pointing to the ableist rhetorics of optimization that drive popular discourse on sexuality, Siebers's primary purpose is to showcase the way disabled people have been excluded from its erotic fold. Nonetheless, these observations have important implications for asexuality. If sexuality is aligned with health, then those who refuse to chase "the ultimate pleasure" are seen as falling away from health norms, transformed into objects of medical scrutiny, intervention, and diagnosis. In her article "How Much Sex Is Healthy?: The Pleasures of Asexuality," Eunjung Kim has remarked upon the ways that individuals thought to possess inadequate levels of sexual drive are "subject to a pathologizing framework that demands a 'cure' and 'help' under the premise that sexual desire is universally and constantly present in adult life and that its absence reflects pathology or causes harm" (159). Despite an increasingly visible asexual community that rejects medical labels in favor of more affirmative models of minority identity, psychiatric professionals nonetheless persist in interpreting the asexual disinterest in sex as a sign of repression, traumatic avoidance, or other forms of psychological blockage.[19]

In such contexts, the rhetoric of sexual liberation risks becoming indistinguishable from "compulsory" sites of sexual rehabilitation. Thus Ela Przybylo explores the peculiar style of Foucauldian "confession" that attends the medicalization of low or absent sexual desire. Using the term "sexuosociety" to refer to the ubiquity of practices, representations, compulsions, and repetitions designed to naturalize sexuality as an innate human drive, Przybylo observes the way that "absence" itself becomes transformed into a tangible lack that must be "confessed" and mobilized into discourse. Though asexuality may be "threatening to sexual subjects," she observes, "it also works to resuscitate sexuality, calling for future articulations of sexuality" and "coercing us into a defence of sexuality" (3). Such diagnostic frameworks, in other words, are accompanied by a set of temporal frameworks through which the asexual individual can only be imagined as either regressively presexual or traumatically postsexual. Their present state of lack is always already defined against a past or future of mythic sexual wholeness.

When Sofia first discloses her inability to have an orgasm to Jamie and James during couples' therapy, the shape her confession takes reproduces precisely these temporal imperatives. The session starts out well enough, but a disagreement between Sofia and Jamie eventually evolves into a screaming match. After regaining her composure, Sofia delivers a mortified apology to her clients, followed by the explanation: "I'm pre-orgasmic." Jamie responds supportively but warily, "Does that mean you're about to have one?" The forward-looking teleology of Sofia's phrasing, coupled with the comic misunderstanding that it produces in Jamie, are telling. Sofia *is* in fact preorgasmic, as her confession of sexual dysfunction initiates a sequence of rehabilitative interventions that will indeed, by the end of the film, result in her first orgasm. Recalling Milks's observations that asexuality is framed as a type of "stunted growth," Sofia's confession already anticipates the orgasm/cure that will usher her presently lacking body into a future state of physical health and emotional wholeness. Sofia's confession is, of course, all the more scandalous since she is herself a "sex therapist." While we might therefore read the scene as offering a compelling critique of medical authority, the result appears to be little more than a straightforward role reversal. The doctor (Sofia) becomes a patient, and the patients (James and Jamie) are redefined as experts who immediately implement a rigorous treatment regimen.

Indeed, in a dynamic that on some level rehearses the historical narrative of the frigid woman who places her sexually dysfunctional body in the capable hands of male doctors, James and Jamie "prescribe" for Sofia a visit to the Shortbus salon—a space that itself opens up new opportunities for confession and therapeutic intervention. First there is Shabbos Goy, the self-identified "orgasmic superhero" who informs her that her lack of orgasm is "unacceptable" and offers to help her "turn on [her] lights." Then there is Justin Bond, who asks her how the "big O is coming" and reassures her that she "has what it takes" if she would only "loosen up." And finally there is Severin, who probes for the traumatic root of Sofia's disorder by grilling her about her childhood. The incitement to discourse that Sofia's asexual "confession of absence" sets in motion thus appears to reveal less about Sofia and more about the significance her orgasm holds for the community around her.[20]

Justin Bond articulates the public value of Sofia's sexuality when he directs her to visualize her sexuality in relation to "a sort of magical circuit board, a motherboard, filled with desire that travels all over the world. That touches you, that touches me. That connects everybody. You just have to find the right connection, the right circuitry. Look at all these people out there: They're trying to find the right connection. And I personally expect a few blown fuses before the night is over. And maybe one of them will be yours." Bond's vision of the salon as a "magical circuit board" of queer erotic sociality resonates with Preciado's description of the "living pansexual body as the bioport of orgasmic force" (43). It also, interestingly, echoes earlier medical framings of the asexual individual as someone who "behaves as though his sexual circuits have been 'shut down'" (267). "In these discourses," Kim explains, "sexuality was imagined as kind of electricity and the human body as a series of circuits that responded to certain stimuli; in this rhetoric, an asexual individual becomes a broken system" (267). It is clear that Sofia understands herself as precisely such a "broken system" when she frames her "problem" as a "clog in my neural pathway, somewhere between my brain and my clitoris." This metaphor is soon literalized in the blackout that—at the moment of Sofia's most intense sexual frustration—abruptly blankets the city in darkness.

But not simply a "broken system," Sofia is also more fundamentally a breaker *of* the system. Like the interruption of electrical flow caused by a literal circuit breaker, her (a)sexual "blackout" constitutes a prophylactic "short circuit" on Shortbus's dynamic and interrelational "motherboard." With Sofia's neural missed connections reimagined as the crossed wires that impede healthy queer sociability, orgasm comes to represent not only a personal triumph but a social duty, as one person's "clog" has the potential to short circuit the entire system. It is in this way that Sofia's and Bond's similar metaphors reflect very different sensibilities regarding the relationship between individual and community. Sofia's circuit board relates solely to her own body, interpreting her lack of "connection" as an isolated medical problem. Bond's circuit board, by contrast, replaces internal wiring with global networking, situating Sofia's blocked or "clogged" desires within an expansive interaction of cultural and interpersonal forces. Rather than traveling merely from the "brain" to the "clitoris," this desire "travels all over the world" and "connects everybody" to everybody else.

It's tempting to read Bond's circuit board as the transgressive alternative to Sofia's seemingly more repressive rendering of her "condition." But while Bond's social model of desire shifts emphasis away from individual "dysfunction," the imperative toward rehabilitation remains—these are broken circuits that call for repair. This insight is related visually as Sofia experiences her orgasm/cure in the final moments of the film during a three-way encounter with a nameless heterosexual couple. A close-up on Sofia's face, bathed in light, reveals her ecstasy. Literalizing Sofia's status as a "bioport of orgasmic force" (43), the film cuts to an aerial shot of the city where lights radiate geographically outward from the site of the salon. Electricity is restored to the city of New York as sexual capacity is restored to Sofia's previously "preorgasmic" body. Here we are presented with a vision of sexual "healing" that resonates with Delany's centrifugal model of civic intimacy: contact begins with a singular "connection" that expands outward, "giv[ing] one a faithful and loving attitude toward one's neighborhood, one's city, one's nation, the world" (*Times Square Red, Times Square Blue*, 126). Ultimately, Sofia's body comes to function like ALAS's patient zero, originating a pandemic of goodwill that reaches beyond geographic boundaries. Indeed, as the aerial shot of the salon eventually widens to a cosmological perspective, we witness the lights expand beyond New York City, lighting up the state, the country, and, ultimately, the entire globe. In the film's final image, this glowing planetary image begins to spin like a record with dizzying speed—literalizing, perhaps, the notion that "revolution" has finally been achieved. Recalling Mitchell's account of queer sexuality as a cipher for American "ingenuity," "optimism," and the "pursuit of happiness," Sofia's moment of orgasmic antiprophylaxis is thus framed as part of a broader patriotic imperative. As the credits roll, the lyrics of the accompanying soundtrack ("Surgery" by Scott Matthews) suggest that Sofia has just experienced a life-saving medical intervention—one that has positive consequences for everyone's public health.[21]

Despite its sexual mandates, *Shortbus* does present some provocative instances of erotic refusal. Though Sofia generally plays the role of the willing patient, she is not entirely uncritical of the ways in which ideologies of compulsory sexuality circulate, reflecting at one point to Jamie and James: "You know, I feel like we're inundated by images of these super deluxe babes in the throes of the ultimate orgasm. I think it's just some myth to sell more magazines." The subtle gender critique embedded in this reflection (women as sexualized objects of consumer desire), takes an even more explicit form when, during an intimate discussion with a small group of lesbians and transmen, Sofia is asked to share a description of what sex feels like to her. Though her reply begins with false enthusiasm, it soon unravels into a narrative of female alienation. She says: "Sex is really awesome. I love sex. We all know that sex feels terrific. I love it, love it a lot. It's a great work out. It feels good.

And I love, you know, loving my husband. It's just, you know, there just comes a point sometimes where it gets to be a lot of pressure and it feels like, 'ah!' like someone's going to kill me and so I just have to smile and pretend to enjoy it, and that way I can survive." As Sofia's superficial insistence that she "loves sex" unravels throughout her monologue, it's important to note that the details she chooses to include as evidence ("it's a great workout") reveal the extent to which compulsory sexuality is wedded to a narrative about health. Furthermore, in framing her experience of sexuality in terms of a perceived violence, she also echoes radical feminist theories about phallocentric sexuality (like those of Andrea Dworkin and Catharine MacKinnon), observations that—while often deeply problematic and dubiously enacted in the legal sphere—are also perhaps too quickly dismissed in our current era of sex-positive queer liberation. Even more striking is the way that Sofia's monologue brings to a screeching halt the room's previously cheerful utopian vibe. While the queers in the room are not exactly unsupportive, there is also a sense that her confession, in disrupting the harmony of the space, has crossed a line—everyone except Severin stares at her with dumbfounded horror.

At this moment, it is Severin who makes what might be interpreted as the gesture of greatest asexual solidarity, snapping a picture of Sofia with her Polaroid camera. Though she is immediately chastised by everyone in the room, including Sofia, for her rude behavior, we might understand her inappropriate photography at this moment as an attempt to document, preserve, and ultimately respect the feminist asexual epiphany she has just witnessed. Severin's choice of medium may be understood as enacting its own peculiar form of asexual resistance. As Matthew Tinckom trenchantly observes, the sexual repression of *Shortbus*'s female characters can be partially explained, within the film's logic, through their lack of fluency with digital technologies. Bond's "magical circuit board," Tinckom suggests, "connects Sofia's orgasm to computers and networks while also framing them in the highly mystified terms of an unseen magic" (702). But while we see neither Sofia nor Severin "engaging in such magic of the digital," they are engaged in alternative "analog" forms of expression. Tinckom observes that "Severin makes photographic images, but they are on Polaroid self-developing film, which produces singular prints with no negatives for replication and dispersal. In short, the women are unfulfilled because their sexuality is not networked to a technology that would allow them to find a partner with 'the right circuitry'" (702). Severin's insistence on hanging onto certain outdated forms of image production—ones that do not lend themselves easily to digital "sharing"—thus codes her sexuality as self-contained, antisocial, and prophylactic. Despite her occupation as a sex worker (or perhaps precisely because of this fact), Severin is careful to safeguard her own experiences of erotic satisfaction within a private realm, refusing to allow them to circulate within the public sphere. With this in mind, we may in fact read Severin as occupying the most exciting and generative site of asexual—or at the very least autoerotic—resistance in the film, as she is constantly turning away from the various forms of sexual relationality she is presented with.

In one of the first essays to treat asexuality as a source of identification, rather than as a pathology, Myra T. Johnson proposes the existence of "two invisible groups": "asexual women" and "autoerotic women." Severin's practices strongly resonate with the latter category, as she explains throughout the narrative that though she enjoys masturbating, she has little to no interest in sharing her sexuality with a partner. Might, then, Sofia and Severin's largely nonsexual friendship be understood as a type of solidarity formed along an "asexual continuum" and in resistance to the structures of compulsory sexuality? This interpretation is, of course, belied by several of the film's events, including a sexual encounter between the two. The encounter itself is presented as asymmetrical and tense; Severin achieves orgasm while Sofia lies beneath her, alienated and uncomfortable. Also problematic is the fact that their friendship is based on the idea that they might each help cure the other of their mutual sexual dysfunction. As Severin remarks to Sofia, "I know I can help you have an orgasm, and maybe you can help me like have a real human interaction with someone." Though their coexistence on the asexual continuum may not always result in active forms of asexual resistance to compulsory sexuality, their pairing does seem to open up some productive alternatives to the ethic of compulsory sexuality that dominates the rest of the film.

For example, when asked by Jesse, her repeat client, to describe her last orgasm, Severin responds, "It was great. It was like time had stopped and I was completely alone." Sexuality, for Severin, is not about solidifying the bonds of queer community but about cultivating for herself a space of sexual privacy. Furthermore, if Sofia's performance of compulsory sexuality includes a reassurance that she "loves loving her husband," then Severin's acts of autoerotic resistance are edged, at times, with an unapologetic dismissal of phallic sexuality. When Jesse asks Severin what "superpower" she most desires, she sardonically replies, "the power to make you interesting." Severin's admission of boredom carries a feminist edge that seems especially productive in cutting through the post-sex-war binary between the "prosex" embrace of all things perverse and the perceived "antisex" stance of the second wave. Severin may not fit easily under the banner of sex-positive queer feminism, but neither is she framed by the radical feminist language of the always-already exploited sex worker. Her avoidance of sexual relationships is not a matter of trauma or victimhood but of indifference. Occupying the major space of queer refusal in the film, Severin is constantly reprimanded for what other characters perceive as her antisocial behavior. Yet it is precisely these refusals that open up a space for her and Sofia to experiment with their own form of homosocial bonding, one that is rife with generative failures. Though Severin approaches Sofia with the hope that they can teach one another how to find, to use Bond's words, "the right connection," this ultimately turns out to be a botched pedagogical project; Sofia does not succeed in teaching Severin to be socially and sexually "permeable" any more than Severin succeeds in helping Sofia produce her first orgasm. And yet, Sofia and Severin's spectacular failure to "educate" one another may open up a space for thinking through alternatives to both Mitchell's and Delany's utopian sexual projects.

After all, Severin's indifference to sexual relationality also manifests in an unruly resistance to treatment. Though she makes a set of half-hearted attempts throughout the film to change her autoerotic ways, by the final scene, Severin remains the only "broken" character who remains stubbornly unfixed. This is reflected in the orgy/sing-along that concludes the film, where Severin, though present, is the only character who is unmoved to participate. Observing the scene, instead, from an armchair in the corner of the room, she ends the film with one last gesture of erotic refusal—though she does find other nonsexual ways to join in the revelry. When a small marching band strolls past her, she playfully swats one of their cymbals. A minute later, as the music swells to a crescendo, she opens her mouth to emit what appears to be a gleeful scream. Though that scream is soon eclipsed by Sofia's orgasm (which, in ending the film, effectively takes the "last word"), these moments might be understood as providing a subtle reminder that empowered connection to oneself and others can be found not only through the act of saying "yes" to sex but also through the act saying "no."

Slowly Turning to Grit

To what extent can we name stone butch untouchability as a variation on asexuality? While these identities are certainly not reducible to each other, the memoirs of disabled trans writer Eli Clare create a space for thinking about how they nonetheless reach into and condition one another. My discussion of Clare's work draws from the assumption that we can identify certain stone identities as contributing to what Ela Przybylo and Danielle Cooper call a "queerly asexual archive" ("Asexual Resonances," 302). To queer the asexual archive is to adopt an interpretive methodology that "trace[s] asexuality in unexpected, and perhaps even undesirable, locations" (304). Emphasizing "asexual 'resonances'—what we understand as a certain texture, sensibility, or implication of asexuality"—this reading practice "shifts the focus from asexual identities to asexual traces, touches, instances" (304). While Clare never explicitly identifies as asexual in his autobiographical writing, there are strong "asexual resonances" in his negotiation of his stone butch identity, his transness, his disability, and his trauma.

One of the most recognizable features of stone butch sexuality is the desire not to be touched by an intimate partner or given direct sexual pleasure. This desire is often informed by personal histories of gendered violence, including sexual assault, public humiliation, and police brutality. In both his 2017 memoir *Brilliant Imperfection* and his earlier memoir *Exile and Pride*, published in 1999, Clare discusses the experiences of rape and recurring childhood physical abuse that led him to vacate his body, to dissociate from feeling, to become nonresponsive. As Ann Cvetkovich observes, stone butch subjectivity can be illuminated by trauma theory's emphasis on "turning numb or not feeling at all, such as Freud's image of the organism warding off sensation through the toughening of the cortical shield" (*Archive of Feelings*, 66). Against imperatives of feminine receptivity, and in contrast to the portraits of masculine "permeability" that I've outlined throughout this book, stone butch sexuality encodes a certain emotional and physical hardening. While the antiprophylactic citizen is defined by his willingness to leave his body perpetually open to sensation, stone butch identifications are most commonly associated with the necessity of "warding off sensation," often through acts of sexual refusal. But while stone butch sexuality may emerge as a relatively straightforward foil to antiprophylactic citizenship, Clare reveals a more complex narrative that troubles the very distinctions between inside and outside, incorporation and defense, sensation and anesthesia.

To understand how antiprophylaxis works differently for Clare, we need to take trauma seriously, acknowledging the way pain can inform, and sometimes even initiate, our journeys through queerness, transness, disability, and asexuality. In *Exile and Pride*, Clare notes the way the "markers of masculinity" he has adopted align with the "markers of disability," including a "heavy-heeled gait," his "halting, uneven speech," and the "tremors in [his] hands, arms, and shoulders," which all "twine together to shape me in the ableist world as either genderless or a teenage boy" (131). Clare writes: "I think about my disabled body, how as a teenager I escaped the endless pressure to have a boyfriend, to shave my legs, to wear make-up. The same lies that cast me as genderless, asexual, and undesirable also framed a space in which I was left alone to be my quiet, bookish, tomboy self, neither girl nor boy. Even then, I was grateful" (130). Here, the presumed equivalence between disability and asexuality, though itself a source of oppression, provides Clare with a necessary refuge from the demands of compulsory heterosexuality as well as compulsory gender.

By decentering sexual pleasure as the exclusive site of queer and crip agency, Clare disrupts a normalizing narrative within disability studies that presents the disabled subject's ability to engage in sexual expression as the index of their humanity. Responding to the persistent cultural refusal to see disabled bodies as sexual, crip theory has usefully claimed the tools of sex positivity to reinvent the disabled body as a site of endless erotic invention and sexual capacity.[22] However, in liberating physical disability from asexual stigma, these writers often miss opportunities to engage with and affirm asexual identifications and practices. Developing a concept of "normate sex," for example, Abby Wilkerson considers the subtle ableism at work in structures of homophobia, transphobia, and intersex oppression. Exploring the way queer, trans, and intersex bodies have been the target of medically pathologizing frameworks and therapeutic interventions, Wilkerson finds a crip value in traditionally queer practices of sexual dissent. But because Wilkerson primarily conceives of disability liberation in terms of sexual liberation, she presents the solution to medical objectification in the form of trans and intersex erotics. In one passage, for example, Wilkerson describes a femme lover's desire for her butch/FTM partner's body as an example of one of the ways that transgender sexuality can be reclaimed. Trans is made "sexy" here, but for whose benefit? And is erotophobia really at the core of the kinds of trans oppression Wilkerson describes? Like Preciado, Wilkerson presents transgender and intersex subjects as erotic minorities whose liberation, like that of disabled subjects, lies in the realm of erotic expression.

But as Robert McRuer cautions, a "crip theory of sexuality," in addition to "thinking seriously about . . . rights and pleasures" should also be "wary of how those *might* get discursively positioned by and around the state" ("Disabling Sex," 114). Against compulsory sexuality, or even compulsory "sexiness," Clare recognizes the importance of making space for individuals who, for a variety of reasons, do not find a source of liberation in sexual expression. In *Brilliant Imperfection*, he reflects on those instances when he's had to "flee queer public space, triggered by some expression of kinky sex or description of violence" (144). In this framework, disidentification with sexuality is no mere index of personal repression or political conservatism. If Preciado celebrates the capacitating qualities of erotic sensation, then Clare refuses to be liberated by "sexual desire and knowledge," instead fashioning stone butch sexual untouchability as an important site of queer expression. Connecting his own sexual refusal to trauma, Clare recalls that, at the age of eighteen, he

> knew nothing about sexual desire. For me sex was bound together with abuse. I had learned the details from my father just as I had learned how to mix a wheelbarrow of concrete, frame a stud wall. Sex meant rape—that simple, that complicated. The only thing I knew about desire was the raw, split-openness that rampaged through me after he was done.... My coming out wasn't as much about discovering sexual desire and knowledge as it was about dealing with gender identity. Simply put, the disabled, mixed-class tomboy who asked her mother "Am I feminine?" didn't discover sexuality among dykes but rather a definition of woman large enough to be comfortable with for many years. (133)

Clare's description of learning how to "mix a wheelbarrow of concrete" or "frame a stud wall" are not incidental here. Concrete hardens and walls protect. By describing the conditions of his abuse alongside the gradual development of these new skills, Clare provides an account not only of his trauma but of his coping mechanisms, strategies that include the construction and maintenance of his stone butch exterior. Exploring the way his disability, queerness, and stone butch gender feel mutually constitutive of his experience of abuse, Clare reflects that "sexual and physical abuse against children isn't only a personal tragedy" but a way of "teach[ing] children bodily lessons about power and hierarchy, about being boys, being girls, being children, being Black, being working-class, being disabled" (129). In this context, Clare's description of himself as a "disabled, mixed-class tomboy" is no mere diversity checklist. Rather, it is a moving account of how systemic oppression regularly produces chronic conditions of physical and psychological precarity.[23] Clare acknowledges that his discussion of sexual trauma opens up a set of "risky" questions about the causal connections between trauma, gender dysphoria, and asexuality (126). It is not always comfortable or easy to discuss trauma in relation to marginalized identities; to do so risks making those identities synonymous with damage, inviting further medicalization and stigma. But by identifying his stone butch identity as a response to trauma, Clare decenters the neoliberal claiming of "pride" as shorthand for superficial, feel-good celebrations of "diversity."

In a recent contribution to *Transgender Studies Quarterly*, Jasbir Puar describes Clare as a "trans man with cerebral palsy," who "has perhaps generated the most material on the specific epistemological predicaments of the 'disabled trans' subject or the 'trans disabled' subject, providing a much-needed intersectional analysis" (78). But intersectional approaches like these, she argues, risk "exceptionalizing both the trans body and the disabled body in order to convert the debility of a nonnormative body into a form of social and cultural capacity, whether located in state recognition, identity politics formations, market economies, the medical industrial complex, academic knowledge production, or subject positioning (or all of the above)" (77). Locating an example of this "social and cultural capacitation" in the exclusion of gender identity disorder from protection under the ADA, Puar remarks that the capacitated trans body, rehabilitated by corrective surgical treatment, has increasingly come to be seen as an able body. Meanwhile, the capacitated disabled body has increasingly come to be seen as a gender normative body, with disabled activism insisting that disabled women be treated *as* women and disabled men *as* men. In these frameworks, "the intersectional subject gets tokenized . . . such that the presence of this subject actually then prohibits accountability toward broader alliances" (78). Making a foil of Clare's presumed attachment to identity politics, Puar advocates instead for a politics of "assemblage" that "refuse[s] to isolate trans and disability as separate and distinct conceptual entities" (78). Against neoliberalism's superficial commitment to diversity and inclusion, Puar calls for new somatechnologies "that refuse the individualizing mandate of neoliberal paradigms of bodily capacity and debility" (80).

Ironically, however, such a reading of Clare mobilizes the very model of intersectionality it seeks to dismantle, with Puar framing Clare's contribution to queer, trans, and disability theory as little more than a product of his interlinked identities. Indeed, despite the obvious gestures toward "pride" in the title of Clare's memoir, the term signifies primarily, throughout the memoir, as one of the ways in which "stolen bodies" can be—ambivalently and provisionally—"reclaimed" from the grind of capitalism, heteronormativity, patriarchy, and white supremacy (132). Far from existing as a set of discrete neoliberal identities, *queer*, *trans*, and *disabled* are presented here as mutually constitutive bodily experiences that center around neither pleasure nor identity but rather the limited agency we exercise within broader disciplinary structures. It's true that *Exile and Pride* does not explicitly use the theoretical language of assemblage and biopolitics, capacity and debility. However, these are precisely the stakes that are illustrated in his memoir's extensive discussion of capitalism—the use capitalism makes of working-class bodies, the forms of toxicity and precarity it produces in search of profit, and the strange alliances it animates in its wake.

In *Brilliant Imperfection*, Clare critically explores the way his own gender transition reflected a temporary collaboration with the medical-industrial complex. Clare wonders to what extent his past desire to "cut off his right arm" due to his tremors can be compared to his later desire to "amputate his breasts" as treatment for gender dysphoria (174). While the former impulse is easy to understand as an effect of internalized ableism, and foregrounds the most coercively normalizing aspects of cure, the latter impulse is less straightforward. Clare resists the *DSM*'s insistence on turning his "desire [for surgery] into a diagnosis," noting that his "slow turn from butch dyke to genderqueer living as a white man in the world was never about curing disorder or fixing brokenness, but rather about desire and comfort—transition a door, a window, a cobalt sky" (177). Clare thus rejects a model that would medicalize his transmasculinity, even as he makes use of it to manage his symptoms of dysphoria.

In negotiating these contradictions, he vacillates between experiences of sensation and experiences of numbness. Reflecting on his desire for top surgery, Clare writes: "I am the stone butch who traces my lovers' breasts. I lavish them with my fingertips, tongue, tremoring touch. Learn how to bite, pinch, suck, drawing our heat to the surface. Yet when my lovers reach toward my breasts, I can't feel their hands on me" (139). Later, he describes himself as "the female-to-male transgender person who lets a scalpel touch my chest. The surgeon slices half-moons around my aureoles, cuts tissue away, and preserves as many nerves as possible. I lie in this operating room, anesthetized and in relationship with medical technology yet again" (176). To be "in relationship with medical technology," in this account, is to risk nerve damage and to become "anesthetized." Here Clare echoes the other prophylactic encounters I've discussed throughout the previous chapters, which frame the medical gaze as one that abstracts the body and dampens sensation.

But this encounter with medicine also opens up new forms of sensual experience. After his top surgery, he reflects: "I am the white guy walking a dirt road between cornfields in the occupied Dakota Territory right after sunset. I take off my T-shirt, tucking into the waistband of my shorts . . . Dusk licks my ribs, sternum, collarbone. I think about how good these ears of sweet corn taste, fresh from the field, husked, boiled, buttered" (176). There is no easy distinction here between the prophylactic and antiprophylactic, between anesthesia and synesthesia, between the abstracted medicalized body and the fleshy material body receptive to taste, touch, and smell. Clare's predicament is not just "epistemological," as Puar suggests, but fundamentally affective as "dusk licks" his newly exposed "ribs, sternum, collarbone." To some extent, the autoeroticism of this vignette echoes Preciado's description of his reaction to testosterone, which activates a "desire to fuck, walk, go out everywhere in the city," initiating a "climax in which the spiritual force of the testosterone mixing with my blood takes to the fore" (21). But while Preciado explicitly sexualizes his encounter with testosterone, linking the "desire to fuck" with the "increased capacity in [his] muscles, [his] brain," Clare's top surgery opens a set of nonsexual pleasures and intimacies that are ultimately inseparable from his disability, his stone butch identity, and his trauma.

Indeed, while Clare's stone butch orientation may lead him to turn away from certain expressions of sexuality and desire, it also opens up new forms of crossing and boundary transgression, including intimate alliances with the nonhuman world. In *Exile and Pride*, Clare recalls that, as a teenager, his "most sustaining relations were not in the human world. I collected stones—red, green, gray, rust, white speckled with black, black streaked with silver—and kept them in my pockets, their hard surfaces warming slowly to my body heat . . . Those stones warm in my pockets, I knew them to be the steadiest, only inviolate parts of myself" (124). In this meditation on nonhuman intimacies, Clare literalizes stone butch identity as a textured encounter with the nature that reaches outward as it also turns protectively inward. The "only inviolate part of himself," Clare's stones—as well as his stone butch orientation—encode a complex response to trauma. But Clare's stones do not function merely as numbing agents, shutting down the possibility of sensation. Warmed by his body heat and rich in color and texture, they are vibrant and vital. Far from existing as dead (or deadening) matter, their animacy generates new, if modified, affective encounters with the outside world.

Clare continues to explore these animacies in his poem "Stone," included in his 2017 memoir *Brilliant Imperfection*, which describes his relationship to a "vivid green-black" stone that he discovered on a beach he visited as a child. "I pick it up," he writes,

> *rub it between my fingers, tracing its round edges,*
> *uneven surfaces. I feel its weight in my hand. Through its*
> *center, some long-ago limpet, barnacle, or steady drip of*
> *water has bored a hole—on one side a lopsided groove and*

> *on the other a small circular opening, stone slowly, slowly*
> *turning to grit. I slip it into my pocket, later thread a leather*
> *cord through the hole, and wear it around my neck, green*
> *and black blurring as the stone absorbs oil from my skin. (49)*

Recognizing the process through which his stone had been "slowly, slowly / turning to grit," Clare dramatizes "slow death" as a complex ecological process. Like the "steady drip of / water" that has "bored a hole" into the stone's surface, "slow death" shifts focus away from those singular instances of spectacular trauma and violence, centering instead on the ongoing practices of institutional neglect that gradually chip away at the vitality of biopolitically disenfranchised populations. Here, the word "bored" gestures not only to the physical effects of slow death as a process of wearing down (*boring* a hole) but also to its chronic, seemingly interminable temporalities (small indignities, repeated often enough, become ordinary, mundane, and even *boring*). In managing these relentless microinjuries, Berlant argues, it is often more pragmatic to develop coping mechanisms than to reach for cures. We become acclimated to the process of slow death through small acts of self-medication and other bad "habits" that make life bearable.

Notably, slow death can help us reframe queer pleasure away from the sexual, acknowledging the ways that we find relief in habitual experiences of numbness or escape rather than the climactic connectivity of orgasm. Clare's tactile communion with the natural world, his habit of picking up rocks and experiencing their weight, shape, and texture, provides one form of escape or method of coping. He identifies with, and to some extent covets, the stone's status as inviolable, insensate matter. But these cross-species and nonorganic intimacies go both ways, as the stone is transformed by its encounter with Clare's body, its colors "blurring" as it "absorbs oil from [his] skin" (49). Simultaneously eroded and vitalized by forces, beings, and objects in its environment, the stone does not represent a prophylactic barrier as much as it reveals the interdependent qualities of its own—and indeed every—ecosystem.

These interdependencies with and among nonhuman nature extend to the "intimate, wordless relationship" he develops with the maple tree that has become his "writing companion" (33), the "rapid scuttling" of hermit crabs who initially betrayed "no signs of life" and "freeze" again upon sensing his motion (81), the "furrowed bark" of a myrtle tree "against his skin" that provides a feeling of "grounding and safety" (124), and the beach shell he finds "alive, muscle of animal protruding, then retracting / in response to my touch" (65). Across these poems, Clare complicates the distinctions we are prone to draw between vulnerability and protection, human and nonhuman nature, organic and inorganic matter, "retract[ion]" and "protrus[ion]," prophylaxis and antiprophylaxis. It becomes impossible, ultimately, to separate the shell from the "muscle of animal" that animates it; both are described as being "alive." And while the "furrowed bark" of the myrtle tree might function as armor, Clare presents it as a second, sensitive skin, no less vulnerable than his own. As we are reminded by the hole in the stone that he "thread[s] a leather cord through" and hangs around his neck, nothing is impermeable.

This notion of ecological interdependence weaves through Clare's autobiographical and theoretical ruminations on the politics of diagnosis and cure. As someone who has been both aided and stigmatized by what he terms the "medical-industrial complex," Clare weighs his proud claiming of disabled identity against his knowledge that disability can also lead to painful physical and emotional states or emerge as a result of environmental damage and global inequalities. He asks:

> how do we witness, name, and resist the injustices that reshape and damage all kinds of body-minds—plant and animal, organic and inorganic, nonhuman and human—while not equating disability with injustice? I feel my grief and rage of environmental losses as small as the disappearance of a single peeper pond and as big as the widespread poisoning of the planet's groundwater. I think about how we might bear witness to body-mind loss while also loving ourselves just as we are right now. I begin to understand restoration—both of ecosystems and of health—as one particular relationship between the past, present, and future. (60)

Clare's observations here resonate powerfully with Alison Kafer's proposal of a "political/relational model" of disability that, while sharing with the social model a critique of medicalizing frameworks, refuses to uphold the opposition between "disability" and "impairment" and takes a more complicated approach to the status of medical intervention and cure. Though we must continue to assert that the problem of disability lies not in the physical body but in the inaccessible environments that restrict that body's mobility (socially, professionally, and sexually), the political/relational model insists that such assertions are incomplete if we are not also asking questions about who has access to health care, who is living closest to polluted lakes and rivers, and who is most at risk for developing conditions like asthma and diabetes or for being a target of sexual assault. In short, it allows us to grapple with disability's complex relationship with institutionally and globally produced conditions of precarity, injury, and trauma.

These queer and crip innovations in biopolitics sit uneasily alongside a traditional model of disability pride. Connecting pain, injury, exhaustion, and depression to the demands of capitalism and a global pharmaceutical industry, they provide a material spin on queer theory's "ugly feelings," and, in this sense, they reconfigure queer theory's embrace of negativity.[24] The crip turn to the negative might ask us, as Alyson Patsavas does, what a cripistemology of chronic physical pain might look like. It refuses, like Merri Lisa Johnson, the "conflation of madness with countercultural adventure," acknowledging how "the distress of failures embodied in lives gone haywire, symptoms run rampant, personal lives devolving into uninhabitable havoc" can sit ambivalently with the pleasures of queer failure ("Bad Romance," 264). It challenges, like Mel Chen, the sanctification of the "vulnerable" white child ostensibly menaced by lead toys while at the same time emphasizing the ways that toxicity can and often does produce disability among "those on the underside of industrial capitalism" ("Toxic Animacies, Inanimate Affections," 276). And it resonates with Heather Love's call to "imagine a politics that allows for damage" (162), which can "simply mean living with injury—and not fixing it" (*Feeling Backward*, 4). Crip states can be painful, anxious, ambivalent, nauseating, foggy, and even, at times, hopeless. To take seriously the sensory lives of debility as well as the impact of trauma requires a more imaginative relation to those seemingly prophylactic practices like avoidance and refusal, reconsidering their capacity to generate new forms of feminist, queer, and crip life.

Epilogue

Against Queer Resilience

If the "vulnerable constitutions" described in the title of this book had a mascot, it might be Tony Matelli's controversial sculpture, *Sleepwalker*, exhibited outdoors at Wellesley College between February and May 2014. Constructed from epoxy, fiberglass, and paint, the hyperrealistic sculpture stands five feet, nine inches tall and takes the shape of a slender male somnambulist. As one *New York Times* writer describes him, "The figure, with a bit of a paunch, is clad only in tight white briefs. His arms are stretched out in front of him, his face reddened and miserable." In this representation of male bodily vulnerability, Matelli intended the sculpture to "contrast with the aggressive, monumental figures that are more typically wrought in statues of men."[1] Rather than memorializing masculine accomplishment, *Sleepwalker* presents a masculinity that is susceptible, uncovered, eternally at risk. In photographs, he often appears as a solitary figure, passively enduring the elements. One image, for example, presents him ankle-deep in snow, an accumulation of white flakes frosting the top of his head and arms.[2] (See Figure E.1.) In an interview, Matelli explains that the figure was explicitly "designed to be in a landscape," as he had wanted to "create something that feels misplaced and vulnerable."[3]

In exploring the relationship between vulnerability and misplacedness, Matelli evokes Rosemarie Garland-Thomson's theorization of "misfit" as a site of crip relationality. Functioning both as a noun (the "person who does not fit") and as a verb ("the act of not fitting"), a misfit "occurs when the environment does not sustain the shape and function of the body that enters

Figure E.1 Tony Matelli's *Sleepwalker* sculpture, installed outdoors on the Wellesley College campus in the winter of 2014. (Photo credit: Darren McCollester/Getty Images News/Getty Images)

it," forcing us to "recognize that bodies are always situated in and dependent upon environments" (598). It is in this way that the misfit reveals the "discrepancy between body and world" to be both socially constructed and materially embodied (593). The "vulnerability" produced through this discrepancy, Garland-Thomson suggests, allows us "to describe the potential for misfitting to which all human beings are subject" (598). Put differently, we all depend on our environments to sustain us, even as some of us bear the privilege of experiencing our "fit" as necessary, natural, and inevitable. No matter what the context, a sleepwalker is always already a "misfit." Out of place by definition, she or he ambles unceremoniously through environment designed for the conscious. But a sleepwalker out of doors is doubly misfit, evoking queer and crip specters of homelessness, perversion, mental impairment, and sexual deviance. Indeed, when one Wellesley student "first saw [the] nearly naked man who appeared to be stumbling on campus," she explains that "she assumed he was a drunk, about to be arrested."[4] Thus the sleepwalker provokes us to recognize the uncomfortable misfit between the privileged university setting and those populations exiled from its boundaries.

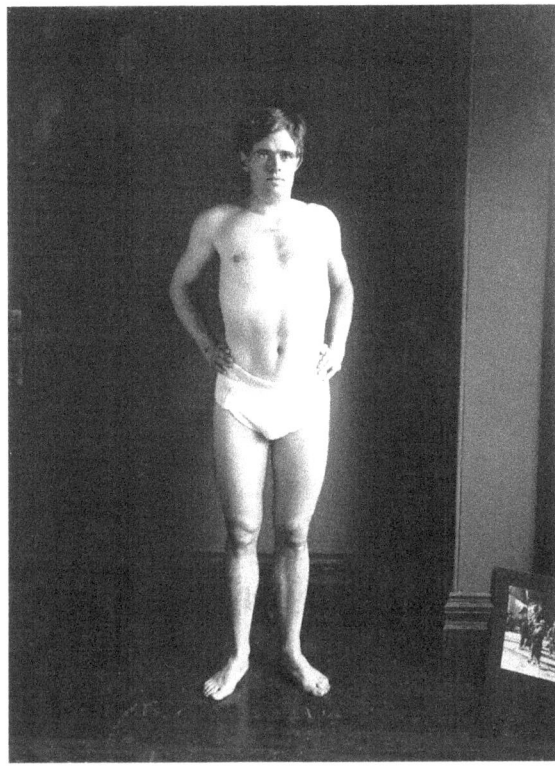

Figure E.2 Jack London poses in his underwear.

We might, for example, imagine the sleepwalker to be one of Delany's "walking wounded," like the compulsive masturbator Joe, abandoned by the mental health profession and exiled from his temporary home in the porn theaters by the gradual gentrification of Times Square. We might also read him as one of Jack London's "road kids" or "tramps," who have been "twisted out of shape . . . and cast adrift by their masters like so many old horses" (126). In a photographic portrait, the context of which is unclear, London himself bears a striking resemblance to Matelli's sculpture. (See Figure E.2.) The adult London stands facing the camera, nearly nude save for a pair of white briefs. Unlike the sleepwalker, London is indoors and awake. His wide-open eyes gaze past the camera as he puffs out his chest, presumably in an attempt to add bulk. And yet, despite the bravado of the pose, London appears vulnerable, exposed, and impossibly awkward. Aside from the obvious and crucial difference of race, the *Sleepwalker* may even emblematize James Baldwin's father who went "mad and died in Bedlam because, being black, he was always 'the last to be hired and the first to be fired'" (126). At the same time, he calls to mind the street boys Eric describes in *Another Country* who are walking wounded insofar as they are walking targets, vulnerable to the violence of a police force that imperils rather than protects their safety.

Symbols of danger and objects of violence, these bodies are both spectacularly visible and pushed out of sight, eroded over time by the slow death of capitalism's sanitizing structures. Berlant identifies the temporality of "slow death" as "endemic" rather than "epidemic" in that it refers to a permanent condition, a gradual wearing down that contrasts with the epidemic's necessary relationship to crisis and emergency. Here, susceptibility is no longer a singular moment or instance to be avoided. Rather, it is interwoven into the very constitution of certain bodies and certain populations as an ongoing condition of precarity. Whether by choice or by circumstance, each of these "walking wounded" dramatize a curious interplay between susceptibility and resistance. As I have argued throughout this book, constitutional vulnerability has offered a potent biopolitical resource for the imaginative refashioning of American identity and American masculinity. By adopting queer-crip practices of exposure and risk, the antiprophylactic citizen is imagined to gradually cultivate physical and political resilience. Rather than objects of "slow death," we might understand them as nurturing, implicitly, an inverse ethics of "slow life." To cultivate slow life through antiprophylaxis, one must be willing to grow a thicker skin, to open oneself up to pain and physical violation. For Jack London, this meant trading the numbness of the anesthetic for the wounding materiality of the callous. For Mitchell, it is indicated by a willingness to "bend over and let in the new." The antiprophylactic citizens who have populated this book remind us that the American body is (or should be) a fundamentally democratic body, and that a truly democratic body is a porous body, a hospitable body, a body that bears out Baldwin's proclamation "that life is dangerous, and that without the joyful acceptance of this danger, there can never be any safety for anyone, ever, anywhere" ("As Much Truth as One Can Bear," 41).[5] But in the rigid commitment to certain forms of antiprophylaxis, what crip insights are lost? What would it mean to argue against queer resilience?

There is, after all, another set of political insights that the *Sleepwalker* animates, one that exists in productive tension with the narrative of vulnerable masculinity I have just related. Here, I want to turn to the student controversy surrounding the sculpture, which tells a very different queer-crip story of sexual trauma, feminist resistance, mental health activism, and accountability to survivors. A flashpoint in the then-nascent trigger warning debates, the sculpture became a rallying point for activist groups on campus who argued that the *Sleepwalker*'s intense realism, coupled with its outdoor location at a women's college, made it "a source of apprehension, fear, and triggering thoughts regarding sexual assault for some members of [the] campus community."[6] One protester's sign, attached to the sculpture, reads: "I am here at the direct expense of the mental health of the students around me." Through this lens, the *Sleepwalker*'s "misplacedness" takes on a troublingly gendered edge—an exposed male body aggressively out of context in the setting of an all-women's college. Students advocating for the sculpture's removal indoors made the case that it constituted an access barrier, limiting the mobility of sexual assault survivors who found themselves newly constrained in their ability to move through campus. As one internet commenter explains, "Some students are even going so far as to plan alternate routes to 'get out of the statue's way' (dir. quote). But, many students are already forcing themselves to 'get used to it' (dir. quote) and to accept it as a situation that they do not have control over."[7] No longer a vulnerable misfit navigating an inhospitable environment, the sleepwalker is here understood to *be* an inhospitable environment for survivors of sexual assault. Against the contours of this inaccessible landscape, undergraduates experience their own "misfit" with an academic culture that refuses to acknowledge the vulnerability of its own student population in their ongoing experiences with violence, trauma, and psychological impairment.

The *Sleepwalker* thus operates in a curiously dual way, emblematizing a potent form of queer-crip vulnerability while at the same time enacting a potentially patriarchal and ableist restructuring of public space. At the same time, students' efforts to remove the statue were met with accusations of sexual prudery and anti–free speech censorship. Emerging from a supposedly "overprotected" and "hypersensitive" student body, the incident was frequently dismissed as an example of political correctness gone awry or as an illustration of the way second-wave feminism's perceived Puritanism continues to persist in the present. My intention here is not to adjudicate the question of whether *Sleepwalker* "belongs" on the Wellesley campus. Rather, I am interested in the rhetorical tension that has emerged within the uproar over the sculpture (and in the discourse on trigger warnings in general) between a celebrated queer-crip *vulnerability*, on the one hand, and a disqualified feminist-crip *sensitivity*, on the other. In what follows, I want to explore what it would mean to claim the kind of "sensitivity" that the antiprophylactic citizen fastidiously (and ironically) guards against. To do so may require us to understand the prophylactic as something other than a simple mechanism of social purification. Indeed, in some cases, it can function as a valuable crip technology.

My desire to reclaim the prophylactic in this epilogue stems, in part, from a recognition of the masculinist and ableist assumptions underlying much anti–trigger warning discourse.[8] Such conversations tend to valorize vulnerability and openness in ways that produce new compulsory narratives. For example, in a *Time* magazine article titled "Man Up, Wellesley: You're a Generation of Sheltered Children," Charlotte Alter identifies the student protest of the sculpture as "the refrain of a generation of sheltered children who grew up to insist on sheltering themselves as adults. They're the grown-up versions of the kids who wouldn't watch rated R movies because they 'might be scary.' They want to purge the world of anything remotely problematic, anything that might offend, might give pause, might cause even a moment of ickiness. If they deem it offensive, it must cease to exist on this earth. It's a weirdly Puritan strain of liberalism." Compare this with Baldwin's own critique of the prophylactic sensibility exactly fifty years earlier, in his 1964 essay "The Uses of the Blues." Baldwin writes:

> Let us talk about a person who is no longer very young, who somehow managed to get to, let us say, the age of forty, and a great many of us do, without ever having been touched, broken, disturbed, frightened—forty-year-old virgin, male or female. There is a sense of the grotesque about a person who has spent his or her life in a kind of cotton batting. There is something monstrous about never having been hurt, never having been made to bleed, never having lost anything, never having gained anything because life is beautiful, and in order to keep it beautiful you're going to stay just the way you are and you're not going to test your theory against all the possibilities outside. America is something like that. The failure on our part to accept the reality of pain, of anguish, of ambiguity, of death has turned us into a very peculiar and sometimes monstrous people. It means, for one thing, and it's very serious, that people who have had no experience have no compassion. (79)

Both of these passages are preoccupied with the temporality of "shelteredness," evoking a nightmare image of the child who has failed to come into adulthood properly. These "forty-year-old-virgins" and "grown up versions of kids" are pathological not for their perversity but rather for their very lack of deviance, their "Puritan" refusal of risk. Here, Baldwin and Alter each reverse the usual terms of reproductive futurism, committing instead to a model that we might term "antiprophylactic futurity." We are urged neither to make the Child safe for the future nor to make the future safe for the Child. Rather, in this queer-crip refiguring of heterofuturity, we are told in no uncertain terms that the Child must be endangered in order to grow up. Hovering on the brink of adulthood, the female students at Wellesley find themselves on a perilous path toward security. They are at risk of risking too little.

One photograph of the sculpture, appearing in a *New York Daily News* feature story, starkly frames this encounter between masculine antiprophylaxis and feminine overprotection. In the foreground, facing the viewer, the sleepwalker's snow-covered body lurches toward the camera, his arms outstretched in a gesture of supplication. In the background, three individuals (presumably Wellesley students) stroll down a paved path, insulated by thick winter coats, eyes faced forward toward their destination.[9] Literalizing Baldwin's image of the person who has "spent his or her life in a kind of cotton batting," these bundled-up figures appear to be actively turned away from "the reality of pain, of anguish, of ambiguity, of death" that the *Sleepwalker* represents. Alongside the photograph, the article copy reveals Matelli's surprise at the protests. Acknowledging the students' freedom to react to his art in unanticipated ways, he admits that he had expected that "the reaction [to the sculpture] would be empathy." Here, the usual feminization of "feelings" is inverted in ways that recall Fitzgerald's project of reclaiming sentiment in *Tender Is the Night*. In this model, sympathy is reclaimed as a virtue, evidencing an admirable ability to take emotional risks. Unmoved by the image of the vulnerable figure in front of them, the trio of "prophylactic dames" is both hypersensitive and emotionally detached. Failing to react with empathy, they appear to confirm the image of the potentially triggered student as one who refuses to look at or engage with difficult realities.

Bearing out this message, Jenny Jarvie's *New Republic* article titled "Trigger Happy" pictures the potentially triggered student as seeking refuge (and perhaps even subterfuge) behind a blindfold. In the stylized photograph at the top of the page, a young woman faces the camera but fails to meet our gaze, eyes shielded by a thick swath of linen fabric. Conventionally attractive and feminine in appearance, she appears to have nothing "wrong" with her and no business claiming disability accommodation—the visual analog to art critic Sebastian Smee's rumination elsewhere that there is a "whiff of a slightly affected fragility" in the petition to remove the sculpture.[10] In this observation, Smee echoes a long history of medical and public suspicion toward women with psychological impairments, who are assumed to lack the credibility to describe their conditions or access needs. Here, the blindfold implicates the demand for trigger warnings as an act of self-deception and willful ignorance—literally pulling the wool over one's own eyes. And yet it is the male *Sleepwalker*, lost in a dream world, whose eyes remain perpetually closed.

Indeed, to dismiss the Wellesley protesters as "sheltered children" is to ignore the somewhat obvious fact that the students most likely to be distressed by the sculpture are precisely those who have not had the luxury of being sheltered from violence. When a Wellesley student takes an alternative route in order to avoid the *Sleepwalker* sculpture, we can assume that she is not fearfully anticipating an abstract future outcome but, rather, acknowledging the embodied afterlives of traumas that have already happened. These traumas may have been personally experienced as isolated incidents or may emerge out of the everyday microaggressions that result from rape culture's long history. From this vantage point, Baldwin's suspicion "that people who have had no experience have no compassion" (79) might better apply to those who dispute the value of trigger warnings but who are not, themselves, at risk of being triggered. Though affects of sympathy and compassion are celebrated in much anti–trigger warning discourse, those same affects remain conspicuously and ironically absent in the mainstream response to those survivors, and their allies, who demand accommodation regarding the sculpture's potential to trigger.

It is, rather, the category of "insensitivity" that emerges most explicitly in these discourses as a masculinized outlaw ideal. Urging Wellesley students to "man up," for example, Alter argues that "there's something spoiled about our knee-jerk reaction to abolish anything that could be considered even remotely insensitive. The message is, 'it's possible that someone somewhere might feel momentarily bad because of this, so get rid of it right this second! And by the way, you're an asshole if you don't agree.'" Here, Alter rehearses a common ableist logic that frames collective requests for reasonable accommodations as unreasonable demands rooted in individual feelings of entitlement ("something spoiled"). To "man up," in this context, is to heroically overcome one's psychological disability, trading one's feminine hypersensitivity for a masculine willingness to endure hardship or discomfort. Note, too, the sleepwalker's own literal insensitivity to his environment. Physically exposed, he is nonetheless impervious to the cold; no matter how much snow accumulates over his half-naked body, he wears the same impassive expression. Frequently pictured in photographs against a stark backdrop of snow-covered trees, his solitary battle with the elements evokes a rugged Darwinian struggle between body and wilderness, a reminder that only the fittest survive.[11] Despite his vulnerability, he is the very picture of toughness and resilience.

Importantly, these distinctions extend beyond the objects themselves, attaching to individuals' ethical orientations to one another. Alter is less bothered by the "sensitivity" of triggered students than she is by the "sensitivity" of the activists organizing empathetically on their behalf. Meanwhile, those who want the statue to stay not only find themselves immune to the artwork's triggering qualities but, more fundamentally, take pride in their "insensitivity" to the protesters' "unreasonable" demands for accommodation. To be "sensitive," according to this logic, is to require prophylactic protection from the unknown, quarantining that which might be perceived as a threat. It is to partake in what Philip Alcabes calls the "anticipatory logic" of the epidemic (219). In his book length study of epidemic discourse, Alcabes illustrates the way these anticipatory logics depend on a "forecasting of future harm" (219) and a related belief that a "risk-free life" is not only desirable but possible to achieve (215).[12] Indeed, those who demand trigger warnings are frequently cast as the worst practitioners of epidemic discourse, taking its anticipatory logics to the most egregious and irrational extremes. What is a trigger warning, after all, if not a "forecasting of future harm"? To be "insensitive," by contrast, is to remain indifferent to future harm, fearlessly bucking tradition and asserting yourself as a contrarian if not a rebel—one of the "assholes" who "disagrees." Fetishizing free speech as "political incorrectness," this ethics of insensitivity takes pride in the perceived risks involved in making one's unpopular opinions vulnerable to critique.

In a queer twist on this valorization of insensitivity, queer scholars have tended to understand such warnings as the latest repackaging of anti-porn feminism's alliance with right-wing efforts to censor "shocking" art and transgressive speech. In her *Bullybloggers* post "Classrooms and Their Dissed Contents," Ann Pellegrini, for example, argues: "In calling for the classroom to be a 'safe space,' the movement for trigger warnings ends up closing down one of the crucial places where students (and teachers, too) can experiment in having and surviving the hurt feelings that may result from differences in viewpoints and differences in moral values. Learning that disagreement does not kill you . . . could even be considered a kind of laboratory in democratic social relations."[13] In this vision, the unfiltered classroom becomes a complex technology for the cultivation of resilient citizens, toughened by exposure to that which, in failing to "kill" them, has made them stronger. Pellegrini's observations follow a series of contributions to the queer blogosphere that treat the trigger warning with suspicion.

For example, in an April 2014 online roundtable, curated by Megan Milks, which gathered a series of queer writers on the topic of trigger warnings in the creative writing classroom, poet C. A. Conrad compared trigger warnings to the Parents Music Resource Center's efforts to censor music, a victory that led to the mandatory labeling of commercial albums that contain "explicit lyrics."[14] Even more provocatively, during the same roundtable,

Sarah Schulman drew an analogy between the institutionalization of trigger warnings and the criminalization of HIV nondisclosure. As in most sex panics, Schulman argues, the real threat of violence comes from the state as it designates vulnerable and marginalized populations as "threats" to be eliminated. In order to avoid enacting these forms of state violence, Schulman suggests, the triggered individual must "learn how to differentiate between the past and present so that they are not blaming, scapegoating or attacking people today for pain that they have not caused but was inflicted by others long ago." Suggesting that "feeling endangered may not mean that one is in danger, but can, in fact, make one very dangerous to others," she thus echoes Alcabes's critique of the policing function of epidemic discourse.

And yet, one of the most potent ironies of the trigger warning debates is the extent to which the backlash against trigger warnings *itself* takes shape around a prophylactic language of epidemic and quarantine. As Andrea Lawlor points out in her response to Schulman, the analogy to HIV criminalization ultimately rings false, since those "living with trauma have much more in common with—and common cause with—people living with other chronic conditions like HIV." By shifting the very terms of the debate from contagion to chronicity, from sexuality to disability, from censorship to accommodation, Lawlor reveals the prophylactic logic behind even the most antiprophylactic of queer discourses. She observes, for example, that in constructing a separate category of innocent victims who are injured by the trauma survivor's misplaced anger, Schulman "creates an image of survivors as 'Typhoid Marys' spreading trauma around like contagion." This framing of trigger warnings as an epidemic threat—one that might "spread" to unsuspecting segments of the general public if not properly dealt with—is even more explicit in Jarvie's "Trigger Happy" article. Jarvie notes with some alarm that while "some consider them to be an irksome tic of the blogosphere's most hypersensitive fringes," trigger warnings have nonetheless "spread from feminist forums and social media to sites as large as the Huffington Post" and are even "gaining momentum . . . at some of the nation's most prestigious universities." As a result, "what began as a way of moderating Internet forums for the vulnerable and mentally ill now threatens to define public discussion both online and off. The trigger warning signals not only the growing precautionary approach to words and ideas in the university, but a wider cultural hypersensitivity to harm and a paranoia about giving offense. And yet, for all the debate about the warnings on campuses and on the Internet, few are grappling with the ramifications for society as a whole." In this commentary, the trigger warning emerges as a recklessly circulating pathogen, one that merits discussion only at the moment that it threatens to cross over from the neglected margins to the normalized mainstream. Ironically, such logic bears a striking resemblance to the moral panics Gayle Rubin describes in her canonical "Thinking Sex." Connecting the panic surrounding certain sex acts to the "panic that has accompanied new epidemics" like HIV/AIDS, Rubin critiques what she calls "the domino theory of sexual peril," which is based on "the fear that if anything is permitted to cross this erotic DMZ, the barrier against scary sex will crumble and something unspeakable will skitter across" (161).

Rubin's essay may appear to provide a counterintuitive pairing with pro–trigger warning activism; one of the main contributions of "Thinking Sex," after all, was to dismantle the very forms of sex negativity that trigger warning activists are so frequently accused of adopting. But perhaps the time has come, to borrow Rubin's own phrase, to think about disability—or, more precisely, to consider how taking disability seriously might shake up the pro- and antisex loyalties that continue to structure the queer and feminist response to the sex wars. Trigger warnings force us to confront difficult questions about which disability accommodations have been, like certain sex acts, "permitted to cross over into acceptability" and which remain "dangerous, psychopathological, infantile, or politically reprehensible" (160). We might say that while wheelchair-accessible buildings (nominally) welcome certain physically disabled bodies into the university's "charmed circle," mental disability continues to remain exiled to the "outer limits." To incorporate trigger warnings into the privileged university setting, it is implied, is to set in motion a slippery slope that will lead to the inevitable intrusion of additional accessibility requirements into our everyday lives. Jarvie completes her epidemic fantasy with the rumination that

> it's only a matter of time before warnings are demanded for other grade levels. As students introduce them in college newspapers, promotional material for plays, even poetry slams, it's not inconceivable that they'll appear at the beginning of film screenings and at the entrance to art exhibits. Will newspapers start applying warnings to articles about rape, murder, and war? Could they even become a regular feature of speech? "I was walking down Main Street last night when—trigger warning—I saw an elderly woman get mugged."

Here, the infectious spread of trigger warnings culminates in the infiltration of the very body itself, entering the mouth of its victim as a diseased utterance. Thus it is ironic when Jarvie critiques trigger warning activists' "growing precautionary approach to words" that defines public discourses as sites that are "full of infinite yet ill-defined hazards." While Jarvie may understand herself as championing a version of the antiprophylactic sensibility, her own approach replicates the anticipatory logic of epidemic discourse. Advocating a swift quarantine (the "growth" of trigger warnings must be "stopped"), Jarvie constructs a prophylaxis against prophylaxis itself.

Also at play in the backlash against trigger warnings is a cripped variation on what Rubin calls the "fallacy of misplaced scale," a phenomenon in which certain sexual acts are "burdened with an excess of significance" and "small differences in value or behaviour are often experienced as cosmic threats" (158). Ironically, this fallacy appears to emerge primarily within the more sophisticated objections to trigger warnings leveled by queer academics in the blogosphere. Even in the most politically savvy critiques, the student who has experienced trauma—and who has developed mechanisms for coping with that trauma in collaboration with feminist and disabled activism—transforms into a scapegoat for our anxieties about neoliberal co-optation. In his controversial *Bullybloggers* post, "You Are Triggering Me! The Neoliberal Rhetoric of Harm, Danger, and Trauma," Jack Halberstam ignited a heated debate on the topic by reading the rise of trigger warnings as evidence of "a post–affirmative action society, where even recent histories of political violence like slavery and lynching are cast as a distant and irrelevant past," and "all claims to hardship have been cast as equal." Those who demand trigger warnings, Halberstam argues, exist in the same camp as those who seek to "obliterate terms like 'tranny' in the quest for respectability and assimilation" and signal the return of a brand of "weepy white lady feminism" that turned away from coalition-building and collective action and toward the individual "wounded self."[15] Following Halberstam, Ann Pellegrini refers to trigger warnings as the "alarm codes of neoliberalism" and Lisa Duggan diagnoses their emergence as part of larger set of political shifts from the "utopian to the pragmatic, from the collective to the individual, from the transformative to the therapeutic."[16] Acknowledging that this schema oversimplifies a "wide range of kinds of social movement politics all through this period," Duggan nonetheless leaves trigger warnings intact as a symbol for the "dangers involved as social movement politics move into institutions." In these visions, the student who requests trigger warnings is cut off from her activist genealogies, emerging as a coddled millennial, steeped in privilege and perpetually tethered to her suburban helicopter parents.

In highlighting capitalism's astonishing ability to adopt, adapt, and ultimately take the teeth out of new vocabularies of social justice, these queer writers launch important critiques of neoliberalism. But while trigger warnings may not be exempt from these dynamics, neither are they fundamentally emblematic or solely illustrative of them. Through the filter of this "misplaced scale," the trigger warning is thus "burdened with excess significance," its very existence triggering memories of homophobic censorship, trans-exclusionary radical feminism, gentrification, anti-porn campaigns, and other painful political histories.[17] Evoking these prophylactic legacies in their connection to "safe spaces," trigger warnings thus became a potent (if misplaced) symbol for all that is chronically unqueer.[18]

But what could be queerer than an honest acknowledgment of the damage we've sustained in our traumatic encounters with heteronormativity and toxic masculinity? Against the teleology of the scar (healed over and sealed off, evidence of a hardship endured and overcome) we might say that there is nothing more antiprophylactic than a wound that never fully closes. As Andrea Smith argues, trigger warnings are intended to collectivize healing, moving the messy practice of dealing with trauma from its proper time and place (hidden away in private, relegated to the past) to the public spaces of the university and the immediacy of the classroom setting. Far from acting as the "alarm codes of neoliberalism," which mandate that we focus on good feelings while banishing bad ones, trigger warnings may thus enable the classroom to be a different kind of "laboratory in democratic social relations," one where trauma, and its political contexts, matter. Let's, then, take seriously Christina Hanhardt's acknowledgment in *Safe Spaces* that "the most transformative visions are those driven less by a fixed goal of safety than by the admittedly abstract concept of freedom" (30). Freedom, in the classroom and the university, might include the autonomy to consent to the contexts in which we allow our healing to happen. It may also mean acknowledging that an investment in safety need not always take shape as a threat to freedom. Bodily defense and bodily exposure are not opposites but, rather, mutually constitutive and inextricable. Sensitivity may simply be the name we give to the vulnerabilities we fail to acknowledge as such. Vulnerability, by contrast, might just refer to the forms of sensitivity we valorize. The coalitions we are in the process of forming between and among marginalized subjects will inevitably involve conflicting access needs and may even, at times, result in situations where the walking wounded wound each other. Antiprophylaxis, if it is to be truly democratic, might therefore ask us to engage in the collective and sometimes risky practice of remaining open to one another's boundaries.

Notes

INTRODUCTION

1. Extending a long history of suspicion directed at passing trans bodies, some commentators additionally (and egregiously) speculated that Manning's claims to be transgender were motivated by her desire to serve her sentence in a women's rather than a men's prison.
2. Elspeth Reeve, "A Portrait of the Mind of Bradley Manning."
3. Ellen Nakashima, "Who Is WikiLeaks Suspect Bradley Manning?"
4. Ellen Nakashima, "Who Is WikiLeaks Suspect Bradley Manning?"
5. In his preface to Roberto Esposito's *Bios*, Timothy Campbell elaborates on the differences between the disciplinary or regulatory biopolitics classically defined by Michel Foucault and Georgio Agamben and an affirmative biopolitics championed by philosophers like Gilles Deleuze, Michael Hardt, and Antonio Negri. While a regulatory biopolitics functions as a "technology of power" (xx) that imposes the regularization of life through statistics, medicalization, and population control, affirmative biopolitics celebrates the "multitude as an affirmative biopolitical actor who resists biopower" (xxvi).
6. See Michael Kimmel, *The Gender of Desire: Essays on Male Sexuality*.
7. See also Ken Corbett, *Boyhoods*.
8. For some notable exceptions see Don Sabo, Tim Dean, Liberty Walther Barnes, Steve Garlick, Melissa N. Stein, and Dana Rosenfeld and Christopher A. Faircloth.
9. For an extended discussion of "bottom values," see Kathryn Bond Stockton's *Beautiful Bottom, Beautiful Shame*.
10. For similar critiques, see Mandy Merck, *In Your Face*, and Tania Modleski, *Feminism without Women*.

11. For more on the relationship between masculinity and masochism, see David Savran, *Taking It Like a Man*.

12. See also Kelly Fritsch and Anne McGuire's recent special issue of *Feminist Formations*, titled "The Biosocial Politics of Queer/Crip Contagions" 30, no. 1 (Spring 2018).

13. Donna Haraway argues for understanding the immune system as a "preeminently twentieth-century object" that functions as a "map drawn to guide recognition and misrecognition of self and other in dialectics of western biopolitics" ("The Biopolitics of Postmodern Bodies," 275). In *Flexible Bodies* (1994), Emily Martin historicizes the way the changing landscape of global politics has shifted understandings of the immune system, from a Cold War portrait of national boundaries breached and defended to contemporary neoliberal celebrations of "flexible" and open-ended systems. See also Paula Treichler's discussion of AIDS as an "epidemic of signification," in "AIDS, Homophobia and Biomedical Discourse."

14. See Ed Cohen, *A Body Worth Defending*, 41.

15. For a nuanced disability studies perspective on metaphors of autoimmunity, see Beth Ferri, "Metaphors of Contagion."

16. "Disability," Rosemarie Garland-Thomson writes, "is the unorthodox made flesh, refusing to be normalized, neutralized, or homogenized," and thus "in an era governed by the abstract principle of universal equality, disability signals that the body cannot be universalized" (*Extraordinary Bodies*, 24). Garland-Thomson observes that freak shows in the United States became popular during a time in which, due to the rise of industrial capitalism, men's bodies were increasingly being seen as standardized, interchangeable cogs. Against such uniformity, she argues, the "freak" embodied both the promise and the fears of American democracy, signaling the American virtues of freedom and singularity alongside the more uncomfortable possibilities of social disorder and anarchy (the threat of individuality gone awry). Emily Russell has recently coined the term "embodied citizenship" to tease out this very paradox by which "the anomalous characteristics that exclude individuals from full access to the political imaginary become the same features that structure their participation" (*Reading Embodied Citizenship*, 15).

17. Charles L. Briggs and Daniel C. Hallin define "sanitary citizenship as 'the ways that states read bodies and bodily practices and assess the biomedical knowledge of individuals and populations,'" a process that "constitutes an increasingly important site for regulating and rationalizing access to privileges of citizenship" ("Biocommunicability," 43).

18. See Washington Irving, *Salmagundi*.

19. As Delano unites with Cereno to quell the San Dominick's slave revolt, the two men's distinct nations (the United States and Spain) become less important than the bond of white rationality that they both, theoretically, share. This model of generalized white "rationality," Nelson observes, did multiple things for white American men of otherwise clashing classes and regional affiliations. First, by dissolving national or ethnic difference under the larger umbrella of whiteness, it helped Americans sever their blood ties with the British (a dissolution that needed to occur in order to justify the American fight for independence). Second, by coding whiteness with properties of rationality and benevolence, it provided a racial identification that justified the slave system and authorized the colonial presence on American soil. And finally, by making

white manhood the common denominator of American citizenship, it helped to neutralize or repress the threat of clashing regional or socioeconomic interests—the anarchic potential of true democracy—under the unifying, if illusory, banner of whiteness.

20. In *An American Obsession*, Jennifer Terry observes that, because the principles of democracy required a commitment to equality in a society still deeply committed to upholding its gender, class, and racial hierarchies, the science of comparative anatomy rose up as a way to both champion democracy and exclude certain bodies from its rights and protections. Siobhan Somerville similarly argues that, far from being merely analogical, "the formation of notions of heterosexuality and homosexuality emerged in the United States through (and not merely parallel to) a discourse saturated with assumptions about the racialization of bodies" (*Queering the Color Line*, 4). Thus the rise of sexual science, and its attendant invention of the primitive body, the sexually deviant body, and the disabled body, offered a way of addressing the paradox of how American democracy can coexist with hierarchical structures.

21. These observations have changed the landscape of disability studies over the past decade and a half, inviting a broader range of approaches to disability and sparking a wave of newer queer-crip collaborations. For example, Ellen Samuels ("My Body, My Closet") and Anna Mollow ("Is Sex Disability?") have theorized the way disability complicates canonical queer concepts like "the closet," "performativity," and "the death drive." Disability autobiography has also provided a rich site of dialogue between the two fields, with memoir and filmic pieces by Eli Clare, Terry Galloway, Loree Erickson, Riva Lehrer, and Kenny Fries powerfully exploring how compulsory heterosexuality and compulsory able-bodiedness can shape bodies and practices. All of this work has been crucially important in advancing scholarly collaboration between these two fields, supplying disability studies with fresh theoretical frameworks while also taking to task queer theory's elision of material conditions.

22. As Elizabeth Grosz illustrates in *The Nick of Time*, Darwinian evolution, despite its eugenic appropriations, is ultimately not a theory of "being" but a theory of "becoming." For Darwin, far more than any linear models of progress, it is a radically unstable ontology of bodily unpredictability and openness that governs the human.

23. I am referring here to Foucault's frequently cited 1997 interview, "Friendship as a Way of Life," as well as Tom Roach's recent (2012) elaborations of the concept in *Friendship as a Way of Life*. Considering the queer activist formations that took shape in the wake of the AIDS epidemic, Roach observes that "such groups transform friendships of shared estrangement into a mode of biopolitical resistance that breaches the boundaries of gender, race, class, and generation and that encourages radically democratic forms of citizenship and civic participation . . . unwedded to the dialectic of identity and difference" (12).

24. See Michael Hardt, "Take the Revolutionary Road."

25. See Frank L. Dewey, "Thomas Jefferson's Law Practice."

26. Alexis Shotwell in *Against Purity* unpacks the prophylactic logic of contemporary antivax rhetoric, arguing that the "belief that vaccinations introduce toxins that would make a child no longer pure is here closely allied with a species of defensive individualism, the sense in which the self is imagined as a fortress, separable from the world and requiring a defense against the world" (11).

27. See John D'Emilio, *Sexual Politics, Sexual Communities*.

28. For a more thorough account of Mad Pride and its relation to disability studies, see Bradley Lewis's "Mad Fight: Psychiatry and Disability Activism."

29. This letter is part of the Kameny papers, archived through the Library of Congress.

30. Ronald Spitzer wrote up a set of proposed revisions the following year that reflected a compromise between the position of the gay activists and the more conservative members of APA. This new position argued that homosexuality was not necessarily a disorder but can be an element of disordered behavior. Relabeled "sexual preference disturbance," psychiatrists' new therapeutic focus was on those who experience distress as a result of their homosexuality. In this way, Spitzer allowed for the possibility of healthy and well-adjusted homosexuality while simultaneously avoiding having to say that homosexuality is "normal" or preferable to heterosexuality. Interestingly, the new designation actually compared homosexuality to other "sub-optimal behaviors" like racism and religious fanaticism. This compromise position finally passed in 1974; a later revision in 1986 removed "homosexuality" entirely. For more on this, see Ronald Bayer, *Homosexuality and American Psychiatry*.

31. In November of 2013, for example, disability scholar Mark Sherry published a controversial essay in the *Feminist Wire* titled "Crip Politics? Just . . . No." In it, Sherry dismissed current academic uses of the word "crip" as a problematic attempt to make disability studies "trendy" and "fashionable" for postmodern and queer textual analysis, maintaining that "crip theory" and "cripistemologies" have little to do with the material realities of disabled lives. I would argue that a careful reading of both *Crip Theory* and the *Cripistemologies* double issue of *JLCDS* reveals a deep and nuanced engagement with the economic and material forces that impact daily survival for disabled people. Nonetheless, Sherry's piece brought to a boiling point some of the historical tensions that have shaped queer theory and disability studies' legacy of uneasy partnership.

32. See Lee Edelman's reading of Tiny Tim in *No Future: Queer Theory* and David Greven's reading of Billy Budd in "Flesh in the Word."

33. For more on biocertification, see Ellen Samuels, *Fantasies of Identification*.

34. See, for example, Jasbir Puar, "Coda: Cost of Getting Better."

35. Of course, the concept of "safe space" is itself a contested rhetorical territory, as I later discuss in more detail. In her illuminating study (*Safe Space*) of how rhetorics of "safety" have shaped queer urban geography, Christina Hanhardt notes that transgender subjects, particularly those of color, were often the first to be targeted by gay "safe space" initiatives, themselves made unsafe by increased threats of surveillance, incarceration, and police violence. Ironically, it is these very forms of precarity that make it crucial to reconsider safety—not as a neoliberal form of property protection or securitization but as a refusal to romanticize the vulnerability of marginalized populations.

CHAPTER 1

1. Following the lead of scholars like Robert McRuer and Carrie Sandahl, my use of the terms "queer" and "crip" can be understood as referring to a variety of practices, meanings, and forms of embodiment that have been constructed in tension with the

era's reigning sexual, physical, and behavioral norms. In reading against the grain of London's "healthy" heteromasculine reputation, my intention is not to uncloset any of London's characters as gay or disabled but rather to trouble the coherence of concepts like "queerness" and "disability," even as I employ them as shorthand.

2. In *Narrative Prosthesis*, David Mitchell and Sharon Snyder write: "The desire to access the seeming solidity of the body's materiality offers representational literatures a way of grasping that which is most unavailable to them. . . . The passage through a bodily form helps secure a knowledge that would otherwise drift away of its own insubstantiality. The corporeal metaphor offers narrative the one thing it cannot possess—an anchor in materiality" (63).

3. Importantly, Rivera's authentic physicality is counterposed against the superficial vanity of his white opponent, Danny Ward. Though Ward possesses a muscular body, his skin is "white as a woman's" and his photographs appear in "all the physical culture magazines." Unlike the feminized superficiality of Ward's body (whose power is only skin deep), Rivera is described as having a "deep chest" and "muscles" that "made no display." Thus Ward's alignment with the inauthentic, feminine performances of culture sets the stage for Rivera's masculine materiality to emerge in relief, a materiality that is deeply intertwined with the authenticity of the natural world.

4. For Georgio Agamben, the "state of exception" that exists at the heart of the sovereignty exists in the sovereign's paradoxical power, in moments of crisis, to suspend law for the sake of preserving law, and in parallel fashion, to kill in the name of preserving life. The power of the sovereign to act both within and outside of the law thus reveals the law's dependence on a largely arbitrary violence and power over physical life. In the phrase "force of law," then, force is to be understood not as the simple administration of law (the punishment of crimes) but the founding moment that establishes the law as such.

5. Of course, in solving one set of problems, the naturalist model of masculinity created another. Primitivism may have been gendered as masculine but it was also often racialized as nonwhite. To slide backward into a more primordial manhood was not just to recover the wellspring of one's masculinity—it was also to identify oneself with the "lower" races. As Gail Bederman explains in *Manliness and Civilization*, when Jim Jeffries (an American boxer nicknamed "the Hope of the White Race") faced off against the African American boxer Jack Johnson (nicknamed "The Negro's Deliverer"), their fight was given as a racial battle that would, if Jeffries were victorious, prove that "white men's capacity for masculine violence was as powerful as black men's—that civilization had not undermined whites' primal masculinity" (41). Thus the coverage described the white Jeffries in both primal terms, as a man with a "vast, hairy body," "legs like trees," and a "long projecting jaw" (41), and intellectual terms, as a man whose "brain" would inevitably give him an advantage over the "emotional" fighting style characteristic of the "Negro." London himself covered this match as a reporter and went on to provide a fictionalized retelling of the event in his 1911 prizefighting novella, *The Abysmal Brute*. In the novella, white masculinity is reclaimed as Pat Glendon Jr. (a fictionalized version of the white Jim Jeffries) prevails over his racialized and animalistic opponents.

6. Indeed, images of Darwinian competition as a physical fight between individuals (rather than as a much slower and more nuanced process involving the evolutionary

fit between species and environment) represent a popular distortion of Darwin's own views. As Kimmel observes, "no sooner had Darwin's Origin of the Species been published in 1859 that social thinkers on both sides of the Atlantic attempted to apply his theories of natural selection and survival of the fittest to human societies—something that Darwin himself had been hesitant to do" (*Manhood in America*, 67).

7. My own use of the term "national manhood" throughout this chapter refers specifically to Nelson's formulation of the concept.

8. London here appears to be echoing Thoreau's "Resistance to Civil Government" but with considerably more optimism regarding the democratic process.

9. As Rita Felski notes in *The Gender of Modernity*, "The stylization and theatricality of aestheticism, exemplified through 'living a life in quotation marks,' was thus to become a defining feature of a 'camp sensibility associated with the homosexual lifestyle of urban elites at the fin de siècle" (103).

10. Indeed, nineteenth-century literary culture is filled with examples of the dispassionate physician, from Hawthorne's extensive catalog of misguided men of science (Chillingworth, Aylmer, Rappacini) to the more sympathetic portrait of Dr. Alec in Louisa May Alcott's *Eight Cousins*. For a compelling and comprehensive account of the ambivalent position that doctors occupied in the nineteenth-century literary imagination, see Stephanie P. Browner's *Profound Science and Elegant Literature*.

11. As Lee Clark Mitchell suggests, "The phrase 'finding one's legs' recurs insistently through the narrative and acquires multiple meanings; it refers not only to striving to rise above the horizontal but also to preserving one's life, discovering one's 'soul,' and defining one's status independent of culture" ("And Rescue Us from Ourselves," 319).

12. This paradigm, of course, produces an interesting problem for heterosexual contact which would, in this schema, produce a feminizing effect on men and a masculinizing effect on women. Toward the end of the novel, London crafts a solution to this paradox, which I discuss in more detail later in the chapter.

13. We might contrast this with Humphrey's attempt to "cleanse" the passages of his own text by censoring the vulgarity of the speech he describes.

14. For more on the link between masculinity and masochism, see David Savran, *Taking It Like a Man* and Kent L. Brintnall, *Ecce Homo*.

15. The ship's name, *The Ghost*, is, of course, important to consider in any discussion of the gendered relationship between body and spirit. There is a certain irony in using a term with so many connotations of disembodiment and spectrality to describe the muscularized, masculine landscape of the ship itself. If the body is commonly understood in religious discourse as the structure that contains the soul, then London's naming here performs an intriguing reversal—it is the "spirit" that composes the usually concrete "structure" and a set of brawny material bodies that constitute what is generally understood to be an intangible soul. Rather than the body containing the spirit, in other words, London presents us with a spirit that contains a set of bodies.

16. See Vinnie Oliveri, "Sex, Gender, and Death."

17. It bears mentioning that Wolf's "perfect" masculine body has, in this scene, just put down a mutiny. Humphrey's appreciation of his brawny physicality is partially related to his new understanding of the contingent nature of law and sovereignty.

Wolf rules *The Ghost* not due to any divine right or abstract moral principle but simply because he can fight a roomful of sailors and emerge with nothing but "bruises and lacerations." It may seem odd for an author like London, known strongly for his Socialism, to celebrate the putting down of a revolt. But it's worth noting that Wolf has described, at other moments in the narrative, his own working-class background and his wage slavery. Wolf does not stand in for the capitalist bourgeoisie as much as he stands for the principle of revolutionary conflict and the fantasy of a state in which muscle does more than signify one's status as an exploited factory worker, carrying with it instead a serious measure of political capital.

18. The forms of male bonding depicted in *Before Adam*—occurring in the free spaces beyond "civilization"—are in many ways reminiscent of the relationship between Huck and Jim in Twain's *Adventures of Huckleberry Finn*. In this context, Huck's own description of his father in the novel is suggestive: "He had been drunk over in town, and laid in the gutter all night, and he was a sight to look at. A body would a thought he was Adam—he was just all mud" (20). Despite the religious reference, the image of Huck's father caked in mud suggests precisely the sort of primordial physicality described later in London's *Before Adam*. In both the title of London's novella and the reference in Twain's novel, then, fatherhood and paradigms of patrilineal descent are displaced by atavism and animal ancestry. If the biblical Adam is given as the original father of all generations, then Big Tooth and Huck's father issue from an even more primordial site of generation.

19. For Freud's explanation of the primal scene, see "From the History of Infantile Neurosis (The 'Wolfman')" in *The "Wolfman" and Other Cases*.

20. London states this desire more explicitly four years later, in an essay titled "The Salt of the Earth." Alongside a set of racist proclamations of white evolutionary superiority, London writes: "The dim perceptions and vague phantasms of the old technology have flickered and vanished in the clear white light of science. Darwin horrified the world, but today our remote relationship with the anthropoid apes is not repulsive. Our cave and arboreal ancestors, hairy of body and prognathous of jaw, have taken their place on the witness stand, and false Adam's lineal claim has been thrown out of court. . . . No matter how much it hurts, the truth must be spoken. Truth—not the heart's ardent logic but the head's colder reasoning" (100). *Before Adam* gives "those arboreal ancestors" their proper place "on the witness stand." Stepping forward to name themselves, these talking primates not only displace those models of patriarchal lineage and religious authority represented by the original "forefather" Adam but represent the realization of London's fantasy of unmediated representation.

21. The term "penny dreadful" was a common term for the nautical adventure literature of the late nineteenth century. This literature was written specifically for consumption by an adolescent readership, often featuring adolescent boys as their protagonists. Its narratives ranged from the more iconic books like Stevenson's *Treasure Island* and Kipling's *Kim* to the mass market "penny dreadfuls" with formulaic titles like *The Boy Highwayman*, *The Boy Pirate*, and *The Boy King of Outlaws*. On the level of both thematics and consumption, the focus was on the education of the adolescent male and these ambivalent bildungsromans found themselves treading a fine line between proper masculine development and the encouragement of immoral or deviant

behavior. As Elyssa D. Warkentin notes, these nautical adventures were "seen either as offering a violent and romanticized alternative to the constructs of nationality and law, or to the contrary, merely using an 'outlaw' thematic to 'produce imperial men'" ("Adventure Literature," 3).

22. Available at http://www.dictionary.com/browse/spread-eagle.

23. London's use of Nietzsche here does not entirely reflect Nietzsche's actual views on evolution, which were more complicated than simple approval. Kimmel, for example, points to the way that some writers of the period "fused Social Darwinism and a bastardized Nietzschean evocation of the Overman" in an attempt to argue "that the survival of the fittest resulted in the 'raw, sturdy Saxon of primitive England'" (*Manhood in America*, 68).

24. Also notable is Maud's occupation as a poet whose "thin volumes" of poetry Humphrey had favorably reviewed in the past. If skill with language is given as the sign of a feminizing modernity, then the "old" Humphrey is even more "feminine" and "modern" than Maud. As a critic rather than an author, Humphrey is someone who writes about writing and is therefore even further removed from the material world than Maud who simply writes.

25. Maud confesses: "You know, I was traveling to Japan for my health. . . . I was not very strong. I never was. The doctors recommended a sea voyage and I chose the longest" (230), but she concludes that her time aboard *The Ghost* has made her a "stronger woman . . . and, I hope, a better woman" (230).

26. See Walter Benn Michaels, Vinnie Oliveri, and Lee Clark Mitchell.

27. As Walter Benn Michaels notes, "The disease that paralyzes before it kills [Wolf] is the triumph of Hump's idealism. . . . The proof of Wolf's soul lies not in its escaping his body but in its being entombed by it." ("Promises of American Life, 1880–1920," 383).

CHAPTER 2

1. See Elizabeth Dill, "That Damned Mob of Scribbling Siblings." Other scholars have also challenged totalized understandings of sentiment as a purely feminine mode, arguing that sentiment was, in fact, absolutely central in constructions of American masculine citizenship. See, in particular, Julie Stern, *The Plight of Feeling*; Dana Nelson, *National Manhood*; Kristin Boudreau, *Sympathy in American Literature*; and Lauren Berlant, *The Female Complaint*.

2. Other factors, too, led to the discrediting of the "sentimental" in the early twentieth century: the rejection of Romanticism in favor of modernism's more experimental, non-representational modes of artistic expression, a collective sense of disillusionment following the Civil War and World War I, and sentiment's increasing association with women's participation in the public sphere.

3. As June Howard observes, "When we call an artifact or gesture sentimental, we are pointing to its use of some established convention to evoke emotion; we mark a moment when the discursive processes that construct emotion become visible" (*Publishing the Family*, 245).

4. See Mary Odem, *Delinquent Daughters*.

5. The queerness of "the child" has emerged as a major inquiry in queer theory over the past decade. See, for example, Steven Bruhm and Natasha Hurley's *Curiouser*, Kathryn Bond Stockton's *The Queer Child*, and *WSQ: Child* (2015), a special issue of *Women's Studies Quarterly*.

6. For another convincing crip critique of *No Future*, see Anna Mollow, "Is Sex Disability?"

7. This point might be made by briefly revisiting a passage that Edelman himself cites in his book, *No Future*, taken from a 1998 essay written in support of a "Parent's Bill of Rights." In it, one of the bill's proponents sounded the following call to action: "It is time to join together and acknowledge that the work that parents do is indispensable—that by nourishing those small bodies growing those small souls, they create the store of social human capital that is so essential to the health and wealth of our nation. Simply put, by creating the conditions that allow parents to cherish their children, we will ensure our collective future" (111–112). For Edelman, this passage demonstrates evocatively the principles of what he terms "reproductive futurism" (111). But what is striking about this passage is not its sentimentality but, to the contrary, the almost clinical portrait of children as a form of "human capital" that circulates through the veins of a "healthy" and "wealthy" body politic.

8. Though academic work on eugenics has traversed a broad range of disciplines including disability studies, African American studies, and feminist studies, scholars of queer studies have not often engaged with the important role of eugenics in constructing a set of national narratives about sexual normativity and sexual transgression. For some notable exceptions to this trend, see Siobhan Somerville's *Queering the Color Line* and Nancy Ordover's *American Eugenics*.

9. Quoted in Ruth Rosen's *Lost Sisterhood: Prostitution in America*.

10. Faulkner's intricate treatment of the racial tensions that marked his era have been thoughtfully explicated by many scholars, and anxieties over the sociopolitical implications of acceptable and unacceptable forms of heterosexual reproduction mark nearly all of his novels. Miscegenation and incest, for example, are two recurring themes within Faulkner's work. Despite—or perhaps precisely because of—the possibility that such pairings will produce offspring, these modes of sexuality are figured as the most queerly abject within his novels. For a comprehensive study of race relations, and the miscegenation anxieties that accompanied them, see Eric Sundquist's *Faulkner: A House Divided*.

11. For a more thorough discussion of enforced sterilization, and its intersections with race, class, and gender, see Edward J. Larson, "'In the Finest Most Womanly Way'"; Johanna Schoen, *Choice and Coercion*; and Rickie Solinger, *Pregnancy and Power*.

12. For a more thorough account of the medicalized governmental treatment of prostitutes, see Allan M. Brandt's *No Magic Bullet*.

13. For a powerful mediation on Carrie Buck and disability politics, see Eli Clare, *Brilliant Imperfection*.

14. For more on the case, see Solinger, *Pregnancy and Power*. Importantly, the ruling against Buck set a precedent for other eugenic sterilization laws throughout the country, laws that were, even into the 1970s, used to sterilize black and lower-class women without their consent.

15. Soon after this, Popeye is "sent to a home for incorrigible children" for abusing animals and is let out five years later when his "impeccable" behavior suggests that he has been "cured." While Popeye's sociopathic leanings may suggest anything but a "feeble" mind, his institutionalization nonetheless places him squarely within those discourses that separated the "fit" from the "unfit."

16. See Ruth Hubbard, "Abortion and Disability."

17. While Faulkner's larger body of work cannot really be described as moralistic, other novels do seem to provide a clearer set of guidelines regarding who the reader is intended to sympathize with. While readers of *Light in August* are led to empathize with the innocent Baby Joey and to morally reject Doc Hines's abhorrent treatment of his mixed-race grandchild, the grotesque depictions of Ruby Goodwin's baby are much more likely to elicit revulsion than sympathy.

18. See Scott DeShong, "Toward an Ethics of Reading Faulkner's *Sanctuary*."

19. Available at http://www.nytimes.com/1981/02/22/books/faulkner-was-wrong-about-sanctuary.html.

20. For a more sustained theorization of how this "mismatch" plays out in public discourses on childhood, disability, and the reproductive/sexual body, see Alison Kafer's "At the Same Time, Out of Time: Ashley X" in *Feminist, Queer, Crip*.

21. In this sense, Benjy seems to prefigure the cognitively impaired Lennie from John Steinbeck's *Of Mice and Men*, published nearly a decade later. But what for Benjy consists only of the public's projection of danger onto his adult body, for Lennie results in the death of a woman. And while Benjy's sterilization is largely denounced by the novel as misguided and unnecessary, the moral implications of George's final act of "euthanasia" is left more ambiguous in Steinbeck's novel.

22. A 1920 reviewer of the novel captures this dynamic well, perhaps, when she observes of Benjy that "it is as if the story of Hans Anderson's *Little Mermaid* had been taken from the nursery and sentiment and made, rather diabolically, to grow up" (79). For the full review, see Evelyn Scott, "On William Faulkner's *The Sound and the Fury*."

23. We might also observe this vacillation between sentimental and scientific registers with respect to *Light in August*'s Lena Grove who fills the narrative with a form of powerful maternal sympathy despite her status as a "delinquent" unwed teen mother.

24. We might here recall Jason's mother's declaration that "Jason can do no wrong because he is more Bascomb than Compson. . . . I look at him every day dreading to see this Compson blood beginning to show in him at last with his sister slipping out" (193).

25. As Dorr puts it, "Although eugenic legislation challenged traditions of local control, it sounded many of the major chords of southern society: white supremacy, paternalism, and the myth of a predatory, atavistic African American population. Many Americans believed that, through government action in support of eugenic policies, the nation's population would become racially and democratically homogeneous" ("Assuring America's Place in the Sun," 263).

26. See M. Thomas Inge, "Fitzgerald, Faulkner and Little Lord Fauntleroy."

27. Indeed, Ophelia's "flower" monologue in Shakespeare's *Hamlet* reads in many ways like a primer for Fitzgerald's own cast of characters, from *Tender*'s "Rosemary" Hoyt and "Violet" McKisco to *Gatsby*'s "Daisy" Buchanan, to even the description of Dick's lace drawers as a "pansy's trick":

> There's *rosemary*, that's for remembrance; pray,
> love, remember: and there is *pansies*. that's for thoughts.
> There's fennel for you, and columbines: there's rue
> for you; and here's some for me: we may call it
> herb-grace o' Sundays: O you must wear your rue with
> a difference. There's a *daisy*: I would give you
> some *violets*, but they withered all when my father
> died: they say he made a good end,—
> (Act IV, Scene V, emphases added)

Available at http://shakespeare.mit.edu/hamlet/hamlet.4.5.html

28. Fitzgerald's own views of eugenics and racial Nordicism are unclear, due in part to his own ambivalent writing on the subject. Several Fitzgerald scholars have noted Fitzgerald's complex and sometimes contradictory treatment of race and miscegenation. While some elements of his fiction display an intense concern for protecting physical integrity of the white woman against the threat of "darker" men, other moments explicitly lampoon the appeals made by writers and orators like Lathrop Stoddard, Henry Goddard, and Madison Grant to safeguard the purity of the white race. According to Alan Margolies, Fitzgerald openly admitted in 1923 that "no one has a greater contempt than I have for the recent hysteria about the Nordic theory" ("The Maturing of Fitzgerald," 108). At the same time, Felipe Smith cites a 1921 letter in which Fitzgerald writes "God damn the continent of Europe. The negroid streak creeps northward to defile the Nordic race. Already the Italians have the souls of blacamoors" (190). Smith also notes that Fitzgerald "warned Wilson that America should 'raise the bars of immigration and permit only Scandinavians, Teutons, Anglo-Saxons, and Celts to enter,' going to far as to suggest that it might have been better after all if the Germans had been allowed to conquer Europe. Fitzgerald also leveled his strongest condemnation of the French in terms of 'racial' unfitness. . . . Fitzgerald's letter reveals not only his strong sensitivity to racial and ethnic difference; it also shows his tendencies to use Africannness as a term of ultimate disapprobation and to see hierarchical classifications of and ethnicity as absolute measurement of human worth" ("The Figure on the Bed," 190–191).

29. Artifice, at the time that Fitzgerald was writing, was becoming increasingly linked to Hollywood's cinematic manipulations. We see this linkage in the text through Fitzgerald's description of the exceedingly (and artificially) sentimental film *Daddy's Girl*.

30. In this respect, Clover and Celeste might be understood as precursors to the wry, no-nonsense New Woman Jordan Baker and the charming, feminine Daisy Buchanan of Fitzgerald's *The Great Gatsby*.

31. We might here recall one of our earliest descriptions of Popeye as a person with the "vicious depthless quality of stamped tin" (4) who walks with his "tight suit and stiff hat all angles, like a modernist lampstand" (7). Far from being coded with qualities of sentiment, Popeye's "viciousness" is here aligned with modernity's cold assembly-line logic as well as the novel's own "depthless" sensational qualities. These two very separate sets of associations expose the sentimental and the scientific/sensational as two sides of the same coin.

32. Of course, what is at this moment a sincere rendering of the sentimental child becomes, by the middle of the same section, hardened into satire during the screening of *Daddy's Girl*: "There she was—the school girl of a year ago, hair down her back and rippling out stiffly like the solid hair of a tanagra figure; there she was—so young and innocent—the product of her mother's loving care; there she was—embodying all the immaturity of the race. Before her tiny fist the forces of lust and corruption rolled away; nay the very march of destiny stopped; inevitable became evitable, syllogism, dialectic, all rationality fell away . . . happier days now, and a lovely shot of Rosemary and her parent united at the last in a father complex so apparent that Dick winced for all psychologists at the vicious sentimentality" (69). Now labeling sentimentality as a "vicious" alibi for a clinically diagnosable "father complex," Dick distances himself from its intimacies by envisioning himself as "an old scientist all wrapped up in his private life" (70).

33. Fitzgerald is here referring to Frances Hodgson Burnett who wrote *Little Lord Fauntleroy*. Elsewhere, Fitzgerald observed that Faulkner's *Sanctuary* and Burnett's *Little Lord Fauntleroy* are in fact "two faces of the same world spirit," a pronouncement that Messenger unpacks with attention to the incestuous subtext underlying *Little Lord Fauntleroy*'s sentimental mother-child bond. What makes Burnett tracts "vicious" for Fitzgerald, in other words, is the extent to which the sentimental in her narratives functions as a smokescreen or—I would add—a kind of feminine "cosmetic" that obscures a more sensational sexual narrative that lies just under the surface.

34. For a more thorough account of this "love-murder," see Mary Ting Yi Lui, *The Chinatown Trunk Mystery*.

35. For more on this, see Lisa Duggan, "Trials of Alice Mitchell." Alice Mitchell's case may also form the background of London's disapproving portrait of Humphrey Van Weyden's masculinity—the "mannish lesbian" is understood to be all the more successful at romancing impressionable girls when her primary competitors are effeminate male intellectuals like Humphrey.

36. In this sense, they almost evoke the "Gold Star" mothers who, entering the narrative much earlier in the novel, remind Dick of the "maturity of an older America. For a while the sobered women who had come to mourn for their dead, for something they could not repair, made the room beautiful. Momentarily, he sat again on his father's knee, riding with Moseby while the old loyalties and devotions fought on around him. Almost with an effort he turned back to his two women at the table and faced the whole new world in which he believed" (101).

37. Tommy's multinational ancestry is worth briefly dwelling on here. Half American and half French, Tommy is first introduced as a mercenary soldier who will fight anyone's war (30). His multinationality is rooted not just in his shifting loyalties but also in his physical body itself. As he opens the window to "find out what caused the increasing clamor below their windows, his figure was darker and stronger than Dick's" (294). In the word "clamor" here, we might recall Fitzgerald's earlier reference to the "clamor of [American] empire." Indeed, while Dick's white masculinity and his status as a doctor had earlier sanitized that empire under his protective umbrella, the "stronger" and "darker" Tommy bears witness to a more unruly scene of empire. If Dick's willingness to merge with others makes him the metanarrative of a dangerously inclusive

America, then Tommy's "strong," "dark" body seems to suggest a remasculinization of the American melting pot ideal, his robust physicality pointing not to a strict preservation of national bloodlines but to a transcendence of them.

38. There is, additionally, a third real-life "case" that haunts the narrative, alluded to in Dick's observation, upon discovering Peterson in Rosemary's bed, that the "paint was scarcely dry on the Arbuckle case" (100). Roscoe "Fatty" Arbuckle was a Hollywood comedian and filmmaker who created a national scandal when he was implicated in the rape and death of aspiring starlet Virginia Rappe.

39. Additionally, the literal "death" of the mother here might be read as the more figurative "death" of the previous century's maternal politics of sympathy and an unmasking of the sensational undercurrents that, ostensibly, lie beneath sentiment's artifice.

40. Dick's status as a national metanarrative is not without its gendered and psychoanalytic implications. In *Eugenic Fantasies*, Betsy Nies draws from the theories of Mikhail Bakhtin, Julia Kristeva, and Mart Douglas to discuss the ways in which psychoanalytic theories of abjection play out in the political sphere through the repudiation of cultural otherness. Nies notes that "the Nordic male now stood as an image of containment, one separated from the mother; his ethnic Other, caught in the throes of living and dying, was forever merged with her figurative presence, inside her in birth, merged with the Kristevan maternal earth in death. . . . Bodily boundaries became national boundaries as the eugenicists made their stand" (14). Nies's study therefore offers a productive starting point for broadening psychoanalytic readings of the novel into more explicitly biopolitical ones.

41. This to some extent recalls Dick's letters to the institutionalized Nicole: "All I said in my letters was 'Be a good girl and mind the doctors'" (130). Indeed, the frequent mention of "rest cures" throughout the novel remind us that liberated womanhood was itself, in that period, often considered a treatable illness. For a comprehensive study of the ways in which femaleness was defined and regulated through medical discourse, see Barbara Ehrenreich and Deirdre English, *For Her Own Good*.

CHAPTER 3

1. See Sid Davis's short "educational" film *Boys Beware*, Sid Davis Productions, 1961, available at https://www.pbs.org/video/american-experience-boys-beware/. See also Jennifer Terry, *Deviant Bodies* and Ronald Bayer, *Homosexuality and American Psychiatry*.

2. See Sally Munt, *New Lesbian Criticism*.

3. Indeed, though it is outside the scope of this essay, the power differential between men and women actively shapes many of the novel's explorations, from Rufus's abusive relationship with Leona to Vivaldo's fraught intimacy with Rufus's sister Ida. For a fuller analysis of Baldwin's treatment of female characters, see Trudier Harris, *Black Women in the Fiction of James Baldwin*.

4. As Baldwin explains in one interview, "My publisher, Knopf, told me I was a 'Negro writer' and that I reached a certain audience. They told me I could not afford to alienate that audience, and that my new book would ruin my career because I was

not writing about the same things in the same manner as I had before. . . . You see whites want Black writers to mostly deliver something as it were an official version of the Black experience. But no true account to Black life can be held, can be contained in the American vocabulary" (quoted in Kenan and Sickels, *James Baldwin*, 126).

5. See Robert Reid-Pharr, *Black Gay Man: Essays*.

6. This understanding was on the one hand rooted in the homophobic equation of homosexuality with weakness and effeminacy (qualities that were perceived as bad for militant uprisings) and the sexist alignment of practices like heterosexual rape with masculinity and strength (qualities that were perceived as good for militant uprisings). Cleaver's dismissal of Baldwin's sexuality was also fueled by the belief that a successful Black Nation depended on the perpetuation of pure black bloodlines, a perpetuation that could only take place via heteronormative reproduction. Ultimately, Baldwin's unwillingness to share Eldridge Cleaver's vision of a heteromasculine Black Nation—his insistence that the relation between black and white Americans was too intimately wedded, too dialectical to be conceived of in terms of simple oppositionality—earned him the nickname "Martin Luther Queen," an epithet that aligned his perceived race betrayal with homosexuality and effeminacy. His queerness, from the perspective of many Black Nationalists, was evidence of his misguided alliances with white people, and those alliances disqualified him from speaking on behalf of the race.

7. Though Bergler claimed to have "no bias against homosexuality," he nonetheless outlined a set of personality traits that symptomatized the homosexual condition, including "a mixture of superciliousness, false aggression and whimpering . . . subservien[ce] when confronted with a stronger person, merciless[ness] when in power, unscrupulous[ness] about trampling on a weaker person" (3). There is, we might note, ample evidence in David's confessional narrations to support most of these charges: he admits to fearing his father's censure (to the point of running away to Europe) while documenting his cruelty toward individuals who carry less social power than himself—specifically, women and effeminate gay men. Indeed, even David's displays of sexism seem to reflect conventional psychiatric wisdom about gay men's misogynistic fear of women—a belief that, as Kenneth Lewes points out, is more reflective of psychiatry's own "gynecophobic stance" (*Psychoanalysis and Male Homosexuality*, 9).

8. While Freud did to some extent frame homosexuality as a result of psychosexual maladjustment, he was also open to more fluid understandings of homosexuality and did not generally regard same-sex desire as something that required (or responded to) medical treatment or cure. For example, in Freud's often cited 1935 "Letter to a Mother," Freud responds to a woman's request for "help" in treating her son's homosexuality by assuring her that while homosexuality may be produced by a certain "arrest in sexual development," it is in fact a legitimate "variation of the sexual function" that "cannot be classified as an illness."

9. Of course, these were not the only voices. Researchers like Alfred Kinsey (in 1948) and Cleland Ford and Frank Beach (in 1951) were simultaneously suggesting that homosexual behavior was more widespread than suspected and therefore was (quantitatively at least) much closer to the "norm" than many suspected. Additionally, Evelyn Hooker's qualitative study of gay men revealed them to be more psychologically stable and happy than other research (drawn specifically from individuals who had

sought help from the medical profession) had suggested. For more on this history, see Ronald Bayer, *Homosexuality and American Psychiatry*.

10. For a fuller account of these therapeutic interventions, see Jonathan Ned Katz, *Gay American History* and Simon Levay, *Queer Science*.

11. Yasmin DeGout also focuses on Baldwin's medicalization of homosexuality, arguing that, while the novel sometimes frames love between men as innocent, redemptive, and healing, it also "creates a psychological history that can be used to explain homoerotic love as behavior that is produced by diagnosable circumstances within a society" ("Dividing the Mind," 430).

12. This is not to suggest that David is racialized in the novel as anything other than white—to the contrary, he opens the novel with a description of his own blond hair and Nordic ancestry. Rather, it is to suggest that David's own projection of racial difference onto the encounter betrays his own anxieties regarding the relationship between queer transgression and interracial intimacy.

13. Baldwin writes: "[The color of my skin] seems to operate as a most disagreeable mirror, and a great deal of one's energy is expended in reassuring white Americans that they do not see what they see. This is utterly futile, of course, since they do see what they see. And what they see is an appallingly oppressive and bloody history, known all over the world. What they see is a disastrous, continuing, present condition which menaces them, and which menaces them, and for which they bear an inescapable responsibility. But since, in the main, they seem to lack the energy to change this condition, they would rather not be reminded of it" (722).

14. When red-light districts in New York and Chicago came under stricter police surveillance during the early part of the twentieth century, much of the sexual underground relocated to black communities. It was in this way that Harlem was gradually transformed into a safe haven for both queer subcultures and individuals (both gay and straight) involved in interracial relationships. As Kevin Mumford convincingly argues in *Interzones*, the origin of most modern queer subcultures can be traced back to the black-and-tan speakeasies of the Jazz Age where interracial affiliations, queer sexualities, and the culture of prostitution overlapped in ways that invited both alliance and conflict.

15. This conflation was not merely subtextual but coded into policy itself, leading to the massive 1950s governmental purge of homosexual employees from the State Department during the "lavender scare." For more on this, see David K. Johnson, *The Lavender Scare*.

16. "Boys Beware." Director Sid Davis. Sid Davis Productions, 1961, available at https://www.pbs.org/video/american-experience-boys-beware/.

17. A striking example of this logic can be found in the 1960 newspaper coverage of Bernon Mitchell and William Marton, National Security Agency analysts who defected to the Soviets. One newspaper headline promises to tell the story "Behind the Scandal of Those Two Traitors: How the Reds Blackmail Homosexuals into Spying for Them." The writer begins his exposé by presenting male homosexuality as a dark agenda hidden behind an all-American masculine façade: "No one could understand how two young men like these—clean cut fellows who looked like typical all-American boys—could betray their own homeland to the Russians. After all, these men came

from solid, church-going families, lived in the kind of small towns for which this country is famous, and seemed as safe from subversion as two men could be." "'How the Reds Blackmail Homosexuals into Spying for Them!'" *Satan Was a Lesbian: Queer Pulp in the Cold War Era*, accessed March 3, 2013, available at http://queerpulp.omeka.net/items/show/120.

18. For more on the politics of gay shame and the critique of gay pride, see David Halperin and Valerie Traub's *Gay Shame* anthology (2009), Jasbir Puar's *Terrorist Assemblages* (2007), and Heather Love's *Feeling Backward* (2009).

19. See Margaret Price, *Mad at School*.

20. Ellen Samuels provides a fascinating account of the rhetoric and ideology of the "disability scam" in *Fantasies of Identification*.

21. Like hysteria, Johnson's feminist peers assured her, BPD "wasn't real," manufactured by male doctors to undermine women's credibility and neutralize female rebellion. Ironically, such claims function to undermine Johnson's credibility in a different way, painting her embrace of diagnostic labels as a convenient evasion of sexual politics rather than, as she sees it, celebrating it as a powerful act of crip solidarity.

22. Baldwin's commitment to black psychological interiority is evidenced, too, in his critique of Richard Wright's *Native Son*. In "Many Thousands Gone," Baldwin notes that "what is missing in [Bigger's] situation and in the representation of his psychology—which makes his situation false and his psychology incapable of development—is any revelatory apprehension of Bigger as one of the Negro's realities or as one of the Negro's roles. . . . He does not redeem the pains of a despised people, but reveals, on the contrary, nothing more than his own fierce bitterness at having been born one of them" (30–31).

23. Quoted in Colm Toibin, "The Henry James of Harlem: James Baldwin's Struggles." *The Guardian*, September 2001. Available at http://www.theguardian.com/books/2001/sep/14/jamesbaldwin.

24. See Elizabeth Donaldson, "Revisiting the Corpus of the Madwoman."

25. We may also hear in Baldwin's remembrance of his father as a "strong, handsome, healthy black man, who liked to use his muscles" a version of London's discovery, among the tramp population, of men who "had once been as good as myself and just as blond-beastly; sailor-men, soldier-men, labor-men, all wrenched and distorted and twisted out of shape by toil and hardship and accident, and cast adrift by their masters like so many old horses" (126).

26. In Agamben's framing, bare life is embodied in the figure of the "homo sacer" whose murder exposes the state of exception that exists at the heart of the sovereign paradigm. Because his death cannot be given meaning through sacrifice and killing him is unpunishable by law, he embodies the state of exception that is the "originary act of sovereignty" (*Homo Sacer*, 85).

27. In his "Talk to Teachers," Baldwin echoes this sentiment, observing that Harlem is populated by "people who live outside the law" and who "wouldn't, for a moment, listen to any of those professions of which we are so proud on the Fourth of July. They have turned away from this country forever and totally" and they "long to see the day when the entire structure comes down" (681). Thus for Baldwin, as well as for London, the "Fourth of July" represents a moment of failed potential—it is up to the present generation, and not the nation's "forefathers," to harness the vital energy of revolution.

28. As Lawrie Balfour notes in *Evidence of Things Not Said*, Baldwin "refus[ed] the choice between integration and separation as a false one" (12), fashioning instead a theory of "race consciousness," which, "by going to the level of assumptions and unacknowledged beliefs . . . provides a way of casting a broad net and pulling in a wide range of conscious and unconscious associations with race and blackness, Americanness and whiteness" (7).

29. For some other accounts, see Ernesto J. Martinez, "Dying to Know: Identity"; James Dievler, "Sexual Exiles"; and Stephanie Dunning, "Parallel Perversions." Notably, however, this focus on interdependency and the breakdown of bodily boundaries is much more common in scholarship on *Another Country* (1963) than it is in scholarship that addresses Baldwin's earlier, and less explicitly "racial," novel *Giovanni's Room* (1956). Scholarship on *Another Country* has focused, for the most part, on the way that Baldwin uses cross-racial and intragender intimacies to craft a model of citizenship based on networked and highly politicized intimacies among differently raced, classed, and gendered bodies.

30. For more on Baldwin's "conversational ethics," see Jack Turner, *Awakening to Race*.

CHAPTER 4

1. See Douglas Crimp, "Mourning and Militancy"; Eric Rofes, *Dry Bones Breathe*; Andrew Sullivan, "When Plagues End"; David Roman, "Not about AIDS," and *Acts of Intervention*; Ann Cvetkovich, *Archive of Feelings*; and Sarah Brophy, *Witnessing AIDS*.

2. Andrew Ross, "Calculating the Risk."

3. While some gay men participated in these public health crusades (see, for example, Gabriel Rotello's inflammatory *Sexual Ecology*), others within the community published work on safe sex practices that theorized "how to have sex" and "how to have promiscuity in an epidemic." As Phillip Alcabes reflects in "The Ordinariness of AIDS," "When we progressives in the public-health field embraced the safe-sex campaign, we also implicitly endorsed the message of individual accountability that the health narrative of the day proffered. Resisting moralism about homosexuality and promiscuity, we instead promoted a new dogma about individual responsibility: Safe sex. Personal risk reduction" (30). See also Richard Berkowitz, Michael Callen, and Richard Dworkin's pamphlet, *How to Have Sex in an Epidemic*; and Douglas Crimp, "How to Have Promiscuity in an Epidemic."

4. Dennis Altman, *The Homosexualization of America*. Simon Watney (*Policing Desire*), too, defended the bathhouses against the attacks waged by moralizing public health officials who saw them as breeding grounds for vice and contagion rather than, as Watney argues, affirmative sites of gay community.

5. As Dean notes, it was not until 1981 that condomless sex between men was rhetorically transformed into the culturally maligned practice of "barebacking." "Although from one perspective," Dean writes, "fucking without condoms represents sex at its most mundane, from another perspective, the history of AIDS has made gay sex without condoms extraordinary, endowing bareback sex with enormous significance" (47). "Barebacking" is therefore a concept that only holds meaning in the context of

the AIDS and post-AIDS era, signifying in this context as excessive risk or recklessness toward one's own health and the health of others.

6. In using the term "biosociality," Dean is following the work of Nikolas Rose and Paul Rabinow. For more on biosociality, see Paul Rabinow, *Essays on the Anthropology of Reason*; and Nikolas Rose, *The Politics of Life Itself*.

7. For a more thorough account of the effect of zoning laws on New York City's queer sexual subcultures, see Michael Warner's *The Trouble with Normal*.

8. For a related analysis of "fellow feeling," disability, and practices of charitable donation, see Sheila Moeschen, *Acts of Conspicuous Compassion*.

9. See also Jeffrey Q. McCune Jr., *Sexual Discretion*.

10. Using the (RED) campaign as an instructive example of the new links that had been created between consumer practices and global health, Einstein describes how the (RED) logo functioned ultimately as a brand image that "connot[ed] to consumers that a percentage of the product's sales price—be it a cup of Starbucks or a red iPod or a Motorola phone—would go to the Global Fund, which works to assuage AIDS in Africa" (2). Einstein identifies practices like these as evidence of a "seismic shift in how we perceive philanthropy and social justice" (2). Though campaigns like (RED) frame themselves in centrifugal terms, with local acts facilitating a global "cure," the effect is ultimately one of centripetal contraction that prophylactically insulates the individual consumer from the global contexts of their giving. The (RED) website, for example, instructs visitors to "Imagine a World without AIDS." As the viewer scrolls down the page, they are presented with a set of statistics delineating the precise (and rising) number of antiretroviral prophylaxis treatments made possible in each African country as a result of donations made to the Global Fund. Without minimizing the crucial importance of treating the virus and preventing its spread in these regions, we might note the way in which the dissemination of literal prophylaxis is linked to a more figurative wave of prophylactic gift-giving that places citizens at a distant remove from the populations receiving assistance.

11. See Robin Morgan, "Theory and Practice: Pornography and Rape."

12. Indeed, Lisa Duggan and Nan Hunter document the ways in which some of the early efforts to outlaw pornography mobilized homophobic rhetorics. In *Sex Wars*, they recount, for example, the way in which Kathleen Mahoney incited "homophobic panic" in her successful 1992 bid to change Canadian obscenity laws by showing the judges "degrading gay movies" in which "the abused men . . . were being treated like women." As Duggan and Hunter note, Mahoney "did not seem to recognize the elasticity of terms like 'degrades' or 'dehumanizes,' nor their easy applicability by homophobes to gay sexuality" (9).

13. Critical race theorists, transnational feminists, and poststructuralist queer scholars have productively challenged many of the universalizing models that anti-pornography feminism rests on. Rich's global and transhistorical model of "lesbian resistance," it has been noted, consolidates an enormous variety of cultural practices under a singular model of "woman-identification," flattening out racial, geographic, temporal, and sexual specificity in the process. Using models of femininity and masculinity that relied on unmarked racial norms (always assuming a universalizable white middle-class subject), second-wave feminism thus could not always account for the uneven forms of agency and victimization that do not fall neatly along a strict male/female binary.

14. One exception includes Jack Halberstam's *The Queer Art of Failure*. Halberstam lists Delany's *Times Square Red, Times Square Blue* among a set of works by gay men in which "utopian joissance seems primarily available only in relation to male-male anal sex between strangers . . . while I am sympathetic to this project of not tidying up sex, I am less than enthusiastic about the archives upon which these authors draw and the resolutely white utopias they imagine through the magic portals of tricking" (150). While I would argue that Delany differs from Edelman and Dean in his attention to race and his emphasis on practices other than anal sex, I agree with Halberstam's account of Delany's masculine and homosocial bias.

15. Delany delivers an early version of this analysis in his essay "On the Unspeakable." While Delany's informal reading of the pornographic films can be understood as an innovative counter to anti-porn feminists' oftentimes reductive accounts of the same films, feminist critics like Constance Penley and Linda Williams had already, a decade earlier, provided a framework and methodology for critically appraising pornographic texts. Williams, like Delany, urges that porn be understood as a genre comparable to other genres, with its own unique narrative structures and devices. Unlike Delany, however, Williams uses that parallel to unpack the porn genre's deeply gendered conflicts even as she celebrates some of its possibilities. For example, while Williams acknowledges that *Deep Throat* was "one of the first pornographic films to concentrate on the problem of a women's pleasure and to suggest that some sexual acts were less than earthshaking," she is careful to qualify that such an exploration does not automatically make the film "a progressive or feminist work" (*Hard Core*, 25). For Williams, then, pornography is neither to be monolithically condemned as the exemplary site of female victimization nor to be understood as a representation of unfettered sexual freedom. Like other genres, it instead represents a complicated negotiation of sexual and gender norms.

16. As John Ellis points out, the presence of "dildos and other substitute penises [in pornography] is quite marked" ensuring that "a male presence is maintained even within scenes of masturbation or lesbianism" (42). See John Ellis, "On Pornography." Dildos, of course, need not be exclusively understood as a "male presence"—academic work on female masculinity and butch sexuality (not to mention the emergent genre of queer porn made for queer audiences) has made a convincing case against seeing these sex toys merely as "substitute penises." Nonetheless, Delany's unwillingness, in this moment, to engage with either body of scholarship is troubling.

17. Linda Williams makes a similar observation in her reading of *Deep Throat* when she argues that "the perverse implantation of the clitoris in *Deep Throat* represents something more than simple horror at the freakishness of female sexual 'lack.' She represents a phallic economy's highly ambivalent and contradictory attempt to count beyond the number one, to recognize, as the proliferating discourses of sexuality take hold, that there can no longer be any such thing as fixed sexuality—male, female, or otherwise. . . . As discourses of sexuality name, identify, and ultimately produce a bewildering array of pleasures and perversions, the very multiplicity of these pleasures and perversions inevitably works against the older idea of a single norm—and economy of the one—against which all else is measured" (*Hard Core*, 115).

18. It's important to mention, here, that this framing differs from some of Delany's earlier writing. In his 1988 memoir *The Motion of Light in Water*, for example,

Delany maintains that he is "not trying to romanticize that time into some cornucopia of sexual plenty. Its densities, its bareness, its intensities of both guilt and pleasure, of censure and of blindness . . . were grounded on a nearly absolutely sanctioned public silence" (175–176). And in an interview on his book *The Mad Man*, Delany provides a less utopian account of sexuality in his definition of "pornotopia": "Pornotopia is not the 'good sexual place.' It is simply *the* 'sexual place'—the place where all can become apocalyptically sexual . . . the place where any relationship can be sexualized in a moment with the proper word or look—where every relationship is potentially sexualized even before it starts" (133). Delany's admission here that a pornotopia is not necessarily the "good sexual place" is important for understanding sexuality's power relations. *The Mad Man*'s unrelenting portrayal of racialized sexual abjection, several scholars have observed, is productive precisely because it allows Delany's characters to claim their sexuality while at the same time resisting a utopian framing of that sexuality. But if *The Mad Man* is "apocalyptically" sexual, then *Times Square Red, Times Square Blue* paints a very different portrait—framed in unequivocally "pleasant terms," the porn theaters are given as precisely the "good sexual place."

19. We might also note the way this language resonates with the growing presence of male "incel" ("involuntary celibate)" communities on the internet. Within incel discourse, women's lack of sexual availability to certain men is cited as a justification for violence, often in the form of mass shootings committed by men who have met with recent romantic rejection.

20. See Eve Sedgwick, *Between Men*, and Katherine Liepe-Levinson, *Strip Show*. In the context of the porn theaters, of course, these homosocial bonds are literalized through the homosexual contacts that take place there. In his study of male-male homoeroticism in the *Penthouse Letters*, Henry Jenkins examines the way that "plausible deniability," within the pornucopic world of the magazine, enables a "passive slide into homoeroticism." The "woman" in the *Penthouse Letters* is thus reduced to "thin membrane" between the two men involved, a process that is structurally echoed in Delany's description of the process by which the absent woman is "flatten[ed]" into an "image on a screen." It might, of course, be argued that the absence of the woman in this context frees her from having to occupy her usual position as a relay point in the homosocial triangle. Whereas her presence is absolutely necessary for the "plausible deniability" that Jenkins describes in the *Penthouse Letters*, the worlds that Delany describes (as well as the subcultures of barebacking that Dean documents) make women an unnecessary part of the biosocial/homosocial exchange.

21. Dean demonstrates a parallel pedagogical imperative in an anecdote he recounts, ironically, about his experience teaching *Times Square Red, Times Square Blue*. "Repeatedly," Dean writes, "my straight female students assure me that the kind of contact with strangers advocated by both Jacobs and Delany is too dangerous for women" (182). Rather than take these objections seriously, Dean uses a passage from Jane Jacobs's 1961 book *The Death and Life of Great American Cities* to simply reiterate Delany's point about the pleasures of contact. Jacobs's recognition that "strangers traversing the street make it safe, especially at night when foot traffic otherwise would diminish," Dean observes, demonstrates precisely why a place like "the White Horse exemplifies the kind of institution necessary for a vital public sphere, and thus for

democracy" (183). Published two years before Betty Freidan's *The Feminine Mystique*, Jacobs's pre-second-wave text seems to here provide Dean with a means of dismissing feminist concerns that drive his students' objections. Pointing out that Jacobs is both "a wife and mother," Dean implies that if Jacobs can manage to get behind stranger sociality, then his female students should follow suit. Mapping Jacobs's (arguably) prefeminist observations onto Delany's more contemporary queer sexual ethics, Dean thus evacuates the entire intellectual and activist history of radical feminism. In this way, Dean deftly switches the terms of the debate, replacing his students' legitimate feminist concerns with the trump card of "democracy." Ultimately, this moment seems like a missed opportunity for an even more radical pedagogical exchange, one in which Dean might have opened himself up to being educated by, as well as educating, these straight female students.

22. For an in-depth exploration of radical feminist and queer sex cultures, see Pat Califia's *Public Sex*.

23. See Margot Weiss, *Techniques of Pleasure*; Christina Hanhardt, *Safe Space*; and Dean Spade, *Normal Life*.

24. For more on "the epidemiology of belonging," see Priscilla Wald, *Contagious*.

CHAPTER 5

1. Because this chapter focuses on how bodies assigned female at birth fit within the structures of antiprophylactic citizenship, I am necessarily leaving out a discussion of transwomen and asexual cismen. There is certainly more to be said about transfemininity and asexual masculinity, identities that also sit uncomfortably within the antiprophylactic frameworks I sketch in this book. My discussions of Chelsea Manning and the arguably asexual Humphrey may serve as starting points for such an investigation.

2. See Lori A. Brotto, "*DSM* Diagnostic Criteria" and Alyson Spurgas, "Interest, Arousal, and Shifting Diagnoses."

3. See Zowie Davy, "*DSM-5* and the Politics of Diagnosing Transpeople."

4. For more on the shifting medical framings of asexuality and its relationship to disability, see Eunjung Kim, "Asexualities and Disabilities," 100–118; and Kristina Gupta, "Asexuality and Disability," 283–301.

5. See L. Brotto, M. Krychman, and P. Jacobson, "Eastern Approaches for Enhancing Women's Sexuality"; and L. Brotto, R. Basson, M. Carlson, and C. Zhu, "Impact of an Integrated Mindfulness," 3–19.

6. See Annamarie Jagose, *Orgasmology*.

7. Of course, queer sex has a long history of being scripted into biopolitical narratives about health, illness, and contagion. As I illustrated in the previous chapter, in the context of the early spread of HIV and AIDS among gay men and the arrival of the Protease Moment a decade and a half later, the defense of queer public sex as a generative world-making practice was a necessary defense against the public health regimes and medical rhetorics that stigmatized gay men as fundamentally diseased and queer sex as medically risky. See Douglas Crimp, "Mourning and Militancy"; and Eric Rofes, *Dry Bones Breathe*.

8. For a wide-ranging overview of asexuality's intersections with queer theory and feminism, see Karli June Cerankowski and Megan Milks, "New Orientations."

9. Perhaps it is this paradoxical formulation that allows Tim Dean to frame barebacking as both communitarian and antisocial. Following Bersani's claiming of sexuality as the "jouissance of exploded limits," in *Unlimited Intimacy*, Dean describes barebacking and bug chasing as a form of "unlimited intimacy" in which "intense pleasure overwhelms self-control, threatening the ego's coherence" (5). But alongside the antisocial "outlaw rhetoric" of barebacking subcultures (9), "a new narrative about sexual citizenship also emerges in which sharing viruses has come to be understood as a mechanism of alliance, a way of forming consanguinity with strangers or friends." Like asexuals, barebackers are assumed to suffer from antisocial life-negating forms of shame and repression. And yet, within queer discourse, the subculture of barebacking, with its immediate relationship to sexual potency and orgasmic capacity, has proven easier to reclaim.

10. In *Feminist, Queer, Crip*, Alison Kafer discusses the temporal logics of ableism, observing that "a future of disability is a future that no one wants . . . disability is seen as the sign of no future" (3).

11. For more on compulsory sexuality, see Kristina Gupta, "Compulsory Sexuality"; C. D. Chasin, "Reconsidering Asexuality and Its Radical Potential"; E. F. Emens, "Compulsory Sexuality"; and Julian Real's "Compulsory Sexuality and Asexual Existence."

12. Lisa Millbank, "The Ethical Prude."

13. Though Sofia, the film's central character, is of Asian descent, the majority of the bodies that populate the salon appear to be white and middle class.

14. As one reviewer notes: "The American flag that Francis Scott Key calls the 'the star-spangled banner' is itself a symbol of unification. In Key's poem, the flag stands in for American resistance against British oppression. In a way, the sex in this scene and in the rest of the film functions as a flag for *Shortbus*. The sex is a flag of resistance and unification that the characters can still fly despite being crippled or numbed to some degree by the events on September 11, 2001, and by arbitrary and suffocating standards of bodily and sexual acceptance." Clifton Smith, "Sex in the Film Shortbus." Available at http://sicmagazine.org/shortbus/.

15. Here I am thinking of Michael Hardt and Antonio Negri's recent theorization of what they term "multitude." For Hardt and Negri, the multitude is the only political figure that can effectively speak back to power and reclaim democracy in the twenty-first century. In an age where corporate power is distributed among a set of global networks, they argue, the body politic must be refashioned into a similarly networked consciousness to succeed at bringing about any kind of meaningful rebellion. "A democratic multitude," they argue, "cannot be a political body, at least not in the modern form. The multitude is something like a singular flesh that refuses the organic unity of the body" (*Multitude*, 162).

16. I provide a more extended discussion of trigger warnings in the Epilogue.

17. It is important to qualify here that all of the *Shortbus* actors got HIV tests before filming and make explicit a commitment to safe sex within the film itself—everyone uses, and is encouraged to use, condoms. Like Delany, Cameron Mitchell

is not literally advocating bug chasing but mobilizing, rather, a crip metaphorics of democratic infection.

18. Jamie's catch phrase is also worth considering from a critical race perspective. We first learn of its origins in his initial counseling session with Sofia where he explains that he played a "white trash kid" adopted by an affluent black family—a satirical inversion of the usual practices of inspirational black tokenism. His character's comedic insistence that he's an "albino" therefore reinterprets his white skin (the usual marker of privilege) as a barrier to his full inclusion. Interestingly, disability (albinism) is framed here as that which provides the promise of racial transcendence, offering Jamie's character a narrative framework in which one can be simultaneously white-skinned and the offspring of black parents.

19. For more on this, see Alyson K. Spurgas, "Interest, Arousal, and Shifting Diagnoses."

20. Jagose gestures toward this dynamic in her reading of the film, arguing that *Shortbus* attempts to negotiate the "double bind of modern sex" by staging a dialectic between "modernity's odd couple": the straight woman and the gay man (89). While the "heterosexual woman bent on her own pleasure" is, for some, the "exemplary figure of modernity," Jagose observes, others have identified the cruising gay man as the exemplar of modernity; his pleasure emerges not through extensive interior work on the private "self" (as with the heterosexual woman) but through a more diffuse network of sexual contacts between strangers across the cityscape (91). Placing these two figures in dialogue, Jagose argues, the film offers "hospitable stranger carnalities" as the solution to the heterosexual women's "coital anorgasmia" (93).

21. "Transplant my heart into yours," Matthews sings, and later, "we're pumping like machinery. . . . It's life / Saving surgery." No isolated procedure, Sofia's orgasm is presented here as a site of a mutually rehabilitative exchange; it is not a singular "she" but a communal "we" whose machinery now "pumps" with newly infused vigor.

22. See, for example, Tobin Siebers, "Sexual Culture for Disabled People."

23. I am building here on a queer theoretical literature that takes trauma seriously and advocates, against progress narratives, for a revaluation of "backward" feelings like shame, anxiety, and depression. See, for example, Heather Love's *Feeling Backward* and "Compulsory Happiness and Queer Existence" and Ann Cvetkovich's *Archive of Feelings* and *Depression: A Public Feeling*.

24. See Sianne Ngai, *Ugly Feelings*.

EPILOGUE

1. Jess Bidgood, "At Wellesley, Debate over Statue in Briefs." *New York Times*, February 6, 2014. Available at https://www.nytimes.com/2014/02/07/arts/design/at-wellesley-debate-over-a-statue-in-briefs.html?_r=0.

2. Lisa Fischman, curator of the exhibit, ruminates that the sleepwalker "appears to have drifted away from wherever he belongs and one wonders . . . how he has gotten so lost, so off course." See Lisa Fischman, "Tony Matelli, Sleepwalker." Davis Museum at Wellesley College. Available at https://www.wellesley.edu/davismuseum/explore-the-collections/artwork-of-the-month/node/42182.

3. Myra Ahmad, "Art Installation Sparks Controversy on Campus," *Wellesley News*, February 14, 2014.

4. Jess Bidgood, "At Wellesley."

5. James Baldwin, "As Much Truth as One Can Bear."

6. Jess Bidgood, "At Wellesley."

7. Available at https://www.change.org/p/1428582/responses/10205/c/32946635.

8. For some excellent disability studies perspectives on trigger warnings, see Alison Kafer, "Un/Safe Disclosures"; Angela Carter, "Teaching with Trauma"; and Melanie Yergeau, "Disable All the Things."

9. Stephen Rex Brown, "Sculptor of 'Sleepwalker' Statue: Wellesley Students Don't GET My Art." *New York Daily News*, February 7, 2014. Available at http://www.nydailynews.com/news/national/sculptor-sleepwalker-statue-wellesley-students-don-art-article-1.1605758.

10. Sebastian Smee, "Threshold States and Dark Wit in Standout Show by Tony Matelli." *Boston Globe*, February 15, 2014. Available at https://www.bostonglobe.com/arts/theater-art/2014/02/15/threshold-states-and-dark-wit-standout-show-tony-matelli/fwMYQ5sQQvaPVUhLoXGbTI/story.html.

11. Indeed, as Matelli explains in one interview, the model on whom the sculpture is based needed to be "in good shape so he could hold that pose for a long time." See Jacklyn Reiss, "Q&A with Tony Matelli, artist behind Wellesley College's scantily-clad sleepwalking statue." *Boston.com*, February 6, 2014, available at http://archive.boston.com/yourcampus/news/wellesley/2014/02/qa_with_tony_matelli_artist_behind_wellesley_colleges_scantily-clad_sleepwalking_statue.html.

12. Exploring a range of epidemic discourses, from the rise of germ theory, to anxieties about immigration and urban poverty, to the AIDS crisis during the 1980s and contemporary alarmism around autism and obesity, Alcabes illustrates the way these anticipatory logics have led us to scapegoat certain groups as high risk, deviant, or unhygienic. In this way, the biological fact (or cultural fantasy) of disease has provided a convenient alibi for marginalizing, quarantining, and even eliminating those populations whose existence makes us uncomfortable. Concluding that "the risk-free life is a mirage" (230). Alcabes powerfully critiques the prophylactic impulse behind contemporary attempts to exclude a variety of social others from full participation in public life.

13. Ann Pellegrini, "Classrooms and their Dissed Contents." *Bullybloggers*, November 27, 2014. Available at https://bullybloggers.wordpress.com/2014/11/27/classrooms-and-their-dissed-contents/.

14. Megan Milks, "On Trigger Warnings: A Roundtable—Part One: In The Creative Writing Classroom." *Entropy*, April 14, 2014. Available at https://entropymag.org/on-trigger-warnings-part-i-in-the-creative-writing-classroom/.

15. Jack Halberstam, "You Are Triggering me! The Neo-Liberal Rhetoric of Harm, Danger and Trauma." *Bullybloggers*, July 5, 2014. Available at https://bullybloggers.wordpress.com/2014/07/05/you-are-triggering-me-the-neo-liberal-rhetoric-of-harm-danger-and-trauma/.

16. Lisa Duggan, "On Trauma and Trigger Warnings, in Three Parts," *Bullybloggers*, November 23, 2014. Available at https://bullybloggers.wordpress.com/2014/11/23/on-trauma-and-trigger-warnings-in-three-parts/.

17. To appropriate Schulman's own language, we might say that such discourses themselves fail to "differentiate between the past and present," which results in "scapegoating or attacking people today for pain that they have not caused but was inflicted by others long ago."

18. As Kathleen Ann Livington points out, trigger warnings might just as easily be read as a "queer gesture" that "attempt[s] to leave behind a record of trauma through disclosure. When a student asks for a trigger warning, they are 'outing' themselves as having a trauma history, in order to be able to access a particular space, such as a college classroom."

Bibliography

Agamben, Giorgio. *Homo Sacer: Sovereign Power and Bare Life*. Stanford, CA: Stanford University Press, 1998.
———. *The State of Exception*. Chicago: University of Chicago Press, 2005.
Ahmed, Sara. *The Promise of Happiness*. Durham, NC: Duke University Press, 2010.
Ahuja, Neel. *Biosecurities: Disease Interventions, Empire, and the Government of Species*. Durham, NC: Duke University Press, 2016.
Alcabes, Philip. "The Ordinariness of AIDS." *American Scholar* 75, no. 3 (2006): 18–32.
Alcott, Louisa May. *Eight Cousins*. New York: Puffin Books, (1875) 1995.
Alter, Charlotte. "Man Up, Wellesley: You're a Generation of Sheltered Children." *Time*, February 6, 2014. Available at http://time.com/5344/wellesleys-boogeyman-wears-tighty-whities/.
Altman, Dennis. *The Homosexualization of America, the Americanization of the Homosexual*, 79–80. New York: St. Martin's Press, 1982.
American Psychiatric Association. *Diagnostic and Statistical Manual of Mental Disorders (DSM-5)*, 5th ed. Arlington, VA: American Psychiatric Publishing, 2013.
Baldwin, James. *Another Country*. New York: Vintage, (1963) 1992.
———. "The Artist's Struggle for Integrity." In *The Cross of Redemption: Uncollected Writings*, edited by Randall Kenan, 50–58. New York: Vintage, (1963) 2010.
———. "As Much Truth as One Can Bear." In *The Cross of Redemption: Uncollected Writings*, edited by Randall Kenan, 34–42. New York: Vintage, (1962) 2010.
———. "A Challenge to Bicentennial Candidates." In *The Cross of Redemption: Uncollected Writings*, edited by Randall Kenan, 126–130. New York: Vintage, (1976) 2010.
———. "From Nationalism, Colonialism, and the United States: One Minute to Twelve—A Forum." In *The Cross of Redemption: Uncollected Writings*, edited by Randall Kenan, 10–18. New York: Vintage, (1961) 2010.
———. *Giovanni's Room*. New York: Penguin, (1956) 2001.

———. "The Harlem Ghetto." *James Baldwin: Collected Essays*, edited by Toni Morrison, 43–53. New York: Library of America, (1955) 1998.

———. "Many Thousands Gone." *James Baldwin: Collected Essays*, edited by Toni Morrison, 19–34. New York: Library of America, (1955) 1998.

———. "Notes of a Native Son." *James Baldwin: Collected Essays*, edited by Toni Morrison, 63–84. New York: Library of America, (1955) 1998.

———. "The Price May Be Too High." In *The Cross of Redemption: Uncollected Writings*, edited by Randall Kenan, 105–108. New York: Vintage, (1969) 2010.

———. "*The Sling and the Arrow* by Stuart David Engstrand." In *The Cross of Redemption: Uncollected Writings*, edited by Randall Kenan, 302–304. New York: Vintage, (1947) 2010.

———. "Talk to Teachers." *James Baldwin: Collected Essays*, 678–686. New York: Library of America, (1963)1998.

———. "Theater: The Negro In and Out." In *The Cross of Redemption: Uncollected Writings*, edited by Randall Kenan, 19–28. New York: Vintage, (1961) 2010.

———. "The Uses of the Blues." In *The Cross of Redemption: Uncollected Writings*, edited by Randall Kenan, 70–81. New York: Vintage, (1964) 2010.

———. "We Can Change the Country." In *The Cross of Redemption: Uncollected Writings*, edited by Randall Kenan, 59–64. New York: Vintage, (1963) 2010.

———. "The White Man's Guilt." *James Baldwin: Collected Essays*, 722–727. New York: Library of America, (1965) 1998.

———. "The White Problem." In *The Cross of Redemption: Uncollected Writings*, edited by Randall Kenan, 88–97. New York: Vintage, (1964) 2010.

Balfour, Lawrie. *The Evidence of Things Not Said: James Baldwin and the Promise of American Democracy*. Ithaca, NY: Cornell University Press, 2001.

Barnes, Liberty Walther. *Conceiving Masculinity: Male Infertility, Medicine, and Identity*. Philadelphia: Temple University Press, 2014.

Bayer, Ronald. *Homosexuality and American Psychiatry: The Politics of Diagnosis*. Princeton, NJ: Princeton University Press, 1987.

Baynton, Douglas C. *Defectives in the Land: Disability and Immigration in the Age of Eugenics*. Chicago: University of Chicago Press, 2016.

Bederman, Gail. *Manliness and Civilization: A Cultural History of Gender and Race in the United States, 1880–1917*. Chicago: University of Chicago Press, 1996.

Bell, Chris. "I'm Not the Man I Used to Be: Sex, HIV and Cultural 'Responsibility.'" In *Sex and Disability*, edited by Robert McRuer and Anna Mollow, 208–228. Durham, NC: Duke University Press, 2012.

Bergler, Edmund. *Homosexuality: Disease or Way of Life?* New York: Collier Books, 1971.

Berkowitz, Richard, Michael Callen, and Richard Dworkin. *How to Have Sex in an Epidemic: One Approach*. New York: News from the Front, 1983.

Berlant, Lauren. *Cruel Optimism*. Durham, NC: Duke University Press, 2011.

———. *The Female Complaint: The Unfinished Business of Sentimentality in American Culture*. Durham, NC: Duke University Press, 2008.

———. "Slow Death (Sovereignty, Obesity, Lateral Agency)." *Critical Inquiry* 33 (Summer 2007): 754–780.

Berlant, Lauren, and Michael Warner. "What Does Queer Theory Teach Us About X?" *PMLA* 110, No. 3 (May 1995): 343–349.

Bersani, Leo. "Is the Rectum a Grave?" *October* 43 (1987): 197–222.

Bierce, Ambrose. "Letter to George Sterling, Feb. 18 1905." In *A Much Misunderstood Man: Selected Letters of Ambrose Bierce*, edited by S. T. Joshi, Tryambak Sunand Joshi, and David E. Schultz, 131–132. Columbus: Ohio State University Press, 2003.

Bland, Lucy, and Laura Doan, eds. *Sexology Uncensored: The Documents of Sexual Science*. Chicago: University of Chicago Press, 1998.

Bordo, Susan. *The Male Body: A New Look at Men in Public and in Private*. New York: Farrar, Straus and Giroux, 2000.

Boudreau, Kristin. *Sympathy in American Literature: American Sentiments from Jefferson to the Jameses*. Gainesville: University Press of Florida, 2002.

Brandt, Allan M. *No Magic Bullet: A Social History of Venereal Disease in the United States since 1880*. New York: Oxford University Press, 1987.

Brier, Jennifer. *Infectious Ideas: U.S. Political Responses to the AIDS Crisis*. Chapel Hill: University of North Carolina Press, 2009.

Briggs, Charles L., and Daniel C. Hallin. "Biocommunicability: The Neoliberal Subject and Its Contradictions in News Coverage of Health Issues." *Social Text* 25, no. 4 (Winter 2007): 43–66.

Brin, David. "The Giving Plague." 1987. *Otherness*. Silverthorne, CO: Spectra, 1994.

Brintnall, Kent L. *Ecce Homo: The Male-Body-in-Pain as a Redemptive Figure*. Chicago: University of Chicago Press, 2011.

Brophy, Sarah. *Witnessing AIDS: Writing, Testimony, and the Work of Mourning*. Toronto: University of Toronto Press, 2004.

Brotto, Lori A. "The DSM Diagnostic Criteria for Hypoactive Sexual Desire Disorder in Women." *Archives of Sexual Behavior* 39, no. 2 (September 2009): 221–239.

Brotto, Lori, Rosemary Basson, Marie Carlson, and Cici Zhu. "Impact of an Integrated Mindfulness and Cognitive Behavioural Treatment for Provoked Vestibulodynia (IMPROVED): A Qualitative Study." *Sexual and Relationship Therapy* 28, no. 1–2 (2013): 3–19.

Brotto, Lori, Michael Krychman, and Pamela Jacobson. "Eastern Approaches for Enhancing Women's Sexuality: Mindfulness, Acupuncture, and Yoga." *Journal of Sexual Medicine* 5 (2008): 2741–2748.

Browner, Stephanie P. *Profound Science and Elegant Literature: Imagining Doctors in Nineteenth-Century America*. Philadelphia: University of Pennsylvania Press, 2005.

Bruccoli, Matthew J. *Some Sort of Epic Grandeur: The Life of F. Scott Fitzgerald*, 2nd ed. Columbia: University of South Carolina Press, 2002.

Bruhm, Steven, and Natasha Hurley, eds. *Curiouser: On the Queerness of Children*. Minneapolis: University of Minnesota Press, 2004.

Califia, Pat. *Public Sex: The Culture of Radical Sex*. Berkeley, CA: Cleis, 1994.

Carter, Angela. "Teaching with Trauma: Trigger Warnings, Feminism, and Disability Pedagogy." *Disability Studies Quarterly* 35, no. 2 (2015).

Cerankowski, Karli June, and Megan Milks. "New Orientations: Asexuality and Its Implications for Theory and Practice." *Feminist Studies* 36 (Fall 2010): 650–664.

Chasin, C. D. "Reconsidering Asexuality and Its Radical Potential." *Feminist Studies* 39, no. 2 (2013): 405–426.
Chauncey, George. *Gay New York: Gender, Urban Culture, and the Making of the Gay Male World, 1890–1940.* New York: Basic Books, 1994.
Chen, Mel. *Animacies: Biopolitics, Racial Mattering, and Queer Affect.* Durham, NC: Duke University Press, 2012.
Chesler, Ellen. *Woman of Valor: Margaret Sanger and the Birth Control Movement in America.* New York: Simon and Schuster, 1992.
Clare, Eli. *Brilliant Imperfection: Grappling with Cure.* Durham, NC: Duke University Press, 2017.
———. *Exile and Pride: Disability, Queerness and Liberation.* Cambridge, MA: South End Press, 1999.
Clark, Keith. *Black Manhood in James Baldwin, Ernest J. Gaines, and August Wilson.* Champaign: University of Illinois Press, 2004.
Cline, Sally. *Zelda Fitzgerald: Her Voice in Paradise.* New York: Arcade, 2002.
Cobb, Michael. *Single: Notes on the Uncoupled.* New York: New York University Press, 2012.
Cohen, Ed. *A Body Worth Defending.* Durham, NC: Duke University Press, 2009.
Combahee River Collective. "Statement." 1977. In *Feminist Theory: A Reader*, 2nd ed., edited by Wendy K. Kolmar and Frances Bartkowski, 311–317. New York: McGraw Hill, 2005.
Cooper, Danielle, and Ela Przybylo. "Asexual Resonances: Tracing a Queerly Asexual Archive." *GLQ: A Journal of Lesbian and Gay Studies* 20, no. 3 (2014): 297–318.
Corbett, Ken. *Boyhoods: Rethinking Masculinities.* New Haven, CT: Yale University Press, 2009.
Crane, Stephen. *Maggie, a Girl of the Streets: A Story of New York.* Boston: Bedford/St. Martin's, (1893) 1999.
Crimp, Douglas. "How to Have Promiscuity in an Epidemic." *October* 43 (1987): 237–271.
———. "Mourning and Militancy." *October* 51 (Winter 1989): 3–18.
Cruz, Denise. "Reconsidering McTeague's 'Mark' and 'Mac': Intersections of U.S. Naturalism, Imperial Masculinities, and Desire between Men." *American Literature* 78, no. 3 (2006).
Cvetkovich, Ann. *Archive of Feelings: Trauma, Sexuality, and Lesbian Public Culture.* Durham, NC: Duke University Press, 2003.
———. *Depression: A Public Feeling.* Durham, NC: Duke University Press, 2012.
Davis, Lennard. *Bending over Backwards: Disability, Dismodernism and Other Difficult Positions.* New York: New York University Press, 2002.
———. *Enforcing Normalcy.* New York: Verso, 1995.
Davy, Zowie. "The *DSM*-5 and the Politics of Diagnosing Transpeople." *Archives of Sexual Behavior* 44, no. 5 (June 2015): 1165–1176.
Dean, Tim. *Beyond Sexuality.* Chicago: University of Chicago Press, 2000.
———. *Unlimited Intimacy: Reflections on the Subculture of Barebacking.* Chicago: University of Chicago Press, 2009.
Decoteau, Claire Laurier. "The Specter of AIDS: Testimonial Activism in the Aftermath of the Epidemic." *Sociological Theory* 26, no. 3 (2008): 230–257.

DeGout, Yasmin Y. "Dividing the Mind: Contradictory Portraits of Homosexual Love in *Giovanni's Room.*" *African American Review* 26, no. 3 (1992).

Delany, Samuel R. *The Mad Man.* New York: Masquerade Books, 1994.

———. *The Motion of Light in Water: Sex and Science Fiction Writing in the East Village, 1957–1965.* New York: Arbor House, 1988.

———. "On the Unspeakable." *Shorter Views: Queer Thoughts and the Politics of the Paraliterary.* Hanover, NH: Wesleyan University Press, 1999.

———. "The Thomas L. Long Interview." *Shorter Views: Queer Thoughts and the Politics of the Paraliterary*, 123–138. Hanover, NH: Wesleyan University Press, 1999.

———. *Times Square Red, Times Square Blue.* New York: New York University Press, 1999.

D'Emilio, John. *Sexual Politics, Sexual Communities: The Making of a Homosexual Minority in the United States, 1940–1970.* Chicago: University of Chicago Press, 1983.

Derrick, Scott. "Making a Heterosexual Man: Gender, Sexuality, and Narrative in the Fiction of Jack London." In *Rereading Jack London*, edited by Leonard Cassuto and Jeanne Campbell Reesman, 110–129. Stanford, CA: Stanford University Press, 1996.

Derrida, Jacques. "Autoimmunity: Real and Symbolic Suicides." In *Philosophy in a Time of Terror: Dialogues with Jürgen Habermas and Jacques Derrida*, edited by Giovanna Borradori, 84–136. Chicago: University of Chicago Press, 2003.

———. *Rogues: Two Essays on Reason.* Stanford, CA: Stanford University Press, 2005.

DeShong, Scott. "Toward an Ethics of Reading Faulkner's *Sanctuary*." *Journal of Narrative Technique* 25, no. 3 (1995): 238–257.

Dewey, Frank L., "Thomas Jefferson's Law Practice: The Norfolk Anti-Inoculation Riots." *Virginia Magazine of History and Biography* 91, no. 1 (1983): 39–53.

Diedrich, Lisa. "Doing Queer Love: Feminism, AIDS and History." *Theoria* 54, no. 112 (April 2007): 25–50.

Dievler, James. "Sexual Exiles: James Baldwin and *Another Country.*" In *James Baldwin Now*, edited by Dwight A. McBride, 161–163. New York: New York University Press, 1999.

Dill, Elizabeth. "'That Damned Mob of Scribbling Siblings:' The American Romance as Anti-novel in *The Power of Sympathy* and *Pierre.*" *American Literature* 80, no. 4 (2008): 707–738.

Doctorow, E. L. *Jack London, Hemingway, and the Constitution: Selected Essays, 1977–1992.* New York: Random House, 1993.

Donaldson, Elizabeth. "Revisiting the Corpus of the Madwoman: Further Notes toward a Feminist Disability Studies Theory of Mental Illness." In *Feminist Disability Studies*, edited by Kim Q. Hall, 91–114. Bloomington: Indiana University Press, 2011.

Dorr, Gregory Michael. "Assuring America's Place in the Sun: Ivey Foreman Lewis and the Teaching of Eugenics at the University of Virginia, 1915–1953." *Journal of Southern History* 66, no. 2 (2000): 257–296.

Dudley, John. "Inside and Outside the Ring: Manhood, Race, and Art in American Literary Naturalism." *College Literature* 29, no. 1 (Winter 2002): 53–83.

Duggan, Lisa. "The Trials of Alice Mitchell: Sensationalism, Sexology, and the Lesbian Subject in Turn-of-the-Century America." *Signs* 18, no. 4 (1993): 791–814.

Duggan, Lisa, and Nan Hunter. *Sex Wars: Sexual Dissent and Political Culture*. New York: Routledge, 1995.

Dunning, Stephanie. "Parallel Perversions: Interracial and Same Sexuality in James Baldwin's *Another Country*." *MELUS* 26, no. 4 (2001): 95–112.

Easton, Dossie, and Janet W. Hardy. *The Ethical Slut: A Practical Guide to Polyamory, Open Relationships & Other Adventures*. Berkeley: Celestial Arts, 2009.

Edelman, Lee. *Homographesis: Essays in Gay Literary and Cultural Theory*. New York: Routledge, 1994.

———. *No Future: Queer Theory and the Death Drive*. Durham, NC: Duke University Press, 2004.

Einstein, Mara. *Compassion, Inc.: How Corporate America Blurs the Line between What We Buy, Who We Are, and Those We Help*. Berkeley: University of California Press, 2012.

Ellis, John. "On Pornography." In *Pornography: Film and Culture*, edited by Peter Lehman, 25–47. New Brunswick, NJ: Rutgers University Press, 2006.

Elman, Julie Passanante. *Chronic Youth: Disability, Sexuality, and U.S. Media Cultures of Rehabilitation*. New York: New York University Press, 2014.

Emens, Elizabeth F. "Compulsory Sexuality." *Stanford Law Review* 66, no. 2 (2014): 303–386.

English, Daylanne K. *Unnatural Selections: Eugenics in American Modernism and the Harlem Renaissance*. Chapel Hill: University of North Carolina Press, 2004.

English, Deirdre, and Barbara Ehrenreich. *For Her Own Good: Two Centuries of the Experts Advice to Women*. New York: Anchor Books, 1978.

Erevelles, Nirmala. *Disability and Difference in Global Contexts: Enabling a Transformative Body Politic*. New York: Palgrave Macmillan, 2011.

Erickson, Loree. "Revealing Femmegimp: A Sex-Positive Reflection on Sites of Shame as Sites of Resistance for People with Disabilities." *Atlantis* 31, no. 2 (2007): 42–52.

Esposito, Robert. *Bios: Biopolitics and Philosophy*. Minneapolis: University of Minnesota Press, 2008.

Faulkner, William. *The Hamlet*. New York: Vintage, (1940) 1991.

———. *Light in August*. New York: Vintage, (1932) 1990.

———. *Sanctuary*. New York: Vintage, (1931) 1993.

———. *The Sound and the Fury*. New York: Vintage, (1929) 1990.

Felski, Rita. *The Gender of Modernity*. Cambridge, MA: Harvard University Press, 1995.

Ferguson, Roderick. *Aberrations in Black: Toward a Queer of Color Critique*. Minneapolis: University of Minnesota Press, 2003.

———. "The Parvenu Baldwin and the Other Side of Redemption: Modernity, Race, Sexuality, and the Cold War." In *James Baldwin Now*, edited by Dwight A. McBride, 233–261. New York: New York University Press, 1999.

Ferri, Beth. "Metaphors of Contagion and the Autoimmune Body." *Feminist Formations* 31, no. 1 (Spring 2018): 1–20.

Fiedler, Leslie. *Love and Death in the American Novel*. New York: Criterion Books, 1960.

Field, Douglas. "Looking for Jimmy Baldwin: Sex, Privacy, and Black Nationalist Fervor." *Callaloo* 27, no. 2 (Spring 2004): 457–480.

Fitzgerald, F. Scott. *The Great Gatsby*. New York: Scribners, (1925) 1995.

———. "Love or Eugenics." In *Fie Fie Fi-Fi: A Facsimile of the 1914 Musical Score, With Illustrations from the Original*, edited by Matthew J. Bruccoli, 66–69. Columbia: University of South Carolina Press, 1996.

———. *Tender Is the Night*. New York: Scribners, (1934) 1995.

Floyd, Kevin. *The Reification of Desire: Toward a Queer Marxism*. Minneapolis: University of Minnesota Press, 2009.

Flynt, Josiah. "Homosexuality among Tramps." In *Studies in the Psychology of Sex*, edited by Havelock Ellis, 359–367. Philadelphia: F. A. Davis, 1915.

Foucault, Michel. *The Birth of the Clinic: An Archaeology of Medical Perception*. New York: Vintage, 1994.

———. "Friendship as a Way of Life." In *The Essential Works of Foucault 1954–1984, Vol. 1—Ethics: Subjectivity and Truth*, edited by Paul Rabinow and translated by Robert Hurley, 135–140. New York: New Press, 1997.

———. *The History of Sexuality, Vol. 1: An Introduction*. New York, Vintage, 1990.

———. *Society Must Be Defended: Lectures at the Collège de France, 1975–76*. New York: Picador, 2003.

Freeman, Chris. "'Something They Did in the Dark': Lesbian and Gay Novels in the US, 1948–1973." In *Modern American Queer History*, edited by Allida M. Black, 131–151. Philadelphia, Temple University Press, 2001.

Freud, Sigmund. "Letter to an American Mother." *American Journal of Psychiatry* 107 (1951): 787.

———. *The "Wolfman" and Other Cases*. New York: Penguin, 2003.

Friedan, Betty. *The Feminine Mystique*. New York: Norton, 2001.

Fries, Kenny. *Body, Remember: A Memoir*. Madison: University of Wisconsin Press, 1997.

Galloway, Terry. *Mean Deaf Little Queer: A Memoir*. Boston: Beacon, 2009.

Galton, Francis. "Hereditary Improvement." *The Eclectic Magazine of Foreign Literature, Science, and Art* 17 (1873): 296–307.

Garland-Thomson, Rosemarie. *Extraordinary Bodies: Figuring Disability in American Culture and Literature*. New York: Columbia University Press, 1997.

———, ed. *Freakery: Cultural Spectacles of the Extraordinary Body*. New York: New York University Press, 1996.

———. "Misfits: A Feminist Materialist Disability Concept." *Hypatia* 26, no. 3 (2011): 591–609.

Garlick, Steve. *The Nature of Masculinity: Critical Theory, New Materialisms, and Technologies of Embodiment*. Vancouver: UBC, 2016.

Gleeson-White, Sarah. *Strange Bodies: Gender and Identity in the Novels of Carson McCullers*. Tuscaloosa: University of Alabama Press, 2003.

Gordon, Linda. *The Moral Property of Women: A History of Birth Control Politics in America*. Urbana: University of Illinois Press, 2002.

Greven, David. "Flesh in the Word: *Billy Budd, Sailor*, Compulsory Homosociality, and the Uses of Queer Desire." *Genders* 37 (2003): n.p. Web. June 7, 2012. Available at https://www.colorado.edu/gendersarchive1998-2013/2003/03/01/flesh-word-billy-budd-sailor-compulsory-homosociality-and-uses-queer-desire.

Grosz, Elizabeth. *The Nick of Time: Politics, Evolution, and the Untimely*. Durham, NC: Duke University Press, 2004.

Gupta, Kristina. "Asexuality and Disability: Mutual Negation in *Adams v. Rice* and New Directions for Coalition Building." In *Asexualities: Feminist and Queer Perspectives*, edited by Karli June Cerankowski and Megan Milks, 283–301. New York: Routledge, 2014.

———. "Compulsory Sexuality: Evaluating an Emerging Concept." *Signs: Journal of Women in Culture and Society* 41, no. 1 (2015): 131–154.

Halberstam, Judith [Jack]. *In a Queer Time and Place: Transgender Bodies, Subcultural Lives*. New York: New York University Press, 2005.

———. "Oh Bondage Up Yours! Female Masculinity and the Tomboy." In *Curiouser: On the Queerness of Children*, edited by Steven Bruhm and Natasha Hurley, 191–214. Minneapolis: University of Minnesota Press, 2004.

———. *The Queer Art of Failure*. Durham, NC: Duke University Press, 2011.

Halperin, David, and Valerie Traub, eds. *Gay Shame*. Chicago: University of Chicago Press, 2009.

Hanhardt, Christina. *Safe Space: Neighborhood History and the Politics of Violence*. Durham, NC: Duke University Press, 2013.

Haraway, Donna. "The Biopolitics of Postmodern Bodies: Constitutions of Self in Immune System Discourse." In *Biopolitics: A Reader*, edited by Timothy Campbell and Adam Sitze, 274–309. Durham, NC: Duke University Press, 2013.

Hardt, Michael. "Take the Revolutionary Road." *The Guardian*, July 4, 2007. Available at https://www.theguardian.com/commentisfree/2007/jul/04/taketherevolutionaryroad.

Hardt, Michael, and Antonio Negri. *Multitude*. New York: Penguin Press, 2004.

Harris, Trudier. *Black Women in the Fiction of James Baldwin*. Knoxville: University of Tennessee Press, 1985.

Hawthorne, Nathaniel. *The Scarlet Letter*. New York: Penguin, (1850) 2003.

———. *Young Goodman Brown and Other Short Stories*. New York: Dover, 1992.

Henderson, Mae G. "James Baldwin: Expatriation, Homosexual Panic, and Man's Estate." *Callaloo* 23, no. 1 (2000): 313–327.

Hines, Maude. "Playing with Children: What the 'Child' Is Doing in American Studies." *American Quarterly* 61, no. 1 (2009): 151–161.

Holland, Sharon. "(Pro)Creating Imaginative Spaces and Other Queer Acts: Randall Kenan's *A Visitation of Spirits* and Its Revival of James Baldwin's Absent Black Gay Man in *Giovanni's Room*." In *James Baldwin Now*, edited by Dwight McBride, 265–288. New York: New York University Press, 1999.

Howard, June. *Publishing the Family*. Durham, NC: Duke University Press, 2001.

Hubbard, Ruth. "Abortion and Disability: Who Should and Who Should Not Inhabit the World?" In *The Disability Studies Reader*, 3rd ed., edited by Lennard Davis, 107–119. New York: Routledge, 2010.

Inge, M. Thomas. "Fitzgerald, Faulkner and Little Lord Fauntleroy." *Journal of American Culture* 26, no. 4 (2003): 342–348.

Irving, Washington. *Salmagundi: or, The Whim-Whams and Opinions of Launcelot Langstsaff [pseud.] and Others*, Vols. 1–2. Printed by Jules Didot, for A. and W. Galignani, 1824.

Jacobs, Jane. *The Death and Life of Great American Cities*. New York: Vintage Books, 1992.

Jagose, Annamarie. *Orgasmology*. Durham, NC: Duke University Press, 2012.

James, Henry. *The Beast in the Jungle and Other Stories*. New York: Dover Publications, 1993.
Jarvie, Jenny. "Trigger Happy." *New Republic*, March 3, 2014. Available at https://newrepublic.com/article/116842/trigger-warnings-have-spread-blogs-college-classes-thats-bad.
Jefferson, Thomas. "To Samuel Kercheval." In *The Life and Selected Writing of Thomas Jefferson*, edited by Adrienne Koch and William Peden, 615–617. New York: Modern Library, 1999.
———. "To the Reverend Doctor G.C. Jenner." In *The Life and Selected Writing of Thomas Jefferson*, edited by Adrienne Koch and William Peden, 531. New York: Modern Library, 1999.
Jenkins, Henry. "'He's in the Closet but He's Not Gay': Male-Male Desire in Penthouse Letters." In *Pornography: Film and Culture*, edited by Peter Lehman, 133–153. New Brunswick, NJ: Rutgers University Press, 2006.
———. *Textual Poachers: Television Fans and Participatory Culture*. New York: Routledge, 1992.
Johnson, David, K. *The Lavender Scare: The Cold War Persecution of Gays and Lesbians in the Federal Government*. Chicago: University of Chicago Press, 2004.
Johnson, Merri Lisa. "Bad Romance: A Crip Feminist Critique of Queer Failure." *Hypatia* 30, no. 1 (2015): 251–267.
———. "Label C/Rip." *Social Text Online*, October 24, 2013. Available at http://socialtextjournal.org/periscope_article/label-crip/.
Johnson, Merri Lisa, and Robert McRuer. "Cripistemologies: Introduction." *Journal of Literary and Cultural Disability Studies* 8, no. 2 (2014): 127–147.
Johnson, Myra T. "Asexual and Autoerotic Women: Two Invisible Groups." In *The Sexually Oppressed*, edited by Harvey L. Gochros and Jean S. Gochros, 96–109. New York: Association Press, 1977.
Kafer, Alison. "Compulsory Bodies: Reflections on Heterosexuality and Able-bodiedness." *Journal of Women's History* 15, no. 3 (2003): 77–89.
———. *Feminist, Queer, Crip*. Bloomington: Indiana University Press, 2013.
———. "Un/Safe Disclosures: Scenes of Disability and Trauma." *Journal of Literary and Cultural Disability Studies* 10, no. 1 (2016): 1–20.
Kahan, Benjamin. *Celibacies: American Modernism and Sexual Life*. Durham, NC: Duke University Press, 2013.
Kameny, Frank. "Victory!!!! We have been 'cured.'" Memorandum regarding the American Psychiatric Association meeting in Honolulu, December 5, 1973. Available at http://www.kamenypapers.org/correspondence/American%20Psychiatric%20Association%20Letter%2072dpi.jpg.
Kaplan, Fred. *Sacred Tears: Sentimentality in Victorian Literature*. Princeton: Princeton University Press, 1987.
Katz, Jonathan Ned. *Gay American History: Lesbians and Gay Men in the U.S.A*. New York: Crowell, 1976.
Kenan, Randall, and Amy Sickels. *James Baldwin*. Philadelphia: Chelsea House, 2005.
Kent, Kathryn. *Making Girls into Women: American Women's Writing and the Rise of Lesbian Identity*. Durham, NC: Duke University Press, 2003.

Kersh, Rogan. "The Rhetorical Genesis of American Political Union." *Polity* 33, no. 2 (2000): 229–257.
Kershaw, Alex. *Jack London: A Life*. New York: St. Martin's Press, 1997.
Kim, Eunjung. "Asexualities and Disabilities in Constructing Sexual Normalcy." In *Asexualities: Feminist and Queer Perspectives*, edited by Karli June Cerankowski and Megan Milks, 249–282. New York: Routledge, 2014.
———. "How Much Sex Is Healthy: The Pleasures of Asexuality." In *Against Health: How Health Became the New Morality*, edited by Jonathan M. Metzl and Anna Kirkland, 157–169. New York: New York University Press, 2010.
Kimmel, Michael. *The Gender of Desire: Essays on Male Sexuality*. Albany: SUNY Press, 2005.
———. *Manhood in America: Cultural History*. New York: Simon and Schuster, 1996.
Klein, Marty. "Pornography: What Men See When They Watch." In *Pornography: Film and Culture*, edited by Peter Lehman, 244–257. New Brunswick, NJ: Rutgers University Press, 2006.
Krafft-Ebing, R., and Northrop Frye. *Psychopathia Sexualis: With Especial Reference to the Antipathic Sexual Instinct*. New York: Bantam, 1965.
Larson, Edward J. "'In the Finest Most Womanly Way': Women in the Southern Eugenics Movement." *American Journal of Legal History* 39, no. 2 (1995): 119–147.
Lehrer, Riva. "Golem Girl Gets Lucky." In *Sex and Disability*, edited by Robert McRuer and Anna Mollow, 231–255. Durham, NC: Duke University Press, 2012.
Levander, Caroline. *Cradle of Liberty: Race the Child and National Belonging from Thomas Jefferson to W. E. B. Du Bois*. Durham, NC: Duke University Press, 2006.
LeVay, Simon. *Queer Science: The Use and Abuse of Research into Homosexuality*. Cambridge, MA: MIT Press, 1996.
Levy, Ariel. *Female Chauvinist Pigs: Women and the Rise of Raunch Culture*. New York: Free Press, 2005.
Lewes, Kenneth. *Psychoanalysis and Male Homosexuality*, 20th Anniversary ed. Lanham, MD: Rowman and Littlefield: 2009.
Lewis, Bradley. "A Mad Fight: Psychiatry and Disability Activism." In *The Disability Studies Reader*, 3rd ed., edited by Lennard Davis, 160–176. New York: Routledge, 2010.
Liepe-Levinson, Katherine. *Strip Show: Performances of Gender and Desire*. New York: Routledge, 2002.
Linton, Simi. *Claiming Disability*. New York: New York University Press, 1998.
Livingston, Kathleen Ann. "On Rage, Shame, 'Realness,' and Accountability to Survivors." Available at http://harlotofthearts.org/index.php/harlot/article/view/237/156.
Loe, Meika. "The Rise of Viagra: How the Little Blue Pill Changed Sex in America." New York: New York University Press, 2004.
London, Jack. *The Abysmal Brute*. Las Vegas, NV: IAP, (1913) 2009.
———. *Before Adam*. New York: McKinlay, Stone and Mackenzie, (1906) 1915.
———. "How I Became a Socialist." In *The Radical Jack London: Writings on War and Revolution*, edited by Jonah Raskin, 124–126. Berkeley: University of California Press, (1903) 2008.
———. *The Iron Heel*. New York: Penguin Classics, (1908) 2006.

———. "The Mexican." *To Build a Fire and Other Stories*, 398–427. Global Language Resources, (1911) 2003.

———. "Revolution." In *The Radical Jack London: Writings on War and Revolution*, edited by Jonah Raskin, 139–157. Berkeley: University of California Press, (1905) 2008.

———. *The Road*. London: Arco, (1907) 1967.

———. "The Salt of the Earth." In *The Radical Jack London: Writings on War and Revolution*, edited by Jonah Raskin, 98–114. Berkeley: University of California Press, (1902) 2008.

———. *The Sea Wolf*. New York: Bantam, (1904) 1991.

———. "The Voters' Voice." In *The Radical Jack London: Writings on War and Revolution*, edited by Jonah Raskin, 58–60. Berkeley: University of California Press, (1896) 2008.

———. "What Shall Be Done with This Boy?" In *Jack London: The Unpublished and Uncollected Articles and Essays*, edited by Dan Wichlan, 157–165. Bloomington, IN: Authorhouse, (1903) 2007.

———. "What Socialism Is." In *The Radical Jack London: Writings on War and Revolution*, edited by Jonah Raskin, 55–57. Berkeley: University of California Press, (1895) 2008.

Longmore, Paul. "Conspicuous Contribution and American Cultural Dilemmas: Telethon Rituals of Cleansing and Renewal." In *Discourses of Disability: The Body and Physical Difference in the Humanities*, edited by David Mitchell and Sharon Snyder, 134–158. Ann Arbor: University of Michigan Press, 1997.

Love, Heather. "Close Reading and Thin Description." *Public Culture* 25, no. 3 (2013): 401–434.

———. "Compulsory Happiness and Queer Existence." *New Formations* 63 (2007): 52–64.

———. *Feeling Backward: Loss and the Politics of Queer History*. Cambridge, MA: Harvard University Press, 2007.

———. "Queers _____ This." In *After Sex: On Writing since Queer Theory*, edited by Janet Halley and Andrew Parker, 180–191. Durham, NC: Duke University Press, 2011.

Lui, Mary Ting Yi. *The Chinatown Trunk Mystery: Murder, Miscegenation, and Other Dangerous Encounters in Turn-of-the-Century New York City*. Princeton, NJ: Princeton University Press, 2005.

MacKinnon, Catharine A. *Toward a Feminist Theory of the State*. Cambridge, MA: Harvard University Press, 1989.

Maddock Dillon, Elizabeth. "Sentimental Aesthetics." *American Literature* 76, no. 3 (2004): 495–523.

Marcus, Steven. *The Other Victorians: A Study of Sexuality and Pornography in Mid-Nineteenth-Century England*. New York: Routledge, 2009.

Margolies, Alan. "The Maturing of Fitzgerald." *Twentieth Century Literature* 43, no. 1 (1997): 75–93.

Martin, Emily. *Flexible Bodies: Tracking Immunity in American Culture from the Days of Polio to the Age of AIDS*. Boston: Beacon Press, 1994.

———. *The Woman in the Body: A Cultural Analysis of Reproduction.* Boston: Beacon, 1987.

Martinez, Ernesto J. "Dying to Know: Identity and Self-Knowledge in Baldwin's *Another Country*." *PMLA* (May 2009): 782–797.

McBryde Johnson, Harriet. "Unspeakable Conversations." In *The Disability Studies Reader*, 3rd ed., edited by Lennard Davis, 573–585. New York: Routledge, 2010.

McCune, Jeffrey Q., Jr. *Sexual Discretion: Black Masculinity and the Politics of Passing.* Chicago: University of Chicago Press, 2014.

McRuer, Robert. *Crip Theory: Cultural Signs of Queerness and Disability.* New York: New York University Press, 2006.

———. "Disabling Sex: Notes for a Crip Theory of Sexuality." *GLQ: A Journal of Lesbian and Gay Studies* 17, no. 1 (2011): 107–117.

McRuer, Robert, and Merri Lisa Johnson. "Cripistemologies: Introduction." *Journal of Literary and Cultural Disability Studies* 8, no. 2 (2014): 127–147.

McRuer, Robert, and Anna Mollow. "Introduction." In *Sex and Disability*, edited by Robert McRuer, and Anna Mollow, 1–34. Durham, NC: Duke University Press, 2012.

McRuer, Robert, and Abby L. Wilkerson. "Introduction." *GLQ: A Journal of Lesbian and Gay Studies* 9, nos. 1–2 (2003): 1–23.

Melville, Herman. *Bartleby and Benito Cereno.* New York: Dover, 1990.

Merck, Mandy, *In Your Face: 9 Sexual Studies.* New York: New York University Press, 2000.

Messenger, Christian K. *Tender Is the Night and F. Scott Fitzgerald's Sentimental Identities.* Tuscaloosa: University of Alabama Press, 2015.

Metzl, Jonathan. *The Protest Psychosis: How Schizophrenia Became a Black Disease.* Boston: Beacon, 2010.

Michaels, Walter Benn. "Promises of American Life, 1880–1920." In *Prose Writing 1860–1920, Vol. 3: The Cambridge History of American Literature*, edited by Sacvan Bercovitch, 285–410. Cambridge: Cambridge University Press, 1994.

Milks, Megan. "Stunted Growth: Asexual Politics and the Rhetoric of Sexual Liberation." In *Asexualities: Feminist and Queer Perspectives*, edited by Karli June Cerankowski and Megan Milks, 100–118. New York: Routledge, 2014.

Millbank, Lisa. "The Ethical Prude: Imagining an Authentic Sex-Negative Feminism." Available at http://radtransfem.wordpress.com/2012/02/29/the-ethical-prude-imagining-an-authentic-sex-negative-feminism/#more-337.

Mitchell, David T., and Sharon L. Snyder. *The Biopolitics of Disability.* Ann Arbor: University of Michigan Press, 2016.

———. *Narrative Prosthesis: Disability and the Dependencies of Discourse.* Ann Arbor, MI: University of Michigan Press, 2000.

Mitchell, Lee Clark. "'And Rescue Us from Ourselves': Being Someone in Jack London's *The Sea-Wolf*." *American Literature* 70, no. 2 (1998): 317–335.

Modleski, Tania. *Feminism without Women: Culture and Criticism in a "Postfeminist" Age.* New York: Routledge, 1991.

Moeschen, Sheila. *Acts of Conspicuous Compassion: Performance Culture and American Charity Practices.* Ann Arbor: University of Michigan Press, 2013.

Mog, Ashley. "Threads of Commonality in Transgender and Disability Studies." *Disability Studies Quarterly* 28, no. 4 (2008).
Mollow, Anna. "Is Sex Disability? Queer Theory and the Disability Drive." In *Sex and Disability*, edited by Robert McRuer and Anna Mollow, 285–312. Durham, NC: Duke University Press, 2012.
———. "Mad Feminism." *Social Text Online*, October 24, 2013. Available at http://socialtextjournal.org/periscope_article/mad-feminism/.
Moraga, Cherrie L. *Loving in the War Years: Lo Que Nunca Paso por Sus Labios*. Boston: South End, 2000.
Morgan, Robin. "Theory and Practice: Pornography and Rape." 1974. *The Word of a Woman: Feminist Dispatches, 1968–1992*, 74–77. New York: W.W. Norton, 1992.
Morrison, Toni. "Unspeakable Things Unspoken: The Afro-American Presence in American Literature." *Michigan Quarterly Review* 28, no. 1 (Winter 1989): 1–34.
Mumford, Kevin. *Interzones: Black/White Sex Districts in Chicago and New York in the Early Twentieth Century*. New York: Columbia University Press, 1997.
Munt, Sally. *New Lesbian Criticism: Literary and Cultural Readings*. New York: Columbia University Press, 1992.
Musser, Amber. *Sensational Flesh: Race, Power, and Masochism*. New York: New York University Press, 2014.
Nakashima, Ellen. "Who Is WikiLeaks Suspect Bradley Manning?" *Washington Post*, May 8, 2011. Available at http://www.washingtonpost.com/lifestyle/magazine/who-is-wikileaks-suspect-bradley-manning/2011/04/16/AFMwBmrF_story.html.
Nelson, Dana D. *National Manhood: Capitalist Citizenship and the Imagined Fraternity of White Men*. Durham, NC: Duke University Press, 1998.
———. "'No Cold or Empty Heart': Polygenesis, Scientific Professionalization, and the Unfinished Business of Male Sentimentalism." *differences: A Journal of Feminist Cultural Studies* 11, no. 3 (1999): 29–56.
Nelson, Maggie. *The Argonauts*. Minneapolis: Gray Wolf, 2015.
Ngai, Sianne. *Ugly Feelings*. Cambridge, MA: Harvard University Press, 2005.
Nguyen, Tan Hoang. *A View from the Bottom: Asian American Masculinity and Sexual Representation*. Durham, NC: Duke University Press, 2014.
Nies, Betsy Lee. *Eugenic Fantasies: Racial Ideology in the Literature and Popular Culture of the 1920's*. New York: Routledge, 2002.
Norris, Frank. *McTeague*. New York: Penguin, 1981.
Odem, Mary. *Delinquent Daughters: Protecting and Policing Adolescent Female Sexuality in the United States, 1885–1920*. Chapel Hill: University of North Carolina Press, 1995.
Oliveri, Vinnie. "Sex, Gender, and Death in *The Sea Wolf*." *Pacific Coast Philology* 38 (Fall 2003): 99–115.
Ordover, Nancy. *American Eugenics: Race, Queer Anatomy and the Science of Nationalism*. Minneapolis: University of Minnesota Press, 2003.
Pascoe, C. J. *Dude, You're a Fag: Masculinity and Sexuality in High School*. Berkeley: University of California Press, 2007.
Patsavas, Alyson. "Recovering a Cripistemology of Pain: Leaky Bodies, Connective Tissue, and Feeling Discourse." *Journal of Literary and Cultural Disability Studies* 8, no. 2 (2014): 203–218.

Powers, Peter Kerry. "The Treacherous Body: Isolation, Confession, and Community in James Baldwin." *American Literature* 77, no. 4 (December 2005): 787–813.

Preciado, Paul B. *Testo Junkie: Sex, Drugs, and Biopolitics in the Pharmacopornographic Era.* New York: Feminist, 2013.

Prendergast, Catherine. "The Unexceptional Schizophrenic: A Post-Postmodern Introduction." *Journal of Literary and Cultural Disability Studies* 2, no. 1 (2008): 55–62.

Price, Janet, and Margrit Shildrick. "Bodies Together: Touch, Ethics and Disability." In *Disability/Postmodernity: Embodying Political Theory*, edited by Mairian Corker and Tom Shakespeare, 62–75. London: Continuum, 2002.

Price, Margaret. *Mad at School.* Ann Arbor: University of Michigan Press, 2011.

Prosser, Jay. *Second Skins: The Body Narratives of Transsexuality.* New York: Columbia University Press, 1998.

Przybylo, Ela. "Crisis and safety: The Asexual in Sexuosociety." *Sexualities* 14, no. 4 (2011): 444–461.

Puar, Jasbir K. "Coda: The Costs of Getting Better: Suicide, Sensation, Switchpoints." *GLQ: A Journal of Lesbian and Gay Studies* 18, no. 1 (2012): 149–158.

———. "Disability." *Transgender Studies Quarterly* 1, nos. 1–2 (2014): 77–81.

———. "Prognosis Time: Towards a Geopolitics of Affect, Debility and Capacity." *Women & Performance: A Journal of Feminist Theory* 19, no. 2 (2009):161–172.

———. *The Right to Maim: Debility, Capacity, Disability.* Durham, NC: Duke University Press, 2017.

———. *Terrorist Assemblages: Homonationalism in Queer Times.* Durham, NC: Duke University Press, 2007.

Quayson, Ato. *Aesthetic Nervousness: Disability and the Crisis of Representation.* New York: Columbia University Press, 2007.

Rabinow, Paul. *Essays on the Anthropology of Reason.* Princeton, NJ: Princeton University Press, 1996.

Rado, Sandor. "A Critical Examination of the Concept of Bisexuality." *Psychosomatic Medicine* 2, no. 4 (October 1940): 459–467.

Raskin, Jonah, ed. *The Radical Jack London.* Berkeley: University of California Press, 2008.

Real, Julian. "Compulsory Sexuality and Asexual Existence." Available at http://radicalprofeminist.blogspot.com/2009/12/compulsory-sexuality-and-asexual.html.

Reeve, Elspeth. "A Portrait of the Mind of Bradley Manning." *The Atlantic*, August 14, 2013. Available at https://www.theatlantic.com/national/archive/2013/08/portrait-mind-bradley-manning/312153/.

Reid-Pharr, Robert. *Black Gay Man: Essays.* New York: New York University Press, 2001.

Rich, Adrienne. "Compulsory Heterosexuality and Lesbian Existence." *Signs* 5, no. 4 (Summer, 1980): 631–660.

Roach, Thomas. *Friendship as a Way of Life: Foucault, AIDS, and the Politics of Shared Estrangement.* Albany: SUNY Press, 2012.

Robinson, Sally. *Marked Men: White Masculinity in Crisis.* New York: Columbia University Press, 2000.

Rofes, Eric. *Dry Bones Breathe: Gay Men Creating Post-AIDS Identities and Cultures.* New York: Routledge, 1998.

Rogers, Thomas. "In Defense of Single People." *Salon*, July 9, 2012. Available at https://www.salon.com/2012/07/09/in_defense_of_single_people/.
Roman, David. *Acts of Intervention: Performance, Gay Culture and AIDS*. Bloomington: Indiana University Press, 1998.
———. "Not about AIDS." *Performance in America: Contemporary U.S. Culture and the Performing Arts*. Durham, NC: Duke University Press, 2005.
Rose, Nikolas. *The Politics of Life Itself: Biomedicine, Power and Subjectivity in the Twenty-First Century*. Princeton, NJ: Princeton University Press, 2007.
Rosen, Ruth. *Lost Sisterhood: Prostitution in America, 1900–1918*. Baltimore: University of Maryland Press, 1983.
Rosenfeld, Dana, and Christopher A. Faircloth, eds. *Medicalized Masculinities*. Philadelphia: Temple University Press, 2006.
Ross, Andrew. "Epilogue: Calculating the Risk." In *Policing Public Sex: Queer Politics and the Future of AIDS*, edited by Strange Bedfellows, 395–400. Boston: South End, 1996.
Ross, Marlon B. "Beyond the Closet as a Raceless Paradigm." In *Black Queer Studies: A Critical Anthology*, edited by E. Patrick Johnson and Mae G. Henderson, 161–189. Durham, NC: Duke University Press, 2005.
———. "White Fantasies of Desire: Baldwin and the Racial Identities of Sexuality." In *James Baldwin Now*, edited by Dwight McBride, 13–55. New York: New York University Press, 1999.
Rotello, Gabriel. *Sexual Ecology: AIDS and the Destiny of Gay Men*. New York: Plume, 1998.
Roughgarden, Joan. *Evolution's Rainbow: Diversity, Gender, and Sexuality in Nature and People*. Berkeley: University of California Press, 2004.
Rubin, Gayle S. "Thinking Sex: Notes for a Radical Theory of the Politics of Sexuality." In *Culture, Society, and Sexuality: A Reader*, 2nd ed., edited by Richard Parker and Peter Aggleton, 150–186. New York: Routledge, 2007.
Russell, Emily. *Reading Embodied Citizenship: Disability, Narrative, and the Body Politic*. New Brunswick, NJ: Rutgers University Press, 2011.
Sabo, Don. "Masculinities and Men's Health: Moving toward Post-Superman Era Prevention." In *Men's Lives*, 7th ed., edited by Michael S. Kimmel and Michael A. Messner, 287–300. Boston: Pearson Allyn and Bacon, 2007.
Samuels, Ellen. *Fantasies of Identification: Disability, Gender, Race*. New York: New York University Press, 2014.
———. "My Body, My Closet: Invisible Disability and the Limits of Coming-Out Discourse." *GLQ: A Journal of Lesbian and Gay Studies* 9, nos. 1–2 (2003): 233–255.
Samuels, Shirley, ed. *The Culture of Sentiment: Race, Gender and Sentimentality in 19th Century America*. New York: Oxford University Press, 1992.
Sandahl, Carrie. "Queering the Crip or Cripping the Queer? Intersections of Queer and Crip Identities in Solo Autobiographical Performance." *GLQ: A Journal of Lesbian and Gay Studies* 9 (2003): 25–56.
Savran, David. *Taking It Like a Man: White Masculinity, Masochism, and Contemporary American Culture*. Princeton, NJ: Princeton University Press, 1998.
Saxton, Marsha. "Disability Rights and Selective Abortion." In *Abortion Wars: A Half Century of Struggle: 1950 to 2000*, edited by Rickie Solinger, 374–393. Berkeley: University of California Press, 1998.

Schoen, Johanna. *Choice and Coercion: Birth Control, Sterilization, and Abortion in Public Health and Welfare*. Chapel Hill: University of North Carolina Press, 2005.

Scott, Darieck. *Extravagant Abjection: Blackness, Power, and Sexuality in the African American Literary Imagination*. New York: New York University Press, 2010.

Scott, Evelyn. "On William Faulkner's *The Sound and the Fury*." In *William Faulkner*, edited by John Bassett, 76–81. New York: Routledge, 2001.

Scott, James C. *Seeing Like a State: How Certain Schemes to Improve the Human Condition Have Failed*. New Haven, CT: Yale University Press, 1998.

Sedgwick, Eve. *Between Men: English Literature and Male Homosocial Desire*. New York: Columbia University Press, 1992.

———. *Epistemology of the Closet*. Berkeley: University of California Press, 1990.

———. *Touching Feeling: Affect, Pedagogy, Performativity*. Durham, NC: Duke University Press, 2003.

Seitler, Dana. *Atavistic Tendencies: The Culture of Science in American Modernity*. Minneapolis: University of Minnesota Press, 2008.

Sherry, Mark. "Crip Politics? Just . . . No." *The Feminist Wire*, November 23, 2013. Available at https://thefeministwire.com/2013/11/crip-politics-just-no/.

Shin, Andrew, and Barbara Judson. "Beneath the Black Aesthetic: James Baldwin's Primer of Black American Masculinity." *African American Review* 32, no. 2 (1998): 247–261.

Shortbus. Dir. John Cameron Mitchell. ThinkFilm, 2006. DVD.

Shotwell, Alexis. *Against Purity: Living Ethically in Compromised Times*. Minneapolis: University of Minnesota Press, 2016.

Siebers, Tobin. "Disability in Theory: From Social Constructionism to a New Realism of the Body." In *The Disability Studies Reader*, 2nd ed., edited by Lennard Davis, 173–183. New York: Routledge, 2006.

———. *Disability Theory*. Ann Arbor: University of Michigan Press, 2008.

———. "Sex, Shame, and Disability Identity: With Reference to Mark O'Brien." In *Gay Shame*, edited by David Halperin and Valerie Traub, 201–216. Chicago: University of Chicago Press, 2010.

———. "A Sexual Culture for Disabled People." In *Sex and Disability*, edited by Robert McRuer and Anna Mollow, 37–53. Durham, NC: Duke University Press, 2012.

Smith, Andrea. B*eyond the Pros and Cons of Trigger Warnings: Collectivizing Healing*, July 13, 2014. Available at https://andrea366.wordpress.com/2014/07/13/beyond-the-pros-and-cons-of-trigger-warnings-collectivizing-healing/.

Smith, Clifton. "Sex in the Film Shortbus." *[sic] magazine*, August 4, 2007. Available at http://sicmagazine.org/shortbus/.

Smith, Felipe. "The Figure on the Bed: Difference and American Destiny in *Tender Is the Night*." In *French Connections: Hemingway and Fitzgerald Abroad*, edited by J. Gerald Kennedy and Jackson R. Bryer, 187–214. New York: St. Martin's Press, 1998.

Socarides, Charles. *Homosexuality*. New York: Aronson, 1978.

Solinger, Rickie. *Pregnancy and Power: A Short History of Reproductive Politics in America*. New York: New York University Press, 2005.

Somerville, Siobhan. *Queering the Color Line: Race and the Invention of Homosexuality in American Culture*. Durham, NC: Duke University Press, 2000.

Spade, Dean. *Normal Life: Administrative Violence, Critical Trans Politics and the Limits of Law*. Durham, NC: Duke University Press, (2011) 2015.

Spurgas, Alyson. "Interest, Arousal, and Shifting Diagnoses of Female Sexual Dysfunction, or: How Women Learn about Desire." *Studies in Gender and Sexuality* 14, no. 3 (2013): 187–205.

———. "Solving Desire." *The New Inquiry*, March 9, 2016. Available at https://thenewinquiry.com/solving-desire/.

Stein, Arlene. "Sisters and Queers: The Decentering of Lesbian Feminism." In *The Gender/Sexuality Reader*, edited by R. Lancaster and M. di Leonardo, 378–391. New York: Routledge, 1997.

Stein, Melissa N. *Measuring Manhood: Race and the Science of Masculinity, 1830–1934*. Minneapolis: University of Minnesota Press, 2015.

Steinbeck, John. *Of Mice and Men*. New York: Penguin, 1993.

Stern, Julia. *The Plight of Feeling: Sympathy and Dissent in the Early American Novel*. Chicago: University of Chicago Press, 1997.

Stiker, Henri-Jacques. *A History of Disability*. Ann Arbor: University of Michigan Press, 2000.

Stockton, Kathryn Bond. *Beautiful Bottom, Beautiful Shame: Where Black Meets Queer*. Durham, NC: Duke University Press, 2006.

———. *The Queer Child, or Growing Sideways in the Twentieth Century*. Durham, NC: Duke University Press, 2009.

Stowe, Harriet Beecher. *Uncle Tom's Cabin*. New York: Penguin, 1986.

Stryker, Susan. *Transgender History*. Berkeley: Seal Press, 2008.

Sullivan, Andrew. "When Plagues End." *Love Undetectable: Notes on Friendship, Sex and Survival*. New York: Vintage, 1999.

Sundquist, Eric. *Faulkner: A House Divided*. Baltimore: Johns Hopkins University Press, 1985.

Terry, Jennifer. *An American Obsession: Science, Medicine and Homosexuality in Modern Society*. Chicago: University of Chicago Press, 1999.

———. *Deviant Bodies: Critical Perspectives on Difference in Science and Popular Culture*. Bloomington: Indiana University Press, 1995.

Thomas, Calvin. *Masculinity, Psychoanalysis, Straight Queer Theory: Essays on Abjection in Literature, Mass Culture, and Film*. New York: Macmillan, 2008.

Thomas, Kendall. "Going Public: A Conversation with Liddell Jackson and Jocelyn Taylor." In *Policing Public Sex: Queer Politics and the Future of AIDS*, edited by Strange Bedfellows, 53–71. Boston: South End, 1996.

Thoreau, Henry David. *Walden; And, Resistance to Civil Government*. New York: W. W. Norton, 1992.

Tinkcom, Matthew. "'You've Got to Get on to Get Off': *Shortbus* and the Circuits of the Erotic." *South Atlantic Quarterly* 110, no. 3 (2011): 693–713.

Treichler, Paula A. "AIDS, Homophobia and Biomedical Discourse: An Epidemic of Signification." *Cultural Studies* 1, no. 3 (1987): 263–305.

Tremain, Shelly, ed. *Foucault and the Government of Disability*. Ann Arbor: University of Michigan Press, 2005.

Truchan-Tataryn, Maria. "Textual Abuse: Faulkner's Benjy." *Journal of Medical Humanities* 26, no. 2 (2005): 159–172.
Turner, Jack. *Awakening to Race: Individualism and Social Consciousness in America*. Chicago: University of Chicago Press, 2012.
Twain, Mark. *Adventures of Huckleberry Finn*. New York: Dover, 1994.
Wald, Priscilla. *Contagious: Cultures, Carriers, and the Outbreak Narrative*. Durham, NC: Duke University Press, 2007.
Warkentin, Elyssa D. "Adventure Literature." In *International Encyclopedia of Men and Masculinities*, edited by Michael Flood, Judith Kegan Gardiner, Bob Pease, and Keith Pringle, 1–3. New York: Routledge, 2007.
Warner, Michael. *The Trouble with Normal: Sex, Politics, and the Ethics of Queer Life*. Cambridge, MA: Harvard University Press, 1999.
Washington, Bryan R. *The Politics of Exile: Ideology in Henry James, F. Scott Fitzgerald, and James Baldwin*. Boston: Northeastern University Press, 1995.
Watney, Simon. *Policing Desire: Pornography, AIDS, and the Media*. Minneapolis: University of Minnesota Press, 1997.
Weiss, Margot. *Techniques of Pleasure: BDSM and the Circuits of Sexuality*. Durham, NC: Duke University Press, 2011.
Wendell, Susan. *The Rejected Body: Feminist Philosophical Reflections on Disability*. New York: Routledge, 1996.
Wilkerson, Abby. "Normate Sex and Its Discontents." In *Sex and Disability*, edited by Robert McRuer and Anna Mollow, 183–207. Durham, NC: Duke University Press, 2012.
Williams, Linda. *Hard Core: Power, Pleasure, and the "Frenzy of the Visible."* Berkeley: University of California Press, 1989.
———. *Screening Sex*. Durham, NC: Duke University Press, 2008.
WSQ: Child, special issue of *Women's Studies Quarterly*, edited by Sarah Chinn and Anna Mae Duane, 3, nos. 1–2 (Spring/Summer 2015).
Yergeau, Melanie. "Disable All the Things: On Affect, Metadata, and Audience." Keynote Address. Computers and Writing Conference, Washington State University, Pullman, WA. June 6, 2014. Available at http://www.digitalrhetoriccollaborative.org/2014/06/24/melanie-yergeau-disable-all-the-things-kn1/.

Index

ability, 4, 11, 15, 120, 144, 145; ideology of, 167, 179–80
able-bodiedness, 172, 178; compulsory, 15, 32, 65
ableism, 9, 32, 71, 99, 126, 177, 180, 187–88, 201; internalized, 191; logics of, 204, 232n10; in *Times Square Red, Times Square Blue* (Delany), 155; whiteness and, 70
ablenationalism, 23, 27
adulthood, 73, 79, 87, 91, 202–203; corruption of, 61; effeminizing, 65; outlaw, 57; queer, 77. *See also* childhood
affect, 10, 27, 119, 156, 168; sexual, 178
Agamben, Giorgio, 41, 122–23, 211n5, 215n4, 226n26. *See also* bare life; state of exception
agency, 28, 139, 159, 173, 190, 228n13; crip, 31, 169; female, 151; lateral, 158; outlaw, 123; queer, 163–64, 188; representational, 56; trans, 163; vulnerable, 126
AIDS, 7–10, 16, 25–26, 133–34, 136–40, 158–59, 176–77, 207, 212n13, 213n23, 231n7; activism, 7, 134; in Africa, 228n9; history of, 227–28n5; as public health crisis, 8–9, 16, 26, 135–36, 138, 140, 177, 227nn3–4, 231n7, 234n12. *See also* barebacking; bug chasing; Dean, Tim; HIV; post-AIDS era
Alcabes, Philip, 205–206, 227n3, 234n12
Alter, Charlotte, 202, 204
Americanism, 83; anti-, 30; spread-eagle, 34, 58, 123

American Psychology Association (APA), 21–22, 106, 118, 214n30
amputation, 25, 45, 48, 126, 153, 156–57, 191. *See also* prosthesis; prosthetics
animal, 6, 10, 62, 65, 80, 194, 217n18
Another Country (Baldwin), 101–104, 117, 199, 227n29
antiprophylactic, the, 12, 93, 136, 173, 192
antiprophylactic citizens, 2, 13, 161, 187, 200–201
antiprophylactic citizenship, 1, 3–4, 7–10, 12, 32, 71–72, 135, 152, 157–59, 161, 166–67, 175–76; ethics of, 126, 128; as founding principle of the United States, 20; in London, 18; racial interdependence and, 30; stone butch sexuality and, 187; structures of, 231n1; women's bodies and, 29
antiprophylaxis, 3, 7, 30, 50, 126, 134, 144, 187, 194, 200, 209; crip virtues of, 177; masculine, 203; orgasmic, 183. *See also* masculinity: antiprophylactic
antipsychiatry movements, 21, 118, 177
asexuality, 42, 49–50, 169–73, 180–81, 185–89, 232n8; medical framing of, 231n4; queer, 167; transmasculine identity and, 31. *See also* Female Sexual Interest/Arousal Disorder (FSI/AD); Hypoactive Sexual Desire Disorder (HSDD); *Shortbus* (Cameron)
atavism, 17, 19, 53–56, 65, 217n18, 220n25
autoimmunity, 10, 12, 212n15

Baldwin, James, 16, 18, 30, 99–105, 107–108, 112–13, 115–31, 199–200, 202–204, 223n4, 225n13, 226n25, 226–27nn27–29; *Another Country*, 101–104, 117, 199, 227n29; "The Artist's Struggle for Integrity, 126, 130; black psychology and, 226n22; conversational ethics and, 227n30; female characters of, 223n3; *Giovanni's Room*, 30, 100, 103–105, 107–19, 227n29; homosexuality and, 224n6, 225n11; "Talk to Teachers," 121–22, 124, 226n27; "The Uses of the Blues," 99, 116, 202; "We Can Change the Country, 122–24
barebacking, 9, 30, 134–35, 137–38, 142, 227n5, 230n20, 232n9. *See also* AIDS; bug chasing; Dean, Tim
bare life, 122, 226n26
Before Adam (London), 28, 53–56, 58, 217n18, 217n20
Bergler, Edmund, 105, 224n7
Berlant, Lauren, 23, 123, 158, 168, 193, 200
Bersani, Leo, 7–9, 26, 168, 170, 232n9
biocapital, 154, 158
biopolitics, 4, 8, 24, 26–27, 191, 212n13; affirmative, 65, 211n5
biopower, 158, 211n5
biosociality, 6–7, 137, 228n6; queer-crip, 136, 139
blindness, 64, 230n18
bodies, 8, 12, 14–16, 20, 128, 159, 163, 169, 198, 200, 212n17, 213n21, 216n15; adolescent, 58, 65; American, 123; asexual, 161; assigned female at birth, 231n1; black, 101, 113, 120–21; defective, 81; gendered, 174, 227n29; homosexual, 70; hypermasculine, 50; intersex, 188; labor of, 61; male, 3, 47, 50, 57, 60, 157; men's, 36, 212n16; nondisabled, 24, 47; pornography and, 176; queer, 22–23; racialization of, 213n20; revolting, 62; revolutionary potential of, 52; stolen, 190; trans, 211n1; transmasculine, 161–62; women's, 29, 44, 69, 72, 148, 165, 167; working-class, 191. *See also* disabled bodies
body, the, 7, 10–14, 33, 38, 127, 191, 197, 212n16, 216n15; biology of, 5; debility and, 23; desires of, 5–6; eruptions of, 17; female, 165; hormones and, 161–62; hypermasculine, 51–52; masculine, 3, 7, 34, 50, 56, 60–61, 161, 216n17; materiality of, 15, 24, 27, 41; naturalism and, 46; permeability of, 178; queer, 4, 22–23, 28, 96; of the sexual deviant, 114; of the sick person, 139; skin of, 164; underdevelopment of, 37. *See also* sensation
body politic, 12–13, 19, 89, 125, 127, 232n15

Bordo, Susan, 5–6
Brilliant Imperfection (Clare), 167, 187–88, 191–92
Brin, David, 133–34, 143, 174, 178
brotherhood, 36, 52, 57; American, 4, 15–16, 38, 45; bug, 9–10, 20, 137 (*see also* barebacking; bug chasing); democratic, 45, 135; revolutionary, 29, 34; universal, 62
bug chasing, 9, 20, 23, 30–31, 134–35, 137–39, 141–42, 157, 232n9, 233n17. *See also* AIDS; barebacking; brotherhood: bug; Dean, Tim; HIV

cancer, 27, 139
capacitation, 23, 27, 190; logics of, 153; orgasmic, 165, 167; queer erotic, 172; sexual, 166
capacity, 16, 27, 153–54, 160, 165, 191; bodily, 171, 190; crip, 154, 158; diminished, 2; fluid model of, 23; of the male body, 6–7; orgasmic, 31, 154, 163–64, 167, 169, 232n9; physical, 36, 136; sexual, 183, 188. *See also* debility
capitalism, 16, 60, 153, 157–58, 163, 166, 190–91, 208; corporate, 146; global, 143; industrial, 195, 212n16; logic of, 159; sanitizing structures of, 200
celibacy, 50, 74
Cerankowski, K. J., 172, 232n8
Chauncey, George, 108–110
Chen, Mel Y., 10, 23, 195
Child, the (Edelman), 69–70, 76, 87–88, 96, 170, 202
childhood, 54, 61, 75, 79, 87, 100, 105, 107; early, 118; nightmares, 111; physical abuse in, 187; sentimental, 88
citizenship, 10, 17, 62, 82, 123, 125, 213n23, 227n29; American, 10, 13–16, 28, 36, 41, 59, 82, 121–23, 213n19; biological, 6–7; black American, 121; democratic, 59; disability and, 89; embodied, 212n16; fraternal, 31; masculinity and, 3, 11, 16, 94, 218n1; nineteenth-century, 17; patriarchal model of, 45; queer, 31, 134, 146, 168–70; sanitary, 212n17; sexual, 30, 176, 232n9; social intimacy and, 158. *See also* antiprophylactic citizenship
Clare, Eli, 16, 31–32, 119, 167, 186–94; *Brilliant Imperfection*, 167, 187–88, 191–92; *Exile and Pride*, 31, 167, 187–90, 192–94
closet, the, 2, 27, 30, 100, 114–18, 176, 213n21
Cobb, Michael, 170–72
contact, 140–42, 144–45, 147–48, 152, 174, 183, 230n21; between bodies, 138; between

INDEX 257

men, 52; heterosexual, 54, 106, 216n12; interclass, 139, 146, 152; physical, 50
corporeality, 34–35, 48
cripistemology, 22–24, 27, 195, 214n31
crip theory, 15, 70, 188, 214n31
Cvetkovich, Ann, 173, 187

Dean, Tim, 9, 31, 134, 137–38, 141–42, 168, 227–28nn5–6, 229n14, 230–31nn20–21, 232n9. *See also* barebacking; bug chasing
death drive, 7–8, 25, 69–70, 78, 170, 213n21
debility, 8, 16, 23–24, 26–27, 33, 136, 157–59, 167, 190–91, 195; disability as, 165; experience of, 31; feminized, 154–55, 161; gendered, 153; in *The Sea Wolf* (London), 49, 65. *See also* capacity; disability
Delany, Samuel, 3, 16, 136, 138–54, 156, 158–59, 168, 170, 175, 229nn14–15, 230n18, 230nn20–21, 232n17; *Times Square Red, Times Square Blue*, 31, 135–59, 173, 229n14, 230n18, 230n21
Deleuze, Gilles, 124, 168, 211n5
democracy, 10–13, 149, 213nn19–20, 231n21, 232n15; American, 15, 18, 68, 121, 125, 128, 175, 212n16; representative, 39–41; sexual, 145, 158; Whitmanesque, 135
Derrida, Jacques, 10–11. *See also* autoimmunity
desire: heterosexual, 37, 42, 167; lesbian, 91; same-sex, 21, 25, 29–30, 69, 100, 103, 105, 107–108, 118, 224n8
Diagnostic and Statistical Manual of Mental Disorders (*DSM*), 31, 106–107, 119–20, 191; Baldwin and, 100; gender variance and, 162, 164–65; homosexuality and, 20–21, 30, 100, 106, 164
disabled bodies, 23–25, 27, 153, 179–80, 188, 190, 207, 213n20. *See also* identity: disabled
disability: nonapparent, 27, 118; political/relational model of, 194; psychiatric, 177; social model of, 24, 182, 194
disability studies, 15, 23–24, 27–28, 80, 96, 104, 118, 124, 153, 179, 188, 212n15, 213n21, 214n28, 214n31, 219n8, 234n8
disidentification, 118, 189
Duggan, Lisa, 89, 208, 228n12
Dworkin, Andrea, 145–46, 149, 184

Edelman, Lee, 69–71, 73–74, 76–78, 83, 87, 96, 170, 219n7, 229n14. *See also* Child, the
Elman, Julie Passanante, 65
effeminacy, 43, 50, 100, 224n6. *See also* femininity; masculinity
Einstein, Mara, 143, 228n10
Ellis, Havelock, 14, 60

embodiment, 3, 65, 127, 214n1; crip, 24, 52, 80; crip/queer, 27; deviant, 23; female, 94; national, 17, 93; queer-crip paradigms of masculine, 37; trans, 31
eugenics, 7, 15–16, 29–30, 67–69, 71–72, 74–76, 79–88, 93–97, 113, 128, 219n8, 219n14, 220n25, 221n28
Exile and Pride (Clare), 31, 167, 187–90, 192–94
exploitation, 16, 31, 113, 145

Faulkner, William, 16, 29, 71–73, 78–81, 84, 96, 219n10, 220n17; *Sanctuary*, 29, 71–80, 84, 222n33; *The Sound and the Fury*, 79–80
feeblemindedness, 29–30, 71, 76–78, 83, 94
Female Sexual Interest/Arousal Disorder (FSI/AD), 165–66. *See also* asexuality
feminism, 208, 232n8; anti-pornography, 145, 152, 205, 228n13; asexuality and, 173; lesbian, 146; sex-positive, 172, 186; radical, 147–48, 152, 172, 184, 186, 209, 231nn21–22; second-wave, 145, 148–49, 172, 185, 201, 228n13, 231n21
feminist-crip, 32, 157, 201
feminization, 48, 50, 112; of the bottom, 9 (*see also* barebacking); of feelings, 203
fitness, 5, 37, 61, 83, 89, 93, 97, 113; racial, 221n28. *See also* unfit, the
Fitzgerald, F. Scott, 16, 67–68, 72, 74, 84–86, 92, 94–96, 119, 221nn28–29, 222n33; *The Great Gatsby*, 113, 221n30; *Tender Is the Night*, 29–30, 71, 84–96, 203. *See also* sympathy
Floyd, Kevin, 14–15
Foucault, Michel, 8, 137, 168, 211n5
fragility, 157–58, 203
freak, 55–56, 65; shows, 212n16
Freud, Sigmund, 54, 68, 106, 187, 217n19, 224n8. *See also* death drive; psychoanalysis
Freudianism, 4, 7, 48, 54, 102, 105–108, 111, 120. *See also* death drive; psychoanalysis
futurism, 83; reproductive, 71, 73–75, 80, 83–84, 87, 96, 170, 202, 219n7; sentimental, 25, 70, 74, 76
futurity, 69, 136–37, 170; able-bodied, 172; antiprophylactic, 202; crip, 30; political, 169; national, 74; reproductive, 71, 73; sentimental, 77

Garland-Thomson, Rosemarie, 197, 199, 212n16
gaze, the, 63; diagnostic, 29, 42; doctor's, 4, 44; Faulkner's clinical, 84; feminine, 44; homoerotic, 51; male, 85, 110; maternal, 47; medical, 43–44, 47, 51–52, 191; scientific, 42, 93

gender, 4–5, 89, 93, 116–18, 146, 213n23, 219n11; binary epistemology, 166; compulsory, 188; critique, 183; crossing, 92, 114; dysphoria, 162, 189, 191; expressions, 3; feminist analysis of, 147; hierarchies, 145, 213n20; identification/identity, 112, 163, 189; inversion, 109; norms, 65, 91, 148, 229n15; stone butch, 189; in *Tender Is the Night*, 30; transition, 70, 191; variance, 164
gender identity disorder, 2, 162, 165–66, 190
Giovanni's Room (Baldwin), 30, 100, 103–105, 107–19, 227n29
Goldstein, Sidney, 72, 78
Grant, Madison, 86–87, 94, 221n28
guilt, 105, 112–13, 119, 230n18

Halberstam, Jack, 63, 173, 208, 229n14
Hanhardt, Christina, 152, 209, 214n35
Hardt, Michael, 18, 211n5, 232n15
health care, 24, 194
Henderson, Mae, 107, 113
heteromasculinity, 32, 34, 37, 42, 62, 215n1, 224n6
heteronormativity, 37, 190, 209
heterosexuality, 50, 63, 146, 213n20, 214n30; compulsory, 32, 65, 150, 173, 188, 213n21 (*see also* Rich, Adrienne). *See also* desire: heterosexual
HIV, 9, 30, 134, 136–41, 206–207, 231n7, 232n17. *See also* AIDS; barebacking; bug chasing; post-AIDS era
homoeroticism, 25, 29, 46, 50–51, 54, 63, 225n11, 230n20
homophobia, 48, 188; Cold War, 115
homosexuality, 22, 76, 95, 100, 102, 106, 213n20, 224nn6–8, 227n3; Cold War medicalization of, 30, 100–101, 114, 120; as disorder, 42, 100, 106–108, 112, 117, 164, 214n30 (*see also Diagnostic and Statistical Manual of Mental Disorders (DSM)*); in *Giovanni's Room*, 105, 107–108, 111, 114, 117, 225n11; London on, 60; male, 73, 225n17; psychiatrization of, 15–16; white, 73, 101, 120, 125. *See also* closet, the
hospitality, 11–12, 85, 94, 127, 175
humanism, 4, 7, 21, 210, 258, 260; classical, 17; in Gibson's early fiction, 72; liberal, 4, 224n1, 258, 268–70; Western, 13. *See also* posthumanism; subject: humanist; transhumanism
hypermasculinity, 46–48, 50–52
Hypoactive Sexual Desire Disorder (HSDD), 165–66. *See also* asexuality
hysteria, 44–45, 55–56, 68, 121, 226n21

identity, 17, 23–24, 30, 70, 170, 190, 213n23; American, 114, 175, 200; crip, 167; disabled, 24–25, 194; gay, 108–109; heterosexual, 102; lesbian, 91; medicalized, 20; minority, 180; queer, 164; regional, 83; sexual, 107, 163; stone butch, 187, 189, 192; trans, 2, 15, 31, 167; transmasculine, 31. *See also* gender: dysphoria; gender: identification/identity; gender identity disorder
identity politics, 47–48, 190
immigration, 86–87, 89, 101, 175, 221n28, 234n12
immigrants, 78, 86, 89, 94
immunity, 10–12, 28, 126, 173. *See also* autoimmunity
impairment, 27, 48, 64, 172, 194, 198, 201, 220n21
incest, 68, 79, 84, 86, 92, 105, 219n10, 222n33
individualism, 61, 133, 145, 213n26; abstract, 48; American, 127–28, 143–44; possessive, 11
injury, 3, 24, 37, 46–51, 61, 64, 157, 195; psychic/psychological, 101, 120, 131; racial, 127; temporality of, 124
inoculation, 11, 19–20
intimacy, 6, 9, 11, 70, 84, 103, 138, 148, 161, 173, 175, 222n32, 223n3; between women, 90, 149; biosocial, 18; civic, 183; embodied, 23 (*see also* bug chasing); forced, 171; homosexual, 127, 135, 146; interclass, 68, 141, 144, 146; interracial, 100, 104, 112–13, 144, 225n12, 227n29; masculine, 39, 53, 59, 146; neighborly, 142; nonorganic, 193; nonsexual, 192; public, 139; queer, 86; social, 140, 158; unlimited, 137, 232n9
Irving, Washington, 15, 35, 45

Jagose, Annamarie, 167–68, 233n20
Jarvie, Jenny, 203, 206–208
Jefferson, Thomas, 18–20, 28, 57, 125
Johnson, Merri Lisa, 23, 118–19, 195, 226n21

Kafer, Alison, 15, 23, 70–71, 194, 232n10. *See also* disability: relational model of
Kim, Eunjung, 180, 231n4
Kimmel, Michael, 4, 216n6, 218n23
Krafft-Ebing, Richard von, 14, 42, 68, 84, 92

lesbian resistance, 173, 228n13
lesbians, 21, 71, 89, 91–92, 94, 104, 114, 145–46, 152, 183, 22n35
Lewes, Kenneth, 106, 224n7
liberalism, 64, 86, 202; white, 16, 101, 117, 125, 127–29

London, Jack, 3, 16–17, 29, 32, 33–42, 44–50, 52–64, 123, 157, 199–200, 215n5, 216n8, 216n12, 216n15, 217n17, 217n20, 226n27; *Before Adam*, 28, 53–56, 58, 217n18, 217n20; "comradeship of the revolution," 34, 58, 61, 123; domesticity in, 37, 49, 5, 60; intellectualism in, 42, 63; "The Mexican," 34–36, 38; "the road" and, 37, 53, 60; *The Road*, 58–61; *The Sea Wolf*, 28, 38–53, 56, 58, 62–65; socialism of, 16, 34, 40, 57–58, 61–62, 217
Love, Heather, 25, 173, 195

Mackinnon, Catharine, 145–46, 149, 184
Mad Pride movement, 21, 214n28
Manning, Chelsea, 1–3, 211n1
male body, 5–7, 14–15, 30, 42–45, 47, 49–50, 53, 56–58, 156; vulnerability and, 3, 197, 201; white, 43, 60–61
manhood, 4, 51, 78, 106, 109, 215n5; American, 15, 19, 29, 36–37; black, 127; ideal of, 3; national, 13–15, 17, 29, 32, 38, 42, 45, 52, 59, 64, 216n7; prophylactic, 38; redefining, 6; white, 41, 59, 213n19
masculinity, 4–9, 11, 16, 22, 50, 161–62, 187, 197, 222n35, 224n6, 228n13; alternative, 32; American, 14–18, 36, 38, 64, 115, 118, 200, 218n1, 225n17; antiprophylactic, 3, 9, 20, 32, 38, 72, 157, 161, 173; asexual, 231n1; capacitated, 155, 159, 161, 167; citizenship and, 16; crip, 153; crisis of, 25, 36, 46, 48, 52; female, 229n16; feminized, 94; in *Giovanni's Room* (Baldwin), 109, 111–12, 115, 117; hegemonic, 2, 6; masochism and, 212n11, 216n14; melancholia/melancholy and, 5; naturalist model of, 215n5; normal, 115; prophylactic, 3, revolting, 13, 29, 34, 52; in *The Sea Wolf* (London), 63; socialist, 34 (*see also* London, Jack); sympathetic, 95; in *Tender Is the Night*, 73, 94–95; toxic, 209; traditional, 108; vulnerable, 200; white, 38, 47–48, 65, 215n5, 222n37; working-class, 29, 37. *See also* femininity; heteromasculinity; hypermasculinity; injury; masochism; selfhood: masculine; transmasculinity
masochism, 7–8, 10, 48, 106, 141, 157, 212n11, 216n14. *See also* masculinity
masquerade, 107, 110
materialism, 10, 38
materiality, 35, 50–52, 200; of the body, 5–6, 15, 19, 24, 27, 41, 49, 215n2; masculine, 215n3; queer-crip, 62, 64
Matelli, Tony, 32, 197–99, 203, 234n11; *The Sleepwalker*, 32, 197–201, 203–204, 233n2

McBryde Johnson, Harriet, 96–97
McRuer, Robert, 15, 23, 144, 188, 214n1
medicine, 7, 23, 28, 94, 100, 125, 162, 191; eugenic, 80; objectivity of, 12, 21; prophylactic, 72; psychiatric, 120
melancholia/melancholy, 93; fraternal, 14, 17, 39, 64
memoir, 28, 31, 58, 60, 70, 119, 138, 213n21; trans, 162. *See also* Delany, Samuel
mental disability, 119, 207
mental disorders, 89, 106
mental distress, 2, 118, 121, 125
mental illness, 21, 106, 177
Messenger, Chris, 85–86, 93, 222n33
metaphor, 81, 92, 126–27, 133, 182; of autoimmunity, 212n15; biometaphor, 5–6; corporeal, 215n2; illness as, 10, 15, 139–40; in *The Sea Wolf*, 42, 46, 54, 56, 59
militancy, 134; black, 120
Milks, Megan, 169–70, 172, 181, 205
miscegenation, 86, 89, 219n10, 221n28
Mitchell, David T., 22–23, 27–28, 35, 80, 215n2
Mitchell, John Cameron, 174–76, 178, 183, 186, 200; *Shortbus*, 31, 167, 173–84, 232n14, 232n17, 233n20
Mollow, Anna, 118, 213n21, 219n6
Morgan, Robin, 145, 149
mourning, 17, 31, 134

nationality, 36, 88, 218n21; multi-, 222n37
negativity, 173, 195; queer, 70–71; sex, 207
Nelson, Dana, 13–14, 38–40, 212n19, 216n7
Nelson, Maggie, 70–71, 157
neoliberalism, 23, 26–27, 31, 143–45, 152–54, 158, 163, 165, 190, 208–209, 212n13, 214n35
normalcy, 22, 34, 113, 179

objectification, 12, 15, 188
openness, 1, 40, 72, 157, 161, 202, 213n22; affective, 95; antiprophylactic, 62, 93; sexual, 31, 177. *See also* permeability; receptivity; vulnerablity
otherness, 72, 87, 102, 112, 223n40

pain, 35, 37, 47–48, 50, 63, 70, 126–27, 130, 167, 187, 195, 200, 202–203, 206, 235n17
paralysis, 50, 52, 64; queer, 45
paranoia, 115, 122, 206; Cold War, 100–101, 120
Patsavas, Alyson, 195
pathology, 23, 42, 44–45, 61, 65, 84, 180, 185
Pellegrini, Ann, 205, 208

performativity, 107, 213n21
permeability, 161, 167, 178; masculine, 187; queer, 177–78. *See also* openness; receptivity; vulnerability
phallic ideal, 5–7
phallus, 5–6
pharmacopornography, 162–64, 166, 176
pornography, 148–50, 163, 174, 229nn15–16; feminist critiques of, 145, 149, 152, 205, 209, 228nn12–13, 229n15; sexual abundance and, 135, 150, 158 (*see also* Delany, Samuel); theaters, 136, 138, 144–46, 148, 151, 153–56, 158, 174, 199, 230n18, 230n20
post-AIDS era, 15, 30, 135–38, 228n5. *See also* AIDS; HIV; Rofes, Eric
poverty, 49, 75, 80, 83, 100, 117, 134, 234n12
precarity, 16, 99, 126, 130, 157, 191, 214n33; of bodies/bodily, 24, 125; conditions of, 159, 195, 200; physical, 4, 123, 189; production of, 27; psychological, 123, 189; of queer populations, 26; socioeconomic, 31
Preciado, Paul B., 31, 162–64, 166–68, 176, 182, 188–89, 192; *Testo Junkie*, 31, 162–64
Price, Margaret, 118, 226n19
privacy, 27, 116, 145–46, 152–53, 185
privatization, 118, 144–45, 152, 171
professionalism, 13, 36–37
prophylactic sensibility, 11, 19, 125, 127, 145, 202
prophylaxis, 50, 95, 166, 194, 208; antiretroviral, 228n10. *See also* antiprophylactic citizenship; antiprophylaxis
prosthesis, 45; narrative, 124. *See also* amputation
prostitution, 60, 73, 75, 100, 113, 225n14
Protease Moment, 135–36, 231n7
Przybylo, Ela, 180, 187
psychiatry, 21, 103, 115, 120, 125, 224n7; Baldwin and, 99, 128–29; history of, 104, 106; pop 102; sexual, 18, 30, 100. *See also* antipsychiatry movements
psychoanalysis, 5, 8, 22, 25–26, 53, 99–100. *See also* Freud, Sigmund
Puar, Jasbir, 23–24, 27, 155–57, 165, 190, 192
public sex, 135, 138, 141, 145, 147, 152, 176; queer, 173, 231n7
public space, 140–41, 201, 209; queer, 188

queer kinship networks, 25, 169
queerness, 2, 22–23, 25–26, 34, 37, 70–71, 157, 187; of the adolescent body, 65; Baldwin's, 104, 224n6; of the Child, 219n5; disability and, 1, 4, 15–16, 22, 25–26, 29, 34, 37, 45–46, 179–80, 189, 215n1; male, 108; in *Sanctuary* (Faulkner), 73, 75, 78; in *The Sea Wolf* (London), 63

Rabinow, Paul, 6, 228n6
racism, 16, 48, 82, 126, 214n30; American, 120, 122; institutional(ized), 101, 121, 123
Rich, Adrienne, 145–46, 150, 228n13
Robinson, Sally, 47–48
Rofes, Eric, 30, 136, 138. *See also* post-AIDS era; Protease Moment
Rose, Nikolas, 6, 228n6
Rubin, Gayle, 163, 168, 170, 207–208

safe sex, 140, 227n3, 232n17; campaigns, 135
Samuels, Ellen, 118, 213n21, 226n20
Sanctuary (Faulkner), 29, 71–80, 84, 222n33
Sandahl, Carrie, 15, 214n1
schizophrenia, 30, 120–23, 125, 128; black, 101, 120–21, 123–24; female, 95
Schulman, Sara, 206, 235n17
The Sea Wolf (London), 28, 38–53, 56, 58, 62–65
Sedgwick, Eve, 25–27, 116, 151
Seitler, Dana, 17, 65
selfhood, 6, 102–103, 143; masculine, 48; nonheteronormative expression of, 171
sensation, 6, 10, 25, 50, 52, 157, 161–62, 187, 191–92; erotic, 164, 167, 189
sexology, 14, 28–29, 37, 90
sexual assault, 148, 187, 194, 201
sexual inversion, 29, 37, 42, 89, 100
sexual inverts, 15, 45
sexuality: crip theory of, 188; female, 81, 89–90, 165; gay male, 70, 145–46; medicalized, 20; queer, 7, 20, 22, 24, 51, 96, 104, 112, 183, 225n14
sexual pleasure, 135, 148, 163–64, 167–68, 178, 187–88; women's, 166
sexual refusal, 31, 146, 164, 169–71, 173, 178, 187, 189
sexual science, 3, 14–15, 17–18, 28, 90, 213n20
sexual subcultures, 114, 135, 145, 151, 174; queer, 228n7
sexual violence, 110, 150, 161
shame, 75, 101, 179, 233n23; asexuality and, 169, 232n9; queer experience of, 27, 117–18, 226n18
Shortbus (Mitchell), 31, 167, 173–84, 232n14, 232n17, 233n20
Shotwell, Alexis, 10, 12, 213n26
Siebers, Tobin, 26–27, 180
Snyder, Sharon L., 22–23, 27–28, 35, 80, 215n2
social justice, 5–6, 40
social model (of disability), 24, 182, 194
Spade, Dean, 23, 152
Spurgas, Alyson, 165–66
state of exception, 36, 41, 215n4, 226n26

stone butch, 191; identity, 187, 189, 192; untouchability, 167, 186; sexuality, 187, 189
subcultures, 141, 174; asexual, 171; bachelor, 109–110; barebacking, 138, 230n20, 232n9; bug chasing, 9; gay male, 112, 145; queer, 170, 225n14, 228n7; sexual, 114, 135, 138, 151, 174
subjects, 144, 146, 155–58, 163; able-bodied, 64, 178; of antiprophylactic citizenship, 72; asexual, 169; black/African American, 101, 120–21, 129; of desire, 15; desiring, 93; disabled, 188; disciplined, 108; feminine, 111; gay/traitor, 115; intersectional, 190; intersex, 188; male, 30, 135; marginalized, 209; masculinized, 48; pharmacopornographic, 164; political, 63, 103; queer, 28, 135; queer-crip, 29; schizophrenic, 124; sexual, 180; transgender, 214n33; white, 100, 117, 119, 228n13
subjectivity, 7, 97, 126, 170; asexual, 167; national, 28; non-American, 114; post-AIDS, 136; queer, 171; stone butch, 187; trans, 161
suffering, 8, 96, 126
surveillance, 214n35; of affect, 156; domestic, 44; maternal, 49; police, 225n14; self, 7; state, 168
sympathy, 69, 71, 75–76, 80–81, 84–87, 92, 95–96, 138, 203–204, 220n17; male, 94; maternal, 220n23, 223n39

Tender Is the Night (Fitzgerald), 29–30, 71, 84–96, 203
Testo Junkie (Preciado), 31, 162–64

testosterone, 31, 161–64, 166, 192
Times Square Red, Times Square Blue (Delany), 31, 135–59, 173, 229n14, 230n18, 230n21
transfemininity, 3, 231n1
transgender, 1–2, 16, 163, 188, 191, 211n1, 214n35. *See also* subjectivity: trans
transgression, 192; bodily, 70; erotic, 168; queer, 225n12; sexual, 73, 86, 89, 219n8
transmasculinity, 32, 70, 162, 164, 166–67, 191. *See also* bodies: transmasculine; identity: transmasculine; transfemininity
trigger warnings, 157, 200, 203–209, 232n16, 234n8, 235n18

unfit, the, 72, 74, 78, 80, 86–87, 220n15. *See also* fitness
United States Constitution, 13, 18–19, 28, 33–34, 59

vulnerability, 1, 3–4, 6, 28, 31–32, 61, 119, 126, 129–30, 161, 173, 194, 198, 202, 209; constitutional, 159, 200; male, 10, 197; masculine, 158; physical, 58, 65, 100; queer-crip, 201

Warner, Michael, 168–70
whiteness, 13–14, 30, 70, 83, 88, 112–15, 212–13n19, 227–28
Wilkerson, Abby, 144, 188
women's safety, 138, 146–47
Wright, Richard, 127, 226n22

Cynthia Barounis is a lecturer in the Department of Women, Gender, and Sexuality Studies at Washington University in St. Louis.

www.ingramcontent.com/pod-product-compliance
Lightning Source LLC
Chambersburg PA
CBHW040747020526
44116CB00036B/2969